Agrarian Elites

Agrarian Elites

American Slaveholders and
Southern Italian Landowners
1815–1861

ENRICO DAL LAGO

LOUISIANA STATE UNIVERSITY PRESS

BATON ROUGE

DESIGNER: Barbara Neely Bourgoyne
TYPEFACE: Adobe Caslon Pro, text; Brioso Pro, display
PRINTER AND BINDER: Edwards Brothers, Inc.

Library of Congress Cataloging-in-Publication Data:

Dal Lago, Enrico, 1966–
 Agrarian elites : American slaveholders and southern Italian landowners, 1815–1861 /
Enrico Dal Lago.
  p. cm.
 Includes bibliographical references and index.
 ISBN 0-8071-3087-7 (alk. paper)
 1. Slaveholders—Southern States—History—19th century. 2. Elite (Social sciences)—
Southern States—History—19th century. 3. Agriculture—Economic aspects—Southern
States—History—19th century. 4. Southern States—History—1775–1865. 5. Southern States
—Economic conditions—19th century. 6. Landowners—Italy, Southern—History—19th
century. 7. Elite (Social sciences)—Italy, Southern—History—19th century. 8. Agriculture—
Economic aspects—Italy, Southern—History—19th century. 9. Italy, Southern—Economic
conditions—19th century. I. Title.

E441.D17 2005
305.5'232'097509034—dc22

                                                                      2005000872

Contents

Maps

Abbreviations

CWH	Civil War History
DBR	De Bow's Review
EEH	Explorations in Economic History
EHQ	European Historical Quarterly
ESLS	Effemeridi Scientifiche e Letterarie per la Sicilia
FR	Farmers' Register
GHQ	Georgia Historical Quarterly
HM	Harper's Monthly Magazine
HR	Historical Research
HW	Harper's Weekly
HWJ	History Workshop Journal
IR	Independent Review
IRSH	International Review of Social History
JAH	Journal of American History
JEH	Journal of Economic History
JER	Journal of the Early Republic
JHS	Journal of Historical Sociology
JMH	Journal of Mississippi History
JPS	Journal of Peasant Studies
JSH	Journal of Southern History
JSoH	Journal of Social History
MI	Modern Italy
NCHR	North Carolina Historical Review
NE	Nuove Effemeridi
NP	New Politics
NQM	Nuovi Quaderni del Meridione
NYT	New York Times
P&P	Past and Present
Pa&Pr	Passato e Presente
PSLA	Il Progresso delle Scienze, Lettere, Arti
QS	Quaderni Storici
RAH	Reviews in American History
RE	Rivista Economica
RISN	Rivista Italiana di Studi Napoleonici
RSA	Rivista di Storia dell'Agricoltura
RSR	Rassegna Storica del Risorgimento
SA	Southern Agriculturalist
SAQ	South Atlantic Quarterly

SCHM	*South Carolina Historical Magazine*
S&D	*Storia & Dossier*
S&S	*Società e Storia*
SH	*Social History*
SoSt	*Southern Studies*
SQR	*Southern Quarterly Review*
SS	*Studi Storici*
SU	*Storia Urbana*
TLS	*Times Literary Supplement*
WMQ	*William and Mary Quarterly*
WUS	*Washington University Studies*

Preface

This book is about the ideology and daily life of two nineteenth-century agrarian elites: the slaveholders of the antebellum American South and the landowners of pre-unification southern Italy. It focuses primarily on the large American slaveholders, or planters, and the large southern Italian landowners, several of whom were noblemen. Although they did not have the same degree of influence and power and they lived in very different economic, social, and political contexts, American slaveholders and southern Italian landowners shared some broadly comparable features. In particular, both elites presided over the production and movement of agricultural commodities in two peripheral areas of the world economy and exploited the work of large masses of mostly landless laborers. Equally comparable is the fact that both elites controlled the social and political life in their local communities—what ultimately led both of them to oppose the centralizing policies of the national governments of which they were part.[1]

A particularly important comparative point relates to the two elites' worldviews. In the present work, I have relied on the close reading of primary sources and on recent studies that seek to mediate between the two opposite interpretations of the elites' ideologies as either premodern or modern, and I have argued that both elites combined precapitalist and capitalist features in different ways and degrees. In my research, I have employed a method similar to the one that historian Joanne Freeman has termed the "ethno-historical study of thought and behavior," a study which—through

1. On the definition of *elite,* see George E. Marcus, "'Elite' as a Concept, Theory and Research Tradition," in George E. Marcus, ed., *Elites: Ethnographic Issues* (Albuquerque, N.Mex., 1989), 7–27. On the roles of the two southern regions in the world economy, see Immanuel Wallerstein, *The Modern World-System,* vols. 1–3 (New York, 1974–1989).

close reading of private and public written evidence, such as letters, diaries, pamphlets, and articles—seeks to find patterns of "shared mentalities"
amid the variety of individual experiences. Through the employment of this
method, I hope I have built a convincing case for the understanding of the
regional worldviews of American slaveholders and southern Italian landowners as comparable—though very different—patriarchal-paternalistic
ideologies that, in both cases, included premodern and modern features.[2]

Interesting similarities emerge from the comparative study of the two landed
elites. Among them, particularly important is the fact that strong regional
variations characterized both American slaveholders and southern Italian
landowners. Within the "many souths" that formed the American South and
the Italian South—or *Mezzogiorno*—articulate members of the two landed
elites often represented very distinctive regional cultures. In this study, I have
paid particular attention to comparisons between American slaveholders who
lived in Virginia, Mississippi, and South Carolina and Italian landowners
who lived in the area surrounding Naples, in Terra di Bari (in present-day
Apulia), and in Sicily. As a general point, Virginia, Mississippi, and South
Carolina hosted some of the oldest and most prestigious planters together
with some of the most recent and wealthiest slaveholders, similar to the
way the Neapolitan area, Terra di Bari, and Sicily hosted a combination of
powerful noble and bourgeois landowning families. In addition, Virginia,
being close to Washington, D.C., resembled the area surrounding Naples,
both in terms of political prestige and economic importance. On the other
hand, Mississippi was a southwestern frontier state that played a crucial
role in both southern and national politics; in this sense, it is comparable to
Terra di Bari, which was a sort of frontier region in geographical terms, and
yet with an unparalleled degree of economic and political importance in the
Mezzogiorno. South Carolina and Sicily, instead, hosted powerful regional
elites with distinctively regional political cultures—elites that, through their
secessionist and separatist policies, triggered the birth of the Confederate

2. See Joanne B. Freeman, *Affairs of Honor: National Politics in the New Republic* (New Haven,
Conn., 2000), 291–292. On the capitalist/precapitalist debate, see Mark D. Smith, *Debating
Slavery: Economy and Society in the Antebellum American South* (New York, 1998); Peter Kolchin,
A Sphinx on the American Land: The Nineteenth-Century South in Comparative Perspective (Baton
Rouge, La., 2003), 79–82; and Enrico Dal Lago and Rick Halpern, "Two Case-Studies in Com-
parative History: The American South and the Italian Mezzogiorno," in Enrico Dal Lago and
Rick Halpern, eds., *The American South and the Italian Mezzogiorno: Essays in Comparative His-
tory* (New York, 2002), 3–24.

and Italian nations in 1861. For this reason, in the present work I have treated comparison between these two specific regions in a separate section.

The differences between American slaveholders and southern Italian landowners are as striking as their similarities. American slaveholders produced mostly particularly valuable cash crops—such as tobacco, rice, sugar, and cotton—and sold them to Europe or the northern United States. They owned plantations and farms worked by slaves who were racially discriminated against and legally considered pieces of property. Also, despite clear regional differences between the older planter aristocracy that lived in the Atlantic Seaboard states stretching from the Chesapeake to Georgia and the newer slaveholding elite that lived on the southwestern cotton and sugar frontiers, American slaveholders were a fairly homogenous master class compared to southern Italian landowners. Unlike the latter, the former inhabited regions that were part of a federal American republic with a democratic system of government and with no inheritance of a class-system or of monarchical institutions in the European sense. Even more important was the fact that they were part of an expanding nation whose population was in the process of settling the western areas of a large continent with plenty of room for farming and herding activities.

Conversely, southern Italian landowners produced mainly grain for the internal market on large landed estates called *latifondi,* except for some areas in which several of them engaged in commercial agriculture producing olive oil, citrus fruits, and wine for sale to northern Europe or the northern United States. They did not exploit a racially discriminated and enslaved workforce; southern Italian peasants were technically free, since the process of emancipation had been completed by the beginning of the nineteenth century. The older families of landowners were part of a former hereditary feudal aristocracy, while the more recent ones belonged to a landed bourgeoisie. Though the Kingdom of the Two Sicilies had only become an independent state less than fifty years before the American Republic, southern Italian monarchical institutions boasted hundreds of years of history and a capital —Naples—whose population of four hundred thousand inhabitants made it hardly comparable to any city of the American South in 1860. Finally, the *Mezzogiorno* lacked the presence of new territories in which the population could move in order to escape overcrowding and in which agricultural enterprises could expand and find fresh land.

In view of these very striking differences, there is little doubt that sustained comparison between American slaveholders and southern Italian landowners, and between the economic, social, and political contexts in which they lived, is a challenging task. Yet, I believe it is also a particularly enlightening exercise, specifically because of its relevance to the explanation of the origins and developments of nationalist ideologies in the southern regions of the United States and Italy in the period leading to 1861—a year that, remarkably, witnessed the birth of both the Confederate States of America and the Kingdom of Italy. Despite the fact that a handful of historians has produced important works arguing in favor of comparing the antebellum American South and the nineteenth-century Italian *Mezzogiorno,* the ideologies of American slaveholders and southern Italian landowners have never been the object of a systematic comparative study. To a certain extent, the present work attempts to follow some of the suggestions that different scholars have made in regard to the possibility of such a comparison, but it also departs quite radically from them in its overall approach and in its conclusions.[3]

The chapters are organized as follows. The prologue provides a theoretical justification for comparison between American slaveholders and southern Italian landowners. Chapter one analyzes the historical development of plantations and *latifondi* and argues that both elites were aware of their regions' economic dependency upon more industrialized areas of the world and, yet, failed in their attempts at implementing programs of economic reform. Chapter two analyzes and compares the constituent elements of the two elites' worldviews—patriarchalism and paternalism—focusing on American slaveholders' and southern Italian landowners' relations with their families and with the laborers on their landed estates. Chapter three looks at the relationship between the two regional elites and their respective national governments, compares the political programs of reform that the two elites embraced, and focuses on the explanation of the success of nationalist ideas in both southern regions. Chapter four analyzes specifically the origins and development of the secessionist/separatist types of regionalism that characterized the landed elites of South Carolina and Sicily and which had important consequences on the creation of the Confederate States of America and

3. See the essays in Dal Lago and Halpern, eds., *American South and Italian Mezzogiorno;* Don H. Doyle, *Nations Divided: America, Italy, and the Southern Question* (Athens, Ga., 2002); and Raimondo Luraghi, "The Civil War and the Modernization of American Society: Social Structure and Industrial Revolution in the Old South before and during the War," *CWH* 18 (1972): 230–267; Raimondo Luraghi, *The Rise and Fall of the Plantation South* (New York, 1978), especially 55–63.

of the Kingdom of Italy. Finally, the epilogue summarizes the development of the Confederate and Italian nations, focusing on the southern elites' failure to maintain an unaltered grip on local power.

During the course of my research, I have received help from many friends, colleagues, and institutions. First of all, I wish to thank my friend and former supervisor Rick Halpern, who encouraged me and helped me transform my vague ideas about comparison into a doctoral dissertation. I also wish to thank those scholars and friends who examined or read my dissertation and gave me extremely helpful comments, particularly Lucy Riall, Anthony Badger, Donna Gabaccia, and Jonathan Morris. Particularly warm thanks go to Bertram Wyatt-Brown, who assisted me in the initial process of publishing the manuscript, and especially to Peter Kolchin, who read the book manuscript for the Louisiana State University Press and provided me with crucial constructive criticisms that helped me a great deal in understanding and sharpening my argument. I also wish to thank the other, anonymous reader of my book manuscript for LSU, and the LSU Press staff, especially Rand Dotson and Mary Katherine Callaway. For as long as she was at LSU, Sylvia Frank Rodrigue also helped me with her extraordinary patience and kindness. Moreover, in the ten years since this project began, many friends and scholars—several of whom participated at the 1999 Commonwealth Fund Conference on the "Two Souths"—have also given me valuable help through their comments, suggestions, and encouragement. In particular, I wish to thank Bruce Levine, Steven Hahn, Don Doyle, Bill Harris, Drew Faust, James Oakes, Catherine Clinton, William Shade, Richard Follett, Anne Boylan, John Dickie, Carl Levy, Ferdinando Fasce, Giovanna Fiume, Marta Petrusewicz, Piero Bevilacqua, Salvatore Lupo, Franco Benigno, Paolo Macry, Giovanni Montroni, Marco Armiero, Luigi Musella, Martin Daunton, Jonathan Israel, and David D'Avray.

Inevitably, in undertaking a research project of this size, I have benefited from the financial support of several institutions. In particular, I wish to thank University College London, and specifically the UCL History Department, for the Departmental Teaching Demonstratorship, which enabled me to finish my Ph.D., for the exchange scholarship with the University of Pennsylvania, and for the Graduate Research Fund and the Hale Bellott Fund. Equally, I wish to thank the National University of Ireland, Galway, for the Millennium Fund and for the Development Fund. I also enjoyed financial support from the Center for the Study of Human Settlement and Historical Change, at the National University of Ireland, Galway, to advance the research on which the book is based.

During the course of my research, I received invaluable help from the staffs of the following institutions: the Virginia Historical Society, the Alderman Library at the University of Virginia, the South Caroliniana Library at the University of South Carolina, the South Carolina Historical Society, the Van Pelt Library at the University of Pennsylvania, the Archivio di Stato di Napoli, the Biblioteca Nazionale di Napoli, the Archivio di Stato di Palermo (Sezione La Gancia), the Biblioteca Regionale di Palermo, the University College London Library (specifically Ruth Dar), and the James Hardiman Library (specifically the Interlibrary Loan Section) at the National University of Ireland, Galway. I also wish to extend specific thanks to the Virginia Historical Society's Director of Manuscripts and Archives, Lee Shepard, for granting me permission to use material from the Spragins Family Papers.

At the National University of Ireland, Galway, I found in the History Department the ideal environment in which to work and do research. I wish to thank all my colleagues and our secretarial staff for making this possible. I wish also to extend specific thanks to my former Head of Department, Nicholas Canny, to my current Head of Department, Steven Ellis, to Geraoid O'Tuathaigh, and to the Dean of Arts, John Marshall, for their enthusiastic support for my research project. I also wish to thank Sinead Armstrong for the time and dedication she has put into making the maps for my book. Finally, I wish to thank my undergraduate and postgraduate students, both at University College London and at the National University of Ireland, Galway.

Among the other friends who have supported me with their help and encouragement, I wish to thank especially Beth Landau, Attilio Castellucci, and Frank Deserino. Enormous thanks go to my parents, Olinto and Rosa Dal Lago, and to my brother Stefano, for their continuous patience and support, and also to my parents-in-law, Petros and Sofia Katsari, for their help at crucial times. My biggest thanks, though, go to my wife, Constantina Katsari. Ever since she came into my life, Constantina helped me in countless ways, giving me her love and support and also allowing me to share my thoughts and constructively criticizing them. Without her, this book would have never seen the light, and to her it is dedicated.

Agrarian Elites

The American South, the Italian *Mezzogiorno,* and Comparative History

A merican and Italian historiographical traditions share a common feature: both include particular fields of study that regard the South as a separate historical entity. A similar idea—that the particularities of the southern region of the country have combined to produce a path to modernization both separate and distinct from northern American and European standards—has guided the efforts of generations of American and Italian historians. In both the United States and Italy, the idea of a "southern question"—with its corollary, the notion of a "southern distinctiveness"—has informed the historiography to such an extent that it is possible to consider it a paradigm.[1]

Also, in both countries, reaction against the premises of the southern question has generated a wave of revisionist historiography that has succeeded in demolishing the validity of previous assumptions, but has also attracted criticism. At the same time, particularly in recent years, both American and Italian historians have emphasized the importance of the comparative dimension for the understanding of the specific characteristics of the southern regions of the United States and Italy. This comparative awareness, in turn, has led to the publication of scholarly works that have shown the promises and potentials of sustained comparison between the American South and the Italian *Mezzogiorno* for the study of topics such

1. See Enrico Dal Lago and Rick Halpern, "Two Case-Studies in Comparative History: The American South and the Italian Mezzogiorno," in Enrico Dal Lago and Rick Halpern, eds., *The American South and the Italian Mezzogiorno: Essays in Comparative History* (New York, 2002), 3–4. On the idea of paradigm, see Thomas Kuhn, *The Structure of Scientific Revolutions* (New York, 1986), viii.

as modernization, backwardness, nationalism, and regionalism—topics that rank high in the agendas of most comparative historians.[2]

The heart of the matter is the fact that in both the American and the Italian cases, the paradigm of the southern question and its critique relate specifically to the particular economic and social features that characterized the southern regions in the nineteenth century, and specifically in the years between 1815 and 1865—the antebellum and Civil War period in the United States and the Risorgimento and unification period in Italy. In Civil War America, the idea of a backward South related to the economic and social characteristics of the slave system—specifically the existence of a planter elite that exploited the work of African American bondsmen and the consequent preeminence of plantation agriculture and scarcity of industrialization and urban development. Comparably, in Risorgimento Italy, the idea of a backward *Mezzogiorno* derived from the established perception of a corrupt, inefficient, and cruel Bourbon absolutist monarchy, which prevented the development of indigenous economic enterprises and kept the majority of southern Italian peasants at the mercy of their landowners.[3]

Doubtless, a great deal of the stereotype was true in both cases. Yet, it is important to remember that in both the United States and Italy, the stereotype became a historiographical paradigm as a result of the process of nation-building. In comparable terms, during the two parallel processes of nation-building that took place in the first half of the 1860s, the American South and the Italian *Mezzogiorno* were ideologically constructed as *imagined*—as much as real—enemies of the nascent American and Italian nations and were forever stigmatized with the original sins of their mid-nineteenth-century features. Clearly, the circumstances that led to the two ideological constructions were very different. On one hand, the slaveholders of the eleven southern states that formed the Confederacy led the majority of the white population of the South to secede from the United States and fight a four-year civil war that cost more than six hundred thousand dead. On the other hand, the Bourbon monarchy based in the *Mezzogiorno* largely

2. See Dal Lago and Halpern, eds, *American South and Italian Mezzogiorno*; and Don H. Doyle, *Nations Divided: America, Italy, and the Southern Question* (Athens, Ga., 2002).

3. See Don H. Doyle, "Slavery, Secession, and Civil War as American Problems," in Don H. Doyle and Michael Griffin, eds., *The South as an American Problem* (Athens, Ga., 1994), 102–125; and Nelson Moe, *The View from Vesuvius: Italian Culture and the Southern Question* (Berkeley, Calif., 2002), 156–186.

imploded as a result of the hostility of a large section of the propertied class, which sympathized with the cause of Italian national unification, but soon grew disaffected with the new Italian state and its inability to maintain law and order at the time of the so-called great brigandage—a major peasant rebellion that caused a five-year civil war with more than five thousand casualties.[4]

Arguably, the deep roots of the two southern questions lay in the particular ways in which the American federal government and the Bourbon and Italian monarchies intended their relation with the two southern ruling classes —American slaveholders and southern Italian landowners—a topic that provides much material for comparison. Yet, it is important to notice that the subsequent stigmatizations of the American South and of the Italian *Mezzogiorno* resulted as much from early criticisms of backwardness as from the establishment of ideological traditions characterized by profoundly negative views of the southern regions following the final defeats of the rebellions of the southern populations in the two civil wars. Therefore, it is also true that the historiographic constructions and deconstructions of the ideas of southern backwardness are closely related to comparable historical trajectories that the two southern regions followed in the processes of formation of the American and Italian nation-states—trajectories in which, in both cases, the elites played crucial roles.[5]

American historians have long attempted to identify the reasons for the South's backwardness and deviation from the United States' economic and social standards—America's southern question. In general, their explanations have relied on the idea of either a "central theme" in southern history or of distinctive characteristics that formed an important part of the region's identity. The search for a constant feature in southern history has led scholars to locate its central theme in particular social and cultural traits—to name but a few, the preservation of white supremacy, the cavalier ideal, the particular culture of violence, the folk way of life, the idea of honor, and the tradition of conservatism—traits which, according to this view, defined the entire culture of the South in its historical evolution. On the other hand, historians have also invested a considerable amount of time and effort investigating

4. See Doyle, *Nations Divided,* 65–89.
5. See Dal Lago and Halpern, "Two Case-Studies," 18–20.

those distinctive social, economic, or political features that Americans have consistently viewed as outstanding and distinctly southern anomalies since the nineteenth century.[6]

Among the southern distinctive features, none has received more historiographical attention than slavery. Ever since the first scholarly studies by U. B. Phillips in the 1910s and 1920s, slavery has been consistently the focus of scholarship that has attempted to either reinforce or demolish the idea of a "distinctive" South through the study and interpretation of its antebellum economic and social system. In particular, in the 1950s, with their sustained analyses of the peculiar institution, Kenneth Stampp and Stanley Elkins contributed a great deal to the identification of the roots of southern distinctiveness by arguing that a particular type of slavery distinguished the antebellum South not just from the North, but also from other slave societies in the Americas.[7]

From the 1960s onward, scholarship on slavery has increased in complexity and sophistication, while particular scholars have emerged as the leaders or founders of historiographical schools that have taken opposite sides in the debate on the idea of southern distinctiveness. Among historians of slavery, Eugene Genovese has given a major contribution in redefining our idea of a distinctive South. As Drew Faust has noticed, "emphasizing what he sees as fundamental differences between North and South, Genovese has explained 'southern distinctiveness' as the product of its pre-bourgeois society." Employing a Marxian analytical framework, Genovese has focused on the master-slave relationship as "the determining factor within southern civilization, affecting class relationship and social structures and defining the ideology of power that gave meaning to the pre-capitalist social order." Indeed, according to Drew Faust, Genovese has identified the master-slave relationship "as southern history's new 'central theme'" and, through its analysis, he "has been

6. See especially Donald L. Smiley, "The Quest for a Central Theme in Southern History," *SAQ* 71 (1972); William J. Cash, *The Mind of the South* (New York, 1941); William Taylor, *Cavalier and Yankee: The Old South and American National Character* (New York, 1961); John Hope Franklin, *The Militant South* (New York, 1956); Bertram Wyatt-Brown, *Southern Honor: Ethics and Behavior in the Old South* (New York, 1982); and Eugene D. Genovese, *The Southern Tradition: The Achievement and Limitations of an American Conservatism* (Cambridge, Mass., 1993).

7. See Ulrich B. Phillips, *American Negro Slavery: A Survey of the Supply, Employment, and Control of Negro Labor as Determined by the Plantation Regime* (Baton Rouge, La., 1968; orig. pub. in 1918); Kenneth M. Stampp, *The Peculiar Institution: Slavery in the Ante-Bellum South* (New York, 1956); and Stanley Elkins, *Slavery: A Problem in American Institutional and Intellectual Life* (Chicago, Ill., 1959).

able to construct an explanation of nearly every aspect of the southern way of life." At the center of Genovese's numerous studies was his idea that the peculiar precapitalist character of the antebellum American South derived from a particular form of paternalism, one through which masters exercised hegemony—understood as cultural and ideological domination—over their slaves.[8]

Since Genovese has advanced his ideas, reactions to his model of southern distinctiveness have been countless. Marxist scholars have mostly accepted his view of a prebourgeois South and have engaged in the analysis of those features of southern society that Genovese had left aside. On the other hand, since the 1970s, neoclassical economists and non-Marxist historians have carried a two-pronged attack against Genovese's idea of a distinctive, prebourgeois and precapitalist antebellum South. Notably, neoclassical economists Robert Fogel and Stanley Engerman have argued in favor of the capitalist character of the South's master class. According to Fogel and Engerman's controversial views, southern plantations had little to envy about northern factories. While southern planters behaved like capitalist businessmen, slaves formed a highly motivated workforce that was little different from factory workers in the northern United States. Arguably, after the publication of Fogel and Engerman's work, the very idea of a distinctive South based on the substantial incompatibility of southern slavery with the modern world has come into question.[9]

Equally influential has been the work of non-Marxist historians such as James Oakes and William Dusinberre in questioning the validity of Genovese's assumptions. Oakes has demonstrated that the large majority of small and medium southern slaveholders included individuals who thought and acted like small entrepreneurs and ran their farms and plantations as if they

8. Drew G. Faust, "The Peculiar South Revisited," in John B. Boles and Edward T. Nolen, eds., *Interpreting Southern History: Historiographical Essays in Honor of Sanford W. Higginbotham* (Baton Rouge, La., 1987), 39. See also Eugene D. Genovese, *The Political Economy of Slavery: Studies in the Economy and Society of the Slave South* (New York, 1965); Eugene D. Genovese, *The World the Slaveholders Made: Two Essays in Interpretation* (New York, 1969); Eugene D. Genovese, *Roll, Jordan, Roll: The World the Slaves Made* (New York, 1974); and Elizabeth Fox-Genovese and Eugene Genovese, *The Fruits of Merchant Capital: Slavery and Bourgeois Property in the Rise and Expansion of Capitalism* (New York, 1983).

9. See Robert W. Fogel and Stanley N. Engerman, *Time on the Cross: The Economics of American Negro Slavery* (New York, 1974); Robert W. Fogel, *Without Consent or Contract: The Rise and Fall of American Slavery* (New York, 1989); and Robert W. Fogel, *The Slavery Debates, 1952–1990: A Retrospective* (Baton Rouge, La., 2003).

were "factories in the field." On the other hand, Dusinberre has shown how even the great rice planters of South Carolina, rather than emphasizing the master-slave relationship and its supposed benefits, brutally exploited and worked their slaves to death in order to achieve high returns in their agricultural enterprises. Genovese's view of southern distinctiveness, based on the idea of a precapitalist form of slavery and its particular emphasis on paternalism, has suffered a particularly strong blow at the hands of both Oakes and Dusinberre.[10]

The debate between Marxist and non-Marxist historians on the distinctive characteristics of the antebellum South is still very much alive. Yet, it is important to notice that a small group of scholars has advocated the possibility of reaching a consensus by conceding that capitalist and noncapitalist features were equally present in antebellum southern society and economy and in the minds and behaviors of southern slaveholders. In particular, Mark M. Smith has shown how, in supervising an enslaved workforce, slaveholders adopted a concept and an ethic of time no different from the ones of contemporary English factory owners. Also, Jeffrey Robert Young has used the concept of "corporate individualism" to describe the slaveholders' ethic as one that effectively incorporated features of capitalism and paternalism in an organic view. And other, more specific, studies—such as Richard Follett's work on Louisiana's sugar planters—have reached similar conclusions. The implications of this recent scholarship on slavery for the idea of a distinctive South are, indeed, far-reaching. Distancing themselves both from Genovese's idea of southern distinctiveness and from the non-Marxist attempts to deny the validity of its foundations, scholars in increasing numbers now hold a view that provides the antebellum South with a regional identity based on economic and social features at once part of the broader American context and distinguished from the ones of the North. In fact, the distinction between South and North was not just a result of the presence or absence of slavery; it also related to the combination of capitalist and noncapitalist elements in the southern economy and ideology—a combination that was

10. See James Oakes, *The Ruling Race: A History of American Slaveholders* (New York, 1982, 153); and William Dusinberre, *Them Dark Days: Slavery in the American Rice Swamps* (New York, 1996). See also William K. Scarborough, *Masters of the Big House: Elite Slaveholders in the Mid-Nineteenth-Century South* (Baton Rouge, La., 2003); and David L. Carlton and Peter A. Coclanis, *The South, the Nation, and the World: Perspectives on Southern Economic Development* (Charlottesville, Va., 2003).

far from being unique when seen in comparison with other regions of the nineteenth-century world.[11]

To be sure, the idea of comparing the nineteenth-century American South with other regions of the world is hardly new. Over the past fifty years, the antebellum South has provided a major field for comparative historians. In their effort to find sustainable ground for comparison, historians have focused specifically on slavery, mostly considering it the distinctive feature that set the South apart from the rest of the United States and from most of the western world. In the 1940s and 1950s, Frank Tannenbaum and Stanley Elkins originally advanced the argument that the unique features of southern slavery depended on the fact that it appeared particularly harsh in comparison with other New World slave systems—a hypothesis that other historians tested with particular comparative studies, contributing a great deal to reinforcing the idea of a distinctive South. Yet, it was the subsequent debate between Marxist and non-Marxist historians of the slave South that proved particularly fruitful when transferred to a comparative dimension. In particular, in the 1960s and 1970s, maintaining his central idea of the pre-bourgeois characteristics of the slave South, Eugene Genovese demonstrated how comparison with other New World slave societies, such as Brazil and the British and French Caribbean, reinforced his particular notion of southern distinctiveness.[12]

Since the 1970s, subsequent comparative studies focusing on the antebellum South have mostly engaged in either supporting or dismissing Genovese's view through sustained comparison with contemporary nineteenth-century societies. In this perspective, it is remarkable that, in their efforts to find new case studies, scholars have increasingly broadened their horizons, going well beyond the limits of comparison with slave societies in the Americas and focusing specifically on societies characterized by different degrees of unfree labor in Africa and Europe. At the same time, broader studies have situated

11. See Mark M. Smith, *Debating Slavery: Economy and Society in the Antebellum South* (New York, 1998); Jeffrey Robert Young, *Domesticating Slavery: The Master Class in Georgia and South Carolina, 1670–1837* (Chapel Hill, N.C., 1999); and Richard J. Follett, *The Sugar Masters: Planters and Slaves in Louisiana's Cane World, 1820–1860* (Baton Rouge, La., 2005).

12. See Frank Tannenbaum, *Slave and Citizen* (New York, 1947); Herbert Klein, *Slavery in the Americas: A Comparative Study of Virginia and Cuba* (Chicago, 1967); Carl N. Degler, *Neither Black nor White: Slavery and Race Relations in Brazil and the United States* (New York, 1971); Genovese, *World the Slaveholders Made*; and Genovese, *Roll, Jordan, Roll*.

the history of the antebellum South in the context of the evolution of slavery and of systems of unfree labor on a world scale, thus broadening our understanding of the distinctive features of the southern peculiar institution in comparison with both New World and Old World unfree societies.[13]

The most recent trend in comparative scholarship focuses on the antebellum South in comparison with nineteenth-century European societies. Studies by Peter Kolchin and Shearer Davis Bowman have focused on eastern Europe and have compared, respectively, American slavery and Russian serfdom and American planters and Prussian Junkers, while other studies—notably the collective volume edited by Enrico Dal Lago and Rick Halpern and Don Doyle's monograph—have focused on comparison between the nineteenth-century American South and the Italian *Mezzogiorno*. It is interesting that George Fredrickson has written of Kolchin's and Bowman's works that "their respective comparisons are used to support contrasting views of the slave society in the Old South and especially of the character of its dominant class." Clearly, in his comparison with Russian serfdom, Kolchin has supported Genovese's view of paternalism as the key southern distinctive feature, while Bowman has compared planters and Junkers in order to support the idea of a distinctive southern path to capitalism. Yet, irrespective of the different ideological convictions—Marxist and non-Marxist —of the two authors, there is little doubt that comparison between southern slavery and other regimes of unfree labor has served well the purpose of questioning previous assumptions on the distinctiveness of the antebellum South.[14]

In fact, comparative historians have become increasingly aware of the fact that—notwithstanding legal definitions of slavery—a wide range of nineteenth-century societies was characterized by different degrees and

13. See George Fredrickson, *White Supremacy: A Comparative Study in American and South African History* (New York, 1981); Anthony Marx, *Making Race and Nation: A Comparison of the United States, South Africa and Brazil* (New York, 1998); David Brion Davis, *The Problem of Slavery in the Age of Revolution, 1770–1823* (Ithaca, N.Y., 1975); David Brion Davis, *Slavery and Human Progress* (New York, 1985); Orlando Patterson, *Slavery and Social Death: A Comparative Study* (Cambridge, Mass., 1982); Robin Blackburn, *The Making of New World Slavery: From the Baroque to the Modern* (London, 1997); Philip Curtin, *The Rise and Fall of the Plantation Complex* (New York, 1990); and Michael L. Bush, *Servitude in Modern Times* (Cambridge, 2000).

14. George Fredrickson, *The Comparative Imagination: On the History of Racism, Nationalism, and Social Movements* (Berkeley, Calif., 1997), 68. See also Peter Kolchin, *Unfree Labor: American Slavery and Russian Serfdom* (Cambridge, Mass., 1987); and Shearer Davis Bowman, *Masters and Lords: Mid-Nineteenth-Century U.S. Planters and Prussian Junkers* (New York, 1993).

forms of unfree labor and by the presence of landowning elites that showed both modern and nonmodern features in their relationships with the workforce and in their position vis-à-vis the world economy. It is in this perspective that we have to see the significance of comparison between the antebellum American South and the nineteenth-century Italian *Mezzogiorno,* since in the latter the presence of a landed elite with premodern and modern characteristics and of an only nominally free working class has led to the long-standing historiographic characterization of its society as unique. In the established historiographic paradigm, the unique features of the Italian *Mezzogiorno* rendered it no less distinctive than the American South and even led to a comparable type of historical problem, Italy's southern question. Significantly, both the essays in Dal Lago and Halpern's edited collection and Doyle's monograph have addressed the similarity between America's and Italy's southern questions as the starting point for comparison between the two regions.[15]

To be sure, when studying the historiography of the Italian *Mezzogiorno,* one cannot help but notice that a paradigm similar to the one that supported the idea of southern distinctiveness in the United States has informed the works of several generations of Italian historians. For well over a century, scholars of the Italian South (*meridionalisti*) have focused on understanding the reasons for the existence of the southern question, blaming the *Mezzogiorno*'s peculiar features—a supposedly backward agrarian economy and semifeudal social relations—for Italy's delay in industrialization. The two great historiographic schools—the Marxist and the Liberal—did not challenge this central assumption, but simply differed in their historical interpretation of it. For Marxist historians, the *Mezzogiorno*'s social development was held back by the failure of the bourgeois revolution during the Risorgimento; for Liberal historians, the history of the *Mezzogiorno* had never showed real potential for social change. The two most influential historians who supported these conflicting views were Antonio Gramsci and Rosario Romeo. Both of them built upon a long tradition of political and historiographic debates

15. See Peter Kolchin, "The American South in Comparative Perspective," and Piero Bevilacqua, "Peter Kolchin's American South and the Italian Mezzogiorno: Some Questions about Comparative History," both in Dal Lago and Halpern, eds., *American South and Italian Mezzogiorno,* 27–32, 61–65; and Doyle, *Nations Divided,* 66–67.

over Italy's southern question and over the role of the *Mezzogiorno* in the distinctive Italian path to modernization.[16]

Elaborating upon the Marxist view of Italian history, Antonio Gramsci argued that the alliance between southern landowners and northern industrialists was of crucial importance throughout the period from unification onward. To Gramsci, the southern question was inextricably linked to the particular form that the capitalist state had taken in Italy. The peculiar weakness of the *Mezzogiorno*'s bourgeoisie, which predated unification, had led to the unfolding of a process that he called "passive revolution." Unable to change the social structure by organizing the masses in a peasant revolution, the *Mezzogiorno*'s bourgeoisie had ended up in a position of subservience to the hegemonic power of the northern bourgeoisie. Thus, according to Gramsci, Italy's North and South stood in an unequal relationship to one another; similar to the city and the countryside, one irresistibly drew the other into a more advanced urban economy. By the 1950s, only a few years after the posthumous publication of Gramsci's *Prison Notebooks,* their fundamental tenets had become the foundations of the most sophisticated and complex interpretation of the process that had led to Italian unification, especially thanks to the work of Marxist historians such as Giorgio Candeloro and Franco Della Peruta.[17]

From the 1950s on, the most prestigious historian in the Liberal school of historiography—whose early greatest advocate had been Benedetto Croce —was Rosario Romeo, an expert in economic history who took the challenge of elaborating a Liberal theory of Italian capitalistic development that could function as an effective alternative to the Marxist one. Holding diametrically opposite views from Marxist historian Emilio Sereni—who had elaborated his own views on the failure of capitalism in the southern Italian countryside—Romeo rejected the possibility of a peasant revolution in the

16. See Massimo Salvadori, *Il mito del buongoverno. La questione meridionale da Cavour a Gramsci* (Turin, 1966); Giuseppe Galasso, *Passato e presente del Meridionalismo* (Naples, 1979); Lucio Villari, ed., *Il Sud nella storia d'Italia* (Rome-Bari, 1977); and Jane Schneider, "The Dynamics of Neo-Orientalism in Italy (1848–1995)," in Jane Schneider, ed., *Italy's "Southern Question": Orientalism in One Country* (New York, 1998), 1–26.

17. See Quentin Hoare and John Nowell-Smith, eds., *Selections from the Prison Notebooks of Antonio Gramsci* (London, 1974), 90–102; John A. Davis, "Antonio Gramsci and Italy's Passive Revolution," in John A. Davis, ed., *Gramsci and Italy's Passive Revolution* (London, 1979), 11–30; Giorgio Candeloro, *Storia dell'Italia moderna*, vols. 1–16 (Milan, 1954–1986); and Franco Della Peruta, *Democrazia e socialismo nel Risorgimento* (Milan, 1965).

Mezzogiorno and argued that southern backwardness had been instrumental to the original accumulation of capital in northern Italy. In his view, the construction of the infrastructures necessary to the industrialization of the North was possible only because of the fiscal pressure that the new Italian state exercised on the *Mezzogiorno*'s agriculture after unification.[18]

Since the 1980s, the traditional view of the *Mezzogiorno*'s "modernization without development"—a phrase which encapsulates the idea of the region's continuing distinctiveness in stark contrast with the industrialized North—has come under attack by a new generation of revisionist historians. Criticizing, and often denying, the idea of distinctive southern Italian features, revisionist historians have established that, far from being characterized by inertia, the *Mezzogiorno*'s nineteenth-century economy included several dynamic areas in which landowners engaged in cash crop production and commercial agriculture. Thanks to the work of historians such as Piero Bevilacqua, Biagio Salvemini, and Salvatore Lupo—whose point of reference is the Southern Institute of History and Social Sciences, or *I.M.E.S.* (*Istituto Meridionale di Storia e Scienze Sociali*)—the rich economy of the coastal plains of Campania, Apulia, Calabria, and Sicily, with their large quantities of olive oil, citrus fruits, and wine exported to northern Europe and the United States, is now known in detail to most students of the *Mezzogiorno*.[19]

Moreover, an increasing number of studies by other scholars has concentrated on the economy and society of southern Italian cities—in some of which industrial production flourished, though on a limited scale—and on the ideology and behavior of urban elites, so as to break the stereotype of the predominance of agriculture as the main cause of the *Mezzogiorno*'s backwardness. One of the most important results of the revisionist wave of historiography has been the denial of a distinctive southern Italian path to modernization. Similar to what happened in northern Italy, in the

18. See Emilio Sereni, *Il capitalismo nelle campagne* (Turin, 1947); Rosario Romeo, *Risorgimento e capitalismo* (Bari, 1959); and Rosario Romeo, *Dal Piemonte sabaudo all'Italia liberale* (Turin, 1963). See also Benedetto Croce, *Storia d'Italia dal 1871 al 1915* (Bari, 1928); and Lucy Riall, *The Italian Risorgimento: State, Society and National Unification* (London, 1994), 50–53.

19. See Jonathan Morris, "Challenging *Meridionalismo*: Constructing a New History for Southern Italy," in Robert Lumley and Jonathan Morris, eds., *The New History of the Italian South: The Mezzogiorno Revisited* (Exeter, 1997), 1–19; Piero Bevilacqua, *Breve storia dell'Italia meridionale dall'Ottocento a oggi* (Rome, 1997); Biagio Salvemini, *L'innovazione precaria. Spazi, mercati e società nel Mezzogiorno tra Sette e Ottocento* (Catanzaro, 1995); and Salvatore Lupo, *Il giardino degli aranci. Il mondo degli agrumi nella storia del Mezzogiorno* (Venice, 1990).

Mezzogiorno the economy included stagnant and active sectors, *rentier* and commercial agriculture, and a number of protoindustrial activities. Though heavily criticized, especially by northern economic historians, this view has formed an important step in the process of moving away from the historiographic debate on the southern question—a debate that most Italian scholars now consider outdated and obsolete.[20]

Equally important has been the discovery that many southern Italian landowners acted with clear economic rationality, even though they were forced to cope with constraints deriving from the fragmentation of the internal market, the lack of infrastructures, and natural disruption due to the population's pressure on the land. In her controversial study of a southern Italian *latifondo*, Marta Petrusewicz has even claimed that self-sufficiency and extreme adaptability to the changing conditions of the world market characterized the great landed estates that were once the very emblem of the *Mezzogiorno*'s distinctively retarded development. Referring specifically to Fogel and Engerman's rehabilitation of the economic performance of southern plantations in the United States, Petrusewicz has constructed an equally iconoclastic model of capitalist rationality for the agricultural activities of southern Italian *latifondi* and has succeeded in dealing a further blow to the idea of backwardness at the heart of Italy's southern question. And, to be sure, virtually all the economic studies by southern Italian revisionist historians have pointed out the fact that on many *latifondi* subsistence and commercial agricultural activities coexisted side by side. In fact, a number of southern Italian landowners seem to have combined the rent that they received from their former feudal estates with the profits they made through the cultivation of cash crops on selected areas of their properties.[21]

In addition, equally important work by other scholars has focused on the ideology of southern Italian liberal landowners in preunification *Mezzo-*

20. See especially Paolo Macry, *Ottocento. Patrimoni, Elites, e ricchezza a Napoli* (Turin, 1988); Nicola Antonacci, *Terra e potere in una città rurale del Mezzogiorno. Le elites di Andria nell'Ottocento* (Bari, 1996); and Alfio Signorelli, *Tra ceto e censo. Studi sulle elites urbane nella Sicilia dell'Ottocento* (Milan, 1999). See also Angelo Massafra, ed., *Il Mezzogiorno preunitario. Economia, società, istituzioni* (Bari, 1988). For a critical view, see Luciano Cafagna, *Dualismo e sviluppo nella storia d'Italia* (Venice, 1990).

21. See Marta Petrusewicz, *Latifundium: Moral Economy and Material Life in a Nineteenth-Century Periphery* (Ann Arbor, Mich., 1996); Salvatore Lupo, "I proprietari terrieri del Mezzogiorno," in Piero Bevilacqua, ed., *Storia dell'agricoltura italiana in età contemporanea*, vol. 2, *Uomini e classi* (Venice, 1990), 105–149; and John A. Davis, "Casting off the 'Southern Problem': Or, the Peculiarities of the South Revisited," in Schneider, ed., *Italy's "Southern Question,"* 205–224.

giorno and has established that not only did they hold prominent positions in government-sponsored economic societies, but they also advocated agricultural improvement through technological innovation and supported the idea of careful land and labor management.[22] At the same time, southern Italian liberal landowners also believed they were the only social group that successfully combined tradition with modernity and was "capable of leading the country toward modernization," even while maintaining as an unchallenged feature of their future "modern" country "the preservation of the old hierarchical order."[23]

Similar to historians of the American South, after reacting with a revisionist wave against stereotypes of backwardness and distinctiveness—inventing, in the process, a new paradigm of capitalist development—historians of the *Mezzogiorno* are now moving toward supporting the idea of coexistence of modern and premodern features both in the economy of the region and in the ideology of its landed elite. This similarity in historiographic development has particularly far-reaching implications, when seen in comparative perspective. In fact, one of the most exciting aspects of southern Italian revisionist historiography is the comparative thrust that clearly informs the most innovative studies. In their efforts to demolish the fundamental assumptions of Italy's southern question, revisionist historians have broadened the view of the *Mezzogiorno,* firmly placing it in the context of economic and social developments on a world scale.[24]

In the introduction to the first issue of *Meridiana*—*I.M.E.S.*'s official publication since 1987—Piero Bevilacqua and Marcello Gorgoni explained the importance of viewing the economic development of the *Mezzogiorno* in European and transnational context, rather than in a sort of negative comparison with the Italian North. Since then, both Bevilacqua and other scholars at *I.M.E.S.* have written fundamental studies that have shown how the agricultural economy of the *Mezzogiorno* not only was fully inserted in the world market through production and sale of specific agricultural

---

22. See specifically, Francesca De Lorenzo, *Società Economiche e istruzione agrarian nell'Ottocento meridionale* (Milan, 1998)

23. Marta Petrusewicz, "Land-Based Modernization and the Culture of Nineteenth-Century Landed Elites," in Dal Lago and Halpern, eds., *American South and Italian Mezzogiorno,* 109. See also Marta Petrusewicz, *Come il Meridione divenne una Questione. Rappresentazioni del Sud prima e dopo il Quarantotto* (Soveria Mannelli, Catanzaro, 1998).

24. See especially Piero Bevilacqua, "Il Mezzogiorno nel mercato internazionale (secoli XVIII–XX)," *Meridiana* 1 (1987): 19–46.

products, but also participated in its own way in the industrial revolution. At the same time, in her work, Marta Petrusewicz has been able to place the *Mezzogiorno* in the context of the comparative suggestions of Immanuel Wallerstein's world-system model, while she has carefully investigated all sorts of ideological connections between southern Italian and European agrarian economic reformers.[25]

Comparative suggestions in revisionist historiography have not simply included economic aspects, but have expanded to other types of specific studies on the ideology and family life of the southern Italian elite, as in Giovanni Montroni's work. In this case, comparative points have often been made in reference to nineteenth-century England and its aristocracy. Yet, it is fair to say that, despite the importance of the above mentioned comparative suggestions, revisionist historians have not yet engaged in a sustained comparison between the *Mezzogiorno,* or one of its regions, and another area of the world. Curiously, several scholars have written important articles on comparative methodology, but none of them has so far put in practice their well-crafted theoretical points on the best way to make historical comparisons. Therefore, in this respect at least, southern Italian historiography lags far behind the historiography of the American South. And yet, there is plenty of room for comparison between the *Mezzogiorno* and other regions of the world, and, to be sure, comparison between the *Mezzogiorno* and the American South is just one of many possible comparisons, even though a particularly enlightening one. Purely from the point of view of historiographic development, even though very different, the two regions share more than one similarity in the fact of having been initially ideologically constructed and subsequently placed at the center of revisionist debates with ultimately comparable results.[26]

25. See Piero Bevilacqua and Marcello Gorgoni, "Mercati," *Meridiana* 1 (1987): 11–18; and Petrusewicz, *Latifundium*, 1–21. See also Piero Bevilacqua, "Clima, mercato e paesaggio agrario nel Mezzogiorno," in Piero Bevilacqua, ed., *Storia dell'agricoltura italiana in età contemporanea*, vol. 1, *Spazi e Paesaggi* (Venice, 1989), 643–667; Lupo, *Il giardino degli aranci*; Salvemini, *L'innovazione precaria*; and Marta Petrusewicz, "Agromania: Innovatori agricoli alla periferia dell'Ottocento," in Piero Bevilacqua, ed., *Storia dell'agricoltura italiana*, vol. 3, *Mercati e Istituzioni* (Venice, 1991), 295–343.

26. See Giovanni Montroni, *Gli uomini del re. La nobiltà napoletana nell'Ottocento* (Catanzaro, 1996), viii–xxvi; Luciano Cafagna, "La comparazione e la storia," *Meridiana* 6 (1989): 15–28; and Carlo Fumian, "Le virtù della comparazione," *Meridiana* 4 (1988): 197–222.

In fact, even taking into account the extraordinary differences between the antebellum American South and the nineteenth-century *Mezzogiorno*, the similarity between issues of historiographic debate on the nature of southern backwardness in the United States and Italy is striking. In both cases, historians have explained the substantial dichotomy and unbalance between the two parts of the country by looking at intrinsic features that made the South "peculiar" long before the 1860s. The weakness of southern entrepreneurial activity, the strength of a powerful landowning class, the failed land redistribution among the lower social strata, and the alliance between northern capital and southern agriculture are all themes that can be discussed within the context of the modern history of both Italy and the United States.[27]

In both the American and the Italian cases, historians have focused their efforts on explaining the different path to modernization followed by the South compared to the North. In both cases, reaction to the paradigms of backwardness and distinctiveness—widely supported by both American and Italian Marxist historians—has led to a discovery of or to an emphasis on the modern features of the southern economy. Also, to a certain extent, particular revisionist historians in both the United States and Italy have engaged in building a new paradigm of "capitalist rationality"—specifically in regard to the southern landed elites' management of plantations and *lati-fondi*—and have attempted to reduce the distance between the historical developments of the southern and northern economies. Finally, in both cases, recent historiographic trends have focused on ways to mediate between the two paradigms and have supported views of coexistence of capitalist and noncapitalist features in southern economy and society.[28]

The recognition of comparability—the acknowledgment of the existence of important similarities within completely different contexts—in terms of historiographic developments is an important first step in the construction of a case for the comparison of the antebellum American South and the nineteenth-century Italian *Mezzogiorno*. In this respect, a breakthrough in

27. See Bruce Levine, "Modernity, Backwardness, and Capitalism in the Two Souths," in Dal Lago and Halpern, eds., *American South and Italian Mezzogiorno*, 233–240; and Doyle, *Nations Divided*, 265–266.

28. See Peter Kolchin, *A Sphinx on the American Land: The Nineteenth-Century South in Comparative Perspective* (Baton Rouge, La., 2003), 79–83.

this process has come from Peter Kolchin's recent treatment of the nine-teenth-century American South in comparative perspective. In *A Sphinx on the American Land,* Kolchin has outlined three ways of comparing the American South: comparison between the South and the North, or "un-south"; comparison between different southern regions and types of South, or "many souths"; and comparison between the South and other regions of the world, or "other souths." Kochin's work, coming at the end of a long line of comparative studies, has brilliantly synthesized the path covered by American scholars in their analyses of the nineteenth-century South and has also anticipated new directions in comparative history. In Kolchin's view, while engaged for a long time in the exercise of comparison between the South and the "un-south," American historians have also produced a num-ber of sustained comparisons of the South with other regions of the world. Only relatively recently, they have discovered the significance of comparison between the many types of South and the many southern regions.[29]

Similarly, as Piero Bevilacqua has noted, Italian historians have spent a long time in understanding the difference between the *Mezzogiorno* and Italy's "un-south" and only recently they have discovered the existence of "many souths" within southern Italy; in the next step, they should engage in comparison between the *Mezzogiorno* and the "other souths" of the world. In both the American and the Italian cases, the latest approaches are the most innovative and they have shown already their potential in a few highly ac-claimed works. In the United States, comparison between the "many souths" has formed the central feature of recent studies by Ira Berlin and Philip Morgan, while in Italy it has been long practiced through the collections of essays on specific regions in the volumes of the *Storia d'Italia Einaudi. Le regioni.* Conversely, in the United States, comparison between the South and "other souths" is a long-established practice that has gradually expanded to include an increasing number of regions of the world, while, at best, it has only been advocated or hinted at by Italian revisionist historians.[30]

Yet, if we move from the plane of comparative historiography to the plane of comparative history, we can take Kolchin's three ways of compar-ing the South as suggestions to firmly place sustained comparative studies within the three contexts of the nation, the region, and the world. In fact, if

29. See Kolchin, *Sphinx on the American Land,* 1–6; and Kolchin, "American South in Com-parative Perspective," 26–59.

30. See Dal Lago and Halpern, "Two Case-Studies," 4–6; and Bevilacqua, "Peter Kolchin's American South," 60–72.

we compare the American South and the Italian *Mezzogiorno,* keeping as a guideline their relation with these three different contexts, we are able to highlight similarities and differences between their historical developments in such a way that they allow us to construct a case for sustained comparison between them. After all, the discovery of important similarities and the analysis of particularly striking differences between two case studies are the two fundamental ingredients of the most effective and comprehensive methods advocated by scholars who have attempted to construct a theory of comparison. In particular, as early as 1928, March Bloch had written in a truly path-breaking study that the general requirements for historical comparison are a certain similarity between the facts observed and certain dissimilarities between situations in which they have arisen.[31]

More than fifty years later, in 1980, outlining the particular comparative method which they termed "contrast of contexts," Theda Skocpol and Margaret Somers described the method's aim as "to bring out the unique features of each particular case ... and to show how these unique features affect the working out of putatively general social processes." The understanding of specific features in the interactions of the antebellum American South and of the nineteenth-century Italian *Mezzogiorno* with nation, region, and world in comparative perspective is, doubtless, an exercise in contrast of contexts. At the same time, it is also a way to practice what George Fredrickson has called "cross-national comparative history" in an effort to undermine the presupposition of absolute uniqueness that lies at the heart of the two paradigms of southern distinctiveness and to define the real elements of identity of the two southern regions.[32]

In general, the world context is the one that provides more similarities between the antebellum American South and the nineteenth-century Italian *Mezzogiorno,* especially if we take Immanuel Wallerstein's world-system approach. From Wallerstein's point of view, in economic terms, both regions were agricultural exporting peripheral areas at the periphery of the world-economy at a time in which Britain was the workshop of the world and the northern United States was undergoing its first wave of industrialization. Peripheral regions, such as the American South and the Italian *Mezzogiorno,*

31. See March Bloch, *Essays in the History of Medieval Europe* (Cambridge, 1965). See also Raymond Grew, "The Case for Comparing Histories," *AHR* 85 (1980): 763–782; and Peter Kolchin, "Comparing American History," *RAH* 10 (1982): 64–81.

32. Theda Skocpol and Margaret Somers, "The Use of Comparative History in Macro-Social Inquiry," *CSSH* 22 (1980): 178. See also George Frederickson, *Comparative Imagination,* 47–65.

were in comparable states of economic dependency on both Britain and the northern United States, to which they exported most of their raw materials. In this respect, as Wallerstein has pointed out, the economic role of the antebellum American South was similar to that of many other regions, from the Caribbean Islands to Andalusia and Sicily—and therefore the *Mezzogiorno*—which were equally at the periphery of the world-system. The implication is that "if one takes a close look at the cultures of these zones, the features which make them different at that time among themselves . . . pale before the striking similarities of the attitudes we associate with 'plantation' or 'seigneurial' zones in the capitalist world-economy." Therefore, taking Wallerstein's suggestions on board, we can imagine all sorts of comparisons between peripheral regions of the world-system, not just between the American South and the Italian *Mezzogiorno*.[33]

Also, Wallerstein's model has the advantage of providing an interpretative comparative framework that takes into account the most striking difference between the plantation and the *latifondo* economy—the existence of slavery in the former and its absence in the latter. In fact, in Wallerstein's view, slavery was just one of many forms that coerced labor—with different degrees of unfreedom—took in the peripheral regions of the world-economy. Therefore, on an ideal scale of systems of unfree labor employed at the periphery of the world-economy, American slavery would be at one end of the spectrum, being the strictest system in legal terms, and would be followed by serfdom and indentured servitude.[34]

The systems of labor relations employed in the nineteenth-century *Mezzogiorno*—ranging from tenancy to sharecropping—would not be excluded from the scale; rather, they would be at the other end of the spectrum. Although legally emancipated, southern Italian peasants could hardly be considered free by twentieth-century standards, since they were exploited, abused, and, in several cases, even discriminated against almost to the extent of being considered a race apart. Clearly, there are striking differences be-

33. Immanuel Wallerstein, "What Can One Mean by 'Southern Culture'?" in Numan Bartley, ed., *The Evolution of Southern Culture* (Athens, Ga., 1985), 57. See also Immanuel Wallerstein, *The Modern World-System*, vols. 1–3 (New York, 1974–1989); and Jean and Peter Schneider, *Culture and Political Economy in Western Sicily* (New York, 1976).

34. See Immanuel Wallerstein, *The Capitalist World-Economy: Essays by Immanuel Wallerstein* (New York, 1979), 119–131. See also Stanley Engerman, "Slavery, Serfdom, and Other Forms of Coerced Labor: Similarities and Differences," in Michael L. Bush, ed., *Serfdom and Slavery: Studies in Legal Bondage* (London, 1996), 18–41; and Bush, *Servitude in Modern Times*, 3–54.

tween the type of legal enslavement of African Americans that characterized the antebellum American South and the combination of economic dependence and psychological subjection that afflicted peasants in the nineteenth-century *Mezzogiorno*. Yet, it is important to acknowledge the place of the two systems of labor relations in the context of the nineteenth-century world-economy, within which they were but two of a range of types of unfree labor employed in peripheral regions.[35]

The regional context offers a rather ambiguous record in terms of similarities and differences between the American South and the Italian *Mezzogiorno*. If the term *region* includes the entirety of each of the two southern areas, even though they shared a comparably peripheral position in the world economy, politically the former was part of the United States since the foundation of the American Republic—apart from the Civil War period of 1861–1865—while the latter became a part of Italy only in 1860–1861. As a consequence, the very idea of southern identity assumed, politically, opposite characteristics in the United States and in Italy in the nineteenth century. In the case of the American South, southern identity related to the socioeconomic features derived from slavery; only in 1861, with the creation of the Confederate States of America, did it become linked to the existence of a nation-state. Conversely, in the case of the *Mezzogiorno*, southern identity was linked to the existence of a sovereign state—the Kingdom of the Two Sicilies—until 1860–1861; yet, afterward, it became linked to what was left of that state's particular socioeconomic features. Significantly, the legacies of these two very different types of identity continued to provide the American South and the Italian *Mezzogiorno* with the main canvases for the depictions of their regional characteristics long after the 1860s.[36]

The term *region* can equally imply the existence of internal variety within the American South and within the Italian *Mezzogiorno*. In this respect, differences between the "many souths" that formed the southern United

35. See Bevilacqua, "Peter Kolchin's American South," 65–67. See also Stanley Engerman, "Introduction," in Stanley Engerman, ed., *Terms of Labor: Slavery, Serfdom, and Free Labor* (Stanford, Calif., 1999), 1–24; and Robert J. Steinfeld, *Coercion, Contract, and Free Labor in the Nineteenth Century* (New York, 2001), 1–25.

36. See Doyle, *Nations Divided*, 69–89; C. Van Woodward, *The Burden of Southern History* (Baton Rouge, La., 1961), 3–29; Gaines M. Foster, *Ghosts of the Confederacy: Defeat, the Lost Cause, and the Emergence of the New South* (New York, 1987); Moe, *View from Vesuvius*, 187–249; and John Dickie, "Stereotypes of the Italian South, 1860–1900," in Lumley and Morris, eds., *New History of the Italian South*, 114–147.

States and southern Italy have played a crucial role in their historical development. In fact, from the economic point of view, in both the American and the Italian cases, agrarian and urban regions coexisted side by side.
Moreover, specific crops—such as cotton, rice, tobacco, and sugar—created
subregions within the agricultural economy of the antebellum American
South. Conversely, other types of crops—such as grain, olives, citrus fruits,
and wine grapes—created comparable subregions within the agricultural
economy of the nineteenth-century *Mezzogiorno*.[37]

Arguably, the fragmentation of the American South and of southern
Italy into different regions had its most far-reaching effects in terms of politics. The differences between the two case studies are, again, striking. In the
nineteenth-century United States, regional sovereignty was recognized and
upheld by the Constitution and by the federal system. Each regional political constituency of the American South was a state with its own regional
government in charge of the local socioeconomic system. In contrast, in
nineteenth-century southern Italy, the absolute monarchical system denied
all instances of regional sovereignty. Though the different provinces of the
Kingdom of the Two Sicilies were characterized by very different socioeconomic features and political cultures, they were free to express the richness
of this diversity mostly at times of political upheavals. And yet, a key similarity was the fact that regional opposition to the policies of the central government played a crucial role in the historical development of both southern
regions. In the American Republic, opposition to centralization led southern
politicians to support the doctrine of states' rights as a precautionary measure
against the federal government's antislavery legislation. Conversely, in the
Bourbon absolutist system, opposition took a conspiratorial form and related
to the provincial elites' critique of bureaucratic centralization and the absence of constitutional liberties. In both cases, the elites' reaction to governmental centralization defined the relationship between regional and national
politics and was at the origin of the most serious national political crises.[38]

In this connection, the national context is both the most problematic
one and the one that offers the clearest view of the interplay between similarities and differences in the comparison between the American South and

37. See Kolchin, *Sphinx on the American Land*, 39–41; and Salvemini, *L'innovazione precaria*,
3–32.

38. See Forrest McDonald, *States' Rights and the Union*: Imperium in Imperio (Lawrence,
Kans., 2000); and Enrica Di Ciommo, "Elites provinciali e potere borbonico. Note per un'analisi
comparata," in Massafra, ed., *Il Mezzogiorno preunitario*, 965–1038.

the Italian *Mezzogiorno.* Due to the particularity of their regional histories, the two southern regions played a fundamental role in the process of definition of American and Italian national identities—yet, in profoundly different ways. Aside from the five-year period of the Confederate experience between 1861 and 1865, the majority of American southerners thought about their national identity in terms that were the same as those of other citizens of the United States. Conversely, at least until 1848, the majority of southern Italians identified their nationality with their loyalty to the Kingdom of the Two Sicilies; only with the experience of the Revolution of 1848 would a large number of wealthy and educated southern Italians increasingly identify as their goal citizenship in a new Italian nation—which eventually they achieved in 1861. Therefore, the American South was an integral part of American national identity for most of its history, aside from the Civil War period, during which it formed a contested Confederate national identity in opposition to the one of the United States. On the other hand, the Italian *Mezzogiorno* was the source of a national identity of its own for most of its history—and of a contested southern Italian national identity in the preunification period—until it was incorporated into the Italian kingdom and, with the loss of its independence, became, de facto, a region within a nation.[39]

And yet, even though the differences mentioned above are crucial, there are also important similarities in the processes of formation of national identities that reached their culmination in the early 1860s in both the United States and Italy. In both cases, the year 1861 witnessed the triumph of nationalist ideas with the birth of a new national institution: the Confederate nation in the American case, the Kingdom of Italy in the Italian one. If this important comparative point has escaped the attention of historians, it is because the scanty references to comparison between the United States and Italy in the 1860s have always placed the emphasis on the similarities between the Union's drive to subdue secession and the Piedmontese kingdom's drive to form a unified Italian nation and have, consequently, constructed the two southern regions as though they formed comparable bastions of opposition to these parallel processes.[40]

39. See Emory Thomas, *The Confederacy as a Revolutionary Experience* (New York, 1979); and Enrica Di Ciommo, *La nazione possibile. Mezzogiorno e questione nazionale nel 1848* (Milan, 1993).

40. See, for example, Carl Degler, "One among Many: The United States and National Unification," in Gabor S. Boritt, ed., *Lincoln, the War President* (New York, 1992), 92–94.

According to this view, both the Bourbon kingdom and the Confederacy resisted northern programs of nation-building with staunchly reactionary policies. American slaveholders and southern Italian landowners in 1860–1861 appeared as the key factors in the opposition to the progressive forces of liberal nationalism in both the United States and Italy. They were akin—according to David Potter—to "the landed proprietors in central Europe who opposed German or Polish or Italian or Hungarian or Bohemian nationalism. All of them were traditionalist. All feared that nationalism was linked with a democracy that they distrusted." Similarly, for Raimondo Luraghi, both American slaveholders and southern Italian landowners were "seigneurial" landed elites whose conservative worldview led them to oppose the two northern bourgeoisies' twin programs of enforcing liberal nationalism and constructing a national market in the United States and Italy.[41]

Yet, this was hardly the case. On one hand, by 1860—and even before then—many southern Italian landowners supported the construction of an Italian nation, even though, quite naturally, they divided according to their different political beliefs. Therefore, rather than opposing liberal nationalism, many southern Italian landowners took part in it and even made possible the creation of an Italian nation based on liberal principles. On the other hand, American slaveholders' reactionary outlook was clearly a consequence of their defense of human bondage. Yet, as many recent studies have argued, their republican convictions were hardly different from those of northerners. They both supported the same principles of liberty, equality, and defense of private property, even though in the South the existence of African American slavery restricted these principles to the white race. And still, this restriction of privileges to a specific class of people was hardly anomalous in "liberal" Europe, where—even without racial discrimination—the distance between landed proprietors and peasants was great. In this respect, nineteenth-century southern Italy was closer to the norm, rather than being the exception. Comparison between the antebellum American South and the nineteenth-century *Mezzogiorno* might help a great deal our understanding

41. David M. Potter, *The South and Sectional Conflict* (Baton Rouge, La., 1967), 290; and Raimondo Luraghi, "The Civil War and the Modernization of American Society: Social Structure and Industrial Revolution in the Old South before and during the War," *CWH* 18 (1972): 230–267. See also Raimondo Luraghi, *The Rise and Fall of the Plantation South* (New York, 1978); and Barrington Moore Jr., *Social Origins of Dictatorship and Democracy: Lord and Peasant in the Making of the Modern World* (New York, 1966), 111–158.

of the similarities and differences between slaveholders' republicanism and landowners' liberalism.[42]

The creation of nations in the American South and in southern Italy in 1861 was, doubtless, the result of different economic, social, and political factors. Yet, in both cases the actual achievement of nationhood largely depended on the determinant role played by the southern elite. In order to fully understand the significance of the role played by the two elites in the two processes of nation-building, we need to reflect upon the comparable functions that slaveholders and landowners performed in connecting the world, the regional, and the national contexts with which the two southern regions interacted. Within the world context, American slaveholders and southern Italian landowners held a prominent position vis-à-vis the largest part of the economy of two regions that were predominantly agrarian; this position allowed them to maintain firm control over relations between their respective regions and the world market. In different ways and degrees, both elites profited from the nineteenth-century world market's demand for cash crops and commercial agricultural products—a demand that originated primarily in England and in the northern United States. The profits that American slaveholders and southern Italian landowners made with the production and sale of agricultural products for the world market and also—especially in the southern Italian case—for the internal market often allowed them to adopt luxurious lifestyles, lifestyles that relied on the exploitation of two very different classes of agricultural laborers. In both cases, the elites rationalized their exploitative practices and their consequent hegemonic social position, seeing them and describing them—especially in the American case—through the lenses of different, but comparable, patriarchal-paternalistic worldviews.[43]

Equally important was the fact that economic and social prominence allowed both American slaveholders and southern Italian landowners to

42. See especially Petrusewicz, *Come il Meridone*, 135–158; Nicola Antonacci, *Dalla Repubblica napoletana alla monarchia italiana. Politica e società in Terra di Bari (1799–1860)* (Bari, 2000); James Oakes, *Slavery and Freedom: An Interpretation of the Old South* (New York, 1990); and Lacy K. Ford, *Origins of Southern Radicalism: The South Carolina Upcountry, 1800–1860* (New York, 1988). See also Maria Malatesta, *Le aristocrazie terriere nell'Europa contemporanea* (Bari-Rome, 2000).

43. See Genovese, *World the Slaveholders Made*, 21–102; Fox-Genovese and Genovese, *Fruits of Merchant Capital*, 3–26; and Luraghi, *Plantation South*, 55–62.

claim different, but comparable, types of political rights. In fact, it was in the realm of politics that the two landed elites played a particularly crucial role in the connection between the regional and national contexts of southern history in the United States and Italy. To begin with, a regional diversity similar to the one that characterized the "many souths" that formed the antebellum American South and the Italian *Mezzogiorno* also characterized American slaveholders and southern Italian landowners. Though holding a broadly similar ideological outlook, American slaveholders differed in their way of life according to the crop they grew, the state they lived in, and the state's particular political culture and historical characteristics. Comparably, southern Italian landowners living in the different provinces of the Kingdom of the Two Sicilies engaged in different types of agricultural businesses and were acutely aware of the importance of regional cultures and traditions, which often stretched hundreds of years back in time. Yet, despite these profound regional differences, in 1861 the majority of American slaveholders joined to form the Confederate States of America, while a number of southern Italian landowners gave their support for the Kingdom of Italy. In both cases, the creation of a nation-state led to the sudden near-obliteration of southern regional identities in the name of a supraregional ideal.[44]

The long-term causes of the contemporary creations of the Confederate and Italian nations in 1861 relate to the developments of two extremely complex socioeconomic and political processes. These processes have never been the subjects of sustained comparison before. While students of nationalism have regularly considered the Italian Risorgimento as a prototype of other national movements, only recently have they included the Confederacy as an important case study, and only recently have southern historians written works with references to the theoretical scholarship on nationalism. Doubtless, a close reading of these studies is crucial for the understanding of the origins and development of nationalist movements in Europe and America in comparative perspective. Yet, I believe that we need to combine their suggestions with a sustained comparative analysis of the specific features of the worldviews of American slaveholders and southern Italian landowners if we wish to take a further step in the understanding of the reasons behind

44. See William Freehling, *The Road to Disunion: Secessionists at Bay, 1776–1854* (New York, 1990), 9–36; and Angelantonio Spagnoletti, *Storia del Regno delle Due Sicilie* (Bologna, 1997), 243–270.

the support for the Confederacy in the American South and for the Italian kingdom in the *Mezzogiorno* in 1861.[45]

In particular, though profoundly different in many respects, both American slaveholders and southern Italian landowners adopted worldviews that gave overarching importance to the defense of individual freedom and private property and postulated resistance to governmental policies and socio-political movements that threatened to violate these principles. On one hand, American slaveholders resisted both the federal government's attempts to interfere with the issue of slavery and the abolitionist movement's pressure to emancipate the slaves, claiming their exclusive rights to freedom and property. Ultimately, their claims formed the ideological bases of the Confederacy—by all means and purposes, a slaveholding nation. On the other hand, southern Italian liberal landowners resisted both the Bourbon government's attempts at implementing absolutist centralization and the pressure of the agrarian masses in regard to land redistribution. They did so by claiming the indispensable nature of landed property and, ultimately, supporting several of the authoritarian measures of the new liberal Italian nation for the sake of its protection.[46]

Remarkably, a comparable phenomenon of "elite resistance to state formation"—an expression borrowed from Lucy Riall—seems to have characterized the American and the southern Italian cases. A comparable defense of perceived republican and liberal principles, which actually disguised comparable fears of losing local power and privileges, seems to have been the guiding idea behind the elites' crusades against the centralizing policies of national governments; in both cases, the crusade ultimately led to the formation of a new national political institution in substitution of the old one. A comparable opposition to the federal government's perceived policy of denial of states' rights and to Bourbon programs of administrative centralization led American slaveholders and southern Italian landowners to support parallel programs of construction of two new nations. As they did

45. See especially Ernest Gellner, *Nations and Nationalism* (Oxford, 1983); Eric J. Hobsbawm, *Nations and Nationalism since 1780* (Cambridge, 1990); Liah Greenfeld, *Nationalism: Five Roads to Modernity* (Cambridge, Mass., 1995); and James McPherson, *Is Blood Thicker than Water? Reflections on Contemporary Nationalism* (New York, 1998).

46. See James L. Huston, *Calculating the Value of the Union: Slavery, Property Rights, and the Economic Origins of the Civil War* (Chapel Hill, N.C., 2003); Oakes, *Slavery and Freedom*, 137–195; and Di Ciommo, *La nazione possible*, 347–361.

so, American slaveholders and southern Italian landowners participated in a process of invention of two new national traditions—the Confederate and the Italian. Though clearly different in a number of respects, in both cases the process of "invention of tradition" occurred according to familiar patterns that Eric Hobsbawm and other scholars have abundantly described.[47]

To be sure, region and nation have also interacted in another comparable way in the American South and the Italian *Mezzogiorno*. In both cases, the feelings of extreme peculiarity harbored by the elite of a specific region— South Carolina and Sicily—have played a crucial role in the exacerbation of conflicts between southern elite and national government. In fact, South Carolina's and Sicily's elites were largely responsible for the unparalleled and continuous assertion of regional distinctiveness through secessionist/separatist politics in the four decades before 1860. Remarkably, with their secessionist/separatist politics aimed at destabilization of the American Union and of the Bourbon kingdom, South Carolina's and Sicily's elites ended up playing crucial roles in the process of formation of the Confederate and Italian nations. Thus, in both cases, paradoxically, extreme regionalism opened the way to the unleashing of nationalism. Therefore, a comparative analysis of the interaction between regional elites and national government in the antebellum American South and in the nineteenth-century Italian *Mezzogiorno* must pay particular attention to the specific case studies of South Carolina and Sicily, and specifically to the extreme regionalist ideologies that characterized the political demands of the South Carolinian and Sicilian elites and which eventually led to the comparable historical phenomena of secession and separatism.[48]

Arguably, the legacy of regionalism in the American South and in the Italian *Mezzogiorno* went far beyond 1860–1861 and was a major cause in the fall of the Confederacy during the American Civil War and in the outbreak

47. See Lucy Riall, "Elite Resistance to State Formation: The Case of Italy," in Mary Fulbrook, ed., *National Histories and European History* (London, 1993), 46–68; Doyle, *Nations Divided*, 90–91; and Eric J. Hobsbawm, "Introduction: Inventing Traditions," in Eric J. Hobsbawm and Terence Ranger, eds., *The Invention of Tradition* (Cambridge, 1983), 1–14. See also Drew Faust, *The Creation of Confederate Nationalism: Ideology and Identity in the Civil War South* (Baton Rouge, La., 1988); Roberto Martucci, *L'invenzione dell'Italia unita, 1855–1864* (Florence, 1999); and Benedict Anderson, *Imagined Communities: Reflections on the Origins of Nationalism* (London, 1983).

48. See Manisha Sinha, *The Counterrevolution of Slavery: Politics and Ideology in Antebellum South Carolina* (Chapel Hill, N.C., 2000); and Francesco Renda, *Storia della Sicilia dal 1860 al 1970*, vol. 1, *I caratteri originali e gli anni dell'unificazione italiana* (Palermo, 1984).

of the southern Italian civil war between 1861 and 1865. Yet, at a more general level, the legacy that American slaveholders and southern Italian landowners handed down to the American South and the Italian *Mezzogiorno* related to their responsibility in the unfolding of the two regions' particular paths to modernization, the substance of earlier historiographic debates on southern backwardness and of American and Italian paradigms of southern distinctiveness. Also, in both cases, the agrarian working class bore the brunt of the region's transition to modernization, since it was through the investment of the profits derived from the exploitation of American slaves and southern Italian peasants that American slaveholders and southern Italian landowners managed to maintain the southern agricultural economies temporarily at pace with changes in the world market.

On the other hand, the rather episodic and unorganized nature of the two elites' efforts to keep up with economic modernization, with little or no consequences in terms of much-needed social reforms—reforms such as slave emancipation in the American South and land redistribution in southern Italy—left the two southern regions in a comparable state of relative backwardness. Though reforms with very different degrees of radical content were eventually enforced in the two regions, backwardness continued to be the main cause behind particular political problems once the two regional landed elites were definitively incorporated into the American and Italian nation-states. Backwardness was also the main factor that led to the American South's and the Italian *Mezzogiorno*'s historiographic stigmatization as retrograde and distinctly anomalous regions—the substance of both America's and Italy's southern questions.

CHAPTER I

Plantations, *Latifondi,* and Commercial Agriculture

The Economic Bases of Social Power

In geographical terms, the American South is the region of the United States located under the Mason-Dixon Line and east of New Mexico. This geographical definition includes the area covered by the eleven southern states that in 1861 seceded from the American Republic to form the Confederate States of America and by the five southern states that remained loyal to the Union. Before 1861, the presence of slavery defined the boundaries of the South in economic and social, rather geographical or political, terms. As a result of the nineteenth-century boom in cotton production, slavery expanded from its original location in the Atlantic Seaboard states—which stretched from Virginia to Georgia—into the areas of the Old Southwest, creating a constantly shifting frontier on the western border of the southern region.[1]

The socioeconomic nature of the characteristics that defined the antebellum American South and the process of dynamic expansion of its frontier were the most important factors that distinguished the region from the nineteenth-century Italian *Mezzogiorno.* Unlike the American South, the Italian *Mezzogiorno* had a long history of settlement that stretched into antiquity and had much clearer geographical boundaries; it included the continental South—the area which covers the lower half of the Italian peninsula from north of Naples to the tip of Calabria—and the island of Sicily. Between 1815 and 1861, the presence of the Bourbon state—the Kingdom of the Two Sicilies—defined the boundaries of the *Mezzogiorno* primarily in

---

1. See James David Miller, *South by Southwest: Planter Emigration and Identity in the Slave South* (Charlottesville, Va., 2002), 1–17.

political, rather than economic and social, terms. Also, unlike the American South, the *Mezzogiorno* did not have a constantly shifting frontier; its only boundary that did not border the sea was in the north of the kingdom, where a fixed line of division existed between the Kingdom of the Two Sicilies and the Papal State.[2]

The geographical differences mentioned above have a particular importance in the context of a treatment of the economic features of the American South and of the Italian *Mezzogiorno* in the first half of the nineteenth century. In the American South, the frontier represented a safety valve in regard to both population pressure and soil depletion; such a safety valve was absent in the *Mezzogiorno,* where chronic problems of overpopulation and soil erosion had long existed. Also, the particular geographical features of the *Mezzogiorno*—that is, the presence of large middle-range mountains and plateaus with little room for valleys and narrow coastal strips—made it a particularly unmanageable territory in agricultural terms; conversely, in the American South, fertile alluvial soils alternated with plains and hills, while mountains were relatively few. Therefore, while in the American South large portions of the territory could be used for farming and could be linked together in a web of market relations that encountered very few natural obstacles, in the *Mezzogiorno* only a few areas near the coasts and on the few plains were suited for farming and had relatively strong links with the market.[3]

As a consequence, two very different types of landed estates characterized the landscapes of the two regions: the American plantation, with its predominance of intensive cultivation and commercial agriculture; and the southern Italian *latifondo,* with its practice of extensive cultivation and stock raising. In the nineteenth century, the impact of the market revolution in the American South and of the commercial revolution in the *Mezzogiorno* led to a renewed emphasis on the commercial character of agricultural production and to a consequent transformation of the agricultural landscapes of the two regions. In both cases, the transformation generated a clear distinction between areas of commercial production with a strong link to the world market and relatively isolated areas that produced mainly for internal consumption. While the plantation economy of the American South underwent

2. See Nelson Moe, *The View from Vesuvius: Italian Culture and the Southern Question* (Berkeley, Calif., 2002), 126–143.

3. See Donald W. Meinig, *The Shaping of America,* vol. 2, *Continental America, 1800–1867* (New Haven, Conn., 1993), 285–295; and Piero Bevilacqua, *Breve storia dell'Italia meridionale dall'Ottocento a oggi* (Rome, 1997), 9–15.

a boom, the *latifondo* economy of the *Mezzogiorno* underwent a profound transformation; in both cases, the process of adjustment led to an increase in the complexity and diversity of agricultural regions and to the establishment of a hierarchy among them in terms of economic importance.[4]

In the American South, the effects of the market revolution—the complex of factors related to the first wave of industrialization in the United States—accelerated the process of creation of a dual economy. According to Harry Watson, in the antebellum period, the southern economy was "divided between commercial western-dominated sectors and highly traditional forms of production that were relatively isolated from the pressures of contemporary capitalism." This division showed clearly in the difference between those areas of the South where plantations and farms produced staple crops—such as rice, tobacco, cotton, hemp, and sugar—and were closer to the sea or to navigable rivers, and those areas where yeoman communities, though isolated, struggled to keep their self-sufficiency and economic independence.[5]

Since the seventeenth century, planters had grown tobacco around the Chesapeake Bay (coastal Virginia and Maryland) and in North Carolina, while they had grown rice primarily in the lowcountry of South Carolina and Georgia. From the beginning of the nineteenth century, Louisiana had been the center of sugar production, while Kentucky and Tennessee produced both hemp and tobacco. Yet, surpassing all other entries in the balance of southern agricultural exports, cotton was on its way to becoming the king crop of the entire region stretching from upcountry South Carolina to Texas. Between 1800 and 1860, planters and slaveholding farmers led the expansion of cotton cultivation and slavery into the area of the Old Southwest that includes the present-day states of Mississippi, Alabama, Arkansas, and Florida (see map 1). Only a few isolated localities in the mountainous regions and in places where transportation was particularly difficult remained

4. See Susan B. Hilliard, "Plantations and the Molding of Southern Landscape," in M. P. Conzen, ed., *The Making of the American Landscape* (London, 1993); and Piero Bevilacqua, "Tra Europa e Mediterraneo. L'organizzazione dello spazio e i sistemi agrari," in Piero Bevilacqua, ed., *Storia dell'agricoltura italiana in età contemporanea*, vol. 1, *Spazi e Paesaggi* (Venice, 1989), 20–23.

5. Harry L. Watson, "Slavery and Development in a Dual Economy: The South and the Market Revolution," in Melvyn Stokes and Stephen Conway, eds., *The Market Revolution in America: Social, Political, and Religious Expressions, 1800–1880* (Charlottesville, Va., 1996), 44–45. See also Morton Rothstein, "The Antebellum South as a Dual Economy: A Tentative Hypothesis," *AH* 41 (1967): 373–383.

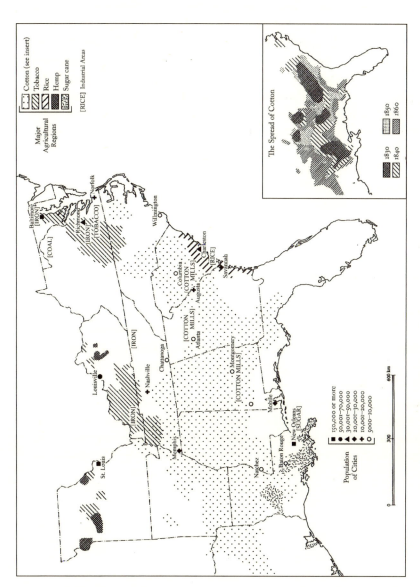

MAP 1. Major Agricultural Regions, Industrial Areas, and Population of Cities in the American South in the Late Antebellum Period

relatively untouched by the influences of the market revolution; these were areas where mostly nonslaveholding farmers and their families lived.[6]

The boom in agricultural production created a hierarchy of economic importance among different regions and areas according to their relation to the market within the dual economy scheme; it also led to the subordination of both transportation facilities and cities to the needs of commercial agriculture. While transportation served mainly the purpose of linking regions of commercial agricultural production to national and international markets, cities served primarily as marketplaces for the export and sale of commercial crops. As a consequence, the South lagged far behind the North in terms of both manufacturing and railroad construction; at the same time, out of a total population of 12.2 million in 1860—4 million of which were slaves mostly working on plantations and farms—only a small percentage lived in cities. Only four cities had more than fifty thousand inhabitants: New Orleans, Louisiana; Baltimore, Maryland; St. Louis, Missouri; and Louisville, Kentucky. Significantly, three of them were located in states bordering the North. Two more cities—Richmond, Virginia, and Charleston, South Carolina—had a population between thirty thousand and fifty thousand; even though both had an unparalleled cultural importance as capitals of the oldest planter aristocracy of the South and also hosted significant manufactures, they were still small and underdeveloped by northern and European standards.[7]

Comparable to the impact of the market revolution in the American South, the influence of the commercial revolution in the *Mezzogiorno*—that is, the participation of southern Italian products in the trade circuits generated by the industrial revolution—resulted in the creation of a hierarchy of importance among different regions according to their relation to the international market. In the model proposed by Biagio Salvemini, the nineteenth-century economy of the *Mezzogiorno* included three types of areas with different degrees of participation in the market. The first type

6. See Keumsoo Hong, "The Geography of Time and Labor in the Late Antebellum American Rural South: *Fin-de-*Servitude Time Consciousness, Contested Labor, and Plantation Capitalism," *IRSH* 46 (2001): 1–27; and Steven Hahn, *The Roots of Southern Populism: Yeoman Farmers and the Transformation of the Georgia Upcountry, 1850–1890* (New York, 1983).

7. See Eugene Genovese, *The Political Economy of Slavery: Studies in the Economy and Society of the Slave South* (New York, 1965), 157–179; and Claudia Dale Goldin, *Urban Slavery in the American South: A Quantitative History* (Chicago, 1976), 11–27.

characterized the largest part of the *Mezzogiorno*—the inland areas of the continental South and Sicily. They were the traditional regions of extensive grain cultivation where *latifondi* alternated with pastures and peasant farms. Similar to the mountainous regions with independent yeoman production in the American South, these areas were either isolated or poorly connected to the market because of both geographical and structural reasons.[8]

Then, Salvemini distinguishes between areas that participated passively and areas that participated actively in the market. The former had mostly "a subordinate role in the organization of market exchanges," while in the latter commercial operators elaborated market strategies and made choices regarding the process of production. Both areas were "fully integrated in the commercial web headed by the strongest capitalist regions of Europe," and both included *latifondi* and commercial farms where grain production alternated with the cultivation of cash crops, such as olives, citrus fruits, and wine grapes. Olive oil was a particularly important product in the coastal regions of Terra di Bari and Terra d'Otranto, in the coastal area of lower Calabria, on the eastern coast of Sicily, and in the region around Naples. Citrus fruits were produced primarily in Sicily, both in the *Conca d'oro*—the area surrounding Palermo—and along the coast around Catania, and in the lower tip of Calabria. Wine production was widespread and was especially concentrated on the coast of both western and eastern Sicily and in the coastal area around Naples (see map 2).[9]

Comparable to what happened in the American South, the commercial revolution in the *Mezzogiorno* led to an increasing subordination of cities to the agricultural needs of the countryside. Even though in the *Mezzogiorno* there was a much older and more diverse urban life than in the American South, in both cases the cities functioned primarily as agricultural markets, since few had industrial activities or proper infrastructures. Despite the efforts of the Bourbon government, most areas of the *Mezzogiorno* lacked roads and railroads. In 1860, the Bourbon capital, Naples, with more than four hundred thousand inhabitants, was one of the largest cities in Europe,

8. See Biagio Salvemini, *L'innovazione precaria. Spazi, mercati e società nel Mezzogiorno tra Sette e Ottocento* (Catanzaro, 1995), 10–20. See also Aurelio Lepre, *Il Mezzogiorno dal feudalesimo al capitalismo* (Naples, 1979), 9–60.

9. Salvemini, *L'innovazione precaria,* 13. See also Giuseppe Civile, "Economia e società nel Mezzogiorno tra la Restaurazione e l'Unità," *S&S* 9 (1980): 705–714; and Piero Bevilacqua, "Forme del paesaggio ed evoluzione dell'habitat. Alcune ipotesi," *Meridiana* 10 (1990): 77–94.

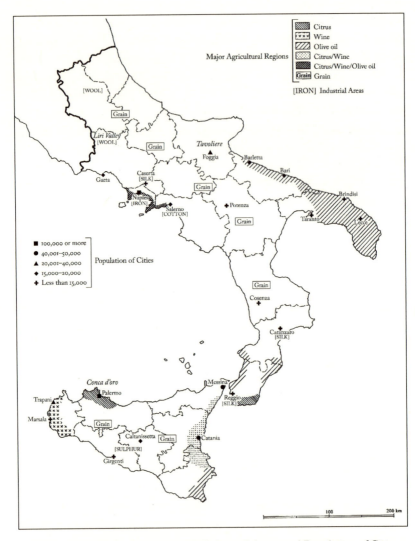

MAP 2. Major Agricultural Regions, Industrial Areas, and Population of Cities in the Italian *Mezzogiorno* in the Early Restoration

and while it had few manufactures, it drove most of the internal market for agricultural products, such as grain. Three other cities—Palermo, Messina, and Catania—each had over forty thousand inhabitants; significantly, they were all located in Sicily and, even though they were important provincial cultural centers, had little industrial activity to speak of. The large majority of the Bourbon kingdom's total population of 9.2 million lived and worked in the countryside or in relatively small towns, many of which were both physically and cultural isolated from the few larger urban centers of fifteen thousand to thirty thousand inhabitants.[10]

Therefore, in the nineteenth century, both the American South and the Italian *Mezzogiorno* were overwhelmingly agricultural regions located at the periphery of the world economy. They participated in the world market to different degrees through the production and sale of crops grown on plantations and *latifondi*—and also on smaller farms. As a consequence, the elites of the two regions—American slaveholders and southern Italian landowners—maintained their power primarily through ownership of land, and especially of the large landed estates that were at once the main centers of agricultural production and the sources of labor for a large part of the agrarian working classes. Though plantations and *latifondi* had somewhat different origins and their responses to the changing conditions of the world market were markedly different, travelers and political economists justly regarded them as the economic bases of the enormous social power of the two regional elites—a power that the elites exercised primarily through the exploitation of their agrarian laborers, whether these were enslaved African Americans or nominally free but landless southern Italian peasants.

Plantations and Latifondi *between the Eighteenth and Nineteenth Centuries*

According to Immanuel Wallerstein, during the sixteenth century a complex interrelation of different factors created a European world-economy that was characterized by a capitalist mode of production. Within the capitalist world-economy, economically stronger regions were located in the "core"

10. See Enrica Di Ciommo, "L'urbanizzazione del Mezzogiorno nella prima metà dell'Ottocento. Aspetti storici e problemi di ricerca," *SU* 45 (1988): 77–102; and Guido Pescosolido, "Dal sottosviluppo alla questione meridionale," in Giuseppe Galasso and Rosario Romeo, eds., *Storia del Mezzogiorno,* vol. 12 (Naples, 1991), 17–90.

and weaker regions in the "periphery" and "semi-periphery." Core regions and peripheral and semi-peripheral regions differed in the way labor was recruited and in the form labor took, especially in regard to the degree of freedom: while in core regions wage labor was the norm, in peripheral and semi-peripheral regions sharecropping and different forms of coerced labor, ranging from serfdom to slavery, were widespread. In time, coerced labor became typically associated with the staple crop agriculture practiced on large landed estates at the periphery of the world-economy, where workers were forced to participate in the production of raw materials—a process that the local elites controlled, together with the export of the materials to the core regions.[11]

From the perspective of the world-economy, plantations and *latifondi* were but two of several types of agricultural structures at the periphery of a capitalist world-system. Large agricultural enterprises employing laborers with different degrees of freedom were widespread throughout southern and eastern Europe, Latin America, and areas of Africa and Asia. An un-precedented increase in the movement of commodities characterized the nineteenth century. The industrial revolution generated a demand for raw materials that converted whole regions of the world into specialized areas of production. As a consequence, a transformation occurred in the economic and social structures of these regions, a transformation that affected the existence of large landed estates. The worldwide demand for items such as cotton, rice, sugar, coffee, grain, citrus, olive oil, and wine changed the func-tion of plantations, *latifondi, haciendas, Rittergüter,* and *çiftlik.* Each one of these types of landed estates specialized in the production of one or more of the agricultural items mentioned above, items that the landed elites in control of the peripheral economies exported, with the help of merchants and middlemen, to the most industrialized regions of the world—namely England and the northern United States—making enormous profits.[12]

11. See Immanuel Wallerstein, *The Capitalist World-Economy* (New York, 1979), 18–29. See also Marcel Van Der Linden, "Global History and 'the Modern World-System': Thoughts at the Twenty-Fifth Anniversary of the Fernand Braudel Center," *IRSH* 46 (2001): 423–459.

12. See Eric R. Wolf, *Europe and the People without History* (Berkeley, Calif., 1982), 310–322. Specifically on *latifondi* and *haciendas,* see Marta Petrusewicz, *Latifundium: Moral Economy and Material Life in a Nineteenth-Century Periphery* (Ann Arbor, Mich., 1996); and Steven J. Stern, "Feudalism, Capitalism, and the World-System in the Perspective of Latin America and the Caribbean," *AHR* 93 (1988): 829–872.

Common to all peripheral societies were the centralization of production in large agricultural units and its focus on a particular variety of staple crops, together with the employment of a large agricultural workforce. While the primary economic function of a large landed estate was the production and sale of particularly valuable cash crops, a significant part of the workforce also worked in the production of additional food crops for internal consumption and subsistence. The emphasis on commercial agriculture differed from case to case. In general, on southern Italian *latifondi,* production of cash crops for sale was less common than on American plantations. On most *latifondi,* grain production covered the majority of the available land, and its sale was aimed primarily at an internal market; yet, cash crops—such as olives, citrus fruits, or wine grapes—often grew side by side or in particular areas of the estates. In contrast, on plantations, cash crops—such as tobacco, rice, cotton, or sugar—took most of the available land; nonetheless, quite a few areas also produced corn and vegetables for subsistence and internal consumption. This basic difference between plantations and *latifondi* resulted from the particular geographical features and constraints of the environments of the American South and the Italian *Mezzogiorno* mentioned above; at the same time, it also had specific historical and structural reasons.[13]

In the late Middle Ages, *latifondi* and plantations lay side by side on the islands of the Mediterranean. First the Arabs and then the Venetian and Genoese merchants developed plantation agriculture involving slave labor in the sugar-producing areas of Cyprus, Crete, Sicily, and southern Spain. Until the fifteenth century, plantations were a localized phenomenon that only partly relied on the relatively small Mediterranean slave trade. For example—according to David Brion Davis—in their sugar plantations in Cyprus, Venetians employed "a mixed labor force of local serfs and Muslim slaves." On the other hand, *latifondi* were widespread and employed mostly local labor, both servile and semi-servile.[14]

13. See John Michael Vlach, "Plantation Landscapes of the Antebellum South," in Edward D. C. Campbell Jr. and Kym S. Rice, eds., *Before Freedom Came: African American Life in the Antebellum South* (Richmond, Va., 1991), 21–50; and Franco Mercurio and Saverio Russo, "L'organizzazione spaziale della grande azienda," *Meridiana* 10 (1990): 58–124.

14. David Brion Davis, *Slavery and Human Progress* (New York, 1985), 59. See also Charles Verlinden, *The Beginning of Modern Colonization: Eleven Essays with an Introduction* (Ithaca, N.Y., 1970); and Sydney W. Mintz, *Sweetness and Power: The Place of Sugar in Modern History* (New York, 1985).

Concurrent economic forces transformed plantation slavery into a global business focusing on the cultivation of staple crops and converted landed estates such as the *latifondi* into agricultural enterprises specializing in the production of particular items. Philip Curtin has identified the sixteenth century as the time of the rise of the modern plantation complex—which he has described as "an economic and political order centering on slave plantations in the New World tropics." Significantly, according to Immanuel Wallerstein, it was also in the sixteenth century that the expansion of European trade in the Atlantic and the consequent opening of a world market led to the specialization of the peripheral areas of the world-economy—where plantations and other types of landed estates were located—in the production and sale of raw materials to regions located in the core. Among the most important consequences of these concurrent processes was a sudden increase in the need for laborers—which led to the enslavement and forced transportation of millions of Africans to New World plantations and to a concurrent reversion to peasant serfdom in the eastern European landed estates. As plantation slavery found profitable markets in the Atlantic and serfdom rose in importance in eastern Europe, in the Mediterranean both systems of unfree labor rapidly declined and left the way clear for the rise of a profitable free-labor economy based on the *latifondi*.[15]

Recently, both Robin Blackburn and Paul Gilroy have convincingly argued in favor of a close relationship between the transformation of plantation slavery into a capitalist venture in the Americas and the rise of the modern world. On the other hand, Robert Fogel has gone as far as seeing the emergence and later improvement of a system based on slave labor and focusing on production for the world market as a process that anticipated features of industrial capitalism. The making of a modern, capitalist version of plantation slavery in the New World found a parallel in the process of conversion of the landed estates in southern and eastern Europe and in the Spanish American colonies into modern agricultural enterprises. Both southern European *latifondi* and Latin American *haciendas* initially went through a period of mixed labor economy, which included servitude in

15. Philip D. Curtin, *The Rise and Fall of the Plantation Complex: Essays in Atlantic History* (New York, 1990), ix. See also Immanuel Wallerstein, *The Modern World-System*, vol. 1, *Capitalist Agriculture and the Origins of the European World-Economy in the Sixteenth Century* (New York, 1974); David Eltis, *The Rise of African Slavery in the Americas* (New York, 2000); John Thornton, *Africa and Africans in the Making of the Atlantic World, 1400–1800* (New York, 1998); and Peter Kolchin, *Unfree Labor: American Slavery and Russian Serfdom* (Cambridge, Mass., 1987), 1–46.

different degrees and forms. Yet, after slavery proved insufficiently profitable, both evolved into nominally free labor systems.[16]

In particular, in Sicily, sugar plantations and slave labor gradually disappeared, while the cultivation of grain and olives by free peasants on the *latifondi* rose in importance. According to Steven Epstein, "it was natural to think of Sicily, just before the voyages of Columbus, as a plantation-style economy." Only the low level of rainfall prevented the cultivation of sugar on a large scale and the consequent transformation of the island and of other areas of the *Mezzogiorno* from "societies with slaves" (in which slavery co-existed with other forms of economic activities and labor systems) to "slave societies" (in which slavery stood at the center of the process of production of staple crops and in which slaveholders were numerous), according to the definition first advanced by Keith Hopkins. Unlike sugar, grain "had a low seasonal demand for labor that could not efficiently use high-priced slaves." As a consequence, slavery disappeared from both Sicily and southern Italy. And yet, it is significant that, as Epstein has recently demonstrated, the "language of slavery"—the complex of references to slavery that remained deeply embedded in the spoken and written language—survived in Italy until well into the nineteenth century, doubtless with some influence also on relations between masters and laborers.[17]

In reverse pattern, in the American South, plantations originally employing a variety of labor arrangements developed into slave-based commercial enterprises. In the late seventeenth and early eighteenth centuries, through what Ira Berlin calls "plantation revolution," southern colonies in North America became slave societies. Unlike the case of Sicily and the *Mezzogiorno,* both the Chesapeake and the Carolinas had the right climate for the subtropical staple crops most efficiently produced with large numbers of slaves and which could command an international market. By the

16. See Robin Blackburn, *The Making of New World Slavery: From Baroque to the Modern, 1492–1800* (London, 1997), 1–27; Paul Gilroy, *The Black Atlantic: Modernity and Double Consciousness* (London, 1993), 41–71; and Robert W. Fogel, *Without Consent or Contract: The Rise and Fall of American Slavery* (New York, 1989), 17–40. See also Christopher Kay, "Comparative Developments of the European Manorial System and the Latin American Hacienda System," *JPS* 2 (1974); and Curtin, *Plantation Complex,* 58–69.

17. Steven Epstein, *Speaking of Slavery: Color, Ethnicity, and Human Bondage in Italy* (Ithaca, N.Y., 2001), 188; and Keith Hopkins, *Conquerors and Slaves* (Cambridge, 1978), 99–102. See also Fernand Braudel, *The Mediterranean and the Mediterranean World in the Age of Philip II,* vol. 1 (New York, 1972), 150–160; and Ira Berlin, *Many Thousands Gone: The First Two Centuries of Slavery in North America* (Cambridge, Mass., 1998), 8–9.

time slavery reached North America in the seventeenth century, Portuguese, Dutch, French, and English planters had already experimented with plantation agriculture and slave labor for two hundred years. Sugar had emerged as the unrivaled commodity, transforming both large areas of northeastern Brazil and the Caribbean into slave societies. Yet, other crops were to make the fortunes of American planters. In the Chesapeake, planters initially met the demand for labor caused by the tobacco boom of the second and third quarters of the seventeenth century with the employment of indentured servants coming from Europe; however, in the 1680s, the concurrent decrease in the number of indentured servants and increase in the number of African slaves available to English traders led to the transformation of Virginia from a society with slaves to a slave society. On the other hand, in South Carolina, the origins of a slave society related to the planting of rice, a staple crop whose early cultivation owed a great deal to the forced migration of Africans shortly after the establishment of the first European settlement in the 1660s.[18]

Significantly, Ira Berlin links the origins of the plantation revolution in the American South to earlier experiments at building plantation complexes in the Mediterranean and in the Caribbean. A parallel revolution with similar profound consequences occurred in southern Italy, when the process of commercialization of the fief led to the conversion of *latifondi* into agricultural enterprises with free landless peasants providing the basis of economic production. Yet, an important difference between the two case studies is that, while plantations in the American South *began* as agricultural estates that focused from the beginning on production for the world market, *latifondi developed* into agricultural enterprises with their participation in the European world-economy. This difference in patterns of development also

18. See Berlin, *Many Thousands Gone*, 8–9; Peter Kolchin, *American Slavery, 1619–1877*, 2nd ed. (New York, 2003), 3–26; and Betty Wood, *The Origins of American Slavery: Freedom and Bondage in the English Colonies* (New York, 1997), 40–93. On Virginia, see Edmund S. Morgan, *American Slavery, American Freedom: The Ordeal of Colonial Virginia* (Chapel Hill, N.C., 1975); Russell R. Menard, "From Servants to Slaves: The Transformation of the Chesapeake Labor System," *Southern Studies* 16 (1977): 355–390; and Anthony S. Parent Jr., *Foul Means: The Formation of a Slave Society in Virginia, 1660–1740* (Chapel Hill, N.C., 2003). On South Carolina, see Peter H. Wood, *Black Majority: Negroes in Colonial South Carolina from 1670 through the Stono Rebellion* (New York, 1974); and Judith A. Carney, *Black Rice: The African Origins of Rice Cultivation in the Americas* (Cambridge, Mass., 2001). See also Richard Dunn, *Sugar and Slaves: The Rise of the Planter Class in the English West Indies, 1624–1713* (Chapel Hill, N.C., 1972); and Stuart B. Schwartz, *Sugar Plantations in the Formation of Brazilian Society: Bahia, 1550–1835* (New York, 1985).

helps to explain the contrast between the marked commercial character of agricultural production on American plantations and the relative scarcity of cash crops grown on southern Italian *latifondi.*[19]

In the eighteenth century, most agricultural production in the southern colonies of North America focused on two crops: tobacco in the Chesapeake and rice in coastal South Carolina and Georgia. By the beginning of the century, the quality and output of South Carolinian rice and Virginian tobacco had no parallels in the world. In turn, the rapid increase in world market demand for tobacco and rice further accelerated the economic and social processes related to the plantation revolution, leading to conspicuous changes in the landscape of the southern colonies. In the areas of tobacco and rice production, the plantation—with its administrative center in the "Big House"—became the dominant feature of the agricultural landscape and the site of the most important economic activities. Doubtless, by the standards of the European landowning nobilities, plantations—aside from a few exceptions—always remained fairly small, with an average size of five hundred to one thousand acres. However, the planters' domination of the economy and society of the regions where they settled was an evident feature from the outset. The transformation of the landscape in these regions reflected both the planters' dominant role and the difference in economic and social standing between them and the agricultural workers, free and unfree. In fact, according to Ira Berlin, the plantation's Big House, "nestled among manufactories, shops, barns, sheds, and various other outbuildings which were called, with a nice sense of the plantation's social hierarchy, dependencies, dominated the landscape, the physical and architectural embodiment of the planters' hegemony."[20]

19. See Maurice Aymard, "La transizione dal feudalesimo al capitalismo," in Ruggero Romano and Corrado Vivanti, eds., *Storia d'Italia,* Annali 5, *Dal feudalesimo al capitalismo* (Turin, 1975), 1187–1192; Emilio Sereni, *Storia del paesaggio agrario italiano* (Bari-Rome, 1961), 190–195; and Aurelio Lepre, "Azienda feudale ed azienda agraria nel Mezzogiorno continentale fra Cinquecento e Ottocento," in Angelo Massafra, ed., *Problemi di storia delle campagne meridionali nell'età moderna e contemporanea* (Bari, 1981), 27–40. See also Immanuel Wallerstein, *The Modern World-System,* vol. 2, *Mercantilism and the Consolidation of the European World-Economy, 1600–1750* (New York, 1981), 128–178.

20. Berlin, *Many Thousands Gone,* 97. See also Wallerstein, *Modern World-System,* 2:160–170, 202–203; Allan Kulikoff, *Tobacco and Slaves: The Development of Southern Cultures in the Chesapeake, 1680–1800* (Chapel Hill, N.C., 1986); Richard Waterhouse, *A New World Gentry: The Making of a Merchant and Planter Class in South Carolina, 1670–1770* (New York, 1989); Clement

To be sure, tobacco was a crop suited for cultivation on both plantations and farms. In fact, for the purpose of taking advantage of the best soil for tobacco growing—which was scattered across the land—the actual units of agricultural production were relatively small, while slaves were often divided into small groups that worked under the supervision of either the planter or an overseer. Tobacco planting was a business that demanded both constant dedication and close supervision of the workforce, especially at the time of tending and harvesting the crop. In fact, in the 1780s, Luigi Castiglioni—an Italian traveler—noticed how in Virginia "the cultivation of this plant [tobacco] calls for a great deal of care and employs a large number of slaves during most of the year."[21]

Almost eighty years after Castiglioni, long after tobacco had ceased to be Virginia's main item of trade, Frederick Law Olmsted reported the case of a planter who "cultivated only the coarser and lower-priced sorts of tobacco, because the finer sorts required more painstaking and discretion than it was possible to make a large gang of Negroes use." For over two centuries, the keys to success in the business of tobacco planting lay in the planters' and farmers' willingness and ability to focus their attention on the crop and in their skills in managing the workforce, dividing it into small, efficient groups. Tobacco cultivation also both encouraged and required the master's residence on the plantation, or on the farm; in turn, the master's constant presence and his preference for supervision of small groups of slaves led to a particularly close relation with his workforce.[22]

Yet, tobacco cultivation caused soil depletion; after three consecutive years of tobacco planting, the land had to rest for twenty years. From as

Eaton, *A History of the Old South* (New York, 1975), 389–390; and Lewis Cecil Gray, *History of Southern Agriculture in the United States to 1860*, vol. 1 (New York, 1933).

21. A. Pace, ed., *Luigi Castiglioni's Viaggio: Travels in the United States of North America, 1785–1787* (New York, 1987), 195–197. See also Lorena Walsh, "Slave Life, Slave Society, and Tobacco Production in the Tidewater Chesapeake, 1620–1820," in Ira Berlin and Philip D. Morgan, eds., *Cultivation and Culture: Labor and the Shaping of Slave Life in the Americas* (Charlottesville, Va., 1993), 170–202.

22. Frederick Law Olmsted, *The Cotton Kingdom: A Traveler's Observations on Cotton and Slavery in the American Slave States, 1853–1861* (New York, 1996; orig. pub. in 1863), 70. See also Ulrich B. Phillips, *American Negro Slavery: A Survey of the Supply, Employment and Control of Negro Labor as Determined by the Plantation Regime* (Baton Rouge, La., 1966; orig. pub. in 1918), 82–83; and John C. Robert, *The Tobacco Kingdom: Plantation, Market, and Factory in Virginia and North Carolina, 1800–1860* (Durham, N.C., 1938), 20–23.

early as the beginning of the eighteenth century, this dynamic had prompted planters to look for new land. Already tobacco's relatively low financial returns and periodic fluctuations in the market had encouraged planters and farmers to experiment with different crops. Wheat emerged from these experiments as the leading substitute crop for tobacco. After the mid-1760s' crisis in Mediterranean wheat harvests and the subsequent rise in prices, wheat cultivation underwent a boom throughout the Chesapeake and, in the words of Philip Morgan, it "became the principal market crop" in several areas. In particular, in the Shenandoah Valley, according to Robert Mitchell, all the major planters shifted from tobacco to wheat production between the 1760s and the 1770s. By the 1850s, in regions such as the Tidewater area of Virginia there was little business left in tobacco planting; significantly, the individual whom Frederick Law Olmsted visited was "one of the few large planters of his vicinity who still made the culture of tobacco their principal business."[23]

Despite the conditions in which Olmsted saw the Tidewater area, several nineteenth-century Virginian planters made a serious attempt to retain a mixed economy on their plantations and grew both tobacco and wheat. However, as time passed, they found it increasingly difficult to face competition over both crops in the market and they chose to expand wheat production at the expense of tobacco. A typical case of a planter who was forced to abandon his plans to keep a regime of mixed economy was that of William Bolling. According to U. B. Phillips, Bolling "set about a hundred thousand tobacco plants and seeded some nine hundred acres in wheat; but an advance in wheat price from ninety cents to $1.90 in the fall of 1828 caused him to add another hundred acres to this crop." Thereafter, eager to exploit the profits of the constant rise in wheat prices, Bolling privileged the cultivation of wheat over tobacco.[24]

In contrast to tobacco, rice cultivation required a large initial effort in terms of both capital and slave supervision. Only wealthy individuals could

23. Philip D. Morgan, *Slave Counterpoint: Black Culture in the Eighteenth-Century Chesapeake and Lowcountry* (Chapel Hill, N.C., 1998), 47; Olmsted, *Cotton Kingdom,* 69. See also Robert D. Mitchell, *Commercialism and Frontier: Perspectives on the Early Shenandoah Valley* (Charlottesville, Va., 1977), 160–188.

24. Ulrich B. Phillips, *Life and Labor in the Old South* (Boston, Mass., 1929), 236. See also John R. Irwin, "Exploring the Affinity of Wheat and Slavery in the Virginia Piedmont," *EEH* 25 (1988): 295–322.

afford the financial burden required to transform the lowcountry swamps of South Carolina and Georgia into well laid out rice fields. An equally large effort went into supervising and instructing slaves on the use of complex technological devices for the clearing of drained and separated square fields. The next step would then be the construction of flood gates in order to regulate the flow of fresh water. Slaves had originally brought the tradition of rice cultivation from Africa. Yet, by the 1780s, when Luigi Castiglioni wrote his journal, rice cultivation in South Carolina had evolved into two fairly sophisticated techniques: "tide fields" cultivation in "marshes near the rivers at some distance from the sea," and "inland fields" cultivation in "large artificially dug ponds" with "rather strong dykes."[25]

After the establishment of rice fields, planters usually left their plantations in the hands of overseers. One reason for this was that rice cultivation did not require the same constant attention as tobacco cultivation. Another reason was the unhealthiness of the lowcountry swamps during the hot summer months. For at least half a year, in order to avoid malaria, most rice planters acted as absentee landowners. On their rice plantations, overseers were often left as the sole persons responsible for all aspects of production and labor management. Usually they were in charge of a very large workforce. The sheer size of the units of agricultural production required large numbers of slaves to work them. At the same time, planters could hope to compensate the initial capital investment in technological devices only with the profits that derived from large-scale agricultural enterprises.[26]

Since planters tended to grow rice on large agricultural units and with a large workforce and since rice cultivation was a costly business restricted to a relatively small number of planter families, a much larger number of slaves usually worked on a single rice plantation in lowcountry South Carolina and Georgia than on a single tobacco plantation in the Chesapeake. Also, rather than working in small groups—as slaves did on tobacco plantations—slaves on rice plantations worked individually according to the so-called task system. Each slave was given a specific task to perform—usually sowing, culti-

25. Pace, ed., *Luigi Castiglioni's Viaggio,* 167. See also Daniel C. Littlefield, *Rice and Slaves: Ethnicity and the Slave Trade in Colonial South Carolina* (Baton Rouge, La., 1981), 56–114; and Gray, *History of Agriculture,* 1:255–290.

26. See David Doar, *Rice and Rice Planting in the South Carolina Low Country* (Charleston, S.C., 1936); and Jeffrey R. Young, *Domesticating Slavery: The Master Class in Georgia and South Carolina, 1670–1837* (Chapel Hill, N.C., 1999), 18–23.

vating, or weeding from half to one acre of rice—and after they finished the task assigned to them, they had the rest of the day for themselves.[27]

In an 1859 article on the South Carolina lowcountry for *Harper's Monthly Magazine,* T. Addison Richards gave a precise definition of the task as the amount of work "daily required of each competent person . . . in accordance with age and condition." Interestingly, Richards also described how, after the laborer had completed the task, he or she usually went "to raise vegetables in his own private garden-patch, or to look after eggs and poultry and pigs, for all of which the master will pay him the market price as to any other trader." In time, this particular feature of the task system had given origin to "slaves' economies," or economies based on the slaves' own production of crops for sale. At the time Richards observed them and described them, the task system and the slaves' economies attached to it were both almost two hundred years old; by then, both had become well-established and crucial features of the social and economic life of lowcountry South Carolina and Georgia.[28]

An important feature of rice cultivation was the fact that rice did not exhaust the soil and had high returns. Therefore, unlike tobacco planters, rice planters did not need to look for new lands and had little incentive to make experiments with the cultivation of other crops. In fact, rice planters had many more reasons to continue to improve the quality of rice in order to make it more profitable. In an important article on the lowcountry's agricultural economy—which he published in *De Bow's Review* in 1854—leading South Carolinian rice planter Robert Allston reviewed the course of planters' experiments in the cultivation of rice. Allston noticed how, ever since its introduction in the seventeenth century, rice had established itself as the lowcountry's principal staple crop. Tracing the history of the different varieties of rice produced in South Carolina, Allston wrote that in the first variety "seed was white, such as is grown in China and Guiana to this day, and such as may still be seen produced on the uplands and inlands of

27. See Philip D. Morgan, "Work and Culture: The Task System and the World of Low-country Blacks, 1700 to 1880," *WMQ* 39 (1982): 563–599; and Joyce E. Chaplin, "Slavery and the Principle of Humanity: A Modern Idea in the Lower South," *JSoH* 24 (1990–1991): 298–315.

28. T. Addison Richards, "The Rice Lands of the South," *HM* 114 (1859): 731. See also Berlin, *Many Thousands Gone,* 164–166; Philip D. Morgan, "The Ownership of Property by Slaves in the Mid-Nineteenth-Century Low Country," *JSH* 49 (1983): 399–420; and Larry E. Hudson, *To Have and To Hold: Slave Work and Family Life in Antebellum South Carolina* (Athens, Ga., 1997).

America." It was only in the late eighteenth century that "the 'gold seed' was introduced, which owing to its superiority, soon entirely superseded the white." In Allston's time, the "gold seed" was "the rice of commerce, and the only grain referred to herein, when rice is mentioned, without being distinguished by some peculiar name or characteristic."[29]

The shift from white seed to gold seed that Allston outlined in his article was a particularly important one in the history of the centuries-old experimentation in rice production and one that was concurrent with other important changes in cultivation techniques. By the end of the eighteenth century, most planters had shifted from flow culture to water culture; in the latter, rice fields were kept flooded—saving both time and capital—rather than being flowed and drained in cycle. However, the most important technological breakthrough was the development of threshing mills. After 1830, the invention of threshing mills allowed the mechanical threshing of the crop, an operation that previously had required much labor to accomplish. This innovation greatly accelerated the process of preparing the finished product for sale on the market. Yet, despite the important advancements in quality and technology of production, and while rice prices remained fairly stable, rice production did not grow exponentially as did production of other staple crops. As a consequence, already in the early decades of the nineteenth century, rice lost its central place in South Carolina's agricultural economy and was replaced by cotton.[30]

Yet, even before cotton replaced rice as the most important crop produced by South Carolina's plantations, throughout the South the slave system underwent a deep structural crisis. In the second half of the eighteenth century, a combination of factors—among them the spread of the humanitarian doctrines of the Enlightenment, the movement for religious reform of

29. Robert F. W. Allston, "Sea-Coast Crops of the South," *DBR* 16 (1854): 606–607. See also William Dusinberre, *Them Dark Days: Slavery in the American Rice Swamps* (New York, 1996), 354–389; John H. Easterby, "Introduction," in John H. Easterby, ed., *The South Carolina Rice Plantation as Revealed in the Papers of Robert F. W. Allston* (Chicago, 1945); and Charles Joyner, *Down by the Riverside: A South Carolina Slave Community* (Urbana, Ill., 1984), 41–89.

30. See James M. Clifton, "Introduction," in James M. Clifton, ed., *Life and Labor on Argyle Island: Letters and Documents of a Savannah Rice River Plantation, 1833–1867* (Savannah, Ga., 1978). See also Joyce E. Chaplin, *An Anxious Pursuit: Agricultural Innovation and Modernity in the Lower South, 1730–1815* (Chapel Hill, N.C., 1993), 227–277; and Peter Coclanis, *The Shadow of a Dream: Economic Life and Death in the South Carolina Low Country, 1670–1920* (New York, 1989), 111–159.

the Great Awakening, and the influence of classic political economists such as Adam Smith and David Ricardo—resulted in the increasing unpopularity of slavery among the educated elites and in public opinion. Philosophers, economists, and churchmen branded the slave system as inhuman and barbaric and argued that slavery not only led to a general degradation of society, but also violated the fundamental tenets of classical capitalism, being based, as it was, on coerced labor and violence. After the 1760s, the economic crisis of the tobacco-growing plantations of the Chesapeake area provided a further confirmation that slavery was an unprofitable economic system.[31]

By the 1770s, a movement for the gradual abolition of slavery—some of whose most vocal representatives were the Quakers—had gained momentum. The American Revolution—both in the spread of the doctrines of liberty and equality that related to it and in the actual revolutionary war—brought a further blow to slavery in the South. By the time the Americans emerged victorious over the British, in 1781, the slave economy had suffered severe disruption throughout the region, especially as a result of the thousands of runaways. Yet, planters were still a strong enough elite to dictate compromises in the drafting of the 1789 Constitution. Though they complied with the provision which set 1808 as the date of the closing of the Atlantic slave trade, ultimately they obtained the federal government's acknowledgment of the legality of slavery and the assurance of constitutional protection of slaveholding interests. At the same time, in the early 1800s, even after a wave of manumissions had swept through the southern states and had led to the abolition of slavery in every state of the North, the slave system and the plantation agriculture succeeded in rapidly regaining strength thanks to the planting of cotton, the crop which was responsible for the last and most spectacular plantation revolution in the antebellum American South.[32]

31. See David Brion Davis, *The Problem of Slavery in the Age of Revolutions, 1770–1823* (Ithaca, N.Y., 1975), 164–254; Robin Blackburn, *The Overthrow of Colonial Slavery, 1776–1848* (London, 1988), 33–67; Kolchin, *American Slavery,* 63–92; and Jan Lewis, "The Problem of Slavery in Southern Political Discourse," in David T. Konig, ed., *Devising Liberty: Preserving and Creating Freedom in the New American Republic* (Stanford, Calif., 1995), 265–297.

32. See William W. Freehling, *The Reintegration of American History: Slavery and the Civil War* (New York, 1994), 12–33; Berlin, *Many Thousands Gone,* 217–227; Duncan J. MacLeod, *Slavery, Race, and the American Revolution* (New York, 1975); Ira Berlin and Ronald Hoffman, eds., *Slavery and Freedom in the Age of the American Revolution* (Charlottesville, Va., 1983); and Paul Finkelman, *Slavery and the Founders: Race and Liberty in the Age of Jefferson* (Westport, Conn., 1996).

* * *

Unlike tobacco and rice plantations in the American South, southern Italian *latifondi* produced massive amounts of grain mostly for the internal market—especially the capital, Naples—and for export throughout Europe. During the eighteenth century, the steady increase in the *Mezzogiorno's* population led to an expansion of grain production, which affected both *latifondi* and smaller landholdings. Even the 1764 economic crisis—which led to famine and a general fall of grain prices—did not alter this general trend in any significant way. Though grain cultivation was widespread in southern Italy, the most important areas where it was produced were the Capitanata region in Apulia, Terra di Lavoro in Campania, the inner parts of Calabria and Sicily, and the plains of Metaponto in Basilicata. In these areas, the *latifondi* were the dominant features of the landscape. These large landed estates were mostly farmed according to centuries-old techniques that allowed peasants to cope with the chronic scarcity of water in the *Mezzogiorno*. Usually, peasants grew grain for one or two years, then they let the land rest, using it for pasture; in the period between these two stages, they might grow fava beans. This system of crop rotation had the advantage of requiring the use of relatively little water; however, the problem with it was that it led quickly to land exhaustion.[33]

In general, the *latifondo* covered a larger and less homogenous area than the average American plantation. The main reason was that, over several centuries, aristocratic families had pursued a policy of aggressive land acquisition that had resulted in the continuous aggrandizement of their fiefs, but not necessarily in the ownership of contiguous property. Also, in between the noble and ecclesiastical fiefs, a number of cities (*università*) and large tracts of common land (*demanio*)—on which peasants exercised customary rights (*usi civici*)—were exempt from feudal law. And yet, the landed aristocracy had managed to increase its holdings through illegal expropriation and land enclosure at the expense of both. Both the large size of the fiefs, which resulted from past policies of land acquisition, and the peasants' constant use

33. See Aurelio Lepre, *Storia del Mezzogiorno d'Italia*, vol. 2, *Dall'Antico Regime alla società borghese (1657–1860)* (Naples, 1986), 50–73; Bevilacqua, *Breve storia*, 15–16; Maurice Aymard, "Il Sud e i circuiti del grano," in Bevilacqua, ed., *Storia dell'agricoltura*, 1:764–771; Paolo Macry, *Mercato e società nel Regno di Napoli. Commercio del grano e politica economica nel Settecento* (Naples, 1974); and Giuseppe Galasso, "Strutture sociali e produttive, assetti colturali e mercato dal sec. XVI all'Unità," in Massafra, ed., *Problemi di storia*, 159–172.

of crop rotation help to explain why diversification in agricultural production was one of the main features of the *latifondo.*[34]

On most *latifondi,* areas extensively farmed with grain alternated with
land for pasture. In some instances, though, grain alternated with olive trees
and vineyards. Especially in regions such as Terra di Bari, Terra d'Otranto,
and Calabria Ultra I and II, feudal estates effectively combined traditional
latifondo cultivation with commercial agriculture or else participated in a
system of exchange that integrated the coastal production of olive oil with
the production of grain and corn in the interior. In the second half of the
eighteenth century, olive oil became such an important item in the export
balance of the Kingdom of Naples that Apulian merchants (*negozianti*)
shipped large quantities of it, especially from the leading port of Gallipoli,
to as far as Marseilles, in France, and to the rising Austrian port of Trieste.[35]

In the eighteenth century, cultivation of cash crops was still limited to a
few coastal regions. Yet, even though in the following century commercial
agriculture rose in importance, in the inner areas of the *Mezzogiorno* grain
continued to be the main item produced in the *latifondi* until well into the
twentieth century. In the 1870s, Tuscan agricultural reformer Sidney Sonnino noticed that Sicilian *latifondi* mostly included "those lands located on
mountains, hills, at the bottom of valleys, or on the plains, which are grown
with grain alternated with natural pastures." Sonnino characterized these
lands as "bare fields" and speculated that those *latifondi* which were "former
feudal estates" reached a size of "1000 or 2000 hectares, and even 6000 hectares or more." Sonnino's characterization of the *latifondo* as a relic of feudalism in which grain and pasture were the only economic activities found parallels in the works of many other economists and intellectuals—the so-called
meridionalisti—and provided the entire southern Italian agriculture with a

34. See Maria Grazia Maiorini, "The Capital and the Provinces," in Girolamo Imbruglia, ed.,
Naples in the Eighteenth Century: The Birth and Death of a Nation State (Cambridge, 2000), 4–21.

35. See Piero Bevilacqua, "Il Mezzogiorno nel mercato internazionale (secoli XVIII–XX),"
Meridiana 1 (1987): 22–25; Patrick Chorley, *Oil, Silk, and Enlightenment: Economic Problems in
Eighteenth-Century Naples* (Oxford, 1968), 20–22; Biagio Salvemini, "The Arrogance of the
Market: The Economy of the Kingdom between the Mediterranean and Europe," in Imbruglia,
ed., *Naples in the Eighteenth Century,* 44–69; Maria Antonietta Visceglia, "L'azienda signorile
in Terra d'Otranto nell'età moderna (secoli XVI–XVIII)," in Massafra, ed., *Problemi di storia,*
41–72; and Augusto Placanica, *La Calabria nell'età moderna,* vol. 1, *Uomini, strutture, economie*
(Naples, 1985), 389–399.

long-lasting stigma. It was only with the recent discovery of the economic history of several regions of the *Mezzogiorno* where commercial agriculture was practiced in or in conjunction with the *latifondi* since the eighteenth century that scholars were successful in demolishing the stereotype of the *latifondo* that relied on the *meridionalisti*'s writings.[36]

Whether they included areas with commercial agriculture or not, *latifondi* were large and diverse landed estates that lacked the internal consistency of a plantation. Yet, in central position—or, rather, in the best possible location—in the *latifondo* was the equivalent of a plantation's Big House: the *masseria*. Particularly in the case of the *latifondi* of northern Apulia and western Sicily, the *masserie* were imposing palaces originally conceived as both the landowner's residence on the estate and the center of the estate's administration. However, since most southern Italian noblemen were absentee landowners, in time the *masseria* became a temporary residence mostly used by the landlord's agent (*amministratore*) during his extended visits to the estate; and yet, it also retained its original function of administrative center. Since the *latifondo* was, usually, much larger than a plantation and included a wider variety of economic activities, its administration also followed a far more complex and rigid hierarchical pattern than that of a plantation. Therefore, the central position and the pattern of construction of the *masseria*—with the landlord's living rooms surrounded by smaller quarters for the personnel, stores, and stables—reflected the hierarchical organization of the administration of the *latifondo*.[37]

The agent was the key factor in the administration, since he represented the link between the landlord and the land. The agent was in charge of a very complex hierarchical system of land lease. At the top of this system were a

36. Sidney Sonnino, "I contadini in Sicilia," in Leopoldo Franchetti and Sidney Sonnino, *Inchiesta in Sicilia* (Florence, 1876), 24. See also Denis Mack Smith, "The *Latifundia* in Modern Sicilian History," *Proceedings of the British Academy* 51 (1965): 85–124; Lucy Riall, "'Ill-Contrived, Badly Executed [and] . . . of No Avail'? Reform and Its Impact in the Sicilian *Latifondo* (c. 1770–1910)," in Enrico Dal Lago and Rick Halpern, eds., *The American South and the Italian Mezzogiorno: Essays in Comparative History* (New York, 2002), 132–154; and Jonathan Morris, "Challenging *Meridionalismo*: Constructing a New History for Southern Italy," in Robert Lumley and Jonathan Morris, eds., *The New History of the Italian South: The Mezzogiorno Revisited* (Exeter, 1997), 1–19.

37. See Angelo Massafra, "Trulli e masserie fra l'Adriatico e le Murge meridionali," in Paola Sereno et al., eds., *Campagna e industria. Itinerari* (Milan, 1981), 69–78; and Anton Blok, *The Mafia of a Sicilian Village, 1860–1960: A Study in Violent Peasant Entrepreneurs* (New York, 1974), 58–59.

type of stewards called the *massari* in the continental *Mezzogiorno* and the *gabelloti* in Sicily. The landlord usually recruited them from the land-owning peasantry and leased most of the *latifondo*'s land to them. *Massari* and *gabelloti* managed the estate, hiring field hands (*braccianti*) to work the land on an occasional basis and, at the same time, subletting large tracts of it to tenants (*coloni*), from whom they collected a rent. During the eighteenth century, due to the chronic absentee habits of the landed aristocracy, *massari* and *gabelloti* became powerful and influential men in charge of maintaining law and order on the *latifondo*. Not only did they act as stewards and rent-collectors, but they also recruited the overseers (*soprastanti*) and the field guards (called *campieri* in Sicily) who were in charge of supervising the workers.[38]

Doubtless, the living conditions of all categories of peasants who worked and lived on the *latifondo* showed a marked degree of exploitation. According to Paolo Mattia Doria—an eighteenth-century Neapolitan economic reformer—"the poor peasant of the Kingdom is the one who bears the full weight of a despotic system, so much so that he is almost reduced to the state of beasts . . . [the peasants'] misery is now such that . . . they only eat bread." Among southern Italian peasants, none were more exploited than the *braccianti,* the day laborers who formed the bulk of the workforce. The *braccianti* were usually recruited from the nearby *agrotowns*—originally feudal settlements whose primary function was to provide reservoirs of laborers—on a daily basis according to the necessities of the agricultural season. The fact that they did not have the means to own or even lease land, together with the fact that they were only hired on an occasional basis, contributed to make the *braccianti* the poorest category of workers in the *Mezzogiorno.* During the sowing, cutting, and harvesting seasons, the *braccianti* were subject to strict control by the *soprastanti,* who, together with the guards, were responsible for keeping discipline on the *latifondo.*[39]

While *braccianti* and *coloni* toiled in the fields, the absentee aristocrats lived a luxurious life as *rentiers* in Naples and other cities, accumulating enormous debts and, consequently, placing even more pressure on the tenants

38. See Aurelio Lepre, *Feudi e masserie. Problemi della società meridionale nel seicento e settecento* (Naples, 1973); and Marcello Verga, *La Sicilia dei grani. Gestione dei feudi e cultura economica fra sei e settecento* (Florence, 1993), especially 59–106.

39. Paolo Mattia Doria, *Massime del Governo Spagnolo a Napoli* (Naples 1973), 112. See also Lepre, *Storia del Mezzogiorno,* 2:82–90; and Franco Mercurio, "Agricoltura senza casa. Il sistema del lavoro migrante nelle maremme e nel latifondo," in Bevilacqua, ed., *Storia dell'agricoltura,* 1:131–179.

to pay higher rents in order to repay their debts. At the same time, the *massari* and the *gabelloti* succeeded in gaining enormous power by acting as middlemen and exploiting the peasantry even more harshly than the landlords themselves. Yet, by the second half of the eighteenth century, the rent-collecting practices of the aristocracy and the legal impediments of feudalism had led to a deep structural crisis in the *latifondo* system. Feudal laws were designed to protect the integrity of the fiefs through generations, preventing the division of the *latifondi*, but at the same time excluding them from the market. The law of primogeniture (*maggiorascato*) dictated that the firstborn male should inherit the whole landed property owned by a noble family. The law also dictated the inalienability of feudal domains: noble families could transfer their land from one generation to the next, but they could not buy or sell it. The inconveniences of a system that did not allow land to be freely available as a marketable good became all the more apparent when the grain economy of the *latifondi* suffered a major setback, placing a further strain on a financial system already under stress from the chronic debt of many aristocratic families. Competition from Russian and American grain on the world market halted the expansion of southern Italian grain production. By the late eighteenth century, most of the grain produced on the *latifondi* was diverted to the internal market to feed the local population of the countryside and the growing city of Naples.[40]

These important economic changes were concurrent with a change of attitude in the public opinion and in the Bourbon administration. In the second half of the eighteenth century, political economists such as Antonio Genovesi and Giuseppe Maria Galanti branded the feudal system as parasitic and monstrous. At the same time, both Prime Minister Bernardo Tanucci and Viceroys Caracciolo and Caramanico attempted, at different times and with little success, to curb the power of the feudal aristocracy, especially in Sicily. By the end of the eighteenth century, decades of debates on the feudal question and attempted reforms had built a momentum of hostile attitudes toward the feudal aristocracy's privileges and absentee practices. Even within the aristocracy itself, liberal noblemen regarded feudal law as an impediment

---

40. See Pasquale Villani, *Il Mezzogiorno tra riforme e rivoluzione* (Rome-Bari, 1977), 171–181; Angelo Massafra, "Una stagione di studi sulla feudalità nel Regno di Napoli," in Paolo Macry and Angelo Massafra, eds., *Fra storia e storiografia. Scritti in onore di Pasquale Villani* (Bologna, 1994); and Marcello Verga, "Il 'Settecento del baronaggio.' L'aristocrazia siciliana tra politica e cultura," in Franco Benigno and Claudio Torrisi, eds., *Elites e potere in Sicilia dal Medioevo a oggi* (Catanzaro, 1995), 87–102.

to the sale and acquisition of property and to the modernization of agriculture. Yet, after the brief and unsuccessful 1799 Neapolitan Revolution, it was Joseph Bonaparte—at the time of the Napoleonic occupation of southern Italy—who, in 1806, decreed the abolition of feudalism in the continental *Mezzogiorno.* In Sicily—which remained a British protectorate and hosted the Neapolitan royal family in exile—it was the Sicilian noble parliament that abolished feudalism with the approval of the Constitution of 1812.[41]

In 1815, after the Napoleonic government fell, restored Bourbon king Ferdinand I confirmed the abolition of feudalism. The transformation of feudal property into marketable land practically allowed noblemen to buy and sell it. According to Gianni Toniolo, "it was, in essence, an adjustment and better definition of property rights, but the land remained in the hands of the aristocracy." Still, several aristocratic families lost their land repaying large debts, while others retained most of their feudal properties and quickly adjusted to their new legal position as simple owners of *latifondi.* Also, despite the Bourbon government's attempts to create a class of small landed proprietors, the sale of noble and ecclesiastical land on the market mostly benefited large landowners who came from the ranks of *amministratori, massari,* and *gabelloti.* Through a combination of legal acquisition of former feudal property and illegal usurpation of common land—which the law abolishing feudalism had extinguished—these new landowners effectively formed a landed bourgeoisie capable of competing with the former feudal aristocracy in matters of local power.[42]

If we were to review the history of plantations and *latifondi* during the eighteenth century, we would identify in both cases the key moments in the century's final decades. At the end of the eighteenth century, both the plantation system in the American South and the *latifondo* system in the Italian *Mezzogiorno* underwent a deep structural crisis. The crops that had made the fortunes of American planters and southern Italian landowners were no

41. See Anna Maria Rao, "The Feudal Question, Judicial Systems, and the Enlightenment," in Imbruglia, ed., *Naples in the Eighteenth Century,* 95–117; Lepre, *Storia del Mezzogiorno,* 2:74–104, 163–210; Angelantonio Spagnoletti, *Storia del Regno delle Due Sicilie* (Bologna, 1997), 31–44; Rosario Romeo, *Il Risorgimento in Sicilia* (Bari-Rome, 1950), 54–77; and Giuseppe Giarrizzo, "La Sicilia dal Cinquecento all'Unità d'Italia," in Vincenzo D'Alessandro and Giuseppe Giarrizzo, *La Sicilia dal Vespro all'Unità d'Italia* (Turin, 1989), 557–669.

42. Gianni Toniolo, *An Economic History of Liberal Italy, 1850–1918* (London, 1990), 39. See also Bevilacqua, *Breve storia,* 3–9; and Domenico Demarco, *Il crollo del Regno delle Due Sicilie. La struttura sociale* (Naples, 1960), 1–10.

longer able to command the world market. In the American South, wheat replaced tobacco in several areas of the Chesapeake, while rice continued to be
grown exclusively in the restricted region of lowcountry South Carolina and
Georgia. In the *Mezzogiorno,* grain quickly lost its central place in the export balance of the Kingdom of Naples, replaced by olive oil, which became
increasingly important in the international market. The economic crises that
hit the crops produced on plantations and *latifondi,* in turn, paved the way for
criticisms of the economic and social systems that revolved around them. In
both cases, political economists, enlightened philosophers, churchmen, and
government representatives branded an agricultural system that depended
particularly on the ownership of large landed estates as backward and unproductive and a labor system that oppressed large masses of human beings
for the idle life of a small class of privileged individuals as exploitative.[43]

In the age of democratic revolutions, the criticisms of the plantation
and the *latifondo* systems reached their peak. In the turmoil of war and disruption that accompanied foreign invasions, the two agricultural economies
suffered further blows. At the same time, the spread of liberal ideas built the
background for legal provisions designed to weaken or destroy plantation
slavery and the *latifondo* feudal system. Yet, in both cases, the momentum
came and went. The legal provisions against slavery disappeared quickly in
the southern states, as the Constitution sanctioned the legality of the slave
system and even protected it. On the other hand, the abolition of feudalism
did little to destroy the power of large landowners, who—whether noble
or bourgeois—were the ones who benefited most from the sale of former
feudal land. Also, if the legal revolution failed in both cases to resolve most
of the problems related to the economic and social systems that revolved
around plantations and *latifondi,* the market revolution in the American
South and the commercial revolution in the *Mezzogiorno* gave new impulse
to the slaveholding and landowning classes of the two regions. Thanks to the
cultivation of new and different crops that could command the international
market, the two southern elites accelerated the process of renewing their
ranks and strengthened their grip over both land and workers.[44]

43. See Immanuel Wallerstein, *The Modern World-System,* vol. 3, *The Second Era of Great Expansion of the Capitalist World-Economy, 1730s–1840s* (New York, 1989), 127–190.

44. See Eric J. Hobsbawm, *The Age of Revolutions, 1789–1848* (London, 1962); R. R. Palmer,
The Age of the Democratic Revolution: A Political History of Europe and America, 1760–1800, 2 vols.

Landed Estates and Commercial Agriculture

From the outset, American planters and southern Italian landowners faced two different types of problems. In the American South, land was abundant and cheap because of the lower population density and the existence of a large unsettled area; slave labor, however, was a rare commodity, especially after the closing of the Atlantic slave trade in 1808. As a consequence, as Shearer Davis Bowman has noted, planters focused on the production of particular staple crops, rather than experimenting with agricultural diversification, while "slavery was well suited to the plantation economy's needs for a supply of gang laborers whose geographical mobility made them highly responsive to constant, often rapid shifts in demand along an advancing frontier." Conversely, in the *Mezzogiorno,* scarcity of land, and especially of valuable agricultural land, was a chronic feature, due to particular geographical problems and to a higher population density; however, labor was cheap and abundant, thanks to the existence of a large mass of landless peasants. Consequently, southern Italian landowners made the best possible use of the land of their *latifondi,* engaging in a wide range of economic activities and in agricultural diversification, all the while keeping a highly flexible system of contractual arrangements with their free workforce so as to be able to respond rapidly to changes in the market demand.[45]

In the nineteenth century, the effects of the market revolution in the American South and the commercial revolution in the Italian *Mezzogiorno,* the emphasis on commercial agriculture, and the emphasis on demand for new staple crops highlighted these fundamental differences between plantations and *latifondi,* increasing the importance of the particular economic and social features attached to them. By the first half of the nineteenth century, American plantations and Italian *latifondi* had acquired characteristics that made them very distinctive economic and labor systems at the periphery of the world economy. The process of adaptation to changing conditions in the world market had transformed them into centers of agricultural activities

---

(Princeton, N.J., 1959–1964); and David Brion Davis, *Revolutions: Reflections on American Equality and Foreign Liberations* (Cambridge, Mass., 1990).

45. Shearer Davis Bowman, "Antebellum Planters and *Vormarz* Junkers in Comparative Perspective," *AHR* 85 (1980): 786.

that, despite the several differences, shared some important elements, elements such as the search for self-sufficiency through diversification of production and the unusual concentration of power in the hands of slaveholders and landowners.[46]

Few historians would dispute the assumption that, in managing their plantations, nineteenth-century American slaveholders strove to achieve a high degree of self-sufficiency. In a 1997 publication, Russell Menard summarized the conclusions of a host of recent studies on the subject and pointed out that, even though planters were often reluctant to experiment with agricultural diversification, their pursuit of self-sufficiency transformed plantations into "enterprises producing a wide range of goods and services for internal use despite their concentration on a single cash-crop." This, in turn, was reflected in the complexity and variety of labor activities that the slaves performed. The nineteenth-century southern plantation, therefore, was a complex economic enterprise that, in addition to fulfilling its primary aim of producing and selling a particular staple crop on the world market, was also at the center of a complex web of economic activities—such as the production of corn and of other subsistence crops—whose impact was almost exclusively local.[47]

Slaves were an integral part of this section of the plantation economy, especially—but not exclusively—in those areas where the task system was in use and the slaves' economies flourished. In fact, as Keumsoo Hong has reminded us, even "the gang and task system were . . . two extremes on the continuum of labor organization, with a variety of intermediate types." Most probably, just as plantations were at once projected into the world market and tied to the local economy, most slaveholders mixed elements of the gang and task systems at their convenience, while slaves strove to keep some independent economic activity, whether they worked on rice, cotton, or sugar plantations. As a consequence, slaves' economies were active in a number of different areas of the antebellum South.[48]

---

46. For a critical view, see Bruce Levine, "Modernity, Backwardness, and Capitalism in the Two Souths," in Dal Lago and Halpern, eds., *American South and Italian Mezzogiorno*, 233–240.

47. Russell R. Menard, "Plantation System," in Randall M. Miller and John David Smith, eds., *Dictionary of Afro-American Slavery* (Westport, Conn., 1997), 579.

48. Hong, "Geography of Time and Labor," 20. See also Ira Berlin, *Generations of Captivity* (Cambridge, Mass., 2003), 184–187; Steven F. Miller, "Plantation Labor Organization and Slave Life on the Cotton Frontier: The Alabama-Mississippi Black Belt, 1815–1840," and Roderick A. McDonald, "Independent Economic Production by Slaves on Antebellum Louisiana Sugar

Whether they implemented the gang or the task system, clearly south-ern slaveholders exercised an unusual degree of power over their enslaved workforce, even by nineteenth-century standards. Yet, ever since the publica-tion of U. B. Phillips's classic work *American Negro Slavery* in 1918, historians have debated fiercely on the nature of the slaveholders' deployment of power and on the organization of the nineteenth-century plantation's labor regime and its implications for our understanding of the slave system as a whole. According to Eric Wolf, the plantation was a "capital-using unit employing a large labor force under close managerial supervision to produce a crop for sale," which combined the three functions of organizational control, pro-cessing, and storage. For their part, neoclassical economic historians have pointed out that, in terms of management, nineteenth-century southern plantations resembled factories because they were—in the words of George Grantham—"eminently suited to respond massively to market opportuni-ties." In particular, Robert Fogel has argued that the high productivity of southern plantations related to the slaveholders' efficiency in managing the workforce; Fogel has referred specifically to the gang system, which a num-ber of slaveholders implemented on cotton plantations.[49]

Conversely, following Eugene Genovese's view on the incompatibility of plantations with the capitalist mode of production, Marxist historians have downplayed the efficiency of plantation management and have argued that a combination of discipline enforcement and paternalism characterized the slaveholders' relationship with their workforce. Recently, an increasing number of scholars seem to have been willing to abandon the idea of an ir-reconcilable opposition between the neoclassical economic and the Marxist interpretations of the slave South. This new trend stems from a number of studies that have clearly demonstrated that there was enormous variety in both the degree of slaveholders' commitment to capitalism and the effects that this had on labor management and productivity. Historians may very well reach a consensus in the near future on the assumption that, in most cases, capitalist practices and precapitalist relations coexisted and a combi-

Plantations,"both in Ira Berlin and Philip Morgan, eds., *Cultivation and Culture: Labor and the Shaping of Slave Life in the Americas* (Charlottesville, Va., 1993), 155–169, 275–299.

49. Wolf, *Europe and the People,* 314; George Grantham, "Agrarian Organization in the Cen-tury of Industrialization: Europe, Russia, and North America," in George Grantham and Carol Scott Leonard, eds., *Agrarian Organization in the Century of Industrialization: Europe, Russia, and North America* (Greenwich, Conn., 1989), 3–4. See also Phillips, *American Negro Slavery;* Gray, *History of Agriculture,* 1:301–302; and Fogel, *Without Consent or Contract,* 72–80.

nation of paternalism, violence, discipline enforcement, and efforts toward maximization of production was the norm on most plantations.[50]

In several ways, the description of the plantation as a self-sufficient enterprise at the center of a variety of economic activities and the debate on the capitalist/noncapitalist nature of slaveholders' activities find a correspondence in similar issues that have engaged southern Italian revisionist historians in their attempt to define the *latifondo* economy of the nineteenth-century Italian *Mezzogiorno*. According to Piero Bevilacqua and other scholars, the nineteenth-century *latifondo* employed a mixed economic regime in which cultivation of subsistence crops for internal consumption coexisted with the raising of livestock and the production of valuable cash crops for sale on the world market. This mixed regime guaranteed both the self-sufficiency and the economic flexibility of the *latifondo* and allowed southern Italian landowners to cope with changes in the world market demand by shifting the emphasis onto different sectors of production, while making minimum investments in innovation. Similar to plantations, a number of *latifondi* participated to the world market through the production and sale of cash crops and, at the same time, were at the center of a web of market relations at the local level.[51]

Yet, the fact that the workforce consisted of free peasants resulted in a substantial difference between the impact of the southern Italian workers' activities on the *latifondo* economy and the impact of the American slaves' activities on the plantation economy. Unlike American slaves, who were the most important source of capital for slaveholders, southern Italian peasants were either field hands who sold their labor on an occasional basis or tenants and sharecroppers who rented tracts of land from either the landowners or their agents. Peasants' exploitation—unlike slaves' exploitation—occurred in terms of economic pressure, rather than in terms of labor organization and

50. See Kolchin, *American Slavery*, 111–127; and Eugene D. Genovese, *Roll, Jordan, Roll: The World the Slaves Made* (New York, 1974), 3–7. See also. Mark M. Smith, *Debating Slavery: Economy and Society in the Antebellum American South* (New York, 1998), 87–94; and, for a case study, Richard J. Follett, "On the Edge of Modernity: Louisiana's Landed Elites in the Nineteenth-Century Sugar Country," in Dal Lago and Halpern, eds., *American South and the Italian Mezzogiorno*, 73–94. For a comparison with the *Mezzogiorno*, see Peter Kolchin, *A Sphinx on the American Land: The Nineteenth-Century South in Comparative Perspective* (Baton Rouge, La., 2003), 79–82.

51. See Piero Bevilacqua, "Latifondo," in *Enciclopedia delle scienze sociali* (Florence, 1996), 162–164; and Petrusewicz, *Latifundium*, xii–xv.

control. Unlike American planters, who were "laborlords first and landlords second," southern Italian landowners were just landlords. Therefore, contractual arrangements over land leases were the key to the masters' control of the workforce, and for this reason usurious practices were the most evident sign of peasant exploitation in the nineteenth-century *Mezzogiorno.*[52]

Economic pressure through usurious practices and exploitative contractual arrangements had a long history in the *Mezzogiorno.* The legal provisions which, at the beginning of the nineteenth century, led to the abolition of the feudal system and to the formation of a new class of bourgeois landowners—most of whom came from the ranks of *massari* and *gabelloti*—did little to eradicate long-established usurious practices. At the same time, the fact that this rising landed bourgeoisie played a passive role in the revolution from above, through which the French and Bourbon governments effectively provided the means to its formation by implementing massive land reforms, cast a historiographic stigma on the new landowners' ability to promote economic and social progress. Until recently, especially Marxist historians—who mostly followed Antonio Gramsci's thought—accused the southern Italian landed bourgeoisie of aping the *rentier* habits of the feudal aristocracy and of being interested only in usurping common land and exploiting the peasantry, rather than being committed to the capitalist transformation of the *Mezzogiorno*'s agriculture. Both the weakness of the bourgeoisie and its feudal origins, in turn, were deemed responsible for the backwardness of the southern Italian agricultural economy.[53]

Since the 1980s, revisionist historians have done a great deal to correct this fundamentally incorrect interpretation. Comparable to the findings of recent scholarship on American slaveholders, revisionist historians of the nineteenth-century *Mezzogiorno* have pointed out the importance of regional variations among southern Italian landowners' land management and capitalist practices and have firmly established the existence of a number of

52. Smith, *Debating Slavery,* 69. See also Marta Petrusewicz, "Wage Earners, but Not Proletarians: Wage Labor and Social Relations in the Nineteenth-Century Calabrian Latifondo," *Review* 10 (1987): 472–476; and Giovanni Arrighi and Fortunata Piselli, "Capitalist Development in Hostile Environments: Feuds, Class Struggles, and Migrations in a Peripheral Region of Southern Italy," *Review* 10 (1987): 661–669.

53. See John A. Davis, "Introduction: Gramsci and Italy's Passive Revolution," in John A. Davis, ed., *Gramsci and Italy's Passive Revolution* (London, 1979), 11–30. See also Lepre, *Il Mezzogiorno dal feudalesimo al capitalismo,* 151–198; and Giorgio Candeloro, *Storia dell'Italia moderna,* vol. 1, *Le origini del Risorgimento* (Milan, 1956), 330–339.

regions in which economic growth clearly relied on the cultivation of cash crops. Recent studies have recast our view of the nineteenth-century southern Italian *latifondo*, "which grew out of the ashes of the *Ancien Régime*," as a "commercially oriented" and rational agricultural enterprise, while seriously questioning the identification of landowners with *rentiers*, since, as Jonathan Morris has pointed out, "many of the mainland *latifondi*, if not directly farmed by the landlords themselves, were certainly managed by resident agents." Whether it was landlords or agents who managed the *latifondi*, several historians consider these particular individuals as representatives of a rising entrepreneurial class. In fact, in addition to being resident on the properties, these same entrepreneurial landlords and agents were also often at the vanguard of projects of agricultural reform and economic modernization.[54]

The implications of the results of the most recent trends in scholarship for the comparative study of the ideologies of American slaveholders and southern Italian landowners are far-reaching. In both cases, it is possible to relate the degree of the elite's commitment to the implementation of capitalist practices in the management of land and/or the workforce to the economic transformations that occurred at the beginning of the nineteenth century. Effectively, the spread of the market revolution in the American South and of the commercial revolution in the Italian *Mezzogiorno* led to a new emphasis on the commercial character of plantations and *latifondi* and formed the background against which two new classes of landed proprietors—the cotton planters and the landed bourgeoisie—rose in wealth and influence. The rapid changes in the world market demand and the emphasis on the production and sale of particular cash crops—cotton in one case and olives, citrus fruits, and wine grapes in the other—effectively accentuated the commitment to capitalist agriculture of the entrepreneurial sections of the two landed elites.[55]

54. John A. Davis, "Casting off the 'Southern Problem': Or the Peculiarities of the South Reconsidered," in Jane Schneider, ed., *Italy's "Southern Question": Orientalism in One Country* (New York, 1998), 213; Morris, "Challenging *Meridionalismo*," 6. See also Salvemini, *L'innovazione precaria*, 3–32; Petrusewicz, *Latifundium*; Salvatore Lupo, "I proprietari terrieri nel Mezzogiorno," in Piero Bevilacqua, ed., *Storia dell'agricoltura italiana*, vol. 2, *Uomini e Classi* (Venice, 1990), 105–149; and Alberto Banti, "Gli imprenditori meridionali: razionalità e contesto," *Meridiana* 6 (1989): 67–89. For a critical view, see Paolo Macry, "Studi recenti sul Mezzogiorno ottocentesco," in Macry and Massafra, eds., *Fra storia e storiografia*, 160–162.

55. See Enrico Dal Lago and Rick Halpern, "Two Case-Studies in Comparative History: The American South and the Italian *Mezzogiorno*," in Dal Lago and Halpern, eds., *American South and Italian Mezzogiorno*, 7–10.

These changes did not just occur in the American South and the Italian *Mezzogiorno.* In each peripheral area of the world economy, progressive landowners responded to the challenge of the readjustment of the world market, experimenting with new technologies and crop rotation and rationalizing the process of production. Though certainly related to a general interest of post-1815 Europe for modernization—as Marta Petrusewicz has argued in the case of southern Italian landowners—this "entrepreneurial liveliness" was actually a tendency among nineteenth-century landed elites on a world scale. Similar to what happened in the American South and in the Italian *Mezzogiorno,* it related to the rise of entrepreneurial classes who made their fortunes by taking advantage of the world market demand for new agricultural products. And yet, the entrepreneurial spirit was not restricted to the new landowning classes. In each case, and particularly in the cases of the antebellum American South and of the nineteenth-century Italian *Mezzogiorno,* it affected many nineteenth-century economic reformers and progressive slaveholders and landowners who belonged to both long-established and rising elite families.[56]

During the nineteenth century, profound changes occurred in the Chesapeake area. From as early as the mid-eighteenth century, soil exhaustion caused by tobacco had forced Chesapeake planters to experiment with crop diversification. By the beginning of the nineteenth century, the tobacco economy was in such a deep crisis that an increasing number of planters relied on wheat as an alternative. Yet, even wheat, especially if grown alone, could quickly lead to a similar problem of soil exhaustion. Ideally, wheat cultivation should have occurred in a system of rotation with other crops that allowed the land to rest in the intervals. Significantly, Virginian agricultural reformers were acutely aware of the importance of crop rotation, and they enthusiastically supported it, even though their experiments soon led them to discover that it could not prevent the dreaded soil exhaustion. For example, Eugene Genovese reports that Virginia's foremost agricultural

56. See Marta Petrusewicz, "Land-Based Modernization and the Culture of Landed Elites in the Nineteenth-Century Mezzogiorno," in Dal Lago and Halpern, eds., *American South and Italian Mezzogiorno,* 95; Maria Malatesta, *Le aristocrazie terriere nell'Europa contemporanea* (Rome-Bari, 1999), 87–127; Douglass C. North, *The Economic Growth of the United States, 1790–1860* (New York, 1966), 36–41; Shearer Davis Bowman, *Masters and Lords: Mid-19th Century U.S. Planters and Prussian Junkers* (New York, 1993), 95–97; and Wallerstein, *Modern World-System,* 3:129–189.

reformer, Edmund Ruffin, "used a fine six-field system, and a fellow Virginian, Colonel Tulley, rotated his wheat with clover and got excellent results."[57]

Agricultural diversification and improved farming techniques were next in importance to crop rotation in the agendas of agricultural reformers. Agricultural diversification was particularly important in the areas where tobacco was still the dominant crop, despite its decline in importance in the international market. Perhaps, the most famous progressive Virginian planter who engaged heart and soul in a battle against the tyranny of tobacco monoculture was John Hartwell Cocke of Bremo. A longtime member of the prestigious Albemarle Agricultural Society—which opened its sessions in Charlottesville in 1817 under the auspices of Thomas Jefferson and James Madison—Cocke became its president between 1854 and 1857. The society also included among its distinguished members John S. Skinner of Baltimore, a pioneer importer of fertilizers and the publisher of the renowned Virginian progressive journal *The American Farmer.*[58]

In 1860, after spending a number of years engaging in agricultural experiments, Cocke published his most influential pamphlet—*Tobacco, the Bane of Virginia Husbandry*. In the pamphlet, Cocke asserted that the preoccupation with tobacco had led planters to care exclusively for its cultivation and even import meat, corn, and hay from the northern states, instead of producing them themselves. Moreover, tobacco exhausted the soil and absorbed labor, and it was also extremely unhealthy. To Cocke, the solution to the problem of the obsession with tobacco and the evils that related to it—as much an economic as a moral issue—was in the planters' employment of agricultural diversification and crop rotation and in the development of agricultural techniques that would restore the soil's fertility.[59]

And to be sure, following Cocke's example, through agricultural diversification, crop rotation, and an emphasis on the cultivation of wheat and corn, many Virginian tobacco planters were able to survive the economic crisis of

57. Genovese, *Political Economy of Slavery,* 96. See also Irwin, "Exploring the Affinity of Wheat and Slavery," 315–318.

58. See Charles W. Turner "Virginia Agricultural Reform, 1815–1860," *AH* 26 (1952): 80–81; and Clement Eaton, *The Mind of the South* (Baton Rouge, La., 1964), 23–43.

59. See John Hartwell Cocke, *Tobacco, the Bane of Virginia Husbandry* (Richmond, Va., 1860). See also M. Boyd Coyner, "John Hartwell Cocke of Bremo: Agriculture and Slavery in the Ante-Bellum South" (Ph.D. diss., University of Virginia, 1961).

the early nineteenth century and reinvent themselves as producers of other types of cash crops—especially wheat—for sale on the world market. In the process, Virginian planters improved dramatically their knowledge of agriculture as a science and also reasserted emphatically their commitment to the system of plantation slavery through the establishment of no less then thirty agricultural societies in Virginia in the period between 1815 and 1860. Each of these societies had its own journal, which offered advice and hosted debates on progressive techniques of farming. Agricultural diversification, crop rotation, and experimentation with scientific agriculture were the common topics of most articles and published letters.[60]

Yet, Virginian planters soon discovered that the profound transformation of plantation agriculture that they had set in motion had far-reaching effects on the entire slave system. As the southern Italian case shows, the cultivation of wheat and other types of grain—unlike the cultivation of tobacco—did not require a permanently stationed workforce and could be handled by a relatively small number of laborers. Therefore, several masters found it more profitable to keep only few specialized field hands and hire out the rest of their slaves. By the 1850s, the practice of hiring out slaves was widespread throughout the areas that specialized in the production of wheat. In fact, Frederick Law Olmsted noticed that "many thousands slaves had been hired in eastern Virginia during the time of my visit" and that "the vast majority of slaves are employed in agricultural labor" on farms, rather than on plantations.[61]

Despite the importance of the shift from tobacco to wheat in vast areas of the Chesapeake, the most far-reaching developments occurred in the South Carolina and Georgia upcountry, where cotton production boomed as a consequence of the market revolution. The expansion of cotton cultivation completely transformed the economy of the Atlantic Seaboard rice-producing states. On the Sea Islands of South Carolina, planters already grew a variety of long staple cotton as a luxury item. Yet, it was the short staple variety of cotton that became the protagonist of a new plantation revolution

60. See Turner, "Virginia Agricultural Reform," 81–89; and Frederick Siegel, *The Roots of Southern Distinctiveness: Tobacco and Society in Danville, Virginia, 1780–1865* (Chapel Hill, N.C., 1987).

61. Olmsted, *Cotton Kingdom,* 91. See also Lorena Walsh, "Plantation Management in the Chesapeake, 1650–1820," *JEH* 49 (1989): 393–406; and Genovese, *Roll, Jordan, Roll,* 390–392.

and was largely responsible for the southern economic recovery at the beginning of the nineteenth century. Unlike long staple cotton, short staple cotton found the perfect environment in the rich and still largely uninhabited soil of the upcountry hills.[62]

After Eli Whitney's 1793 invention of the cotton gin—which mechanically separated the fiber from the seed—cotton production accelerated and its cost decreased; consequently, short staple cotton entered a long phase of expansion and its cultivation gradually spread throughout the southern interior. The invention of the cotton gin and the expansion of cotton cultivation occurred at the same time in which the world market demand for cotton increased as a consequence of the growth of textile factories in England and in the northern United States. Southern plantations supplied the cotton mills of both regions, where the majority of the world's manufacturing centers were located. From 1800 to 1860, cotton production grew exponentially until it reached a total amount of 4.5 million bales—which made it the most important entry in the list of American exports before the Civil War.[63]

As cotton production grew, its cultivation moved from its original center in upcountry Georgia and South Carolina to the regions of the southern frontier, or Old Southwest. In the western lands, cotton production originally centered around Natchez, on the rich alluvial soils of the Mississippi River, where the local cotton planters who started their business at the beginning of the nineteenth century became some of the wealthiest individuals in America. From upcountry South Carolina and Georgia and from the Mississippi River, cotton expanded to Florida, Alabama, Mississippi, Arkansas, and Texas, creating the largest area of cotton production in the world. After the Jackson and Van Buren administrations enforced the removal of the southeastern Indian tribes in the 1830s, no more obstacles existed for the agricultural colonization of the southern interior. Thousands of southern planters relocated together with their slaves in the western regions, fleeing the economic crisis of the Atlantic Seaboard states. Many more slavehold-

62. See Joyce Chaplin, "Creating a Cotton South in Georgia and South Carolina, 1760–1815," *JSH* 57 (1991): 171–200; Anthony G. Smith, *Economic Readjustment of an Old Cotton State: South Carolina, 1820–1860* (Columbia, S.C., 1958), 1–18; Lacy K. Ford, *Origins of Southern Radicalism: The South Carolina Upcountry, 1800–1860* (New York, 1988), 5–19; and Joseph P. Reidy, *From Slavery to Agrarian Capitalism in the Cotton Plantation South, 1800–1880* (Chapel Hill, N.C., 1992).

63. See North, *Economic Growth*, 66–74; Charles Sellers, *The Market Revolution: Jacksonian America, 1815–1846* (New York, 1991), 396–428; and Gavin Wright, *The Political Economy of the Cotton South: Households, Markets, and Wealth in the Nineteenth Century* (New York, 1978), 11–15.

ing and nonslaveholding yeomen joined them and set out to start their own business in the rich cotton lands of the Old Southwest.[64]

As cotton cultivation colonized the southern interior, a dual economy emerged in most of the settled regions while, at the same time—as Harry Watson has noticed—"the dependence of southern plantations on export agriculture and the vagaries of international prices and credit terms remained constant." In fact, the almost complete reliance on the world market demand for cotton left the southern economy even more vulnerable to periodic crises of overproduction and price falls. Yet, as long as the demand for cotton rose and fresh land was available, the southerners' westward migration continued in a seemingly endless stream. As planters and less wealthy slaveholders migrated westward with their families, they confronted the problem of finding a suitable workforce for their plantations and farms. A few resolved the problem by taking their slaves on the journey westward. The overwhelming majority relied on the internal slave trade. After the Atlantic slave trade became illegal in 1808 and slave prices rose exponentially, smugglers and slave traders made fortunes through a large network for the purchase and sale of slaves on the southeast-southwest route. Whether they dealt with slaves who were sold by impoverished Chesapeake planters to frontier slaveholders or whether they dealt with kidnapped free blacks who were illegally enslaved, internal slave traders uprooted hundreds of thousands of African American families in what Ira Berlin has recently termed the "Second Middle Passage."[65]

The expansion of cotton cultivation did not just cause unspeakable grief to African American slaves, it also had important repercussions on the white population. According to William Freehling, "upland short-staple, green-seed ordinary cotton . . . was a crop with which the poor made their fortune. One could grow upcountry cotton on cheap land, without slaves, or, as an

64. See Meinig, *Shaping of America,* 3–32; Miller, *South by Southwest;* John Hebron Moore, *The Rise of the Cotton Kingdom in the Old Southwest: Mississippi, 1770–1860* (Baton Rouge, La., 1988); Daniel S. Dupre, *Transforming the Cotton Frontier: Madison County, Alabama, 1800–1840* (Baton Rouge, La., 1997); and Edward E. Baptist, *Creating an Old South: Middle Florida's Plantation Frontier before the Civil War* (Chapel Hill, N.C., 2002). See also Anthony F. Wallace, *The Long, Bitter Trail: Andrew Jackson and the Indians* (New York, 1993).

65. Watson, "Slavery and Development," 47. See also Berlin, *Generations of Captivity,* 166–169; Frederick Bancroft, *Slave Trading in the Old South* (Baltimore, Md., 1931); Michael Tadman, *Speculators and Slaves: Masters, Traders, and Slaves in the Old South* (Madison, Wisc., 1989); Robert H. Gudmestead, *A Troublesome Commerce: The Transformation of the Interstate Slave Trade* (Baton Rouge, La., 2003); and Walter Johnson, *Soul by Soul: Life Inside the Antebellum Slave Market* (Cambridge, Mass., 1999).

alternative, with several slaves." Cotton cultivation suited both large planters and small farmers and it soon became the business of individuals and
families who belonged to all social classes. As a consequence, while planters
continued to be relatively few, the slaveholding class as a whole grew constantly and rapidly in number.[66]

By 1860, slaveholders totaled 385,000 individuals. Within this figure,
yeomen who owned from one to five slaves were half of the slaveholding
population, while owners of ten to twenty slaves formed 38 percent of it; at
the peak of the pyramid, the top 12 percent was made of planters, or owners
of twenty or more slaves. As the slaveholding population grew, the interests
of the yeomanry in many southern regions increasingly became entangled
with slavery—a factor that had momentous political consequences. At the
same time, those yeomen who did not own slaves either yielded to the enormous pressure of the market economy and aspired to become slaveholders
or, in a few cases, managed to live outside the logics of the cotton market
and of plantation slavery, but generally not for long.[67]

Aside from the already established planters, most slaveholders who
engaged in the business of cotton planting on the southwestern frontier
belonged to a new, self-made gentry. As James Oakes has shown, the small-
and medium-size slaveholders who migrated to the Old Southwest were
more interested in profit than in a refined life and conceived their plantations as "factories in the field." Yet, as far as we know, even those slaveholders
who became large cotton planters and moved toward a more refined lifestyle
in the southwestern regions retained a distinctively entrepreneurial attitude
vis-à-vis plantation agriculture and slave management.[68]

Commenting upon the rise of the new cotton gentry, a southern lawyer
wrote in *Harper's Weekly* in 1859 that "the sudden acquisition of wealth in the

66. William W. Freehling, *Prelude to Civil War: The Nullification Crisis in South Carolina,
1816–1836* (New York, 1966), 19.

67. The statistics are in Smith, *Debating Slavery*, 15–16. See also Eugene D. Genovese, "Yeomen Farmers in a Slaveholders' Democracy," *AH* 49 (1975): 331–342; Watson, "Slavery and Development," 44–48; Ford, *Origins of Southern Radicalism*, 44–96; Hahn, *Roots of Southern Populism*;
and Stephanie McCurry, *Masters of Small Worlds: Yeoman Households, Gender Relations, and the
Political Culture of the Antebellum South Carolina Low Country* (New York, 1995), 37–91.

68. See Oakes, *Ruling Race,* 153–191; and Steven F. Miller, "Plantation Labor Organization
and Slave Life on the Cotton Frontier: The Alabama-Mississippi Black Belt, 1815–1840," in
Berlin and Morgan, eds., *Cultivation and Culture*, 155–169.

cotton-growing region of the United States, in many instances by planters commencing with very limited means, is almost miraculous." Characterizing the new slaveholder as "patient, industrious, frugal, and self-denying," the lawyer described how "nearly the entire amount of their cotton crops is devoted to the increase of their capital. The result is, in a few years, large estates, as if by magic, are accumulated." Doubtless, the reasons for the distinctive entrepreneurial attitude of cotton planters and slaveholders related to the particular conditions of the frontier, and especially—as Mark Smith has pointed out—to "the time it took to clear new land and the greater need for early return on investment." These were also the themes that the southern lawyer implicitly hinted at in his article when he praised the new cotton gentry's industriousness and adaptability.[69]

Yet, an equally important reason for the distinctive entrepreneurial attitude of cotton planters and slaveholders was the fact that cotton plantations and farms were organized rather differently from both tobacco and rice plantations. Planters and slaveholders were usually resident, with or without an overseer, throughout the year and closely supervised a workforce divided into large gangs. Slaves planted the seed in the spring and tended the crop until cotton bolls ripened in the fall; then they picked the cotton, ginned it, and packed it in bales. The labor pace was much more exhausting than under the task system; slaves had little time to do other activities except on Sundays. The close master-slave relationship that characterized the cotton plantation, together with its full involvement in the capitalist world economy, made the problem of labor management absolutely crucial, especially at times of fluctuation in the market's demand for cotton. Also for this reason, more than other types of slaveholders, cotton planters tried particularly hard to achieve total control of their workforce. In fact, as Mark Smith has pointed out, they even attempted to rationalize the work pace through all kinds of time-measuring devices in true factory fashion.[70]

Yet, as Ira Berlin has noted, if "the tick of the clock paced the new order, domesticity was its idiom." Planters and slaveholders systematically adopted

69. "A Southern Lawyer," *HW* (February 1859); Smith, *Debating Slavery,* 27.

70. See Mark Smith, *Mastered by the Clock: Time, Slavery, and Freedom in the American South* (Chapel Hill, N.C., 1996), 108–111. See also Daniel R. Hundley, *Social Relations in Our Southern States* (Baton Rouge, La., 1979; orig. pub. in 1860), 175–185; Olmsted, *Cotton Kingdom,* 167–169; Kenneth M. Stampp, *The Peculiar Institution: Slavery in the Ante-Bellum South* (New York, 1956), 82–85; and Hong, "Geography of Time and Labor," 8–11.

a paternalistic rhetoric to describe the master-slave relationship, one that combined success and efficiency in work management with the masters' constant interest and often intrusion in the slaves' lives. Slaves, in turn, resisted their masters' intrusions and their imposition of their will upon them in a variety of ways, and, through a process of continuous bargaining, they achieved partial acknowledgment of their needs. In Eugene Genovese's thought, this process was at the heart of a particular type of paternalistic relationship between master and slaves, one that implied mutual obligation and reciprocity. As Genovese has explained in *Roll, Jordan, Roll*, paternalism forced masters to implicitly recognize the humanity of their slaves and, at the same time, gave slaves room to manipulate their condition in order to carve out some room for autonomous behavior.[71]

The case of Thomas B. Chaplin, a cotton planter of St. Helena Island, off the coast of South Carolina, is a particularly illuminating example of the process of bargaining between master and slaves over work on the plantation. Chaplin was an important figure in the local community and a prominent member of the St. Helena Agricultural Society. From his family, he had inherited the renowned cotton plantation of Tombee, to which he moved with his wife in 1840. From the beginning, Chaplin attempted to assert his will over his slaves; yet, he often ended up being disappointed at their response. In several instances, Chaplin's field hands resisted his orders regarding particular assignments, either faking a misunderstanding or performing other tasks instead of the ones to which they had been assigned. On one particular occasion, in late May 1851, after a serious drought and consequent shortage of cotton, Chaplin desperately needed his slaves to plant new cotton ("supplying"), rather than having them waste time covering the dead plants with dirt ("hauling"). Although he had not given precise orders, the slaves understood exactly the urgency of the situation; however, they led him to believe that they had misunderstood the priorities of their tasks, due to a lack of communication. On May 31, Chaplin wrote a few notes of disappointment in his plantation journal: "I have not been out to see what the hands are doing. Saw some hauling cotton. . . . My Negroes were hauling cotton when their own sense should tell them they ought to be supplying."[72]

71. See Berlin, *Generations of Captivity*, 204–205; Genovese, *Roll, Jordan, Roll*, 3–8; 321–322; Phillips, *American Negro Slavery*, especially 291–307; Drew G. Faust, *James Henry Hammond and the Old South: A Design for Mastery* (Baton Rouge, La., 1982), especially 69–104.

72. Thomas Chaplin's plantation journal, May 31, 1851, in Theodore Rosengarten, *Tombee: Portrait of a Cotton Planter* (New York, 1986), 533.

Through a series of minor incidents such as this, the slaves resisted their masters' efforts to completely regulate their life and pace of work and managed to implement autonomous decisions; the final result of this bargaining process was the masters' recognition of their slaves' needs and—implicitly—of their humanity. As Theodore Rosengarten has pointed out, despite the fact that the master was "perpetually exercising some means of surveillance or control, either through his formal institutions or in mundane contact with his slaves," the slaves were able to resist by "physically and mentally withdrawing from the field" and "creating elbow room to rest, pray, plot, love, heal, or for no other reason than to remain human." Nevertheless, it is also important to remember that Chaplin's slaves had more room for bargaining than slaves on upcountry cotton plantations, simply because Sea Island cotton planters usually employed the task system, rather than the much more strict and exhausting gang system, which was in use on most upcountry cotton plantations and farms.[73]

Comparable to what happened on American plantations, on southern Italian *latifondi* the changes in the overall structure of the nineteenth-century world economy also produced momentous transformations. After southern Italian grain proved no longer competitive in the world market, its producers increasingly turned to internal consumption. At the same time, the commercial revolution allowed other agricultural products to find their way to the international markets. According to Giovanni Montroni, "the progressive decline of the export of both silk and grain shifted the attention of southern producers first on olive oil and then on citrus and wine." In fact, in the first half of the nineteenth century, the *Mezzogiorno* exported large quantities of olive oil to England and France, citrus to both America and Europe, and wine to England.[74]

Olive oil was produced in several areas of southern Italy and went to supply—mainly as a lubricant—English textile mills and French wool and soap factories. As cotton did with the American South, olive oil provided the *Mezzogiorno* with its own distinctive contribution to the industrial revo-

73. Rosengarten, *Tombee,* 158, 68–92.

74. Giovanni Montroni, "Introduzione," in Montroni, ed., *Agricoltura e commercio,* 11. See also Francesca Assante, "Le trasformazioni del paesaggio agrario," in Angelo Massafra, ed., *Il Mezzogiorno preunitario. Economia, società, istituzioni* (Bari, 1988), 29–54; Bevilacqua, "Il Mezzogiorno nel mercato internazionale," 26–31; and Piero Bevilacqua, "Clima, mercato e paesaggio agrario nel Mezzogiorno," in Bevilacqua, ed., *Storia dell'agricoltura,* 1:651–660.

lution. The total volume of olive oil exported leapt from 19,119 tons in 1832 to 34,899 tons in 1855. The region around Naples, the lower tip of Calabria, and Terra di Bari and Terra d'Otranto in Apulia were among the most important areas of olive oil production. Between 1835 and 1855 half of the entire production of the Bourbon kingdom—an average of 300,000 *cantaja*—came from Terra di Bari. Although olive oil also went to Sicily and other regions of the *Mezzogiorno*, a good deal of it was shipped to the soap factories of Marseille in France.[75]

Similar to olive trees, citrus trees were grown in groves (*giardini*) along the coast of several areas of the *Mezzogiorno*, especially Calabria and Sicily. In particular, in the Conca d'oro, around Palermo, citrus fruit production had started under the Arabs and had grown constantly during the early modern period. In the nineteenth century, Sicily exported oranges and lemons to the long-distance markets of northern Europe and North America. Starting from the 1830s, employment of the new steamships increased the speed and decreased the cost of transport across the Atlantic. By 1839, more than 373,648 boxes of citrus fruits were shipped each year from the harbor of Messina alone.[76]

Aside from olive oil and citrus fruits, a very important agricultural product was wine. Wine production was widespread throughout southern Italy since ancient times, but in the nineteenth century it received a new impulse from the world market demand. At the end of the eighteenth century, in Sicily, the English merchants Woodhouse and Ingham had started producing a sweet wine called marsala. During the course of the nineteenth century, local entrepreneurs—the most important of whom was Vincenzo Florio—transformed the production of marsala into a regional industry whose products gained the appreciation of all of Europe. By 1840, wine was Sicily's most important agricultural product; its exports for that year reached a total value of 1.4 million ducats.[77]

75. See Bevilacqua, *Breve storia*, 18–19; Spagnoletti, *Storia del Regno*, 260–261; Pietro Tino, *Campania felice? Territorio e agricolture prima della grande trasformazione* (Catanzaro, 1997), 35–37; Salvemini, *L'innovazione precaria*, 123–158.

76. Salvatore Lupo, "Tra società locale e commercio a lunga distanza. La vicenda degli agrumi siciliani," *Meridiana* 1 (1987): 82; Salvatore Lupo, *Il Giardino degli aranci. Il mondo degli agrumi nella storia del Mezzogiorno* (Venice, 1990), 15–32; and Orazio Cancila, *Storia dell'industria in Sicilia* (Bari-Rome, 1995), 48–55.

77. See Cancila, *Storia dell'industria*, 34–47; R. Trevelyan, *Princes under the Volcano* (London, 1972); Simone Candela, *I Florio* (Palermo, 1986), 54–79; Rosario Lentini, "Una nuova cultura

These important changes in agricultural production and export were concurrent with the process of abolition of the feudal system, which resulted in substantial accumulation of land at the hands of a new landowning class. The members of this new class were bourgeois landowners whose fathers often had been *amministratori, massari,* or *gabelloti* for important aristocratic families and had sometimes risen to acquire a noble title. While several of them continued the absentee practice of management that had characterized their former noble landlords, many others joined with the most progressive section of the aristocracy to rationalize estate management and apply modern ideas to the administration of the *latifondi.* Emblematic is the example of the Barraccos, the most famous case of a bourgeois family that rose to prominence through land acquisition and marriage within the noble ranks in the first half of the nineteenth century. At the time of its largest extent, the *latifondo* owned by Alfonso Barracco—the family's patriarch—reached thirty thousand hectares and covered almost entirely the central area of Calabria, between the Sila Mountains and the Ionian Sea.[78]

As Marta Petrusewicz has shown, the Barraccos held a view of *latifondo* management that aimed at transforming it into a functional and efficient enterprise. The key to this process was the administration, which was complex and multilayered and which supervised economic activities as diverse as "a whole mosaic of tenancy forms, a multiple-crop system, industrial production, and a great variety of farming techniques ranging from the archaic to the most modern and sophisticated, as well as a complex web of markets." Together with grain, nineteenth-century *latifondi* such as the Barracco estate also produced cash crops—olives, citrus fruits, and wine grapes—for sale on the world market. On another Calabrian estate, one owned by Agostino Serra, duke of Terranova, tenants grew both grain and citrus fruits together with olives, from which they made oil. In fact, reading the documents of the estate's administration, one cannot help but think that olive oil was the most important item that Serra produced on his *latifondi* throughout the 1830s and 1840s. Arguably, Serra's decision to privilege the production of olive oil was proof of his entrepreneurial spirit, since—according to Mariarosaria

del vino," in Francesco Pillitteri, ed., *L'economia dei Florio. Una famiglia di Imprenditori borghesi dell'Ottocento* (Palermo, 1990), 71–86. See also Enrico Iachello, *Il vino e il mare. "Trafficanti" siciliani nella Contea di Mascali tra '700 e '800* (Catania, 1991).

78. See Alberto M. Banti, *Storia della borghesia italiana. L'età liberale* (Rome, 1996), 74–75. See also Petrusewicz, *Latifundium,* 6–32; and Giovanni Montroni, *La società italiana dall'unificazione alla Grande Guerra* (Rome-Bari, 2002), 67–68.

Giorgio—in the first half of the nineteenth century olive oil was "the road by which Calabria was . . . taken into the circuits of the national and international markets."[79]

The rationality of *latifondo* management lay in the ability to emphasize sectors of commercial agriculture or to retreat to internal consumption according to the fluctuations of the world market demand. According to Maria Malatesta, in the case of the Barraccos, the rational management of the *latifondo* lay in "a kind of suspended equilibrium [achieved] by protecting the agricultural products from the market's fluctuations, keeping at the same time the production costs at a low level." Since it was impossible for southern Italian landowners to apply a lot of pressure on the management of a free labor force—as American slaveholders did with their slaves—their response to the market demand focused on the employment of a system of production that was highly flexible because of its agricultural diversification. As with Agostino Serra's decision to emphasize olive oil production because of its commercial value, in most cases entrepreneurial landowners focused on the cultivation of those agricultural products that the market needed and at the particular times in which it needed them. Products such as citrus, olive oil, and wine enjoyed a boom in market demand throughout the nineteenth century. As a result, a number of landed proprietors took advantage of the boom, converting large areas of their landed estates to the cultivation of cash crops without completely abandoning grain production.[80]

Nineteenth-century agricultural reformers understood that the strength of the *latifondo* lay in the coexistence of different crops and in the combination of intensive and extensive agriculture. Therefore, they advised landowners to supplement the cultivation of grain with the production of one or more cash crops. In an article that he published in the government's periodical *Annali Civili del Regno delle Due Sicilie* (Civilian Annals of the Kingdom of the Two Sicilies) in 1838, Raffaele Pepe—a leading agricultural reformer from Molise—recommended the planting of cash crops, or "tree

79. Petrusewicz, *Latifundium,* 6; Mariarosaria Giorgio, "Produzione e commercio dell'olio nell'azienda calabrese dei Serra di Gerace (1836–1847)," in Montroni, ed., *Agricoltura e commercio,* 49. See also Demarco, *Il crollo del Regno,* 1–52; Agnese Sinisi, "Le aziende calabresi dei principi Serra di Gerace nella prima metà del XIX secolo," in Massafra, ed., *Problemi di storia,* 91–116; and Giovanni Montroni, *Gli uomini del re. La nobiltà napoletana nell'Ottocento* (Catanzaro, 1996), 74–75.

80. Malatesta, *Le aristocrazie,* 53. See also Lupo, *Il giardino degli aranci,* 74–79; and, for a critical perspective, Davis, "Casting off the 'Southern Problem,'" 212–214.

crops," because "the planting of trees never fails" and because "plantations are a capital that increases through the years and without expenses." In particular, Pepe recommended the planting of olive trees and the setting up of "a vineyard with carefully selected tendrils to make better wine; because, if wine is not excellent, if it does not have a name on the market, it is a fruitless business." At the time in which Pepe wrote his article, wine was rapidly becoming a leading entry in the *Mezzogiorno*'s export. Not surprisingly, he encouraged southern Italian landowners to take advantage of the favorable juncture, arguing that "arts and manufactures now make great use of wine *spirit,* therefore distillation has become a very profitable industry."[81]

Since the production of cash crops mostly required the planting of trees, the technical term which agricultural publications used for it was "tree cultivation" (*coltura arborea*), as opposed to grain cultivation (*coltura a grano*), which did not need trees to support it. Most southern Italian entrepreneurial landowners linked the ownership of olive and citrus groves and vineyards to the very idea of agricultural progress precisely because of the high value of tree cultivation on the market. Many recently ennobled and bourgeois landowners—such as the Barraccos and the Nunziantes in Calabria, the Fortunatos in Basilicata, and the Turrisi Colonnas in Sicily—owned, together with grain-producing *latifondi,* landed estates where they grew cash crops, or else they reserved extensive areas of their *latifondi* for tree cultivation. In fact, according to Alberto Banti, it was the large size of the landholdings that allowed bourgeois landed proprietors such as the Barraccos to be "owners of grain-grown *latifondi* inland, and, at the same time, owners of citrus or olive groves, or even vineyards, on the coast."[82]

In those areas of the *Mezzogiorno* where tree cultivation was prevalent, commercial agriculture and production for the world market were widespread and the local agricultural economy was particularly strong. Especially in the area around Naples and on the coasts of Apulia, Calabria, and Sicily, increasing numbers of landowners displayed an extraordinary amount of wealth. In his work on Sicilian peasants, Sydney Sonnino penned a particularly impressive description of the irresistible advance of tree cultivation and commercial agriculture on the Sicilian coasts. In the 1870s, Sonnino noticed

81. Raffaele Pepe, "Sopra alcuni argomenti di economia agraria," *ACRDS* 16 (1838): 32. See also Lupo, "I proprietari terrieri," 108–111.

82. Banti, *Storia della borghesia,* 75. See also Lupo, "I proprietari terrieri," 105–118.

that, on the eastern and southwestern coasts of Sicily, tree cultivation had progressively transformed both the landscape and the economy of several areas where "every year there were new plantations, methods of cultivation were improved," while "agriculture tended to make progress and strove to become intensive and improve the quality of its products."[83]

Special types of land lease called "improvement leases" (*contratti a miglioria*) bound the tenants of the commercial sectors of production to provide for the improvement of the lots they rented; the tenants—often landless *braccianti*—had to pay an annual rent and at the same time plant or take care of vineyards or olive groves. The land lease lasted from ten to fifteen years, during which time the tenants were the beneficiaries of the fruits of the trees that they had planted, usually with enormous effort; however, when the contract expired, they had to return the lot and the fruits to the landlord without any compensation. Often, this meant that the peasants had to leave the land that they had stewarded for ten years just when the olive trees started to bear fruits and the vineyards started to produce at full scale. In fact, this is an example of how, according to Augusto Placanica, "the needs of specialized cultivation pushed the landed proprietors to place the burden of innovation on the laborers." And, to be sure, landlords often used the *contratto a miglioria* in an exploitative way. Still, despite its exploitative features, especially in the areas of citrus production, the *contratto a miglioria* often represented a compromise between the landowner's need to improve his *latifondo* with profitable tree cultivation without the burden of direct management and the peasants' increasing demand for land.[84]

In general, tree cultivation needed especially intensive care, mainly because of the constant irrigation it required. In the case of citrus groves, while the landowners supplied the land, the plants, and the water, the tenants grew the citrus fruits, guarded the groves, and irrigated them constantly. On citrus groves, *contratti a miglioria* could last up to twenty years. In this case, landowner and tenants shared the crop, with an increase in the landowner's share with the passing of time. As Francesco Galassi has demonstrated, "share-

83. Sonnino, "I contadini in Sicilia," 78. See also Piero Bevilacqua, "Il paesaggio degli alberi nel *Mezzogiorno* d'Italia e in Sicilia (fra XVIII e XX secolo)," *AIAC* 10 (1988); and Tino, *Campania felice*, 33–52.

84. Augusto Placanica, "Il mondo agricolo meridionale: usure, caparre, contratti," in Bevilacqua, ed., *Storia dell'agricoltura*, 2:303. See also Demarco, *Il crollo del Regno*, 138–139; and Adrian Lyttleton, "Landlords, Peasants, and the Limits of Liberalism," in Davis, ed., *Gramsci and Italy's Passive Revolution*, 126–127.

cropping provided an efficient way to tackle problems specific to Mediterranean crops . . . in particular the high risk and the need for strict supervision to protect the valuable capital embodied in tree crops." In the case of the most productive citrus groves, according to Salvatore Lupo, landowners fixed the tenants' share at a maximum of one-eighth of the total crop. Yet, there were also landowners who struck more equitable deals with the peasants working on their land.[85]

In particular, Lupo cites Sidney Sonnino's mention of the contract in use in Baron Niccolò Turrisi Colonna's citrus groves; according to this type of contract, which contemporaries viewed as highly progressive, the peasants' share was one-fourth of the crop. Though we have little information available, the speculation that some sort of contractual bargaining between Turrisi Colonna and his laborers might have led him to strike a relatively more favorable deal for them reminds us, with the obvious differences, of the bargaining process between master and slaves on Thomas Chaplin's cotton plantation. Significantly, Niccolò Turrisi Colonna was the son of a former *gabelloto,* an advocate of agricultural modernization, and the owner of a famous model farm at Bonvicino, in Sicily. Turrisi Colonna's attitude was emblematic of the progressive ideas held by liberal noblemen and bourgeois landowners—ideas that emphasized the importance of reciprocity in their relations with the peasants and that were broadly comparable to the paternalistic attitudes of American planters toward their slaves.[86]

Arguably, when dealing with progressive landowners such as Turrisi Colonna, southern Italian peasants could have a chance to alter the provisions of the *contratto a miglioria* and to transform it, through bargaining, into a more equitable and reciprocal compromise with a partial recognition of their own rights. In fact—according to Salvatore Lupo—in regard to citrus production, "the *contratti a miglioria* were held in high esteem by contemporary [nineteenth-century] observers, who saw in them an example of collaboration between peasants and landlords." Indeed, although exploited, peasants working in the commercial sectors of agriculture of the *latifondo* had a greater chance of establishing boundaries of agreement within which to operate because of the landowners' commitment to rationalization of production.

85. John Cohen and Giovanni Federico, *The Growth of the Italian Economy, 1820–1960* (New York, 2001), 38. See also Francesco Galassi, "Mezzadria e sviluppo tecnologico tra Otto e Novecento," *RSA* 33 (1993): 91–123; and Lupo, *Il giardino degli aranci,* 88–89.

86. See Lupo, *Il giardino degli aranci,* 88–89; and Sonnino, "I contadini in Sicilia," 70–95.

In this sense, their situation was comparable to the one of slaves on cotton plantations, since, especially on the latter, the masters' interest in the production and marketing of the staple crop led them often to adopt an attitude of compromise toward the slaves' affirmation of their own rights so as to both diffuse labor conflict and reach a high level of efficiency and productivity.[87]

To recapitulate, nineteenth-century southern Italian *latifondi* and American plantations shared two important common features: first, a mixed economy, either more oriented toward sale on the world market or toward internal consumption; and second, the ability to respond to fluctuations in the market demand either by changing the shape of labor management or by shifting the emphasis onto different sectors of production. In general, plantations and *latifondi* had a hybrid character of both capitalist and noncapitalist enterprises. The ability to respond to market fluctuations and the production of particular cash crops for sale on the world market gave the majority of plantations and a number of *latifondi* a capitalist character. Conversely, the combination of subsistence and commercial agriculture and the nonexistence or the relatively minor importance of a free labor market gave them a mixed character. In the American South, the nonexistence of a free labor market resulted primarily from the enslavement of the workforce. In the Italian *Mezzogiorno*, however, the relatively minor importance of the free labor market depended mainly upon the persistence of distinctive relations of authority between landowners and peasants. In this respect, it is highly significant that, even while acknowledging evident differences with the exploitative features of the antebellum American South's slave system, Piero Bevilacqua has described "the specific forms of subordination which psychologically and morally tied the peasants to the landowners" in the nineteenth-century *Mezzogiorno* as a "much more subtle kind of slavery."[88]

---

87. Lupo, *Il giardino degli aranci*, 89. See also Immanuel Wallerstein, *The Capitalist World-Economy: Essays by Immanuel Wallerstein* (New York, 1979), 202–221; and Stanley L. Engerman, "Introduction," in Stanley L. Engerman, ed., *Terms of Labor: Slavery, Serfdom, and Free Labor* (Stanford, Calif., 1999), 1–24.

88. Bevilacqua, "Peter Kolchin's American South," 66–67. See also David Roediger, "Pre-Capitalism in One Confederacy: A Note on Genovese, Politics, and the Slave South," *NP* 11 (1991): 90–95; Smith, *Debating Slavery*, 90–91; Petrusewicz, "Wage-Earners, but Not Proletarians: Wage Labor and Social Relations in the Nineteenth-Century Calabrian Latifondo," *Review* 10 (1987): 471–503; and Marta Petrusewicz, "The Demise of *Latifondismo*," in Lumley and Morris, eds., *New History of the Italian South*, 20–41.

However, in both cases, the particular relation between masters and laborers did not just emphasize the noncapitalist character of the agricultural economy; it also offered laborers a resource for action toward the improvement of their conditions. Especially on those plantations and *latifondi* that were owned by progressive planters and landowners, relations between masters and laborers tended to move in the direction of defining boundaries of action. On one hand, this happened because of the masters' necessity of maintaining a production regime that responded to the market demand. On the other hand, the move toward compromise was a product of the particular ideological outlook that related to the rise of new entrepreneurial classes—an outlook that emphasized paternalism and reciprocity in the relationship between the master and the workforce.

Commercial Dependency and Industrial Weakness

Nineteenth-century agricultural entrepreneurs in the American South and the Italian *Mezzogiorno* can be best described as "dependence elites." According to Jane and Peter Schneider and Edward Hansen, dependence elites are one of two basic elite types—the other being "development elites"—associated with regional processes of modernization. While development elites tend to "stress the role of the state in economic planning" and also "seek to mobilize national resources and people for national aims," dependence elites tend not to take initiatives on a national scale, tend to "place more emphasis on markets than on the state," and tend to not make further investments with the capital accumulated through international trade.[89]

Dependence elites flourish where the state is inherently weak and regional upper classes can take advantage of their economic power to fill the gap left by state institutions at the political level. Such situations were typical of regions such as the American South and the Italian *Mezzogiorno* at the periphery of the nineteenth-century world economy. While in the American South the state was weak because of the limited powers of the federal government before the Civil War, in the *Mezzogiorno* the state was weak because of the limited support enjoyed by the Bourbon absolute monarchy.

89. Peter Schneider, Jane Schneider, and Eric Hansen, "Modernization and Development: The Role of Regional Elites and Non-Corporate Groups in the Mediterranean," *CSSH* 14 (1972): 345.

Moreover, in both regions, a very powerful elite whose fortunes related to the sale of cash crops in the world market had emerged at the beginning of the nineteenth century: the cotton planters in the American South and the landed bourgeoisie in the Italian *Mezzogiorno*. The type of entrepreneurship that these two groups represented was emblematic: both were heavily dependent on the fluctuations in the market demand for the particular crops that they grew on their landed estates. As dependence elites, they relied mainly on their unstable role in the world market as a source of economic power. At the same time, they were unable to promote projects of autonomous development that would have released their regions from dependency on the economic needs of more industrialized areas of the world, such as England and the northern United States.[90]

In the course of the nineteenth century, the effects of the market revolution in the American South and of the commercial revolution in the *Mezzogiorno* highlighted the inherent weaknesses of the two predominantly agricultural economies. Aware of the dangers of a situation of dependency, from the early 1800s on, enlightened economists and reformers focused their attention on devising ways to improve the economic performance of the two regions. Throughout the period 1815–1860, the central problem that economic reformers in the American South and in the Italian *Mezzogiorno* sought to address was the development of a strong and autonomous regional economy. As they did this, they stressed the importance of improvements in commercial agriculture as a natural resource of their regions, but they did not disdain the promotion of manufacturing. As a result of the work of economic reformers, progressive intellectuals and members of the elites, especially in the 1820s, 1830s, and 1840s, both the American South and the Italian *Mezzogiorno*, witnessed a flourishing of local and regional agricultural societies, agricultural journals, and even specialized agricultural schools; moreover, in both regions leading agricultural spokesmen traveled in different areas and wrote detailed reports on their conditions and needs.[91]

90. See Joseph J. Persky, *The Burden of Dependency: Colonial Themes in Southern Economic Thought* (Baltimore, Md., 1992), 61–92; Genovese, *Political Economy of Slavery*, 124–155; Paolo Pezzino, *Il paradiso abitato dai diavoli. Società, elites, istituzioni nel Mezzogiorno contemporaneo* (Milan, 1992), 22–23; and Salvemini, *L'innovazione precaria*, 5–12. For a critical view, see Lupo, *Il giardino degli aranci*, 9–11.

91. See Watson, "Slavery and Development," 43–73; and Marta Petrusewicz, *Come il Meridione divenne una Questione. Rappresentazioni del Sud prima e dopo il Quarantotto* (Soveria Mannelli, Catanzaro, 1998), 34–38.

In the American South, reformers such as George Tucker, Jacob N. Cardozo, and Thomas Roderick Dew, inspired by the works of British classical political economists, advocated the advantages of crop diversification and free trade. According to Genovese, these "leaders of southern economic thought . . . were trying to use the economic science of the age to justify claims to the moral and practical superiority of slavery as a social system." In fact, throughout the South, agricultural societies gathered planters and intellectuals who were as committed to the spread of scientific knowledge in agriculture as to the defense of slavery. By addressing issues that varied according to the area and the variety of crops and labor systems, agricultural societies essentially promoted the same ideas; in the words of Steven G. Collins, they "encouraged better farming techniques, efficient plantation management, crop diversification, and technological progress."[92]

Among the leading economic journals—which functioned primarily as a forum of debate over these ideas—were Edmund Ruffin's *The Farmers' Register* and John Skinner's *The American Farmer* in Virginia, and John D. Legaré's *The Southern Agriculturalist* in South Carolina. In particular, *The Southern Agriculturalist*—the official journal of South Carolina's State Agricultural Society—started its publication as early as 1828; its director, Legaré, was particularly keen to stress the importance of crop diversification and planting profitability, the two main issues that he thought South Carolinian planters needed to attend to. Legaré was convinced that his journal could be an effective medium of communication for agricultural knowledge, and during its eighteen years of publication he managed to maintain a careful balance between promotion of scientific experimentation and spread of agricultural education and provided a model for other similar publications sponsored by agricultural societies throughout the South.[93]

To be sure, in Virginia, experiments in crop diversification had begun somewhat earlier, because tobacco cultivation had induced soil exhaustion in several areas already by the second half of the eighteenth century. A real breakthrough occurred when Edmund Ruffin discovered that marl could

92. Eugene D. Genovese, *The Slaveholders' Dilemma: Freedom and Progress in Southern Conservative Thought, 1820–1860* (Columbia, S.C., 1992), 55; Steven G. Collins, "System, Organization, and Agricultural Reform in the Antebellum South, 1840–1860," *AH* 75 (2001): 4.

93. See Allen Kaufman, *Capitalism, Slavery, and Republican Values: Antebellum Political Economists, 1819–1848* (Austin, Tex., 1982); and Theodore Rosengarten, "*The Southern Agriculturalist* in an Age of Reform," in Michael O'Brien and David Moltke-Hansen, eds., *Intellectual Life in Antebellum Charleston* (Knoxville, Tenn., 1986).

restore the fertility of tobacco plantations; he first reported the results in *The American Farmer* in 1821, and then propagandized them in his own periodical, *The Farmers' Register,* from 1833. This was Ruffin's earliest feat and the highest point of his career as an agricultural reformer—a career that led him to continue experimenting for the next thirty years of his life, even though he stopped publishing *The Farmers' Register* in 1843. In those ten years leading to 1843—years that ended with the publication of the results of his agricultural survey of South Carolina—Ruffin was instrumental in the making of what Clement Eaton has called "a renaissance of agriculture in Virginia, Maryland, and the Carolinas." His tireless efforts inspired many important advocates of agricultural innovation—fellow planters such as Virginian John Hartwell Cocke of Bremo and South Carolinian James Henry Hammond, who admired him and were also his personal friends.[94]

Yet, according to both William Mathew and David Allmendinger, Ruffin's early retreat to privacy shows that, despite being the most revered and successful southern agricultural reformer of his age, he ultimately failed to both reach and interest a large readership of southern slaveholders in regard to the theme of agricultural improvement through scientific experimentation. Above all, Ruffin's ultimate failure at effectively reforming southern agriculture was a clear proof of the incompatibility of the slave system with the most radical and also most efficient ways of improving the plantation economy as a whole. In William Mathew's words, as a representative of the master class, Ruffin "came increasingly to see his reforms as means of rescuing the slave society of the Old South." And as sectional conflicts over slavery intensified, Ruffin came to share with most southern agricultural reformers the idea that the protection of the South's slave system was far more important than the issue of implementation of a much needed program of improvement of the region's agricultural economy.[95]

In comparable terms to southern agricultural reformers in the United States, several southern Italian economists—among whom were Francesco

94. Clement Eaton, *The Growth of Southern Civilization, 1790–1860* (New York, 1963), 179. See also Edmund Ruffin, "First Views which Led to Marling in Prince George County," *FR* 7 (1839): 659–697; and Edmund Ruffin, "Observations on the Earliest Marled District of Prince George County," *FR* 8 (1840): 484–497.

95. William M. Mathew, *Edmund Ruffin and the Crisis of Slavery in the Old South: The Failure of Agricultural Reform* (Athens, Ga., 1988), 198. See also David F. Allmendinger, *Ruffin: Family and Reform in the Old South* (New York, 1990), 23–56; and Avery Craven, *Edmund Ruffin, Southerner: A Study in Secession* (New York, 1932).

Fuoco, Antonio Scialoja, and Francesco Ferrara—relied on British classical economic thinkers and supported a free-trade policy. However, unlike what happened in the American South—where progressive members of the elite spontaneously promoted agrarian associations—in the Italian *Mezzogiorno* agrarian reformers gathered in regional institutions called Economic Societies of the Provinces (*Società economiche delle province*), institutions that the Bourbon government sponsored and monitored. As a consequence, the leading economic journals—such as Ignazio Rozzi's *Il Gran Sasso d'Italia* (The Gran Sasso of Italy), Federigo Cassitto's *Giornale Economico di Principato Ultra* (The Economic Journal of Principato Ultra), and Ferdinando Malvica's *Effemeridi scientifiche e letterarie per la Sicilia* (Scientific and Literary Notes for Sicily)—were regional publications that had close links with the local Economic Societies of the Provinces, while their directors also served as the societies' secretaries.[96]

Despite the fact that the southern Italian economic journals had a marked governmental and regional outlook, their concerns on improvement of regional economic performance found supporters among both the progressive aristocracy and the landed bourgeoisie, regardless of their ideas on the Bourbon monarchy. In this sense, we can compare the southern Italian economic publications to the periodicals promoted by the State Agricultural Societies in the American South; both were vehicles through which the peripheral elites voiced their needs for programs of economic reform on a national scale and with a special emphasis on the particular characteristics of the different regions. For example, in 1838, when he started publishing *Il Gran Sasso d'Italia,* Ignazio Rozzi aimed at promoting the economic development of the region of Abruzzo Ultra—where he served as secretary of the local Economic Society—through scientific agriculture. Yet, among the reforms that Rozzi advocated in his journal, there were also wide-ranging national programs, including the formation of an Agrarian Bank for the farmers' credit, and the foundation of an Italian Philantropic Society, for the "economic, physical, and intellectual improvement of the peasant."[97]

As a prominent landed proprietor actively involved in the promotion of the economic development of his region, Federigo Cassitto epitomized the

96. See Petrusewicz, *Come il Meridione,* 49–57; and, on Ferdinando Malvica, Giovanna Fiume, *La crisi sociale del 1848 in Sicilia* (Messina, 1982), 41–68.

97. Ignazio Rozzi's quotation in Demarco, *Il crollo del Regno,* 125. See also G. De Lucia, ed., *Ignazio Rozzi e la storia dell'agricoltura meridionale* (Teramo, 1971); and Renata De Lorenzo, *Società economiche e istruzione agraria nell'Ottocento meridionale* (Milan, 1998), 49–91.

characteristics of the progressive landed elite of the *Mezzogiorno*. In 1814, Cassitto joined the Economic Society of Principato Ultra, and in 1834 he became its secretary. In the following twenty years, Cassitto coordinated a wide range of activities and transformed the local Economic Society into a center of agrarian experimentation and promotion of provincial economic development. In particular, Cassitto promoted the diffusion of cash crops, such as cotton, linen, olives, and wine grapes and opposed the traditional focus on grain cultivation in the region; he also encouraged crop rotation and gave special prizes to those landed proprietors who were willing to make experiments.[98]

Until 1848, Cassitto published the results of his efforts at promoting his region's economic progress in the *Giornale Economico di Principato Ultra*, a publication that the progressive landed elite held as a model for the diffusion of agricultural knowledge. Yet, Cassitto's exclusive interest in agriculture led him to stubbornly refuse to encourage the development of manufactures, fearing that industrial production would leave the agricultural sector without a consistent labor force. In fact, Cassitto's anti-industrial ideology shows how widespread was the idea of an incompatibility between promotion of agrarian interests and expansion of industrial activity among the Bourbon kingdom's propertied classes, not the least because landowners thought that industrialization would lead to radical changes in social relations and to a diminishment of their power. Comparable to the American planters' commitment to slavery at the cost of southern economic improvement, the southern Italian landowners' perceived incompatibility between agrarian and industrial interests had a negative influence on the efforts to promote economic development in the *Mezzogiorno*; more than likely, it was a factor that played an important role in the limited success of reform programs in most of the Bourbon kingdom's provinces.[99]

Arguably, the two leading economic publications in the American South and the Italian *Mezzogiorno* were *De Bow's Review* and the *Annali Civili del Regno delle Due Sicilie*. They had in common an impressively wide circula-

98. See Walter Palmieri, "Tra agronomia e amministrazione: Federico Cassitto," *Meridiana* 33 (1998): 125–162.

99. See De Lorenzo, *Società economiche*, 72–73; Renata De Lorenzo, *Istituzioni e territorio nell'Ottocento borbonico: la Reale Società Economica di Principato Ultra* (Avellino, 1987); Gaetano Cingari, *Problemi del Risorgimento meridionale* (Messina-Firenze, 1965), 51–52; and Silvio De Majo, "La lavorazione delle fibre tessili nell'Ottocento," in Paolo Macry and Pasquale Villani, eds., *La Campania* (Turin, 1990), 317–370.

tion and a tendency to address issues that went far beyond the limited horizons of local economic policies; significantly, they also shared a commitment
to stress the need to build the foundations of a sound regional economy
through improvements in both agriculture and manufacturing. However, as
we might expect, *De Bow's Review* was a wholly private enterprise, while the
Annali Civili was the chief publication of the Royal Institute of Encouragement (*Reale Istituto di Incoraggiamento*), the Bourbon administrative organ
that promoted and supervised the activities of the Economic Societies of
the Provinces. *De Bow's Review* started its publication in 1846 in New Orleans, and its director was South Carolinian James B. De Bow; by 1850, it
had more than five thousand subscribers. The journal hosted articles written
by prominent planters, agricultural reformers, and industrial entrepreneurs
who strongly supported De Bow's views on the equal importance of agrarian
and manufacturing interests. De Bow maintained that the South needed to
complement agriculture with industry in order to overcome its economic
dependence on the North and on Britain. To further promote his ideas, he
envisioned and advocated the creation of a Southern Commercial Convention to gather planters and industrialists from all over the South—which he
eventually saw come to life in the 1850s.[100]

In 1833, thirteen years before the publication of *De Bow's Review* in the
American South, in the Italian *Mezzogiorno* the Bourbon government began
issuing the *Annali Civili,* whose interests and aims were largely comparable.
The publication was the brainchild of Raffaele Liberatore, an economic
reformer who was convinced, as James De Bow was, that agriculture and
manufacturing were equally essential factors of economic growth. With the
help of famous economists and high civil servants, such as Carlo Afan De
Rivera, Liberatore created a periodical that focused on issues of progress
and reform in both industry and agriculture. By the mid-1830s, the *Annali Civili* reached already a large readership among the progressive landed
elites of the Bourbon kingdom; from 1839, it also featured a section on the
Economic Societies of the Provinces, in which the societies' secretaries reported periodically on agricultural and industrial progress in their particular
regions. The fact that both *De Bow's Review* and the *Annali Civili* shared a
distinctive emphasis on the equal importance of industry and agriculture

---

100. On *De Bow's Review,* see Diffee William Standard, "*De Bow's Review,* 1846–1880: A
Magazine of Southern Opinion" (Ph.D. diss., University of North Carolina, 1970); Laurence
Shore, *Southern Capitalists: The Ideological Leadership of an Elite, 1832–1885* (Chapel Hill, N.C.,
1986), 34–37; and Genovese, *Political Economy of Slavery,* 180–240.

had important implications. In the predominantly agricultural worlds of the American South and of the Italian *Mezzogiorno,* the validity of both De Bow's and Liberatore's arguments often fell on deaf ears. Both southern slaveholders and southern Italian landowners were usually reluctant to engage in manufacturing. Doubtless, there were important differences in the degree of industrialization, since, for example, by 1860 the American South could boast more than ten thousand miles of railroads against the few kilometers worth in the *Mezzogiorno.* Yet, on the whole, both regions lagged far behind the more industrialized areas of the world.[101]

Among the states of the American South, Virginia and Maryland had the greatest output from manufacturing activities, with a particularly high concentration of factories in Richmond and Baltimore. Indeed, according to William Link, by the 1850s, thanks to its iron foundries and tobacco factories, "Richmond had become the leading manufacturing city in the antebellum South." Outside Richmond, the most important southern industries included forges and ironworks in Virginia and Tennessee, tobacco manufactures in Virginia and North Carolina, and textile mills in North and South Carolina and Georgia. Yet, although by 1860 three-fifths of all American smoking tobacco came from the South and one-fifth of the national output of textile mills came from the slave states, southern industries never rivaled their counterparts in Pennsylvania and New England.[102]

Only a handful of southern industrialists were as famous as the most renowned planters. Among them there was Joseph Reid Anderson, who in 1848 became president of Richmond's Tredegar Iron Works, a factory that employed eight hundred workers, most of whom were slaves, both skilled and unskilled. An equally famous promoter of southern manufacturing was Daniel Pratt, a native of New Hampshire. In 1838, Pratt moved to Alabama, where he founded Prattville, near the state capital of Montgomery. Pratt modeled his town after New England's industrial villages and supplied it with

101. On the *Annali Civili,* see Rosario Villari, *Mezzogiorno e contadini nell'età moderna* (Rome-Bari, 1977), 91–93; Petrusewicz, *Come il Meridione,* 49–50; and Petrusewicz, "Land-Based Modernization," 106–107.

102. William A. Link, *Roots of Secession: Slavery and Politics in Antebellum Virginia* (Chapel Hill, N.C., 2003), 32. See also Genovese, *Political Economy of Slavery,* 180–220; Robert Starobin, *Industrial Slavery in the Old South* (New York, 1966); and Frederick Bateman and Thomas Weiss, *A Deplorable Scarcity: The Failure of Industrialization in the Slave Economy* (Chapel Hill, N.C., 1987).

several mills and a factory for the production of cotton gins, which employed as many as two hundred laborers and produced six hundred gins a year.[103]

Arguably, the most renowned southern industrialist was William Gregg, a Virginian who visited New England and subsequently settled in South Carolina. In 1845, Gregg published his *Essays on Domestic Industry,* in which he maintained that poor whites—rather than slaves—ought to become factory workers. Gregg was especially interested in cotton mills and in 1846 built his own in Graniteville, near Augusta, Georgia. Similar to Daniel Pratt's project, Gregg's idea was to recreate a New England mill village, an aim he largely accomplished when he succeeded in employing as many as three hundred laborers; in Graniteville, the laborers slept and worked within his premises under strict rules. Thanks to his achievements in cotton manufacturing, Gregg became the leading spokesman on the need for a strong southern industry, a subject on which he wrote a number of articles in *De Bow's Review.* The basic problem, according to Gregg, was that most planters did not value investment in industry as much as investment in agriculture; consequently, state governments had little or no interest in promoting manufacturing. Those entrepreneurs, such as Gregg, who thought differently discovered that the South lacked both basic infrastructure and specific legislation to protect industrial production.[104]

In a long article that he published in *De Bow's Review* in 1860, Gregg discussed the failure of the South to provide patronage for its own industries and argued that nations achieved commercial power—the first step to political power—only with the aid of a strong economy that relied on manufactures. Therefore, he concluded that if southerners remained "an exclusively agricultural people, neglecting all other industrial occupations . . . [they would] become vassals of some power," instead of achieving independence. Gregg finished his article with a plea to the southern states' governments to "encourage the extension of manufactures, and by all means encourage and give our patronage to every product of Southern domestic industry."[105]

103. See Robert L. Lewis, *Coal, Iron, and Slaves: Industrial Slavery in Maryland and Virginia, 1715–1865* (Westport, Conn., 1979); and Curtis J. Evans, *The Conquest of Labor: Daniel Pratt and Southern Industrialization* (Baton Rouge, La., 2001).

104. See Genovese, *Political Economy of Slavery,* 186–191; Walter Licht, *Industrializing America: The Nineteenth Century* (Baltimore, Md., 1995), 35–38; and Ernest M. Lander, *The Textile Industry in Antebellum South Carolina* (Baton Rouge, La., 1969).

105. William Gregg, "Southern Patronage to Southern Imports and Domestic Industry," *DBR* 29 (1860): 778.

In Gregg's thought, economic power and political power were strictly related; politically strong nations had a strong economy. A strong economy was one in which industry and agriculture coexisted and the interests of both collaborated to make a nation self-sufficient. Few southerners were as aware as Gregg of the possible disastrous consequences of the South's weakness in industrialization. The southern ruling elites and the state governments—which represented their interests—continued to rely on an almost exclusively agricultural economy, while Gregg felt they ought to encourage the spread of manufactures and protect the products of the local industry. Only if industry gained the same importance as agriculture in the mind of southern planters and entrepreneurs, he believed, could the American South reach a position of economic self-sufficiency and free itself from the "degrading shackles of commercial dependency" on northern and British industrial products.[106]

The antebellum American South's weakness in industrialization found a parallel in the scarcity of major manufacturing centers that characterized the nineteenth-century *Mezzogiorno*. However, in the *Mezzogiorno*, dependence on the industrialized regions of the world took a characteristically visible form, since Swiss, German, English, and French entrepreneurs owned and managed a number of important factories, especially in the textile sector. The Bourbons' early attempts to control the kingdom's industrial production had led to the 1789 foundation of the colony of San Leucio, in Terra di Lavoro, a model industrial village with several textile mills, which—similar to Prattville and Graniteville—included houses for more than two hundred workers. Later, in 1840, Ferdinand II sponsored the foundation of the ironworks at Pietrarsa, near Naples, which employed more than eight hundred workers and produced mainly implements for the royal navy.[107]

Aside from the Bourbon government's projects in industrialization, there were few successful private enterprises owned and managed by south-

106. See John McCardell, *The Idea of a Southern Nation: Southern Nationalists and Southern Nationalism, 1830–1860* (New York, 1979), 91; and T. Downey, "Riparian Rights and Manufacturing in Antebellum South Carolina: William Gregg and the Origins of the Industrial Mind," *JSH* 65 (1999): 77–108.

107. See Aurelio Lepre, *Contadini, borghesi, ed operai nel tramonto del feudalesimo napoletano* (Naples, 1979), 195–197; M. Battaglioni, ed., *La Fabbrica del Re. L'esperimento di S. Leucio* (Rome, 1984); and Luigi De Rosa, *Iniziativa e capitale straniero nell'industria metalmeccanica del Mezzogiorno, 1840–1904* (Naples, 1968), 1–28.

ern Italian entrepreneurs. Most of them were located within the borders of the present-day region of Campania, which, as to manufacturing centers, had a role comparable to the one of Virginia and Maryland in the American South. Among the most important private enterprises were Gregorio Macry's ironworks at Capodimonte, which started their production in 1833; by 1850, Macry & Henry employed 550 workers. Yet, the best example of successful indigenous enterprise was, arguably, the wool-producing "industrial district" of the Liri Valley. In 1860, the seven factories built by Simoncelli, Muzio, Cino, and Ciccodicola provided employment for twenty-eight hundred workers and produced altogether six thousand quintals of wool.[108]

An equally important manufacturing sector was silk, which was particularly strong in Terra di Lavoro, Calabria, and Sicily; by 1860, both Catanzaro and Reggio, in Calabria, had emerged as major centers of silk production. Even more important was the cotton industry, both because of its size and because of its connections with foreign capital. For this latter reason, cotton production was firmly controlled by foreigners. During the first half of the nineteenth century, a number of southern entrepreneurs made repeated efforts to start a cotton industry with the support of the Bourbon government. For example, in 1819, the baron of Fiddoni, a Sicilian entrepreneur, wrote to the prince of Linguaglossa that he "wished to introduce, and build at my expenses in Sicily, some machines for the spinning of cotton, which will be . . . extremely useful for the exclusive profit of our national industry." Yet, as happened in other similar cases, Fiddoni's efforts to build a cotton industry promoted and controlled by southerners—specifically Sicilians—met with little success.[109]

As a result, since the early nineteenth century, Swiss entrepreneurs dominated cotton manufacturing from their base in Campania with the outright support of the Bourbon government and with the help of Swiss banks. Giovanni Giacomo Egg, a Swiss entrepreneur, erected the first cotton loom in Caserta, in Terra di Lavoro, in 1812; by 1843 his factory had five hundred looms, employed thirteen hundred workers, and produced four thousand quintals of cotton a year. Davide Vonwiller, another Swiss entrepreneur, opened his first cotton mill near Salerno in 1812; by 1838 his six hundred workers produced

108. See Demarco, *Il crollo del Regno,* 54–100; Bevilacqua, *Breve storia,* 20–32; and Tommaso Pedio, *Economia e società meridonale a metà dell'Ottocento* (Lecce, 1999), 47–65.

109. Baron of Fiddoni to the prince of Linguaglossa, 22 July 1819, Linguaglossa Family Papers, ASP. See also Orazio Cancila, *Storia dell'industria in Sicilia* (Bari-Rome, 1995), 72–75.

eight thousand quintals of cotton a year. Altogether, cotton manufacturing counted more than five thousand workers in different areas of Campania and was entirely managed by ten Swiss families. Significantly, Lorenzo
Zichichi has used the expression "industrial colonization" to describe the
phenomenon.[110]

To be sure, the fact that one of the *Mezzogiorno*'s major industries was
in the hands of foreign entrepreneurs underscored the problem of commercial dependency. With few native entrepreneurs in the industrial sector,
there was little capital invested in industry in comparison to agriculture;
most landed proprietors did not value investment in manufacturing at the
same level as investment in land. Aware of the crucial connection between
industrial development and commercial dependency, in the *Annali Civili
del Regno delle Due Sicilie,* Raffaele Liberatore and his clique of economic
reformers called for the creation of a strong manufacturing sector managed by southerners under the government's patronage. According to Enrico
Thomas, the author of an important article on paper manufacturing in the
first issue of the *Annali Civili,* industry brought prosperity; therefore, "there
is no hope of prosperity for the people, when there is no industry together
with trade and agriculture." Interestingly, even though he acknowledged that
the economy of the *Mezzogiorno* "lagged behind in these studies," Thomas
was confident that "now she will make up for the lost advantage, now that
she has started moving and that she is being helped by the powerful hand of
the government."[111]

The issues touched upon by Enrico Thomas in the *Annali Civili* had a
lot in common with the ones that William Gregg wrote about in his famous
article in *De Bow's Review.* Economic reformers and entrepreneurs in both
the American South and the Italian *Mezzogiorno* considered industry and
agriculture to be the bases of strength and independence of every nation;
the wealth and prosperity of the people depended on a balanced economy
that gave equal importance to both. Also, in both cases, reformers considered the government responsible for the promotion and protection of indigenous manufactures and for the improvement of agricultural education. They

110. Lorenzo Zichichi, *Il colonialismo felpato. Gli svizzeri alla conquista del Regno delle Due
Sicilie (1804–1848)* (Palermo, 1988), 72. See also Silvio De Majo, *L'industria protetta. Lanifici e
cotonifici in Campania nell'Ottocento* (Naples, 1989); and John A. Davis, *Società e imprenditori nel
regno borbonico (1815–1860)* (Bari-Rome, 1979), 111–131.

111. Enrico Thomas, "Della fabbricazione della carta nei domini di qua del Faro," *ACRDS* 1
(1833): 81.

thought that only with the adoption of a long-term program of development that included these policies could the government achieve tangible results in economic terms. Therefore, in both cases, the reformers' path toward the ultimate aim of ending commercial dependency passed through the realization of the need for a wide-ranging governmental program of economic growth.[112]

More to the point, in both cases, reformers linked the idea of their region's independence from the economies of more industrialized areas of the world—namely Britain and the northern United States—with its consequent strength in political terms vis-à-vis the international arena. In this sense, in both the American South and the Italian *Mezzogiorno,* programs of economic reform had a distinctive political character. In advocating the formation of a strong regional economy through the integration of industry and agriculture, economic reformers manifested their wish to work toward the creation of a sound economic base for a strong political institution with markedly regional features. Yet, in their efforts to uplift the two regions from their positions of commercial dependency and build the bases for strong economies, reformers had to come to terms with the power of the two regional landed elites. In both the American South and the Italian *Mezzogiorno,* the reformers' success depended on their ability to win the progressive sections of the elite to the cause of modernization and coopt them to work together within their vision of economic nationalism. In both cases, reformers succeeded only partially in their aim.

In the American South, awareness of economic dependency on more industrialized and economically stronger regions of the world led to a very tortured relationship with plantation slavery and cotton production. Cotton was, indeed, "King"—as James Henry Hammond argued in a famous speech—since it provided both the South and the United States with their major item of trade. Since the early 1800s, the total production of cotton had increased exponentially. Cotton had enabled thousands of aspiring planters to leave the soil-depleted areas of the Atlantic Seaboard states and settle the fertile regions of the Old Southwest. However, cotton ruled over a shaky ground, since its prices were subject to periodic rise and fall according to the world market demand. Cotton gave prosperity to the South, but at the same

---

112. See E. Herriott, "Wants of the South," *DBR* 29 (1860): 215–227; and Raffaele Liberatore, "Discorso Preliminare," *ACRDS* 1 (1833): 15–22.

time it epitomized the region's commercial dependency on the industrial-ized countries it supplied. Moreover, cotton production depended on planta-tion slavery and on reliance on a type of monocrop culture that led to soil exhaustion. Not surprisingly, on the issue of commercial dependency, only cotton planters who were also extreme southern nationalists, such as Robert Barnwell Rhett, thought that monocrop agriculture guaranteed southern economic strength, while businessmen such as William Gregg thought that the road to self-sufficiency passed necessarily through economic diversifica-tion and the spread of industrialization.[113]

The Southern Commercial Conventions, which met regularly from 1852 to 1857, addressed the problem of economic nationalism, seeking to reach a compromise between slaveholding interests and economic diversification. The majority of the conventions' members were lawyers and merchants who had business in southern cities and looked favorably on industrialization; as a result, the conventions often included reports from committees on manu-facturing and mining that encouraged the development of industrial pro-duction in the southern states. Nevertheless, within the membership of the conventions, slaveholders were a very respectable minority that held a sig-nificant amount of power; they used their power and influence to obtain the conventions' unconditional support for the plantation economy and the slave system. Indeed, according to Vicky Johnson, "the agenda of the Conventions remained focused on material prosperity within an agrarian economy"; for this reason, the "convention debates show little evidence of conflict between planters and commercialists or industrialists." In other words, the Southern Commercial Conventions achieved a great deal in terms of unifying the elite over issues that related to the strengthening of the southern economy while also addressing the problems of economic diversification and industrializa-tion. However, they never challenged the primacy of staple crop agriculture and plantation slavery over other forms of economic activity. Convention members—who represented the southern elite's wealthiest and most pro-gressive section—enthusiastically supported the development of industry only as long as it helped the South's agricultural economy; a proof of this is the fact that they encouraged the expansion of railroads mainly as a means

113. See Persky, *Burden of Dependency,* 87–96; Genovese, *Political Economy of Slavery,* 85–105; Emory Thomas, *The Confederate Nation: 1861–1865* (New York, 1979), 7–8; and J. H. Soltow, "Cot-ton as Religion, Politics, Law, Economics, and Art," *AH* 68 (1994): 6–19.

to improve the links between the South's agricultural exporting areas and the world market.[114]

In fact, the experience of the Southern Commercial Conventions showed that planters had a major influence in the southern elite's commitment to perpetuate slavery and plantation agriculture as the South's natural economic resource and as the basis of its distinctive way of life. To be sure, cotton planters had gathered in special conventions since 1839 to discuss crop-related business. By the 1850s, the cotton planters' conventions had become increasingly political and forthright in acknowledging the link between plantation agriculture and southern nationalism. Then, in 1860, E. N. Elliott published an edited collection of speeches written by prominent planters and significantly entitled *Cotton Is King.* The collection was intended as much as a work in defense of slavery as a statement on the intimate link between the socioeconomic system that focused on plantation agriculture and cotton production. Significantly, in his introduction, Elliott linked the plantation economy and the slave system to the South's regional distinctiveness and called slavery the "one great question dividing the American people ... by a geographical line."[115]

Doubtless, through their commitment to preserve the South's peculiar institution, slaveholders effectively perpetuated the region's economic dependency and prevented its economy from developing along self-sufficient lines. Only a handful of businessmen and merchants dared to voice their fear that slavery retarded the South's development, keeping its economy in a state of backwardness and preventing the investment of significant sums of capital in long-term projects of industrialization and economic diversification. The construction of a strong national economy required reliance on trade in a wide range of articles, from manufactured items to cash crops, whose production the slave-based agricultural system could not support. However, by 1860, the ideas of those few businessmen—such as William Gregg—who understood the inadequacy of the slaveholders' view of economic nationalism and who remarked that the problem lay in the idea of the preservation of slavery

114. Vicky Vaughn Johnson, *The Men and the Vision of the Southern Commercial Conventions, 1845–1871* (Columbia, Mo., 1992), 5, 7. See also Shore, *Southern Capitalists,* 52–58.

115. E. N. Elliott, "Introduction," in E. N. Elliott, ed. *"Cotton Is King," and Proslavery Arguments* (Augusta, Ga., 1860), 3. See also McCardell, *Idea of a Southern Nation,* 104–134; and Weymouth Jordan, "Cotton Planters' Convention in the Old South," *JSH* 19 (1953): 318–335.

as the distinctive southern characteristic were increasingly unpopular in the midst of the sectional conflicts that were about to precipitate into civil war.[116]

Regardless of the problems related to the primacy of slavery in the southern economy, the planters' characterization of the South as a cotton kingdom also obscured the fact that within the southern states there were important regional differences in terms of agricultural systems and crop production. For example, in Louisiana planters made enormous profits from the cultivation of sugar, a crop that remained largely untouched by the economic crises that periodically hit southern agriculture. In Virginia, even with the expansion of wheat, tobacco had retained its importance, and by 1845 its production was on the road to recovery. And in the lowcountry of South Carolina and Georgia, planters continued to grow rice, a crop whose price remained steady throughout the antebellum period. Compared to them, cotton planters and farmers were in dire straits several times during the 1830s and 1840s. During the panic of 1837, cotton prices fell to less than five cents a pound, and throughout the depression of the late 1830s and early 1840s cotton prices continued to fall, reaching their lowest point between 1841 and 1845; only in the late 1840s did prices rise again and was cotton able to regain its preeminence in the southern economy.[117]

The panic of 1837 signaled the beginning of the worst economic depression of the antebellum period and showed the weakness of the southern agricultural economy. The depression hit particularly hard both tobacco and cotton production. Significant for the understanding of the mood of agricultural operators at the time is a letter that commercial agent Samuel D. Rawlins wrote in July 1837 to Humberston Skipwith, whose Virginian plantation in Mecklenburg County produced both tobacco and cotton. Rawlins complained about the sudden depreciation of "the two great staples of our country [cotton and tobacco]" and the "almost entire withdrawal of commercial confidence" and maintained that "never since this country possessed any commerce have difficulties to an equal extent prevailed." In view of these difficulties, it is fair to say that it was only in the wake of the 1850s' rapid rise in the world market demand for both cotton and tobacco and the sub-

116. See Genovese, *Political Economy of Slavery*, and John M. Grammer, *Pastoral Politics in the Old South* (Baton Rouge, La., 1996). For a different view, see William K. Scarborough, *Masters of the Big House: Elite Slaveholders of the Mid-Nineteenth-Century South* (Baton Rouge, La., 2003), 226–234.

117. See Wright, *Political Economy of the Cotton South*, 90–96; Sellers, *Market Revolution*, 353–355; Robert Russell, *Economic Aspects of Southern Sectionalism, 1840–1861* (Urbana, Ill., 1932); and Scarborough, *Masters of the Big House*, 128–140.

sequent boom in agricultural production that the majority of slaveholders and commercial agents found a renewed confidence in the strength of the economy of the South.[118]

A major difference between the American South and southern Italy was the role that the Bourbon monarchy played in the latter. In general, the Bourbon government actively supported a policy of economic protectionism in regard to southern manufactures and, at alternate times, it enjoyed the support of the most state-oriented part of the progressive section of the landed elite, of several businessmen, and of the majority of the industrialists. After the 1815 restoration of the Kingdom of the Two Sicilies, the Bourbon ministers attempted to create an administrative system in which monarchical absolutism coexisted with the view of a highly centralized and modern state. In recent years, revisionist historians have uncovered a great deal about the Bourbon administration's efforts at reforming and modernizing the kingdom. The reformist impulse reached its peak in the 1830s, during the early part of the reign of Ferdinand II—a time that also witnessed a temporary collaboration between the Bourbon monarchy and the liberal landowners who were in control of the kingdom's commercial agricultural activities. The Bourbon government's reform programs focused especially on improvements in the infrastructures of the different regions of the kingdom and on land reclamation in a number of areas that were still infested by malaria. Governmental intervention manifested also in the construction of imposing public buildings—mostly markets and offices—for the cities' economic and administrative activities. At the same time, in the different regions, local enterprises in the manufacturing sector received particular encouragement and help from the government's protectionist policies.[119]

Particularly important, especially in relation to the building of infrastructures, was the activity of the *Corpo di Ponti e Strade* (Committee of Bridges and Roads), whose director was—from 1824—Carlo Afan De Rivera, a firm believer in the necessity of the government's direct intervention. As Costanza D'Elia has pointed out, under Afan De Rivera, the Committee of

118. Samuel D. Rawlins to Humberston Skipwith, 28 July 1837, Skipwith Family Papers, VHS, RASP. See also Fogel and Engerman, *Time on the Cross,* 89–94; and Roger L. Ransom, *Conflict and Compromise: The Political Economy of Slavery, Emancipation, and the Civil War* (New York, 1989), 55–57.

119. See Spagnoletti, *Storia del Regno,* 214–234; Enrica di Ciommo, *La nazione possibile: Mezzogiorno e questione nazionale nel 1848* (Milan, 1993), 33–50; and Alfredo Buccaro, *Opere pubbliche e tipologie urbane nel Mezzogiorno preunitario* (Naples, 1992).

Bridges and Roads represented the embodiment of an idea of "bureaucratic dirigisme," according to which modern competent administrators believed that the government's role was to actively promote public works, overcoming private interests for the sake of the common good (*stato demiurgo*). This view was in opposition with an older, yet still very lively, tradition of enlightened and paternalistic governmental reformism (*stato padre*). During the thirty years in which he was director of the Committee of Bridges and Roads, Afan De Rivera attempted to assert the pervasiveness of his model of bureaucratic dirigisme by becoming the heart and soul of the Bourbon government's most extensive programs for road construction and land reclamation.[120]

Equally important was the activity of the Royal Institute of Encouragement, whose foundation dated to 1810, and of its offspring, the Economic Societies of the Provinces. According to Marta Petrusewicz, by the 1830s the fourteen societies in the continental *Mezzogiorno*, together with several others in Sicily, formed "the largest network of their kind on the Italian peninsula." Apart from promoting agricultural experimentation and educating farmers and peasants through agricultural schools, the societies provided an important forum for the progressive elites to discuss a number of economic problems that were relevant to their particular regions. Yet, the societies' local journals—such as the ones directed by Ignazio Rozzi and Federigo Cassitto—and meetings were much more than simply vehicles of information and forums of debate over agricultural topics. They served the purpose of spreading the regional elites' ideas about economy and society in the local context. In this sense, as Marta Petrusewicz has noted, the societies were "the best instruments of the re-forging of the landed elite's hegemonic role" at the local level.[121]

In fact, the Economic Societies of the Provinces addressed particular problems that related to local economic development under the guidance of renowned agronomists—such as Federigo Cassitto—who served as their secretaries. In principle, the societies' aim was in line with the Bourbon governmental policy of combining agricultural modernization with the encouragement of manufacturing. Accordingly, each society included two different sections—Rural Economy and Civil Economy—which took care of

120. See Costanza D'Elia, *Stato padre, stato demiurgo. I lavori pubblici nel Mezzogiorno (1815–1860)* (Bari, 1996), 41–49.
121. Petrusewicz, "Land-Based Modernization," 107. See also Marta Petrusewicz, "Agromania: innovatori agrari nelle periferie europee dell'Ottocento," in Piero Bevilacqua, ed., *Storia dell'agricoltura italiana in età contemporanea*, vol. 3, *Mercati e Istituzioni* (Venice, 1991), 295–343.

promoting progress in the agricultural and industrial sectors. The principles and the organization of the Economic Societies of the Provinces reflected the ideas of the Bourbon kingdom's progressive intellectual and enlightened administration on economic nationalism, ideas according to which it was the government's responsibility to create the opportunities for economic growth. Arguably, the importance given to the Societies represented the Bourbon monarchy's most ambitious attempt to build a strong national economy, creating opportunities to integrate industry and agriculture at the local level. Yet, despite the principles that informed the Societies' work, many progressive landowners who were active members of a local Society in their province were firmly convinced of the primacy of agriculture over industry. Equally, many shared Federigo Cassitto's suspicions toward industrialization and were far keener to encourage the spread of agricultural knowledge and agrarian experimentation than to promote the development of manufacturing.[122]

In this respect, we can compare the role of the Economic Societies of the Provinces in the *Mezzogiorno* to that of the Southern Commercial Conventions in the American South. Both institutions served as important forums for debates on regional issues and for the activities of economic reformers. Also, both helped to unify the progressive sections of the landowning elites in the acknowledgment of the need to address the issues of agricultural progress and of the strengthening of the regional and national economy. Yet, both the Economic Societies of the Provinces and the Southern Commercial Conventions failed to break the monopoly of agrarian interests in their respective region's economy or to prevent their promotion at the expense of manufacturing activities.[123]

To be sure, economic crises also periodically hit the Bourbon kingdom's agricultural products—especially grain and oil, which were particularly subject to falls in market prices. The worst crises happened in 1816–1817, in 1853–1854, and in concurrence with the political upheavals of 1820 and 1848. Still, the landed elite—especially its progressive sections—considered agriculture as the most honorable activity and the only secure source of wealth. Repeatedly, they referred to the kingdom as an "agricultural nation." Comparable to the planters' commitment to slavery in the American South, the landowners' commitment to agriculture in the *Mezzogiorno* revealed their aim to assert

122. See De Lorenzo, *Società economiche,* 49–91; and Walter Palmieri, "L'offerta di stato' nell'agricoltura meridionale del primo Ottocento: trasformazioni e vincoli," *Meridiana* 25 (1996): 133–166.

123. See Petrusewicz, *Come il Meridione,* 39–62; and Demarco, *Il crollo del Regno,* 11–24.

the region's distinctive character, preserving at the same time a hierarchical labor system.[124]

The ideological implications of the landowners' commitment to agriculture emerge clearly from the writings of intellectual members of the elite, such as literary critic Francesco De Sanctis, and especially of liberal economists, such as Francesco Fuoco. While De Sanctis claimed that "the word 'landowner' has a kind of magic effect on the spirit," Fuoco wrote that "the property of land is a central feature of society." In comparable terms to American planters, southern Italian landowners preferred to live in a nation of farmers with a few large property owners rather than in a strong and self-sufficient country with a diversified economy. Not surprisingly, according to Raffaele De Cesare, by the 1850s the *Mezzogiorno* elite's commitment to land and peasants, rather than industry, had led to a situation whereby "the kingdom was lagging far behind in industrialization." A similar observation would have easily applied to the antebellum American South to describe the results of the slaveholding elite's commitment to land and slaves.[125]

For well over two centuries, the elites of the American South and the Italian *Mezzogiorno* had based their fortunes on the ownership of landed estates and on the formal and informal obligations that forced their legally unfree and their nominally free laborers to work for them. In the eighteenth century, American slaveholders were a highly commercialized elite that made immense profits with the southern system of plantation slavery. On the other hand, southern Italian landowners belonged to a feudal aristocracy whose rights to live as *rentier* exploiting peasant labor passed from generation to generation. At the beginning of the nineteenth century, consistent changes occurred in both the American South and the Italian *Mezzogiorno*. In the American South, the combined effects of the market revolution and of the restructuring of the world economy led to a boom in the production of specific crops, especially cotton. This economic change, in turn, was instrumental in the rise of a new and increasingly larger class of cotton planters and of a number of slaveholding farmers. In the *Mezzogiorno*, the effects of the commercial revolution led to an increasing importance in the export of particular

124. See also Aurelio Lepre, "Produzione e mercato dei prodotti agricoli: vecchio e nuovo nelle crisi della prima metà dell'Ottocento," in Massafra, ed., *Il Mezzogiorno preunitario*, 122–131, 133–147.

125. Francesco De Sanctis's and Francesco Fuoco's quotations are in Petrusewicz, *Come il Meridione*, 86; Raffaele De Cesare, *La fine di un regno* (Milan, 1969; orig. pub. in 1895), 321.

agricultural products, such as olive oil, citrus fruits, and wine. At the same time, the abolition of feudal law led to the transformation of the nobility into a class of landed proprietors and to the rise of a new landed bourgeoisie.

Arguably, the rise of cotton planters in the American South and of landed bourgeois in the *Mezzogiorno* brought with it an emphasis on an entrepreneurial spirit that was reflected in the management of both land and laborers. This, in turn, prompted an increasing number of progressive slaveholders and landowners to discuss the implementation of programs of reform in order to save their region from commercial dependency. However, despite the best intentions of the progressive members of the elites, who were mostly convinced of the primacy of agriculture over other economic activities, the programs and activities of reform showed serious flaws in both regions. In the American South, even the Southern Commercial Conventions—doubtless the most advanced attempt at reconciling agrarian and industrial interests—staunchly defended plantation slavery. While, in the *Mezzogiorno,* the Economic Societies of the Provinces—the Bourbon government's instrument for the promotion of agriculture and industry at the local level—were dominated by large landed proprietors who downplayed the importance of manufacturing. In both regions, the perceived incompatibility between agriculture and industry ultimately proved an important factor in the failed transformation from a dependent and agrarian-oriented economy to an independent and diversified economy. Clearly, there were structural limits to the promotion of industry and to its compatibility with plantation slavery in the American South and with *latifondo* agriculture in the *Mezzogiorno.* Yet, there is little doubt that both American slaveholders and southern Italian landowners were more concerned about the possible loss of their power and status as landed elites than about the economic development of their respective regions.

CHAPTER 2

The Constituent Elements of the Elites' Worldviews

Patriarchalism and Paternalism

I n the first half of the nineteenth century, the worldviews of the landed elites of the American South and of the Italian *Mezzogiorno* included comparable elements of two different types of ideology. Deferential attitudes within the family and in society often related to patriarchalism—the dominant ideology of the eighteenth century—and were part of the daily life of especially, but not exclusively, the most conservative families within the two elites. At the same time, the rise of new propertied classes in both regions was concurrent with the spread of a paternalistic ideology at whose core were both capitalist practices and liberal attitudes. Constant exchange and intermarriage ensured that most members of the two elites combined elements of both ideologies in different degrees and in such a way that, in both cases, it is possible to speak of a range of behaviors from more conservative—or patriarchal—to more progressive—or paternalistic. Arguably, the behaviors of most American slaveholders and southern Italian landowners grouped somewhere in the middle, combining patriarchal and paternalistic elements into two specific and coherent worldviews.[1]

The adoption of attitudes and behaviors that related to patriarchalism formed part of a conscious attempt by members of the two elites to uphold

---

1. On patriarchalism as conservative and paternalism as progressive among American slaveholders, see Philip D. Morgan, *Slave Counterpoint: Black Culture in the Eighteenth-Century Chesapeake and Lowcountry* (Chapel Hill, N.C., 1998), 284–296. My definition of paternalism as a progressive ideology at whose core were capitalist practices may seem closer to Robert Fogel and Stanley Engerman's ideas than to Eugene Genovese's, even though, as Mark Smith has noted, Genovese himself had written in 1968 that "no one would argue that a strong dose of capitalism did not exist in the South. The argument turns on the proportions and their signifi-

the importance of eighteenth-century aristocratic values well into the nineteenth century, both within the family and in society. Within the family, the patriarchal ethos provided a normative standard of behavior based on obedience and respect for paternal authority by children and wives. In society, it implied a deferential behavior by the lower classes toward the upper classes and especially by workers toward their masters. Between the eighteenth and the nineteenth centuries, the concurrent rise in several regions of the world of entrepreneurial classes that were advocates of modernization and of capitalistic and liberal values led to the emergence of a paternalistic ethos in both the American South and the Italian *Mezzogiorno*. Advocates of paternalism believed in the necessity of relations of reciprocity both within the family and in society. They manifested an affectionate behavior toward their children—with whom they interacted with mutual respect—and they extended the idea of reciprocity to relations with their workforce. Consequently, they constructed an ideology according to which mutual obligations caused them to attend to the well-being of their laborers in return for the work that the latter performed for them.[2]

---

cance." See Eugene D. Genovese, "Marxian Interpretations of the Slave South," in Barton J. Bernstein, ed., *Toward a New Past: Dissenting Essays in American History* (New York, 1968), 119; and Mark M. Smith, *Debating Slavery: Economy and Society in the Antebellum American South* (New York, 1998), 92–94. We may very well discover that a "strong dose of capitalism" was an integral part of the slaveholders' paternalistic ideology, as the examples in the last section of the present chapter would suggest, or else—as Peter Parish has pointed out—that "the balance between paternalism and profit seeking varied from master to master according to a whole range of factors, including size of holding and economic conditions—and also time"; see Peter J. Parish, *Slavery: History and Historians* (New York, 1989), 54. For Genovese's clearest explanation of the incompatibility of slaveholders' paternalism with bourgeois capitalism, see Eugene D. Genovese, *Roll, Jordan, Roll: The World the Slaves Made* (New York, 1974), 661–665. See also, among the scholars who have supported the same view, especially Elizabeth Fox-Genovese, *Within the Plantation Household: Black and White Women of the Old South* (Chapel Hill, N.C., 1988), 55–56; Douglas R. Egerton, "Markets without a Market Revolution: Southern Planters and Capitalism," *JER* 16 (1996): 207–221; and Peter Kolchin, *American Slavery, 1619–1877*, 2nd ed. (New York, 2003), 170–173.

2. On patriarchal ideology, see Bertram Wyatt-Brown, "The Ideal Typology and Ante-Bellum Southern History: A Testing of a New Approach," *Societas* 5, no. 1 (1975): 5–6; and Paolo Macry, *Ottocento. Famiglia, elites e patrimoni a Napoli* (Turin, 1988), xiv–xv. On patriarchal and paternalistic—or aristocratic and bourgeois—concepts of the family, see Anne C. Rose, *Victorian America and the Civil War* (New York, 1992), 146–147; and Giovanni Montroni, "La famiglia borghese," in Piero Melograni, ed., *La famiglia italiana dall'Ottocento a oggi* (Rome-Bari, 1988), 132–137.

Though related to the ideology of liberalism and to the entrepreneurial ethos that characterized the rising middle classes of nineteenth-century
America and Europe, in the American South and in the Italian *Mezzogiorno*
the spread of paternalism was also rooted in particular social and economic
features that were peculiar to the two regions. In the American South, the
end of the Atlantic slave trade in 1808 and the constant need for higher profits forced many planters to focus on the well-being of their slaves and, thus,
adopt an attitude that later provided the background for their paternalistic
justification of slavery as a positive good. In the *Mezzogiorno*, instead, paternalistic attitudes and behaviors related to the progressive ideas of several
nineteenth-century agronomists, landowners, and enlightened members of
the elite who were convinced that the fair treatment of laborers, and of the
lower classes in general, was both economically and morally viable.

In general, in both regions, the spread of paternalism was part of the
nineteenth-century phenomenon of ideological modernization of the landed
elite. Among both American slaveholders and southern Italian landowners, especially the most progressive individuals embraced both capitalistic
and liberal values. While they engaged in the search for profit, they also
acknowledged the importance of implementing contractual reciprocity in
dealing with their workforce and adapted the particular features of the paternalistic ethos to the needs of two socioeconomic systems in which non-
market relations, deference, and exploitation were the norm. Both for this
reason and also as a result of ideological exchange and intermarriage between different sections of the elites, the majority of American slaveholders
and southern Italian landowners combined elements of patriarchalism and
elements of paternalism in two specific patriarchal-paternalistic worldviews
that comparably embraced capitalistic and liberal values while implying, at
the same time, that the lower classes ought to show a deferential attitude
and respect for the existing social order.

For the purpose of clarity, in this chapter I explain the main features of
the constituent elements of the two patriarchal-paternalistic worldviews—
patriarchalism and paternalism—and how they developed in the antebellum American South and in the nineteenth-century Italian *Mezzogiorno*,
illuminating their comparable characteristics through specific case studies
drawn from the analysis of behaviors and practices of particularly representative and articulate members of the American slaveholding elite and of the
southern Italian landowning elite—both noble and bourgeois. In comparable
terms, behind the general adoption of a patriarchal-paternalistic worldview,

in both elites the most conservative individuals—several of whom belonged to the oldest aristocratic families—tilted naturally toward privileging behaviors and practices that related to the patriarchal ethos, while the most progressive individuals—many of whom either belonged to the rising classes or to liberal groups within the oldest aristocracies—tilted naturally toward privileging behaviors and practices that related to the paternalistic ethos. Generally speaking, though, different elements of patriarchalism and paternalism combined together in an ideological continuum and gave origin, in the two cases, to two specific—and, yet, comparable—patriarchal-paternalistic worldviews that characterized the minds of the master classes, old and new, of the American South and of the Italian *Mezzogiorno*. Also for this reason, it is better to refer to an articulated patriarchal-paternalistic ideology in the case of American slaveholders and to an implicit patriarchal-paternalistic worldview in the case of southern Italian landowners, even though the combination of patriarchal and paternalistic elements resulted in both cases in the creation of a powerful tool for the landed elite's justification of its economic and social prominence based on the exploitation of the lower classes.

Aristocratic Patriarchalism in the Nineteenth Century

Within the two specific patriarchal-paternalistic worldviews that characterized the minds of American slaveholders and southern Italian landowners, patriarchalism was the older ideological element. In the eighteenth century, the patriarchal ethos had informed the daily life of the major aristocratic families of both the American South and the Italian *Mezzogiorno*. Rigid authoritarianism and deference within the family and respect for hierarchy and status in society were its distinctive characteristics. The figure of the father—*pater familias*—at the same time head of the household and head of the social system, demanding absolute obedience from his wife and children and from his servants and slaves, was at its core. The demand for obedience and for respect for the authority, in turn, often led to resort to violence and to brutal punishments, which were the norm for both disobedient children and ill-disciplined servants and slaves. Well into the nineteenth century, attitudes and behaviors that related to patriarchalism were very much part of the daily life of some of the most prominent families of both southern regions. In the American South, several individuals who belonged to the planter aristocracies of Virginia and South Carolina continued to follow practices related to patriarchal ideology and still regarded deference and respect for hierarchy and status as the foundations of family life and of the entire social order; the same was true of several members of the Neapolitan and Sicilian landed aristocracies in the Italian *Mezzogiorno*.[3]

In its essence, patriarchal ideology aimed to preserve social order through recognition of the importance of fixed roles in family and society. Consequently, formality characterized relations between heads of households who privileged the patriarchal ethos and their wives and children, while discipline and detachment characterized relations between masters and laborers on the landed estates. In both cases, the underlining idea was that women, children, and members of the lower classes were—in the words of Peter Bardaglio— "naturally suited for subordination, and the male heads of the household . . . were naturally fitted to command this subordination." Still according to Bardaglio, in the nineteenth-century American South, the "preservation of the social order, not just domestic tranquility, rested on the smooth and effective functioning of the patriarchal network," a network in which everybody knew his or her exact place and function in society. Similarly, in his description of the main features of the nineteenth-century southern Italian patriarchal family, Paolo Macry has noted how "within the household the roles are fixed, the power of the father is strong and unchallenged; wife, children, and servants are tightly subordinated to him. The paradigm is hierarchical and the relationships, even the ones between master and servants, are deferential rather than contractual."[4]

In his famous 1839 work *Democracy in America,* Alexis De Tocqueville described the "aristocratic family" with characteristics that closely matched the ones of a patriarchal household. He saw correctly that this particular

3. On eighteenth-century patriarchal ideology, see Morgan, *Slave Counterpoint,* 269–284; Allan Kulikoff, *Tobacco and Slaves: The Development of Southern Cultures in the Chesapeake, 1680–1800* (Chapel Hill, N.C., 1986), 165–204; Enrico Dal Lago, "Patriarchs and Republicans: Eighteenth-Century Virginian Planters and Classical Politics," *HR* 76 (2003): 492–511; Cara Anzilotti, *In the Affairs of the World: Women, Patriarchy, and Power in Colonial South Carolina* (Westport, Conn., 2002); Robert Olwell, *Masters, Slaves, and Subjects: The Culture of Power in the South Carolina Low Country, 1740–1790* (Ithaca, N.Y., 1998), 193–200; Maria Antonietta Visceglia, *Il bisogno di eternità. I comportamenti aristocratici a Napoli in età moderna* (Naples, 1988), 11–93; Orazio Cancila, "Introduzione," in Orazio Cancila, ed., *Noi e il Padrone* (Palermo, 1982), ix–xxviii; and Antonino Morreale, *Famiglie feudali nell'età moderna. I principi di Valguarnera* (Palermo, 1995), 64–104.

4. Peter W. Bardaglio, *Reconstructing the Household: Families, Sex, and the Law in the Nineteenth-Century South* (Chapel Hill, N.C., 1995), 27; Macry, *Ottocento,* xiv.

type of family functioned according to a hierarchy based on both age and sex. At the top of the hierarchy stood the husband/father, who was "not only the civil head of the family, but the organ of its traditions, the expounder of its customs, the arbiter of its manners." Wife and children listened to him with deference, addressed him with respect, and loved him and feared him at the same time. According to Tocqueville, this deferential attitude was the main reason why in the correspondence of aristocratic families the letters showed a style "always correct, ceremonious, stiff, and so cold that the natural warmth of the heart can hardly be felt in the language."[5]

In a previous chapter, Tocqueville wrote about relations between masters and servants in aristocratic societies. Some of his observations fit well the description of the effects of patriarchalism in both the American South and the Italian *Mezzogiorno*. In particular, Tocqueville wrote that in aristocratic societies, "the master readily obtains prompt, complete, respectful, and easy obedience from his servants, because they revere in him not only their master, but their class of masters." As for the master, he not only orders the servants' actions, but also "to a certain extent, he even directs their thoughts." As a consequence, "among an aristocratic people the master gets to look upon his servants as an inferior and secondary part of himself, and he often takes an interest in their lot by a last stretch of selfishness."[6]

Arguably, Tocqueville's description of the main features of aristocratic societies had a lot in common with eighteenth-century American and southern Italian descriptions of society functioning according to the patriarchal ethos; both cases showed clearly how social hierarchy was taken for granted and how the implication was that the lower classes—free and unfree—ought to be obedient and deferential toward the upper classes. According to an eighteenth-century Virginian lawyer, "societies of men could not subsist unless there were a subordination of one to another. . . . That in this subordination the department of slaves must be filled by some, or there would be a defect in the scale of order." Federico Di Napoli, an eighteenth-century Sicilian nobleman, echoed the Virginian lawyer's comments when he wrote that "the good rule . . . from which the people gain . . . can only come from subordination . . . so that people know how to obey and their superiors dispense justice with the authority that we have given them."[7]

5. Alexis De Tocqueville, *Democracy in America*, part 2 (London, 1994; orig. pub. in 1839), 194, 195.

6. Tocqueville, *Democracy in America*, part 2, 179.

7. The Virginian lawyer is quoted in Morgan, *Slave Counterpoint*, 258; Federico Di Napoli, "Libro Verde di Resuttano," in Cancila, ed., *Noi e il Padrone*, 99.

Among the comparable elements of patriarchalism that survived in the nineteenth-century patriarchal-paternalistic worldviews of American slaveholders and southern Italian landowners, the stress on subordination was of paramount importance; it implied obedience and deference and, at the same time, led to a lack of communication between upper classes and lower classes. In fact, masters who emphasized the importance of patriarchal attitudes tended largely to live separate lives from those of their laborers and to have very rare personal contacts with slaves and peasants. The distance between masters and laborers was even greater if the planter or the landowner was an absentee landlord, as happened in most of southern Italy and in some areas of the American South, especially coastal South Carolina. In this case, relations with slaves and peasants became distant problems that overseers and agents were in charge of resolving. And yet, unlike what happened in the Italian *Mezzogiorno*, in the American South, especially on absentee-owned plantations, overseers resorted routinely to violence to enforce discipline and ensure the slaves' obedience. The overseer's whip was always the symbol of the master's authority, whether the planter was a resident or an absentee landlord, and slaves received routine floggings for all sorts of reasons besides the one of not completing their task properly.[8]

In fact, this constant presence of violence was one of the main differences between nineteenth-century American plantations and southern Italian *latifondi*. In the *Mezzogiorno*, there was not nearly as much violence involved in the enforcement of discipline as in the American South, primarily because agrarian workers were legally free. However, the threat of violence was always present; often landowners had armed guards who represented their authority on the *latifondi* and who did not hesitate to use weapons in case of a workers' revolt. Ultimately, in both the American and the southern Italian cases, the masters' combination of a detached attitude in regard to workers' conditions with the attempt to maintain authoritarian relations led to a situation in which either violence or the threat of it was an integral part of daily life on landed estates. Especially in the cases of absentee ownership of plantations and *latifondi*, distant and detached masters gave agents and overseers a free hand to discipline the workforce with whatever means they deemed necessary.[9]

8. See Kenneth Stampp, *The Peculiar Institution: Slavery in the Ante-Bellum South* (New York, 1956), 43–44, 175–181.

9. See Brenda Stevenson, *Life in Black and White: Family and Community in the Slave South*

* * *

In both the antebellum American South and the nineteenth-century Italian *Mezzogiorno*, correspondence between fathers and children shows how the masters' efforts to assert their authority following patriarchal rules of behavior greatly influenced the personal lives of their sons and daughters. Planters and landowners who privileged the patriarchal ethos expected their children to receive a proper education and uphold the reputation of the family name. They constantly watched and severely constrained their sons' public behavior with a number of unwritten rules. In particular, in the American South, according to Michael P. Johnson, the "authority of the father structured patriarchal families" and led to regarding the reputation of the family name as being "the most obvious evidence of the planter's glorification of the father." The duty of the planter's son was to honor his father, and "to honor one's father, one deferred to his authority, studied his wishes, and obeyed his commands. In short, one remained subordinate." Respectability, virtue, dignity, and sense of duty were qualities that planters who followed patriarchal rules of behavior demanded from their sons. They punished the lack of these qualities, increasing the emotional distance between themselves and their sons and assuming a detached attitude toward them.[10]

The correspondence between James Coles Bruce and his father, James Bruce—a wealthy Virginian planter—illustrates this point. The Bruces were a family that came originally from the southside region of Virginia; they owned several tobacco plantations and farms in the Virginian counties of Halifax, Charlotte, Pittsylvania, and Roanoke and in neighboring counties of North Carolina. The total value of James Bruce's patrimony was more than $4 million—which made him one of the wealthiest individuals of the antebellum American South. In 1826, James Coles Bruce attended Harvard University in Cambridge, Massachusetts. He wrote frequent letters to James Bruce, addressing him with the affectionate expression "My Dear Father"; yet, the letters show that his father had little confidence in him. In fact, despite James Coles's best efforts, James Bruce scrupulously maintained an

---

(New York, 1996), 166–205; Leslie H. Owens, *This Species of Property: Slave Life and Culture in the Old South* (New York, 1976), 79–80; Aurelio Lepre, *Il Mezzogiorno dal feudalesimo al capitalismo* (Naples, 1979), 126–137; and Anton Blok, *The Mafia of a Sicilian Village, 1860–1960: A Study of Violent Peasant Entrepreneurs* (New York, 1974), 54–68.

10. Michael P. Johnson, "Planters and Patriarchy: Charleston, 1800–1860," *JSH* 46 (1980): 49–50. See also Bertram Wyatt-Brown, *Southern Honor: Ethics and Behavior in the Old South* (New York, 1982), 117–174.

emotional distance with his son, either by chronically delaying his replies to him or by overstating the frequent misunderstandings between them.[11]

In one of his frequent complaints about James Bruce's lack of reply, James Coles wrote on May 14 of how his father's last letter had "the date of the 17th of February." He then speculated on his father's behavior and attempted to explain his delayed reply with a list of possible reasons, among them a dissatisfaction with his conduct which had provoked an exaggerated reaction: "I have attributed your silence to absence from home, ill health, and displeasure; if it be the latter, I can only say that it has been most immerited on my part. Nothing can be more chilly to a person of sensibility than neglect from a father." In fact, James Bruce's attitude toward James Coles reminds us that planters who followed patriarchal rules of behavior gave their confidence to their sons and took it away from them at will. They decided how close the father-son relationship ought to be and when to increase or decrease the distance between them. Doubtless, particularly sensitive sons, such as James Coles, felt neglected by their fathers' arbitrary changes of attitude, especially if they were away from home for study and they saw a constant delay or lack of reply in the post.[12]

In a previous letter, while protesting against James Bruce's unjust accusation of having wasted a large sum of money, James Coles wrote in disbelief that "I once thought that your confidence in my prudence and discretion was too firm to be shaken by a circumstance so slight." Declaring his innocence, he attempted to convince his father that "the distance which separates us, I assure you, has no effect in influencing my conduct" and that "dissipation and extravagance I have never entered into, and never in the course of my life have I been so attentive to my studies as I am at the present time." Particularly significant were the words with which James Coles closed his letter to his distant and authoritarian father, claiming his right to enjoy both his trust and his confidence. After apologizing "for the uneasings which you must experience before the reception of this letter," he continued, "I hope you will see your mistake and return me the confidence which an accident has robbed me of. You wish me to consider this letter confidential, I obey you."[13]

Planters who privileged the patriarchal ethos—as was the case of James Bruce—demanded from their sons that they conform to the codified rules

11. On James Coles Bruce, see Willie Lee Rose, ed., *A Documentary History of Slavery in North America* (New York, 1976), 337–338.

12. James Coles Bruce to James Bruce, 14 May 1826, Bruce Family Papers, UVA, RASP.

13. James Coles Bruce to James Bruce, 30 January 1826, Bruce Family Papers, UVA, RASP.

of behavior of their family and class; only then could their sons hope to earn their father's attention and trust. According to these rules, a planter's son ought to behave in an exemplary way while he was away from home study-ing. He could hardly indulge in any enjoyment and he ought to constantly regard his behavior as an indicator of the moral standard of the upper class. Only if he followed parental advice and conformed to the rules that both family and society imposed upon him could a planter's son hope to earn his fathers' confidence in reward for the fulfillment of his duty. Yet—as in James Coles's case—at the slightest mistake, relations between father and son rap-idly deteriorated and the son needed to work hard to earn again his father's trust. Perhaps also as a consequence of this harsh training, James Coles Bruce set out to become a role model for his family and class. After study-ing at Harvard and at the University of Virginia, he married Eliza Wilkins in 1829; he then served in the Virginia state legislature for a number of years and also traveled extensively. He was successful in the management of his plantations and spent his last years looking after his considerable wealth. According to Shearer Davis Bowman, by the time he was in his early sixties, James Coles Bruce "was the only member of the 1861 [Virginia] secession convention who, according to the 1860 census, owned more than a hundred slaves (134 to be exact) in a single county."[14]

Different—but equally strict—rules of codified behavior characterized the expectations that planters who privileged the patriarchal ethos had about their daughters. Southern elite families raised daughters constantly remind-ing them, from a very early age, that their main goal in life was to marry a rich planter; in fact, society regarded those daughters who did not suc-ceed in marrying to be a disgrace to the family's reputation. Eligible men met girls at balls, parties, or at church, and began courting them when they reached the age of sixteen. By that age, most southern elite girls would have completed their education. Female elite education in the antebellum South aimed mainly to transform girls into attractive women for potential suit-ors and prepare them for their future married life. Consequently, teaching focused on behaving properly, in a lady-like manner, and on learning to be obedient, purposeful, and pious.[15]

14. Shearer Davis Bowman, *Masters and Lords: Mid-19th Century U.S. Planters and Prussian Junkers* (New York, 1993), 181.

15. See Sally G. McMillen, *Southern Women: Black and White in the Old South* (Arlington Heights, Ill., 1992), 77–80; and Ann Firor Scott, *The Southern Lady: From Pedestal to Politics, 1830–1930* (Chicago, Ill., 1970), 30–31.

Elite girls learned these fundamental precepts of patriarchal ideology, along with several supposed women's skills—such as drawing and sewing —and studied a variety of different subjects, ranging from languages to history and music, at special female academies, which they usually entered when they were twelve and in which they stayed for a number of years. Yet, despite the often decisive influence that formal education had on shaping the minds of growing southern elite girls, a good deal of schooling and training actually happened at home. In the domestic environment, a planter complemented his daughter's patriarchal education by training her to be obedient to her father so that she would, then, be able to be obedient to her future husband.[16]

A particularly interesting document on the informal education of daughters in southern elite families, and one that sheds light on the expectations of planters who privileged the patriarchal ethos, is Elizabeth Allston Pringle's published autobiography, *Chronicles of Chicora Wood.* Elizabeth was the daughter of Robert Allston—one of the richest rice planters in the South Carolina lowcountry—and Adele Petigru—the youngest sister of prestigious Charleston lawyer James Louis Petigru. In 1832, after Allston married Petigru, together they moved to his rice plantation at Chicora Wood, on the Waccamaw River. Elizabeth's recollections start from this point and take the reader to the time of her own marriage, in 1870, through family tales, character sketches, and reports of conversations that add a great deal to our understanding of patriarchal ideology and its everyday practice in an elite family. Elizabeth's admiration for her father's patriarchal authority, his strong will, determined character, and ability to teach his wife and children discipline and obedience, is clear and shows in several episodes.[17]

In one of the most meaningful conversations that Elizabeth reported in her recollections, Robert Allston's aunt Blythe explained to Elizabeth's mother, Adele Petigru, the meaning of her life as plantation mistress in

16. See Anya Jabour, "Grown Girl, Highly Cultivated: Female Education in an Antebellum Southern Family," *JSH* 64 (1998): 23–64; and Christine Ann Farnham, *The Education of the Southern Belle: Higher Education and Student Socialization in the Antebellum South* (New York, 1994).

17. See Elizabeth Allston Pringle, *Chronicles of "Chicora Wood"* (Atlanta, Ga., 1922). On the Petigru and Allston families, see Jane H. Pease and William H. Pease, *A Family of Women: The Carolina Petigru in Peace and War* (Chapel Hill, N.C., 1999); and James H. Easterby, "Introduction," in James H. Easterby, ed., *The South Carolina Rice Plantation as Revealed in the Papers of Robert F. W. Allston* (Chicago, 1945), 1–6.

connection to the patriarchal virtues of discipline and restraint. Blythe first told Adele that the plantation mistress's life "is a life of self-repression and effort," and yet "a very noble life, if a woman does her full duty in it." Blythe then concocted a remarkable statement—which sheds light on the meaning of marriage in patriarchal ideology—when she told Adele that "to be the wife of a rice planter is no place for a pleasure-loving, indolent woman, but for an earnest, true-hearted woman, it is a great opportunity, a great educa-tion." The educational aspects lay in the fact that "to train others one must first train oneself; it requires method, power of organization, grasp of detail, perception of character, power of speech; above all, endless self-control."[18]

The education of women in elite families that followed patriarchal rules of behavior emphasized the importance of self-repression and self-control as the indispensable qualities that a planter's daughter and a planter's wife—a wife who obeyed her husband without questioning his authority—ought to have. As a consequence, training in self-discipline was the most important learning activity and one which women started at an early age and continued even after their marriage. Plantation mistresses such as Adele Petigru—who, both before and after marrying, received a training in patriarchal values that stressed the importance of discipline and self-restraint—tended to internal-ize those values and pass them on to their daughters after having accepted them as a substantial part of a woman's duties in life.[19]

At the same time, planters who privileged the patriarchal ethos taught their daughters discipline and submission so that they learned from their mistakes and did not repeat them with their future husbands. In her rec-ollections, Elizabeth described an episode in which her father—Robert Allston—taught her a lesson in discipline she never forgot. When she was three, Elizabeth stole a peach from the sideboard of the dining room and, apparently, Allston failed to realize it. Subsequently, he asked her to tell him the truth about the stolen peach and she lied to him. He then let her know that "that is a terrible thing to have done, and I must punish you, so that you may never fall so low again." That very night, Allston gave Elizabeth a severe

---

18. Pringle, *Chronicles*, 77–78. See also Pease and Pease, *Family of Women*, 19–20; and Johnson, "Planters and Patriarchy," 50.

19. See Bardaglio, *Reconstructing the Household*, 23–35. On resistance to patriarchy, see Ann Firor Scott, "Women's Perspectives on Patriarchy in the 1850s," *JAH* 66 (1974): 52–64; Victoria Bynum, *Unruly Women: The Politics of Social and Sexual Control in the Old South* (Chapel Hill, N.C., 1992); and Laura F. Edwards, "Law, Domestic Violence, and the Limits of Patriarchal Authority in the Antebellum South," *JSH* 65 (1999): 733–770.

switching and then put her into bed. The following morning, when Elizabeth woke up, she was "happy and peaceful, and, above all, filled with a kind of adoration" for her father. In fact, she wrote, "I never ceased to feel grateful to papa for the severity of my punishment. It *had* to be remembered, and it meant the holding aloft of honesty and truth, and the trampling in the dust of dishonesty and falsehood. No child is too young to have these basic principles taught to them." Aside from the specificity of the episode, the story is a good example of what Bertram Wyatt-Brown has described as the southern elite families' "tendency . . . to seek ways whereby children would internalize virtues and fears of wrongdoing, chiefly through conscience and guilt."[20]

Elizabeth received her punishment for trespassing her father's authority by eating a peach without asking for his permission. The severity of the punishment reminded her that she could not subvert the hierarchical and authoritarian principles that ruled family life according to the patriarchal ethos without suffering terrible consequences. Though harsh, the training in discipline and submission to her father's authority had the purpose of preparing Elizabeth for her married life, when she would have to submit to her husband's authority or suffer severe social consequences. Apparently, Elizabeth not only learned the lesson but also internalized the patriarchal principles in such a way that she came to see the episode as a proof of her father's love for her. After all, Allston wished for his daughter to learn from as early an age as possible the quality she needed most as plantation mistress: the ability to be submissive and self-restrained with the male head of the household, whether it was her father or her husband. In her adult life, Elizabeth continued to adore her father. Later on in life—partly out of love for Allston's successful rice planting activity and partly out of a wish for self-fulfillment against patriarchal prejudices—Elizabeth went back to the family estate at Chicora Wood and dedicated a good deal of time to the business of rice cultivation. During the years after the Civil War—while the patriarchal world in which she had grown up was in shambles—Elizabeth won her own personal battle, becoming a successful rice planter, as her father had been before her. She described this experience in her book *A Woman Rice Planter*, which she published in 1913.[21]

*   *   *

20. Pringle, *Chronicles*, 110–111; Wyatt-Brown, *Southern Honor*, 155.

21. See Elizabeth Allston Pringle, *A Woman Rice Planter* (New York, 1913). See also Catherine Clinton, *The Plantation Mistress: Woman's World in the Old South* (New York, 1982), 59–86.

A greater detachment than the one between American planters and their sons and daughters characterized relations between southern Italian land-owners—especially noblemen—who privileged the patriarchal ethos and followed patriarchal rules of behavior and their children. In particular, southern Italian noblemen demanded from their children respect for the codified rules of the aristocracy both in matters of public conduct and in the choice of the marriage partner. Unlike what happened in the American South, in the Italian *Mezzogiorno* several aristocratic families still complied with the law of primogeniture (*maggiorascato*), and this contributed to create greater distance between parents and children. Also, aside from issues of primogeniture, matters related to the preservation and transmission of the family patrimony—rather than matters related to personal feelings—often dictated the choice of the spouse in aristocratic households. In his analysis of nineteenth-century wills written by Neapolitan noblemen, Paolo Macry has pointed out that "the Neapolitan code of 1819 acknowledged the masculine character of family hierarchies and protected the continuity of family pat-rimony." On the other hand, regarding the law of primogeniture, Giovanni Montroni has concluded that "the analysis of the use of the *maggiorascato* has confirmed the preference of southern aristocrats for models of succes-sion which, even if not egalitarian, smoothed out excessive differences" in the treatment of sons. Still, some of the major constraints on spousal choice derived from unwritten, codified rules of aristocratic behavior that protected the honor of the family name and demanded that noblemen and noble-women marry their equals.[22]

The correspondence between Diego Pignatelli, duke of Monteleone, and his wife, Maria Carmela Caracciolo, the duchess, illustrates this point particularly well. The dukes of Monteleone belonged to one of the most il-lustrious southern Italian noble families and, traditionally, they always mar-ried within the highest ranks of the Sicilian aristocracy. In addition to be-ing dukes of Monteleone, the Pignatelli were also princes of Castelvetrano, in Sicily—where they had extensive landholdings—and owned mines in Mexico as a result of the seventeenth-century marriages of a branch of the family with the Cortès, the descendants of the Spanish conquistador. In fact, the Pignatelli ranked extremely high among the titled families of the Sicil-ian aristocracy. According to Raffaele De Cesare, "until the beginning of the

22. Macry, *Ottocento*, 9; Giovanni Montroni, *Gli uomini del Re. La nobiltà napoletana nell'Ottocento* (Catanzaro, 1996), 59.

[nineteenth] century they possessed the largest capital in the island," since they "had a higher income than 200,000 ducats."[23]

In 1815, the duke of Monteleone was in search of a suitable wife for his son Giuseppe Pignatelli. He wished him to marry a woman of comparable aristocratic credentials, but Giuseppe was in love with a woman of the lesser nobility. In December, the duke wrote a long letter to his wife in Naples and told her how in the summer, after he left for his Sicilian feudal estates, "I received a letter in which they told me that my son was in love with a noble girl, but not of the same standing." The duke acted immediately: "I summoned him, while I was in Menfi, I reproached him, and he agreed that the girl was not convenient to him, but he said that he did not like at all the young daughter of Paternò." Clearly, Giuseppe had protested his feelings to his father and had let him know that he had no intention to marry the noble spouse the duke had chosen for him. Yet, Giuseppe had little say in matters of spousal choice and had to obey his father's wishes. For his part, the duke had definite ideas on Giuseppe's partner. Two years later—in 1817—in another letter to his wife, he made a list of possible spouses for his son; all belonged to the highest ranks of the aristocracy and several were relatives of the Pignatelli. At the end of the letter, the duke commented, "I would consider myself lucky if he [Giuseppe] chose one of his cousins, either the daughter of Cutò or the daughter of Campofranco, perfect people, with good and healthy manners."[24]

The following year, even though previously in love with another woman, Giuseppe complied with his father's wishes and married Bianca Lucchesi Palli, the daughter of the prince of Campofranco and one of the possible spouses the duke had included on his list. The 1818 marriage between Giuseppe Pignatelli and Bianca Lucchesi Palli led to the birth of seven daughters. Interestingly, Giuseppe seems to have acted much like his father in regard to his own children's choice of spouses. In his analysis of Palermo's social scene in the nineteenth and twentieth centuries, Orazio Cancila mentions that Giuseppe Pignatelli had problems in finding the perfect spouses for his daughters in terms of both aristocratic titles and wealth; possibly the problems derived also from the fact that Giuseppe's and his daughters' ideas on the perfect spouse coincided very little.[25]

23. Raffaele De Cesare, *La fine di un regno* (Milan, 1969; orig. pub. in 1895), 380–381.

24. Diego Pignatelli to Maria Carmela Caracciolo, 20 December 1815; Diego Pignatelli to Maria Carmela Caracciolo, 12 June 1817, Aragona-Pignatelli-Cortès Family Papers, ASN.

25. See Orazio Cancila, *Palermo* (Bari-Rome, 1988), 16.

Arguably, in both American and southern Italian elite families that followed patriarchal rules of behavior, the children's respect for their father's authority and obedience to his wishes were beyond question. And yet, in southern Italy, the respect that the children owed to their father in elite families related to the respect which young noblemen owed to both social and family traditions—traditions according to which they ought to marry noblewomen of their same social standing. When they demanded that their children obey traditional rules of social behavior, noblemen insisted that they respect those traditions that maintained heads of the household in a position of unchallenged authority over the other members of the family. According to these traditions—as the case of Giuseppe Pignatelli shows—children ought to agree with their father's choice of their spouse and obey his wishes, even though his selection rarely coincided with their own.[26]

Patriarchal rules were particularly strict in the case of the marriage of daughters of prominent noblemen. As in the antebellum American South, in the nineteenth-century Italian *Mezzogiorno* elite girls received from a very early age an education that stressed the fact that their goal in life was to marry wealthy and prominent elite men. However, unlike what happened in the American South, there was very little schooling and formal education in the nineteenth century *Mezzogiorno*. As a consequence, the parents' role in teaching their daughters patriarchal values and expectations on a daily basis within the household was far more influential in shaping their characters and beliefs than any external stimulus. Southern Italian elite girls grew up far more convinced of the necessity of believing in patriarchal values acquired through this type of informal, family-centered, education than elite girls in the American South. In both cases, though, informal education in families that followed patriarchal rules of behavior stressed the importance of the daughters' self-restraint and submission to the authority of both parents, and of the father in particular.[27]

In the *Mezzogiorno*, this was especially true in the case of marriage, since it was felt that daughters—even more than sons—ought to comply with

26. On patriarchal families, see also Marzio Barbagli, *Sotto lo stesso tetto. Mutamenti della famiglia in Italia dal XV al XX secolo* (Bologna, 1996), 88.

27. On patriarchal values and the history of Italian families, see Ronald P. Saller and David I. Kertzer, "Historical and Anthropological Perspectives on Italian Family Life," in David I. Kertzer and Ronald P. Saller, eds., *The Family in Italy: From Antiquity to the Present* (New Haven, Conn., 1991), 13–14; and Marzio Barbagli and David Kertzer, "Introduction," in Marzio Barbagli and David Kertzer, eds., *Storia della famiglia italiana, 1750–1950* (Bologna, 1992).

their parents' spousal choice. Contrary to what happened in the American South, elite families often forced those daughters who did not succeed in marrying suitable noblemen to become nuns and live in convents, so that they did not shame the family name by living on their own. Although this custom was much less widespread than in previous times, there were several cases of Neapolitan and Sicilian aristocratic families that, still well into the nineteenth century, forced their daughters to take the veil.[28]

A famous case was the one of Enrichetta Caracciolo, who in 1864 published the recollections of her life as a nun in a Neapolitan convent in a book entitled *Misteri del chiostro napoletano* (Mysteries of the Neapolitan Cloister). Born in 1821, the daughter of Gennaro Caracciolo—prince of Forino—and Teresa Cutelli, Enrichetta belonged to a prestigious Neapolitan aristocratic family. Her father served as a high officer in the Bourbon army. In 1827, the Bourbon administration assigned him to the post of commander-in-chief of the province of Reggio, in Calabria Ultra I, and his family—including the six-year-old Enrichetta—followed him. While the family was in Calabria, three of Enrichetta's elder sisters married local noblemen, and by the time she was fourteen, she was one of only two single daughters in the family. Although she dreamt of meeting an eligible man and marrying him as her sisters had done, patriarchal family rules allowed Enrichetta very few opportunities to do so. "The education that our mother gave us was extremely rigorous"—she wrote in her recollections—"she measured the time during which we were allowed to stay on the balcony to enjoy the sight of the public walk; the least transgression of these rules was treated with a severe punishment."[29]

As her last elder sister approached the time of her marriage, Enrichetta fell in love with the young son of a local civil servant, whose name was Domenico. Despite the disapproval of both Enrichetta's mother and Domenico's father, the relationship continued for a year and, in 1840—when Enrichetta was nineteen—the two engaged to be married. Unfortunately, Enrichetta's father unexpectedly died and her family momentarily returned to Naples. Following her husband's death, Enrichetta's mother increased her authoritarian behavior, repressing her and attempting to instill in her

28. On aristocratic nuns, see H. Hills, "Monasteri femminili aristocratici a Napoli e Palermo nella prima età moderna e la conventualizzazione della città," in Giovanna Fiume, ed., *Il Santo Patrono e la città. San Benedetto Il Moro* (Venice, 1999).

29. Enrichetta Caracciolo, *Misteri del chiostro napoletano* (Florence, 1986; orig. pub. in 1864), 7–8, 14. See also Alfonso Scirocco, "Il dibattito sulla soppressione delle corporazioni religiose nel 1864 e I 'Misteri del chiostro napoletano' di Enrichetta Caracciolo," *Clio* 28 (1992).

mind patriarchal values of submission and self-restraint. After Domenico threatened not to marry Enrichetta if she did not join him in Calabria, her mother proceeded to declare the engagement dissolved, against Enrichetta's prayers and tears. Shortly afterward, Enrichetta's mother decided that, not finding any suitable spouse for her daughter, she would have her locked in a convent for her own benefit. In a remarkable scene, Enrichetta protested her right not to become a nun against her will and her mother silenced her with the argument that, as a parent, she enjoyed absolute authority over her daughter: "I am the only arbiter of your fate . . . both human laws and divine laws impose obedience upon you, and, for the sake of God, you will obey!"[30]

As in every household that followed patriarchal rules of behavior, also in the Caracciolo family obedience and submission were particularly important features of the normal conduct of children toward their parents. The decision that Enrichetta's mother took when she forced her to spend the next twenty years of her life in a convent reasserted the strength and importance of the mother's parental authority over her daughter. Both Elizabeth Allston Pringle's mother and Enrichetta Caracciolo's mother are examples of women who, after internalizing the values attached to patriarchal ideology, attempted to transmit those values to their daughters. At the same time, Enrichetta's case also shows that in patriarchal families, while the father/husband's authority was absolute, in the case of his absence or death, the mother took his place as head of the household and imposed her own will over the children, ensuring the perpetuation of the patriarchal system of authoritarian family relations.[31]

An interesting case of resistance to oppression on issues of courtship and spousal choice in an elite family that followed patriarchal rules of behavior arises in a series of letters that the princess of Lampedusa sent to the prince of Sant'Antimo in 1832. In that year, the princess of Lampedusa, who belonged to a prestigious Sicilian aristocratic family, was in search of a suitable spouse for her daughter. Apparently, Vincenzo Ruffo, prince of Sant'Antimo, a prominent Calabrian nobleman, had let the princess of Lampedusa's daughter believe that he wished to marry her; however, he thought it was only a misunderstanding without consequence. Yet, Lampedusa's daughter took

30. Caracciolo, *Misteri,* 48; see also 18–46.

31. On points of comparison between patriarchy in the American South and the Italian *Mezzogiorno,* see J. William Harris, "Gender in the Recent History of the U.S. South and Some Prospects for Comparative History," in Enrico Dal Lago and Rick Halpern, eds., *The American South and the Italian Mezzogiorno: Essays in Comparative History* (New York, 2002), 155–172.

the matter extremely seriously and—in an interesting reversal of Enrichetta Caracciolo's case—threatened to lock herself in a convent if Sant'Antimo did not agree to marry her. In a particularly sincere letter, the princess wrote him that she was preoccupied with her daughter's behavior: "regarding . . . my daughter I would have liked from you a positive answer, since I am extremely worried."[32]

Furthermore, the princess wrote that "every time I talk to her about a possible marriage with somebody, she says that she does not want to get married . . . and she says that if I force her she will lock herself in a convent . . . Please, write to me about your true intentions." After this exchange, the princess continued to write Sant'Antimo and attempted to convince him to change his mind about marrying her daughter, but to no avail. This case shows that a daughter who was eligible for marriage could use the threat of her decision to enter a convent as a weapon against her parents' authoritarian pretensions. From this perspective, it seems that in southern Italian elite families there sometimes was more room for negotiation than Enrichetta Caracciolo's story suggests.[33]

In both the American South and the Italian *Mezzogiorno,* heads of households who privileged the patriarchal ethos attached great importance to the family name. In particular, in the American South, family names identified individual planters, linking them to well-known dynasties of slaveholders. The diaries and letters of a number of planters and plantation mistresses show that prestigious names such as—for example—Lee, Ball, or Manigault identified an individual as the member of a powerful slaveholding aristocracy whose origins stretched as far back as the seventeenth century. Patriarchal expectations demanded that children show particular devotion toward the history of the family name and seek to continue the family tradition of managing plantations and owning large numbers of slaves. In fact, according to Michael P. Johnson, "the ultimate way for a son to honor his father was to become a planter-patriarch himself." Several prominent planters who sent their sons away from home to study asked them to behave according to

32. Princess of Lampedusa to Vincenzo Ruffo, prince of S. Antimo, 20 August 1832, Ruffo di Bagnara Family Papers, ASN.

33. Princess of Lampedusa to Vincenzo Ruffo, prince of S. Antimo, 20 August 1832, Ruffo di Bagnara Family Papers, ASN. For a critical view of southern Italian patriarchy, see Giovanna Fiume, "Making Women Visible in the History of the Mezzogiorno," in Dal Lago and Halpern, eds., *American South and Italian Mezzogiorno,* 173–196.

patriarchal expectations honoring the family name and showing that they were conscious of its importance. Especially when planters pursued a political career, they placed particular pressure over their sons and expected them to honor the family tradition and their father's reputation with an impeccable behavior at all times. The planters' engagement in politics demanded consistency between the public image of their family and their pretensions to represent the community. The sons' residence in another state for study, then, became a pretext for planters to be particularly insistent and demanding in their patriarchal expectations and in their control of their children's public behavior.[34]

For example, Robert Allston had good reasons to be particularly careful about the impact of his sons' behavior on the family reputation and on his public image. The owner of 630 slaves scattered on five rice plantations in South Carolina's Georgetown district and the husband of Adele Petigru, Allston was also a prestigious politician. After graduating from West Point in 1821, Allston sat in the South Carolina House between 1828 and 1832. During the 1840s, Allston served in the South Carolina Senate and then became the Senate president. His political career reached its peak when he became governor of South Carolina between 1856 and 1858. Doubtless, Allston had the ambition of seeing his son, Benjamin—the elder brother of Elizabeth Allston Pringle—follow in his footsteps and become both an equally successful rice planter and a state politician of national stature.[35]

Between 1849 and 1850, while Allston served in the South Carolina Senate in Columbia, Benjamin studied at West Point. Clearly, Benjamin's behavior at such a strict and prestigious school could have had an impact not just on the Allston family, but also on Robert Allston's personal reputation, especially given the fact that in his youth he had attended the same institution. As a consequence, a thick correspondence developed between Adele Petigru and Benjamin, one in which Adele—acting on behalf of her husband—filled her letters with recommendations on his behavior, such as, "I would have you so conduct yourself that anyone might be pleased to claim you as a relative." Adele also specifically returned time and again to the issue of fulfilling patriarchal expectations of obeying senior individuals in positions of authority—as in the case of West Point instructor Mr. Cotes—and even underlining the most important concepts in the text of her letters, so

34. Johnson, "Planters and Patriarchy," 56.

35. On Robert Allston, see William Dusinberre, *Them Dark Days: Slavery in the American Rice Swamps* (New York, 1996), 285–291; and Easterby, "Introduction," 11–19.

that Benjamin would not miss them: "you must now set in, in earnest to study, and I *beseech* you give Mr. Cotes no *cause* to complain of you, on the contrary deserve and gain his respect and esteem." Moreover, at times Adele reinforced her points also with references to the teachings of the established authority of the church: "I went to the church this morning, the upper church. Mr. Glennie gave an excellent sermon, impressing upon us the necessity of *obedience* as well as faith, obedience being the proof of our faith, the evidence of its being a living faith."[36]

Benjamin's position as the elder son in the Allston family put particular pressure on him; patriarchal expectations demanded a model behavior on his part, one that would lift him above the crowd and would allow him to become an honorable gentleman. To this end, his father was ready to resort to any means to instill in his son's mind the idea that his main preoccupation ought to be the acquisition of a gentlemanly behavior accompanied by respect for authority. Allston's means clearly included severe beatings, as the content of several of Adele's letters to Benjamin implied. In one letter in particular, Adele told Benjamin of rumors of disturbance at his school. She then reported Allston's reaction and his precise words to Benjamin, so that he could almost hear his own father make a chilling comment on his behavior: "When your father heard of it [the disturbance], he said 'I am very glad Ben had nothing to do with it. There is nothing I would flog him for so soon as resisting or insulting his teacher . . . I trust he has learnt his catechism to better purpose and that he is *incapable* of such an act.'"[37]

Clearly, Allston thought that he had successfully taught Benjamin the proper rules of behavior that fulfilled patriarchal expectations; Benjamin's impeccable conduct on this and other occasions testified to his father's success and honored the Allston family's reputation. Also, Robert Allston's insistence on Benjamin's behavior and on his respect for the family reputation sought to prepare his son for a future political career. Yet, after graduating from West Point in 1853, Benjamin Allston stayed in the army for four years. After that, he returned to follow his father's example and become a rice planter. However, in 1861, he received a commission in the Confederate

36. Adele Petigru Allston to Benjamin Allston, 6 August 1850; Adele Petigru Allston to Benjamin Allston, 4 January 1849; Adele Petigru Allston to Benjamin Allston, 14 December 1849, Robert F. W. Allston Papers, SCHS (original text underlined).

37. Adele Petigru Allston to Benjamin Allston, 3 January 1849, Robert F. W. Allston Papers, SCHS (original text underlined).

army and fought in the Civil War. After his return, Benjamin made a second attempt at becoming a rice planter, but he failed; disappointed, he turned to religious life and became an Episcopalian minister.[38]

There were several comparable features in the importance that aristocratic households in both the American South and the Italian *Mezzogiorno* attached to the family name; among them, a key element was the fact that, in both cases, the most significant reason for this particular behavior related first and foremost to the preservation of the family patrimony, rather than to abstract qualities. Southern Italian patriarchal noblemen acted according to a type of reasoning that Paolo Macry has termed "logic of the surname" (*logica del cognome*). The wills that Neapolitan aristocrats wrote in the first half of the nineteenth century revealed a constant worry about the dispersion of the family patrimony and a consequent constant attempt to link it from generation to generation to the family name. However, contrary to what happened in the American South, prestigious names such as Monteleone, Caracciolo, or Notarbartolo did not just identify an individual as a member of an ancient and still powerful aristocratic clan. In the *Mezzogiorno,* identification with a family of the titled aristocracy brought with it all the weight of a much older tradition of social prominence that related to a long history of ownership of former feudal land.[39]

According to Macry, "the strong link between surname and family patrimony" that began under the feudal system became, "in time, a strategic element in the preservation of a status whose social identity and source of income related to the ownership of extensive landed properties and family palaces." Southern Italian noblemen expected their sons to have a particular reverence toward traditions and know about their family's history and origins in relation to particular landed properties and palaces, but only to take minimal care of the administration of the family estates while preserving them intact. On the other hand, even more than American planters, southern Italian noblemen worried about the reputation of the family name and often instructed their sons to follow rules of behavior that related to patriarchal expectations of obedience and deference. Rather than being preeminently local politicians who only occasionally rose to national stature—as in the case of American planters—southern Italian noblemen often held

38. See Easterby, "Introduction," 14.
39. Macry, *Ottocento,* 5–81.

privileged posts in the Bourbon administration of the Kingdom of the Two Sicilies. Sometimes they were in charge of diplomatic missions or offices and, as a consequence, had frequent contact with the nobilities of other European countries. In this latter case, they put particular pressure on their sons' behavior so that they upheld both the national and international reputation of their family name.[40]

For example, Nicola Maresca descended from a prominent noble family of the Bourbon kingdom. The Marescas were dukes of Serracapriola in Capitanata, part of present-day Apulia; they were traditionally close to the Bourbon dynasty and covered important positions in the kingdom's administration. Nicola Maresca's father, Antonino Maresca, was the second duke in the line of succession and served as minister of King Ferdinand IV in Russia while also working as the Neapolitan ambassador in Vienna; Nicola's mother, Anna Wiasenski, was a Russian princess. Continuing the family tradition, Nicola began to work in the Neapolitan kingdom's administration and soon embarked on diplomatic missions. He entered the world of international diplomacy in 1811, when he was just twenty-one, as assistant minister at the court of Czar Alexander I, in St. Petersburg. Though Antonino's credentials guaranteed him the respect of every diplomat in Europe, Nicola still had to show that he could successfully follow in his father's footsteps and uphold the international reputation of the Maresca family name. He was well aware of the importance of his performances in international diplomacy and of its consequences for the family.[41]

One of Nicola's first diplomatic missions occurred in 1816, when he was one of the signers of the treaties that ratified the restoration of the Neapolitan Bourbon king as Ferdinand I and the creation of the Holy Alliance between the reactionary powers of post–Napoleonic Europe. On that occasion, Nicola's disappointment with the disrespectful behavior of other European diplomats caused him to write a long letter to his father in Naples. In that letter, Nicola voiced his frustration with the words "I am one of the King's Ministers, and not just a young man to despise." Then he acknowledged the position of respect which Antonino enjoyed and asked for his help: "I beg you to talk to the clerks in the chancery. . . . I think that in the letters

40. Macry, *Ottocento*, 24.

41. On the Maresca family, see Saverio Russo, "Agricoltura e pastorizia in Capitanata nella prima metà dell'Ottocento," in Angelo Massafra, ed., *Produzione, mercato e classi sociali nella Capitanata moderna e contemporanea* (Foggia, 1984), 295–308.

sent to me they should write my title of Assistant Minister . . . all this [his diplomatic mission] if I were not your son, would be constantly a reason for suspecting me." Since Nicola Maresca had followed his father Antonino's diplomatic career, his behavior in the European courts had a particular influence on the Maresca family's image and reputation. Yet, the real issue at stake was the fact that Antonino expected Nicola to follow closely in his footsteps and obey him, acknowledging his senior position until the time in which the son would be able to earn the same respect that the Maresca family had enjoyed during the father's own years of diplomatic activity.[42]

Doubtless, Nicola knew that his chances to earn respect for the Maresca family name and recognition as an accredited diplomat depended on his close study and repetition of Antonino's behavior in international meetings. Nicola worshipped Antonino, respected him, and loved him, but at the same time he probably envied him and wished to be as successful as his father in upholding the reputation of the Maresca family name. To achieve this aim, Nicola knew he had to follow a set of unwritten rules of conduct, the first of which implied that he ought to submit to Antonino's authority, as a son ought to submit to the father/head of the household in a family that followed patriarchal rules of behavior. Significantly, Nicola closed his letter with the words "I proclaim myself your most obedient and affectionate son for life"—an expression that showed that he acknowledged and was ready to abide by the patriarchal rules of conduct in family relations and, therefore, submit to his father' authority both within and outside the household.[43]

Eventually, Nicola became both a respected diplomat and an important public figure in the high echelons of the Bourbon administration. In 1822, after Antonino's death, he became the third duke of Serracapriola. Yet, by then, the Maresca had fallen out of the king's favor as a result of their role in the 1820 Neapolitan Revolution; not until 1839 would Ferdinand II restore Nicola's former privileges, asking him to join the Bourbon legation in Paris. Aside from a brief period in the Revolution of 1848—during which he served as prime minister in the Neapolitan constitutional government—throughout the 1840s and 1850s Nicola continued to cover important diplomatic positions. Even after the fall of the Kingdom of the Two Sicilies, he continued to be loyal to the Bourbons. Significantly, in an 1861 letter that King Francis II

42. Nicola Maresca to Antonino Maresca, 3/15 March 1816, Maresca Family Papers, ASN.
43. Nicola Maresca to Antonino Maresca, 3/15 March 1816, Maresca Family Papers, ASN.

sent to Nicola from Gaeta—where the Piedmontese troops were about to besiege the last contingent of the Bourbon army—the king referred to Nicola's "honored career" and to him in particular as "a loyal and faithful man."[44]

Families such as the Allstons and the Marescas—families in which patriarchal attitudes and rules of behavior were part of the daily life—kept in high esteem the respect with which society surrounded aristocratic clans. This respect was part of a system of values that identified men of property, and especially heads of elite families, with men of honor. Particularly in those elite families that clearly privileged the patriarchal ethos, the father's identification with a man of honor related to his role as head of the household and main bearer of the family name. After their father's death, the sons inherited both his position and his role. As a consequence, unwritten rules of aristocratic dignity conditioned the behavior of the sons and obliged them to earn respect so as to uphold the reputation of the family name. Originally, the reputation of the family name related to the family's historical claim to specific lands. The addition of the place where the family originally owned property to the family name—as in "Hammonds of Redcliffe" or "Lanza of Trabia"—indicated the family's inclusion into a class of established elite landowners. As a consequence, in both the American South and the Italian *Mezzogiorno*, elite landowners who followed patriarchal rules of behavior considered the preservation of original family properties a crucial matter and one strictly related to the continuation of the family's privileged role in society.

The link between the elite families' ownership of specific lands and their claims to privileged positions in society strongly suggests that both American planters and southern Italian landowners with patriarchal attitudes held similar views about social relations within the family and on the family's estates. The same emphasis on deference and obedience that led to detachment between fathers and sons also characterized relations between masters and laborers on the landed estates. Detachment often increased when masters delegated the management of their lands to overseers and agents. On one hand, delegation of management resulted from the fact that some of the wealthiest American planters and most of the largest southern Italian landowners owned property scattered in different regions. On the other hand,

44. Francis II to Nicola Maresca, 3 January 1861, Maresca Family Papers, ASN. On Nicola Maresca, see Carlo di Somma and Gaetano Fiorentino, "Cenni biografici," in Gaetano Fiorentino, ed., *Ricordi Napoletani. Uomini, scene, tradizioni antiche, 1850–1820* (Naples, 1991).

landowners' absenteeism was a widespread practice among large sections of the landowning elite—especially the aristocracy—in the *Mezzogiorno*, and among specific sections of the slaveholding elite—particularly the rice-growing planters—in the American South.[45]

Potentially, the practice of delegation of estate management to overseers and agents could increase the distance and detachment between masters and laborers to such an extent that it could almost create two separate worlds. This was especially the case when planters and landowners with patriarchal attitudes were neither interested in contact with their laborers nor in problems related to the management of workers' activities. In fact, in this case, both the lack of interest and the continuing reliance on overseers and agents led to a chronic problem of finding suitable individuals who could effectively substitute for the masters in the management of plantations and *latifondi*. And, to be sure, both American planters and southern Italian landowners counted on the help of their sons or of other members of the family to work for them as agents, rather than overseers. However, while most southern Italian landowners owned properties in different regions and were in constant need of local agents, only a few American planters had the same problem. In most cases, planters only needed overseers to manage their plantation—overseers whom they usually recruited among the local yeoman farmers. On the other hand, most southern Italian landowners who needed agents to take care of their scattered properties usually recruited them among the local landed proprietors. As a consequence, while overseers were the crucial individuals in the mechanism of plantation management, agents were the crucial individuals in the management of the *latifondo*.[46]

According to Peter Kolchin, increasingly in the nineteenth century overseers "belonged to a professional group who made their careers managing plantations." State agricultural societies attempted to transform overseers into a professional category, establishing clear guidelines for their performance and even offering prizes to those who followed them; yet, despite these efforts, dissatisfaction with the results of delegation of plantation management was widespread and most planters—especially those who were

---

45. On absenteeism, see John W. Blassingame, *The Slave Community: Plantation Life in the Antebellum South* (New York, 1979), 271–277; and Montroni, *Gli uomini del Re*, 79–93.

46. On plantation and latifondo management, see William K. Scarborough, *The Overseer: Plantation Management in the Old South* (Baton Rouge, La., 1966), 67–101; and Marta Petrusewicz, *Latifundium: Moral Economy and Material Life in a Nineteenth-Century Periphery* (Ann Arbor, Mich., 1996), 149–184.

absentee landlords—were constantly replacing overseers and looking for better ones. In comparison to plantation overseers, only few of the individuals who worked as agents (*amministratori*) in the landed estates of southern Italian absentee landowners were professionals. According to Giovanni Montroni, in most cases, southern Italian landowners chose their representatives from among "those categories of people who enjoyed prestige and authority in the local communities," such as local landed proprietors, members of the lesser nobility, or even priests. The southern Italian agent usually had to take care of several landed estates at the same time and select a number of collaborators who worked at specific tasks in the highly complex administrative system of the *latifondo*. As a consequence, his job was more difficult than the one of American agents and overseers, both of whom were usually in charge of only one plantation. Also for this reason, even more than among American planters, dissatisfaction over the results of delegation of land management was widespread among southern Italian landowners and led to the frequent replacing of agents among most elite families.[47]

Virginian Richard Baylor was among those American planters who employed both agents and overseers in the management of their estates. The Baylor family was originally from Essex County, Virginia. In the 1850s, Richard Baylor purchased Sandy Point plantation in Charles City County and employed his cousin Thomas Gregory Baylor to act as his agent. The correspondence that the two entertained between 1855 and 1858 illustrates some of the problems related to patriarchal ideas of management. The exchange shows that Richard Baylor had told his cousin to instruct the new overseer—Mr. Thomas Lipscomb—to use a firm hand with the slaves; yet, the overseer seems to have used threats and intimidations to mask his own incompetence at keeping discipline on the plantation. In the course of the three years, Thomas Gregory wrote frequently to Richard Baylor about slaves' complaints against Lipscomb. In an 1855 letter, he reported about a "most serious charge made against Mr. Lipscomb today by one of the servants." The charge showed how Lipscomb's use of serious intimidations in treating the workforce not only was completely unnecessary, but also led to a dangerous escalation in the slaves' violent reaction: "the Negro says he told Mr.

47. Kolchin, *American Slavery*, 103; Montroni, *Gli uomini del Re*, 92. See also Charles G. Steffen, "In Search of the Good Overseer: The Failure of the Agricultural Reform Movement in Low-country South Carolina, 1821–1834," *JSH* 63 (1997): 753–802; and Marco Armiero, "Tra proprietari e proprietà: gli agenti locali della famiglia Riario Sforza," *Meridiana* 20 (1994): 135–166.

L[ipscomb] he would kill him if he ever caught him engaged thus again." Yet, Richard Baylor's detached attitude toward problems of plantation management ensured that Lipscomb continued in his position. That fact gave Thomas Gregory much reason for frustration with his cousin: "several complaints of a similar character [of slaves against Lipscomb] have reached me in the past 6 months, but you said I had no business to listen to Negro lies."[48]

In subsequent letters, Thomas Gregory told Richard Baylor about his continuous efforts to maintain a calm attitude toward Lipscomb, despite the fact that the situation was already out of control. At the same time, Thomas Gregory continued to blame Lipscomb for his inability to control the slaves despite his continuous threats to use violence against them. In fact, the slaves responded to these threats by showing that they were perfectly conscious that the master was both distant and detached and that neither his agent nor his overseer could enforce his authority simply by threatening them, as the following excerpt from an 1856 letter written by Thomas Gregory shows: "Mr. Lipscomb upon taking the reins told the Negroes not to come to my house or he would flog them and soon after some one [*sic*] attempted to break my Big House."[49]

Two years later, in 1858, one of Richard Baylor's slaves—John Washington —escaped from Sandy Point and reached Thomas Gregory's house at Petersburg. Thomas Gregory asked his cousin to come and take him, but he received no answer, so he kept Washington with him for a while and put him to work. Meanwhile, the slave told Thomas Gregory that the reason for his escape was that "he would not live any longer with Mr. Lipscomb," apparently because Lipscomb had passed from simple threats to outright use of violence. Thomas Gregory noticed that "besides the fact that Mr. Lipscomb gives his wife and daughter no peace, he [Washington] is otherwise persecuted by Lipscomb," and yet—he continued—"Mr. L. could not take too much authority over him and make him do as he pleased. . . . John tells me they had him whipped for stealing a hog. I would much sooner have suspected L. than John from the knowledge I have of the two men." A week passed and Thomas Gregory still received no answer from Richard Baylor. Lipscomb,

48. Thomas Gregory Baylor to Richard Baylor, 16 December 1855, Baylor Family Papers, VHS. On Richard Baylor's Sandy Point estate, see also William K. Scarborough, *Masters of the Big House: Elite Slaveholders of the Mid-Nineteenth-Century South* (Baton Rouge, La., 2003), 138–139.

49. Thomas Gregory Baylor to Richard Baylor, 23 February 1856, Baylor Family Papers, VHS.

then, went to Petersburg to fetch Washington, but the slave had already fled from there.[50]

Clearly, Lipscomb's incompetence in disciplining the workforce and his clumsy attempts to hide it with intimidations and violence show that he was hardly suited for the job of overseer. Acting according to his duties, Thomas Gregory Baylor wrote Richard Baylor both about his own problems as agent and about the complaints that the slaves had about the overseer; yet, Richard Baylor never changed his attitude toward the management of his estate. Ironically, in January 1855, Lipscomb had signed Terms of Agreement according to which "he [the overseer] will faithfully, honestly and diligently apply himself and perform all the duties of a manager or overseer ... and faithfully obey all the reasonable wishes and commands of the said Richard Baylor." Yet, a letter from Lipscomb to Richard Baylor that accompanied this document shows that, already by November of the same year, the overseer had found reasons to complain—significantly, in very poor English—both about his pay and about his need of an assistant to do his job properly. Richard Baylor agreed with his requests, mainly to avoid possible troubles related to Lipscomb's management; yet, when troubles came nonetheless, he simply ignored them. Manifesting a clear patriarchal attitude toward plantation management, Richard Baylor preferred to have little to do with problems related to the supervision of his workforce. After he had delegated his authority to his agent and his overseer, he considered these problems their sole responsibility; yet, his detachment, silence, and absolute reliance on both contributed in creating even more problems in the relations between them and the slaves.[51]

Documents such as the Terms of Agreement between Richard Baylor and Thomas Lipscomb were fairly typical. The reason why they did not include specific instructions was that several slaveholders considered it a waste of time to write detailed contracts with particular clauses since, very often, overseers had no intention of abiding by the rules. For example, in 1822, Robert Allston's aunt Blythe drafted and signed very simple and straightforward Terms of Agreement with her new overseer, William T. Thompson, terms according to which he took the charge of two of her rice plantations.

50. Thomas Gregory Baylor to Richard Baylor, 7 July 1858; Thomas Gregory Baylor to Richard Baylor, 14 July 1858, Baylor Family Papers, VHS.

51. Terms of Agreement between Thomas P. Lipscomb and Richard Baylor, attached to Thomas P. Lipscomb to Richard Baylor, 6 November 1855, Baylor Family Papers, VHS.

Yet, Thompson failed to comply with the contract and in particular violated "the clause forbidding him to keep for himself more than two cows and two calves."[52]

To be sure, the basic duties of overseers were similar on every plantation: aside from the activities related to the business of producing and selling staple crops, they included taking care of the food provisions and managing the workforce. At the very least, overseers ought to periodically inspect the food storage to prevent stealing and ought to keep discipline among the slaves, using the whip when necessary. Yet, even if they were on average more competent than Thomas Lipscomb, overseers and agents working on absentee-owned plantations felt additional pressure because planters left them in charge of all the tasks related to plantation management and often gave them little or no advice when problems arose. Effectively, they often represented the authority of distant and detached masters. In turn, distance and detachment created additional problems when absentee planters followed patriarchal rules of behavior, as Richard Baylor clearly did. In this case, planters demanded that their agent and overseer enforce the master's authority with whatever measures they deemed necessary, as long as they were able to discipline the workforce on their own—a policy which, clearly, created additional problems.[53]

The detached attitude of absentee planters who followed patriarchal rules of behavior found a parallel in the carelessness that several southern Italian landowners—especially noblemen—showed toward the absentee management of their *latifondi*. Most of southern Italy's large landowners had agents who took care of their family estates. Yet, aside from the fact that some agents acted more professionally than others, the relationship between landlord and agent varied a great deal and depended almost exclusively on the landowner's attitude toward his properties and the workers. The letters that

52. Easterby, ed., *South Carolina Rice Plantation*, 22.

53. For a more elaborate overseer contract, see "Rules on the Rice Estate of Plowden C. Weston, South Carolina (1846)," in Rick Halpern and Enrico Dal Lago, eds., *Slavery and Emancipation* (Malden, Mass., 2002), 210–212. See also John S. Bassett, "The Duties of the Overseer," in John S. Bassett, ed., *The Southern Plantation Overseer as Revealed in His Letters* (Northampton, Mass., 1925), 15–16; Scarborough, *Overseer*, 20–50; and James O. Breeden, ed., *Advice among Masters: The Ideal in Slave Management in the Old South* (Westport, Conn., 1980), 291–304.

Filippo Muscianisi wrote to Michele Spadafora, marquis of Policastrello, in the 1840s and 1850s are a fairly typical example of exchange between an agent and an absentee landowner in southern Italy. Muscianisi acted as Spadafora's agent on the landed estate of Spadafora S. Pietro, one of several properties with extensive *latifondi* that this prestigious noble family owned in northeastern Sicily. In particular, the Spadafora S. Pietro property included several lands in which the marquis engaged in the production of wine and olive oil. Muscianisi wrote him frequent and detailed letters informing him periodically about the conditions of both the wine grapes and the olives. Yet, Spadafora often delayed his replies.[54]

In an 1855 letter, which Muscianisi wrote after a particularly long period without reply, he let Spadafora know that "I am extremely worried because I have not received a letter from you with the last mail." The truth was that, in this particular instance, Muscianisi needed Spadafora's help and advice on problems of workers' management. In the postscript to the same letter, Muscianisi explained that Spadafora's instructions to lower the cost of the olives that the tenants (*coloni*) were to collect for the following year had provoked their reaction. The tenants refused to comply with provisions that the last contract (*patto colonico*) between them and Spadafora did not include. Understandably, Muscianisi asked for further instruction on how to proceed; yet, Spadafora's delay in replying only confirmed that Muscianisi had to try and resolve the problem on his own.[55]

In a previous letter, Muscianisi had mentioned the fact that Spadafora and the overseers of his estate had different views from the tenants on the use of the surplus wine that the estate produced. Significantly, Muscianisi praised the firm hand of the field guard (*campiere*) in keeping discipline among the workers: "for your knowledge, I wish to let you know that the *campiere* Todaro from San Domenico [another Spadafora estate] has so far been very strong in carrying out his duty, and there is nothing to say against him." In fact, from Muscianisi's letters, it emerges that the *campiere* was crucial in the administration of absentee-owned family estates such as Spadafora S. Pietro, because he helped to keep a tight control over the workforce, especially in cases of labor protest. On a few occasions, a *campiere*

54. For a detailed study of Sicilian aristocratic families' management of *latifondi* in the previous century, see Marcello Verga, *La Sicilia dei grani. Gestione dei feudi e cultura economica fra Sei e Settecento* (Florence, 1993), 59–106.

55. Filippo Muscianisi to Michele Spadafora, 26 November 1855, Spadafora Family Papers, ASP.

wrote directly to Spadafora and, in extremely deferential terms, explained to the marquis the role that he played in the administration of the estates. In an 1845 letter from San Domenico, *campiere* Giuseppe Milici addressed Spadafora as "Excellency" and "Master" and called himself "an old servant of yours." Then, professing his loyalty to the marquis, he assured him, "on my conscience, that no tenant, out of the old and natural subjects of Your Excellency . . . has ever damaged either an olive tree or any other property of Your Excellency that has been placed under my guard." Spadafora never replied to any of Giuseppe Milici's letters. Aristocratic upbringing, combined with a detached attitude toward absentee landownership, led the marquis to act according to patriarchal rules of behavior. Similar to Richard Baylor, Spadafora demanded deference from both his workers and his dependents, but he could not bother to be interested in their lives or deal with their problems.[56]

Just as American slaves could appeal directly to the planter in case of misconduct on the part of the overseer, southern Italian tenants could send petitions (*suppliche*) directly to the landlord. These petitions were originally appeals to the feudal lord against abuse of power in the conduct of his landed estate, and they maintained a similar function even after the abolition of feudalism. Yet, on the landed estates that belonged to the Spadafora family, only in a few cases did tenants send petitions directly to the marquis.[57]

In 1849, Francesco Calapriste signed as "Your Humble Tenant" a collective letter that addressed the problems of poor administration and work exploitation in San Domenico, the estate where Giuseppe Milici was *campiere*. Writing in very poor Italian, Calapriste told Spadafora of the abuse that "us poor tenants" had suffered at the hands of the agent, who had paid them very little for the oil they had produced, and of the subsequent relief which the marquis's instructions, telling the agent to raise their pay, had brought them: "Excellency, we can see that the hand of the Lord has reached us already through your agent, since the principle that us tenants can have a fair return for our efforts and therefore not be robbed has been understood."

56. Filippo Muscianisi to Michele Spadafora, 17 September 1855; Giuseppe Milici to Michele Spadafora, 24 October 1845, Spadafora Family Papers, ASP. On Sicilian campieri, see Blok, *Mafia of a Sicilian Village*, 61.

57. On slaves' appeals, see Peter Kolchin, *Unfree Labor: American Slavery and Russian Serfdom* (Cambridge, Mass., 1987), 275–277. On peasants' exploitation and *latifondo* absentee management, see Domenico Demarco, *Il crollo del Regno delle due Sicilie. La struttura sociale* (Naples, 1960), 123–133; and Orazio Cancila, *Gabellotti e contadini in un comune rurale della Sicilia (secoli XVIII–XIX)* (Caltanissetta-Rome, 1974).

Though in this case he had directly intervened, Spadafora never replied to Francesco Calapriste, both because he wished to keep a detached attitude toward the tenants' problems and also because he had, doubtless, given new instructions to his agent more to avoid further trouble with his workers than out of genuine interest for their conditions.[58]

To be sure, in both the Italian *Mezzogiorno* and the American South, the combination of absentee landownership with patriarchal attitudes led to an increase in the practice of workers' exploitation. Agents and overseers alike felt as if they had very little control over the workforce and, as a consequence, forced the workers to respect the authority of their absentee landlord through harsh management and the threat of violence. Though hardly comparable to the fear induced by routine punishments on American plantations, the threat of violence played an important role on several southern Italian landed estates. Two letters that Mario Cristofano—who was agent on the Calabrian estate of Bulgarano in 1835—wrote to Silvio Bonanno, prince of Linguaglossa, shed light on the role of violence in the absentee administration of the *latifondo*. Apparently, at Bulgarano some *coloni* were in the habit of robbing the Bonanno estate of its grain and barley provisions. Cristofano, then, decided to place "together with Turrisi [the overseer, or *soprastante*] during harvesting time . . . two more, or even three mounted *campieri*, who would patrol the threshing floors in the night, causing some terror."[59]

Yet, this measure turned out to be insufficient and, less than two months later, Cristofano decided to hire an adjunct overseer, "Don Gaetano Di Maura, a very honorable person, knowledgeable about the countryside and used to handle all kinds of arms." These letters show how—comparable to what happened on American plantations—on southern Italian absentee-owned estates agents and overseers used the threat of violence to maintain law and order, while they also hired *campieri* for the specific purpose of disciplining the workforce. At the same time, the *campieri* also clearly policed and controlled the activities of workers after hours, providing a sort of night watch, similar to slave patrols in the plantation districts. Arguably, on both absentee-owned American plantations and southern Italian landed estates, the employment of harsh security measures and the frequency of either violent punishments or their threat was a result of the agents' and overseers' efforts

58. Francesco Calapriste to Michele Spadafora, 23 October 1849, Spadafora Family Papers, ASP.

59. Mario Cristofano to the prince of Linguaglossa, 29 May 1835, Linguaglossa Familiy Papers, ASP.

at enforcing the authority of absentee proprietors who were both physically and psychologically removed from management problems.[60]

In general, in both the American South and the Italian *Mezzogiorno,* patriarchal attitudes were a vestige of the eighteenth-century world. The deference and obedience that characterized those elite families in which the heads of the household imposed patriarchal rules of behavior on their wives and children were increasingly at odds with nineteenth-century values and expectations. The rigidity of social roles, which the members of the landed elites who adopted the patriarchal ethos considered fixed and immutable in regard to both relations within their households and relations with the workforce on their landed estates, found a growing challenge in the ideas of equality and reciprocity which were the offspring of nineteenth-century liberalism. At the same time, the aristocratic disdain that caused several absentee American planters and southern Italian landowners to maintain a clear distance between themselves and the workers on their landed estates was increasingly at odds with the bourgeois economic and social values of the "age of capital." These values stressed the importance of rationalization of production through direct, as opposed to absentee, management and of contractual relations with the workforce, as opposed to enforcement of discipline, on plantations and *latifondi*. In turn, the adoption of such values questioned the economic and social viability of attitudes and behaviors that related to the patriarchal ethos, and also challenged the strength of adaptation of eighteenth-century aristocratic ideas to the rapidly changing nineteenth-century world.[61]

Family, Paternalism, and Reciprocity

Several American and Italian historians have noticed that, between the end of the eighteenth and the beginning of the nineteenth centuries, patriarchal ideology underwent profound changes in both the American South and the Italian *Mezzogiorno*. Family relations became more egalitarian and sentimental, as opposed to authoritarian, while a more humanitarian approach characterized relations between masters and laborers. A new ethos—paternalism

60. Mario Cristofano to the prince of Linguaglossa, 15 July 1835, Linguaglossa Family Papers, ASP. On slave patrols, see Sally E. Hadden, *Slave Patrols: Law and Violence in Virginia and the Carolinas* (Cambridge, Mass., 2001).

61. See Eric J. Hobsbawm, *The Age of Capital, 1848–1875* (London, 1975).

—stressed the importance of reciprocal relations in the interaction between the father/master and his subjects both within the family and in society. Heads of households based their relationships with their wives and children on the recognition of the needs of both and on reciprocal trust and affection. Masters based their relationships with the workers on the recognition of reciprocal rights and duties that both ought to observe and respect.[62]

During the course of the nineteenth century, within the two specific patriarchal-paternalistic worldviews that characterized the minds of the elites of the American South and the Italian *Mezzogiorno,* paternalistic attitudes and behaviors, with their emphasis on reciprocal relations rather than on implicit recognition of authority, became increasingly commonplace among many prominent families. Several of these families belonged to the progressive sections of the two landed elites. Progressive American planters and progressive southern Italian landowners shared a similar disdain for deference and hierarchy and, at the same time, had comparable capitalistic concerns that focused on the efficiency of their workforce and the productivity of their landed estates. In fact, referring to the American planters' adoption of attitudes related to the paternalistic ethos and to their concurrent capitalist concerns, Robert Fogel and Stanley Engerman have argued that "paternalism is not intrinsically antagonistic to capitalist enterprise . . . [it] may actually raise profits by inducing labor to be more efficient than it would have been under a less benevolent management. There is no reason to rule out the possibility that paternalism operated this way for slaveowners."[63]

For her part, Marta Petrusewicz has linked directly her analysis of the southern Italian *latifondo* as a "rational and efficient system of production

62. On the American South, see Rhys Isaac, *The Transformation of Virginia, 1740–1790* (Chapel Hill, N.C., 1982), 308–310; Bardaglio, *Reconstructing the Household,* 23–24; Morgan, *Slave Counterpoint,* 284–296; Jan Lewis, "The Problem of Slavery in Southern Political Discourse," in David T. Konig, ed., *Devising Liberty: Preserving and Creating Freedom in the New American Republic* (Stanford, Calif., 1995), 283–297; and Willie Lee Rose, "The Domestication of Domestic Slavery," in William W. Freehling, ed., *Slavery and Freedom* (New York, 1976), 18–36. On the *Mezzogiorno,* see Valeria Del Vasto, *Baroni nel tempo. I Tocco di Montemiletto dal XVI al XVIII secolo* (Naples, 1995), 69–70; Barbagli, *Sotto lo stesso tetto,* 359–363; Macry, *Ottocento,* 10–11; and Aurelio Lepre, "Azienda feudale ed azienda agraria nel Mezzogiorno continentale fra Cinquecento e Ottocento," in Angelo Massafra, ed., *Problemi di storia delle campagne meridionali nell'eta moderna e contemporanea* (Bari, 1981), 27–40.

63. Robert W. Fogel and Stanley L. Engerman, *Time on the Cross: The Economics of American Negro Slavery* (New York, 1974), 73. For a critical view, see Peter Kolchin, *A Sphinx on the American Land: The Nineteenth-Century South in Comparative Perspective* (Baton Rouge, La., 2003), 25–29.

and a stable and livable form of social organization" to Fogel and Engerman's work and has claimed that rationality and efficiency were characteristics of "such systems in the peripheral areas of the world economy, especially outside Europe." Both efficiency and rationality were needed in order to achieve the capitalist goal of maximization of production; and arguably, both loomed large in the ideas and practices of management of American slaveholders and southern Italian landowners who privileged the paternalistic ethos. Progressive members of both elites sought to achieve their aim through a partial recognition of the workers' needs. In their minds, such recognition eventually would guarantee peace and stability in labor relations.[64]

In general terms, the goal of those members of the two elites who adopted paternalistic attitudes was to seek from—as opposed to force upon—both workers and members of the family the acceptance of a social order that continued to acknowledge the privileged positions of the masters/heads of households. To this end, while within the family fathers ought to be prepared to recognize their duties toward their wives and children, in society members of the upper classes ought, at the very least, to acknowledge the needs of members of the lower classes. Consequently, a certain degree of affection characterized paternalistic relations between heads of households and their wives and children, while a sort of masked benevolence characterized paternalistic relations between both slaveholders and landowners and the workers on their landed estates. In fact, referring to the ambivalent nature of paternalistic relations in the American South in comparison to other areas of the world, Eugene Genovese has written that "southern paternalism, like every other paternalism . . . grew out of the necessity to discipline and morally justify a system of exploitation. It encouraged kindness and affection, but it simultaneously encouraged cruelty and hatred."[65]

In both the American South and the Italian *Mezzogiorno*, the adoption of paternalistic attitudes in elite families went hand in hand with the spread of ideas about the importance of affection and intimacy in family life. According to these ideas, family life ought to focus on feelings and emotional attachment, rather than on respect for authority and fixed roles. Doubtless, Tocqueville had a similar model in mind when he wrote about the "democratic family" in *Democracy in America*. In fact, he described it as

64. Petrusewicz, *Latifundium*, 4. For a critical view, see Paolo Macry, "Studi recenti sul Mezzogiorno ottocentesco," in Paolo Macry and Angelo Massafra, eds., *Fra storia e storiografia. Studi in onore di Pasquale Villani* (Bologna, 1994), 151–162.

65. Genovese, *Roll, Jordan, Roll*, 4.

one in which "the father exercises no other power than that which is granted to the affection and the experience of the age; his orders would perhaps be disobeyed, but his advice is for the most part authoritative." Linking his analysis of the family to the analysis of democratic institutions, Tocqueville went on to say that "in democratic countries . . . the language addressed by a son to his father is always marked by mingled freedom, familiarity, and affection, which at once show that new relations have sprung up in the bosom of the family"; for this reason, "under democratic laws, all the children are perfectly equal . . . as no peculiar privileges distinguish or divide them."[66]

As in Tocqueville's description of the "democratic family," in the model of the affectionate family that related to the spread of paternalistic attitudes, relations between fathers and children occurred largely on an egalitarian and reciprocal basis. This particular feature showed in the family letters, which, also according to Tocqueville, had very little sign of the formality that characterized correspondence among aristocratic families, or families that privileged the patriarchal ethos. Therefore, in both the American South and the Italian *Mezzogiorno,* the adoption of paternalistic attitudes in family relations led to important changes in the daily life of elite households—changes that related to the acknowledgment of the necessity of balanced and reciprocal relations between the head of the household and his wife and children. Within the family, then, reciprocity combined with an emphasis on emotional support and trust—as opposed to authority and discipline—in the relations between husbands and wives and between fathers and children.[67]

In the American South, planters who privileged the paternalistic ethos showed their sons that they had confidence in them and that they trusted their sense of responsibility and duty. Since relations between parents and children focused increasingly on the importance of reciprocal relations rather than respect for authority, fathers gave advice to their sons about their behavior, but they did not expect them to comply automatically with their own standards. Consequently, planters with paternalistic attitudes often had close and affectionate relationships with their children, they wrote frequent letters,

66. Tocqueville, *Democracy in America,* part 2, 195–197.

67. On the American South, see Jan Lewis, *The Pursuit of Happiness: Family and Values in Jefferson's Virginia* (New York, 1983); and Jane Turner Censer, *North Carolina Planters and Their Children, 1800–1860* (Baton Rouge, La., 1984). For Italy, see Barbagli, *Sotto lo stesso tetto,* 325–374; and Filippo Mazzonis, "Premessa," in Filippo Mazzonis, ed., *Percorsi e modelli familiari in Italia tra '700 e '900* (Bologna, 1997), 9–12.

they replied often, and they showed a genuine concern for their problems, especially when their sons lived or studied away from home.[68]

The correspondence that Virginian planter Thomas Lanier Spragins entertained with his sons, Fayette, Thomas, and Leonidas, illustrates the above points particularly well. Originally from Halifax County, Virginia, Spragins owned several plantations on which, in addition to growing tobacco, he experimented with the cultivation of wheat, corn, and other types of grain. In the 1830s, Spragins's sons Fayette and Thomas studied at Princeton University, in New Jersey. In an 1839 letter that he wrote to both of them, Spragins explained that he had sent his sons to Princeton to have the education they needed in order to return and start their own business in the South, "where there will be more avenues to promotion and aggrandizement for the young and enterprising than in the northern states." In other words, Spragins wished to help his sons to become southern entrepreneurs; he was a progressive planter, who, in addition to being committed to agricultural innovation and reform, was convinced that the southern agrarian economy was potentially stronger than the northern one.[69]

Between 1832 and 1839, Spragins wrote frequent letters to his sons at Princeton. Their exchange shows that their relationship was informal and affectionate and that they shared a mutual trust, at the roots of which lay a respect for their reciprocal rights and duties. Typically, Spragins addressed Fayette and Thomas with the affectionate expression "dear sons." He usually began his letters to them with an account of the interest and delight that he had gained from reading their last letter and with his reassurance to them that he eagerly looked forward to receiving their next one. Often, Spragins wrote about "the pleasure of receiving letters" from his children; apparently, he liked receiving them frequently and he gained special pleasure when he did not expect them.[70]

68. See Rose, *Victorian America*, 168–169; Joan E. Cashin, "The Structure of Antebellum Planter Families: 'The Ties That Bound Us Was Strong,'" *JSH* 56 (1990): 55–70; and Censer, *North Carolina Planters*, 20–65. See also Wylma Wates, "Precursor to the Victorian Age: The Concept of Marriage and Family as Revealed in the Correspondence of the Izard Family of South Carolina," in Carol Bleser, ed., *In Joy and in Sorrow: Women, Family, and Marriage in the Victorian South* (New York, 1991), 3–14.

69. Thomas Lanier Spragins to Fayette and Thomas Spragins, 3 August 1839, Spragins Family Papers, VHS.

70. Thomas Lanier Spragins to Fayette and Thomas Spragins, 5 September 1832; Thomas Lanier Spragins to Fayette and Thomas Spragins, 5 September 1839, Spragins Family Papers, VHS.

In the same letter in which he explained to his sons the reasons for sending them to Princeton, Spragins also defined his ideas about reciprocal relations within the family. First, he reminded Fayette and Thomas of their obligation to perform well at such a prestigious school, and then he encapsulated in a simple but effective phrase the nature of reciprocity: "my sons . . . recollect that your opportunities have been and will be good for improvement and distinction . . . 'when much is given, much is required.'" In elite families such as the Spragins—which clearly followed paternalistic rules of behavior—mutual agreement between fathers and sons defined the nature of their reciprocal rights and duties and the correct way to respect them. In the case of Spragins's sons, in return for the fact that their father had provided them with educational opportunities, they ought to fulfill their moral obligation by honoring the family with high grades at school.[71]

Still in the same letter, Spragins also revealed his ideas on morality and gave his sons advice about correct behavior: "you have now arrived to an age and a crisis at which it requires great moral courage and extraordinary fortitude to sustain you . . . the force of example is very great and the force of habit is more so, hence the importance of correct habit in early life." To further clarify his point, Spragins discussed the effects of a son's bad behavior and explained that the son caused his father enormous grief because he broke a previously established bond of reciprocal moral obligations: "how painful [it] must be to a tender parent to have sons at school spending the hard earnings of their affectionate father in idleness and dissipation; a reverse of conduct how pleasing and delightful."[72]

The latter point was one on which Spragins routinely insisted in his correspondence. When he gave his sons specific advice, he asked them to control their habits and to not indulge in dissipation and idleness. In fact, he spent a great deal of time reminding his sons that their choices in conducting their lives influenced their ability to fulfill their moral obligations toward their "tender parent." He wrote his three sons separately on this particular issue, so as to make his point absolutely clear. Spragins was particularly concerned about his youngest son, Leonidas, who lived at the Rockingham family estate, in Virginia. In a letter he wrote to him in 1839, Spragins warned him

71. Thomas Lanier Spragins to Fayette and Thomas Spragins, 3 August 1839, Spragins Family Papers, VHS.

72. Thomas Lanier Spragins to Fayette and Thomas Spragins, 3 August 1839, Spragins Family Papers, VHS.

about the danger of underestimating the importance of the moral obligations which bound him to be a model student: "be exemplary in all of your
conduct, permit not the immoral and wicked boys to lead you astray, but be
studious and pursue the path of rectitude and do nothing which you will
afterwards be ashamed of, keep good company and recollect the old adage
'evil communication corrupts good manners.'" As Spragins's case shows,
morality was a central concern for planters who privileged the paternalistic
ethos. Since affection and reciprocal obligations—rather than authority—
bound parents and children, a father expected his children to show enough
common sense to comply with the family's moral standards, but he could
not force them to follow them. As a consequence, a father's advice sought to
cause his son to reflect upon his need to maintain high moral standards so
as to reciprocate his parent's moral obligation toward him and also preserve
the honor of the family.[73]

Yet, even though respect for reciprocal moral obligations, rather than
obedience to authority, characterized relations between parents and children
in elite families that followed paternalistic rules of behavior, intimacy and
affection were not as common in the correspondence between American
planters and their sons as the Spragins example suggests. In fact, according
to Steven Stowe, often, while children wrote parents about experiences of
"intimacy" and "enjoyment of emotional closeness" in the closed society of
the college where they studied, parents routinely wrote their replies to them
elaborating upon "themes of authority, stressing the academy as a means to
moral ends and practical achievements." This might very well be an indication
of the fact that, according to Jane Turner Censer, "planters did not mind-
lessly relinquish power. Rather, they came to express authority differently," as
part of a reciprocal exchange of obligations. In return for their parents' care,
children ought to show that they had received and internalized the parents'
moral standards and the related values of hard work and self-control. Only
then would planters show their willingness to listen to their children and
acknowledge their needs. Then, "a blend of respect for adolescents' and young
adults' wishes and affection characterized parent-child interaction in planter
families," as the case of the Spragins family shows.[74]

73. Thomas Lanier Spragins to Leonidas Spragins, 19 September 1839, Spragins Family
Papers, VHS

74. Steven Stowe, *Intimacy and Power in the Old South: Rituals in the Lives of the Planters*
(Baltimore, Md., 1987), 154–155; Censer, *North Carolina Planters*, 60, 64.

The planter families' adoption of attitudes related to the paternalistic ethos had particularly far-reaching consequences in the realm of gender relations within the household. Though women's roles continued to suffer from a clear subordination to the rules of a male-dominated society—especially in legal matters—the spread of ideas on the importance of affection and mutual understanding in the family contributed a great deal to cast in a better light relations between husbands and wives and between fathers and daughters. Plantation mistresses and planters' daughters who belonged to elite families that privileged the paternalistic ethos wrote numerous letters and diaries in which they showed that they shared a previously unknown degree of intimacy and affection with the head of the household. For their part, planters behaved purposefully, combining the emphasis on affection with the respect for the rights and duties of reciprocal relations, which was at the root of paternalistic ideology, so as to mask the existence of male domination in gender relations within the household. In so doing, they gained the confidence and trust of the female members of the family. As husbands, planters showed their acquiescence in sharing feelings with their wives; as brothers, they showed their willingness to communicate with their sisters; and as fathers, they showed their eagerness to listen to their daughters. Yet, in the process—as Elizabeth Fox-Genovese has noted—"the beneficent paternalism of the father was ever overshadowed by the power of the master, just as the power of the master was tempered by the beneficent paternalism of the father."[75]

With the planters' adoption of attitudes related to the paternalistic ethos, relations between fathers and daughters became particularly delicate. The emphasis on reciprocity and egalitarian relations within the family implied that fathers ought to treat their sons and daughters equally. Consequently, planters who chose to privilege the paternalistic ethos gave equal importance to the feelings and wishes of all their children, while at the same time giving particular attention to their daughters' need for affection. In fact, according to Steven Stowe, several planters "encouraged both sons and daughters" to write them often; yet, the letters that planters wrote their daughters focused specifically on their emotional fulfillment "in an intimate fashion most parents did not use with boys." For example, reassuring his daughter, Elizabeth, of his willingness to listen to her, South Carolinian planter John Richardson

75. Fox-Genovese, *Plantation Household*, 101.

encouraged her to trust him with the words "yes! My Dear Girl! These are subjects that can never become uninteresting or viewed with indifference by your tender Father."[76]

And yet, the planters' attention to their daughters' need for emotional fulfillment was part of a conscious manipulation of their feelings aimed at diverting their attention from the real issue of power unbalance within the household. Though they were very careful not to impose their will upon their children, through their adoption of paternalistic ideas on reciprocal family relations, planters successfully masked the extent to which their daughters continued to have little room for independent action. Similar to planters who showed a preference for patriarchal attitudes, planters who showed a preference for paternalistic attitudes worried about affecting their daughters' lives and aimed at influencing their decisions especially in matters related to courtship and marriage. Yet, the paternalistic planter's was a more subtle type of control, one that focused on the psychological effects of the discourse of reciprocity, as in the case of relations between fathers and sons. A father expected her daughter to return his efforts to provide her with emotional support and treat her on equal terms with his sons by manifesting through her particular behavior her will to accept the rules of a male-dominated society. In fact, the real principles that regulated relations between planters with paternalistic attitudes and their daughters continued to relate to the particular expectations regarding the female gender in the white slaveholding South—a culture in which social ideas of femininity demanded that girls trained to become future wives and mothers and that women's roles identified with those of keepers of the household. As Elizabeth Fox-Genovese has remarked, though "southerners borrowed from the interlocking discourses of companionate marriage, motherhood, and domesticity," above all "they emphasized women's obligation to manifest purity, chastity, and obedience, and cultivate their special calling for motherhood."[77]

Building on this powerfully evocative social model, planters who embraced the paternalistic ethos successfully constructed a gender culture that emphasized women's roles as wives and mothers and justified its characteristics

76. John P. Richardson to Elizabeth Richardson, 9 March 1809, quoted in Stowe, *Intimacy and Power*, 148.

77. Fox-Genovese, *Plantation Household*, 200–205. See also McMillen, *Southern Women*, 9–10.

not as parts of a fixed and immutable social system, but as elements of the proper sphere of women's activity, a private sphere in which they could find sentimental fulfillment. At the same time, relying on the reciprocal model of family relations, planters claimed that, in return for women's acceptance of the South's male-dominated social order, they offered protection to their wives and daughters—according to Drew Faust—"from threats posed by the slave system upon which white male power rested." As a consequence, the daughters and wives of planters who privileged the paternalistic ethos tended to accept an inequity in gender relations that they had come to rationalize as part of a system of reciprocal rights and duties, a system which gave them a reason to abide to what Joan Cashin has called a "culture of resignation."[78]

Illuminating in this respect is the case of the relationship between North Carolinian William Gaston and his eldest daughter, Susan. A prominent member of the planter class, Gaston served as judge in the North Carolina State Supreme Court and was the owner a large family house in Newbern and of a two thousand–acre plantation at Brice Creek, both in North Carolina. In 1819, Gaston's third wife died as a result of childbirth complications, following the same destiny of the previous two and leaving him with five children to raise on his own. Determined not to marry again, Gaston set out to raise his children with the help of Susan and his son Alexander. Later, he sent both of them to Philadelphia to complete their studies.[79]

Between 1822 and 1823, while Susan was at Philadelphia, Gaston kept a tight control over her behavior and made a serious attempt to influence her mind with the help of his friend Joseph Hopkinson, at whose house his daughter lived. Gaston had definite ideas on the type of woman he wished his daughter to become and masked with fatherly attention his concern for her ability to fulfill her social role. In the words of Steven Stowe, "[Gaston's] thoughts on care for her easily expanded into suggestions on carefulness

78. Drew G. Faust, *Southern Stories: Slaveholders in Peace and War* (Columbia, Mo., 1992), 127. See also Joan E. Cashin, "Introduction: Culture of Resignation," in Joan E. Cashin, ed., *Our Common Affairs: Texts from Women in the Old South* (Baltimore, Md., 1997), 1–42; Fox-Genovese, *Plantation Household*, 64–65; Rose, *Victorian America*, 145–192; and Jane E. Friedman, *The Enclosed Garden: Women and Community in the Evangelical South, 1830–1900* (Chapel Hill, N.C., 1985). On women's life beyond the household, see Cynthia A. Kierner, *Beyond the Household. Women's Place in the Early South, 1700–1835* (Ithaca, N.Y., 1998); and Elizabeth Varon, *We Mean to Be Counted: White Women and Politics in Antebellum Virginia* (Chapel Hill, N.C., 1998).

79. Stowe, *Intimacy and Power*, 166–167.

for the womanhood she embodied." As time passed, Gaston increasingly "expressed his strict standards for her in such reasonable words of love and duty that their very impersonality became the mark of true parental care." Gaston revealed the strictness of the behavioral standard he had in mind for his daughter in an 1823 letter to Hopkinson, in which he wrote that "when a girl sees much society her mind is liable to become dissipated . . . and she is too apt to fancy herself a woman."[80]

In 1826, after Susan returned to the family house in Newbern, Gaston entrusted her with the task of raising her younger brothers and sisters, while also taking care of the management of the household slaves; it was almost as if she were training to become a future plantation mistress. And, to be sure, by this time Susan's ideas about womanhood and Gaston's ideas about her daughter's fulfillment of her gender role coincided on several points. Soon afterward, Susan began to receive the courtship of potential suitors; in her letters, she dutifully reported the details of every marriage proposal to her father. In one of his replies to Susan, Gaston appeared particularly keen to clarify that he did not aim to control her decisions in matters of courtship, but rather to offer her his parental advice, his "best counsel (when asked) and my tenderest sympathy." Yet, according to Steven Stowe, Gaston's insistence on advising Susan showed how "in such ways was the authority of the father clothed in loving selflessness."[81]

Then, in 1827, Susan became engaged to lawyer Robert Donaldson and she wrote her father about her wish to marry him. Soon after, Gaston sent Donaldson a letter in which he wrote that he approved of their union. In the same letter, Gaston also clarified his ideas about the reciprocal obligations and duties that lay at the heart of his paternalistic relation with his daughter. First, Gaston let Donaldson know about the deep attachment he felt toward his daughter and about how "in consenting to the union with my child I feel that I am about to bestow a gift the value of which none can know so well as myself. She has long been the pride, the joy, the solace of my heart." Then, Gaston wrote a wish which he clearly intended also as a statement and which encapsulated and explained the nature of Susan's roles as his daughter and as Donaldson's wife: "God grant that she may discharge

---

80. Stowe, *Intimacy and Power,* 171, 173; William Gaston to Joseph Hopkinson, 4 January 1823, quoted in Stowe, *Intimacy and Power,* 172.

81. William Gaston to Susan Gaston, 2 October 1826, quoted in Stowe, *Intimacy and Power,* 174.

the duties which she may owe to you with the same unequalled, inimitable excellence which has characterized her in the performance of those that were due to her Father!"[82]

Gaston's wish to Donaldson was a masterpiece of ideological rhetoric, and it perfectly synthesized the essence of the particular features of reciprocity that bound both father and daughter and husband and wife in paternalistic relations. Gaston told Donaldson that Susan had discharged her duties toward her father honoring the reciprocal relation that bound the two of them. At the same time, he clarified to Donaldson that he expected his daughter to behave in the same way toward him once they were married. Susan ought to have an equally reciprocal relation with her husband and discharge her obligations in exchange for the fact that he provided for her welfare, protection, and emotional fulfillment. Gaston's description of Susan as "the pride, the joy, the solace of my heart" was characteristic of the type of sentimental language of family relations that planters with paternalistic attitudes had adopted. With his wish, Gaston really meant that Susan's successful discharge of her duties showed that she had understood the importance of fulfilling her gender role, behaving as a model daughter, and that she was prepared to assume the behavior of a model wife and mother.[83]

In Gaston's eyes, Susan's commitment to discharging her duties and obligations was her best quality—which, in fact, was a daughter's best quality for any planter who privileged the paternalistic ethos. Therefore, the real meaning of Gaston's letter was that of a reassurance to Donaldson that he had been able to instill in Susan's mind the idea of reciprocal obligations to such an extent that he did not have to worry about her fulfillment of her gender role. Yet, Susan's willingness to honor her reciprocal obligations implicitly testified of her acceptance of her gender role in the male-dominated society of the slaveholding South and of her resignation to the expectations and rules that related to it.[84]

Comparable to American planters who adopted paternalistic attitudes, southern Italian landowners who privileged the paternalistic ethos sought to have close relations with their children and used a great deal of affectionate

---

82. William Gaston to Robert Donaldson, 2 June 1827, quoted in Stowe, *Intimacy and Power*, 175.

83. See Stowe, *Intimacy and Power*, 174–176.

84. See, in this connection, Marli F. Wiener, *Mistresses and Slaves: Plantation Women in South Carolina, 1830–1880* (Urbana, Ill., 1998), 53–71.

terms in their letters to them. As among American planters, the concept of reciprocity was at the heart of paternalistic relations within southern Italian landowning families. Fathers expected their children to reciprocate the affection and care that they showed for them and they tended to clarify the nature of their respective moral obligations. While presenting themselves as non-authoritarian and benevolent parents, landowners who followed paternalistic rules of behavior sought to instill in their children's minds the awareness that they owed respect to their parents and that they ought to be willing to follow parental advice. This interpretation has a great deal in common with Marzio Barbagli's description of the characteristics of the "intimate marriage" family as one that—contrary to the patriarchal family—included "a more flexible role system, less related to gender and age, and in which the relations of authority were more balanced."[85]

In sketching the characteristics of the liberal culture whose ideas informed family law in the *Mezzogiorno* in the 1860s, Paolo Macry has underlined the importance of the equal status—though with a different degree of power—of parents and children within the household, and the idea that in the modern family "the authority of the father—whose task is to educate and direct—is tempered" by the mother's affection. Far from being a legal innovation of the 1860s, this view of the family related to the social and cultural changes that took place between the eighteenth and the nineteenth centuries, a time in which—according to Giovanni Montroni—the *Mezzogiorno* witnessed the appearance of an egalitarian model of family relations. In fact, the letters that several southern Italian noblemen and landowners wrote from that period on show a high level of intimacy and affection and represent a clear indication of the importance of equality in the relations between different members of the household. Montroni has used the term "bourgeois" to describe the tone—both intimate and paternalistic—of some of the correspondence between noble parents and their children.[86]

A particularly illuminating example of a relationship between a noble landowner with paternalistic attitudes and his children is in the correspondence that Agostino Serra, duke of Terranova, entertained with his adoptive son and daughter. In 1801, Agostino Serra married the daughter of the prince of Cassano, but the marriage did not produce heirs. In 1836, Serra adopted the twenty-four-year-old Luciano Brunas, and in 1838 his sister

85. Barbagli, *Sotto lo stesso tetto*, 19.
86. Macry, *Ottocento*, 9. See also Montroni, *Gli uomini del Re*, 37–44.

Giulia. According to Giovanni Montroni, "several elements suggest that the two were [Serra's] natural children." In other words, there is reason to believe that the relationship between Serra and Luciano and Giulia Brunas was by all means and purposes a relation between a father and his actual son and daughter, even though it lacked legal acknowledgment for the probable reason that Luciano and Giulia were born from Serra's extramarital affair with a commoner. Among the strongest elements that support this hypothesis is an analysis of the voluminous correspondence between Serra and his two adoptive children, a correspondence which shows that the noble landowner manifested a rather unusual degree of care and interest for the lives of both Luciano and Giulia Brunas and in which at no point did he give any suggestion that he was not their natural father.[87]

The Serra family inheritance included extensive landholdings located in Calabria, among which were the estates of Gioia and Cannavà. In particular, on the Calabrian estate of Cannavà, Serra engaged in large-scale entrepreneurial activity; he produced large quantities of olive oil, citrus fruits, and wine and took care of their sale on the market. For this reason, several scholars have seen the Serra estates in Calabria as an example of capitalist enterprise in the nineteenth-century *Mezzogiorno*. Moreover, Serra showed an unusual degree of attention to problems related to both land and work management. Though residing in Naples for most of the time, he was clearly favorable to the idea of direct management and he implemented it on his own estate through his son, Luciano Brunas. According to Giovanni Montroni, Serra took particular care of his landholdings, wishing to "improve the systems of conduction and cultivation" through the employment of modern agricultural techniques. In this sense, Serra was certainly a progressive noble landowner akin to the Barraccos and other progressive members of the landed bourgeoisie who contributed a great deal in the transformation of the nineteenth-century *latifondo* into a capitalist enterprise through crucial innovations, such as the direct management of the landed estates and the rationalization of production.[88]

87. See Montroni, *Gli uomini del Re*, 36–38.

88. On Agostino Serra, see Agnese Sinisi, "Le aziende calabresi dei principi Serra di Gerace nella prima metà del XIX secolo," in Massafra, ed., *Problemi di Storia*, 91–116; Mariarosaria Giorgio, "Produzione e commercio dell'olio nell'azienda calabrese dei Serra di gerace (1836–1847)," in Giovanni Montroni, ed., *Agricoltura e commercio nel Mezzogiorno tra '700 e '800* (Naples, 1996), 43–68; and Montroni, *Gli uomini del Re*, 79–85.

Between 1837 and 1840, during the period in which Luciano Brunas managed the family estates in Calabria, Serra wrote him more than a letter per week. His letters always opened with the phrase "my dear son" and included long descriptions of his ideas and expectations about Luciano's proper behavior. In fact, Serra's advices to Luciano resembled Thomas Spragins's advices to his children to observe a behavior that would not displease their parent; yet, Serra's letters also emphasized to a greater degree the egalitarian nature of paternalistic family relations and the particular features of reciprocity in the father-son relationship. Repeatedly, Serra asked Luciano to consider him a friend and to trust him for the reason that he did not attempt to impose his authority on him, but rather to help him with his guidance. In a letter he wrote to Luciano in 1837, Serra clarified that "I am not the kind of father who is jealous of his authority when I know for sure that nobody acts to usurp it . . . I enjoy seeing, together with the son's affection and love, the friend's trust." Serra's proclaimed friendship between himself and his son established a particular bond of affection and mutual moral obligations that reinforced the egalitarian and reciprocal nature of their relationship.[89]

The indispensable conditions for friendship were reciprocal trust and willingness to tell each other the truth, no matter how painful, as Serra revealed in a previous letter: "when you talked to me about matters on which I did not share your feelings, I have never really rejected you for this, but, considering you more than a son, a friend, I have always told you the reasons why I was keen to follow my own opinion." By asking his son to be his friend, Serra ensured that he had Luciano's trust and that the young man would listen to his advice. In the end, Serra's advice tended to be that of a parent more than that of a friend, especially in matters of management. "On the conduction of business, I won't tell you anything," he wrote Luciano in another letter, "you are cautious enough to behave well and with the required kindness: make yourself loved, and at the same time show both firmness and shrewdness."[90]

The particular nature of the reciprocal relation between Serra and Luciano shows specifically in the way the noble landowner reacted when, in 1839, his son manifested his wish to marry. Instead of questioning Luciano about the

89. Agostino Serra to Luciano Brunas Serra, 27 December 1837, Serra di Gerace Family Papers, ASN. See also Montroni, *Gli uomini del Re,* 36–37.

90. Agostino Serra to Luciano Brunas Serra, 6 December 1837; Agostino Serra to Luciano Brunas Serra, 25 November 1837, Serra di Gerace Family Papers, ASN.

social standing and wealth of the family of the future bride, Serra asked him to consider the fact that his wife would enter their family as a new daughter. He told Luciano that his wish was that he marry a woman who was both sensible and with proper family habits, regardless of her wealth. Serra was less than sure that the person Luciano wished to marry had these qualities; therefore, he disapproved of his choice. However, he attempted to provide a balance to his argument by pointing out that Luciano would have felt profoundly unhappy if the woman he loved lacked precisely the type of qualities that his father sought in her. In a long and detailed letter, Serra told Luciano that the fact that he was no longer a boy, but a grown-up man, should have caused him to "act accordingly, in order to not sacrifice your peace, and mine as well." He then proceeded to clarify to Luciano that, "regarding the business of you getting married, I do not think in terms of a bigger, or a smaller dowry, since Providence has placed us in a wealthy enough condition," but rather "I would like to live the time that is left as much quiet as possible, and certainly if I did not see you happy, I would not be either."[91]

Since balanced exchange—as opposed to deferential respect—was at the heart of reciprocal relations between landowners who adopted paternalistic attitudes and their children, a father could manifest his disapproval of his sons' spousal choice only by pointing out the discomfort which both would feel if the choice were wrong. When he told Luciano that he considered his future wife as an additional daughter, Serra reminded him of the relation of reciprocity between them. The ties of mutual obligation that bound father and son demanded from Luciano that he take into account Serra's opinion. Yet, the real issue at stake in Luciano's marriage was likely to be the reputation of the family name. Serra did not wish to welcome into his family a person who would not act and speak according to the Serra family's high standards. To discourage Luciano from his intention to marry without imposing his authority, Serra asked him to act according to his sense of duty toward the family. Similar to the effect that Thomas Spragins's advice had on his children, Serra's advice caused Luciano to reflect upon the nature of the father-son relationship and the expectations that reciprocity and mutual obligations placed upon him as a member of the family. According to Montroni, the fact that Serra and his son had such a close and affectionate

91. Agostino Serra to Luciano Brunas Serra, 14 December 1839, Serra di Gerace Family Papers, ASN. See also Montroni, *Gli uomini del Re*, 42–43.

relationship did not necessarily imply that "in matters of spousal choice sentimental reasons could prevail over elements such as wealth and status." Still, Serra was at least willing to consider the qualities of Luciano's future bride in terms that did not relate exclusively to family name and dowry. And yet, in 1843, Luciano married Giovanna Filangieri, who belonged to one of the most illustrious Neapolitan aristocratic families.[92]

The southern Italian landowners' adoption of paternalistic attitudes also profoundly affected gender relations within the family. A new language of intimacy and affection characterized relations between husbands and wives and fathers and daughters in those households that privileged the paternalistic ethos. The egalitarian model of family relations gave equal importance to all members of the household, whether they were males or females. Egalitarian ideas also informed the formulation of a law on inheritance according to which, after the death of the father, sons and daughters were to share the family patrimony on equal terms. In practice, several noblemen ignored the law and continued to privilege male heirs over female heirs. Still, this legal change is a significant example of the phenomenon of the rise in number of egalitarian practices that accompanied the southern Italian landowners' adoption of paternalistic attitudes. In his analysis of the Neapolitan aristocratic families, Paolo Macry has argued that the real change in the nineteenth century was in "the juridical culture's emphasis on principles." According to Macry, the principles of equality among individuals and of intimacy and solidarity in family relations demanded the abolition of hierarchies in the household, even though noblemen continued to prefer that their male heirs inherit the family patrimony, mainly because of the risk of disappearance of the family name.[93]

The reciprocity implicit in egalitarian family relations showed explicitly in the frequent correspondence of several elite families. The importance of intimacy and affection emerged clearly from the direct way of addressing one another, through the use of the informal pronoun *tu*—rather than the formal *voi*—and from the existence of genuine reciprocal concern, especially over matters of health. The characteristic display of affection by landowners with paternalistic attitudes toward the female members of the family led to increasing closeness and to an unknown degree of participation of heads of house-

92. Montroni, *Gli uomini del Re,* 43–44.
93. Macry, *Ottocento,* 10. See also Ida Fazio, "Le ricchezze e le donne," *QS* 101 (1999): 539–550.

holds in the private lives of their wives, and even more so of their daughters. This, in turn, created a bond of reciprocal obligations between fathers and daughters similar to the one that characterized relations between fathers and sons. In return for their fathers' show of affection and attention, it was believed daughters ought to follow, or, at the very least, listen to and reflect upon, parental advice.[94]

Mirroring the behavior of American planters who privileged the paternalistic ethos, through the rhetoric of reciprocity southern Italian landowners who adopted paternalistic attitudes continued to keep tight control over the lives of their daughters. Rather than imposing their authority, they filled their daughters' minds with even stricter expectations that related to their gender role and with ideas about the need to respect the reciprocal nature of family relations without disappointing their fathers. In fact, among elite families of the Italian *Mezzogiorno*, the expectations that related to the female gender roles demanded that elite girls trained to become attractive to both noble and bourgeois potential suitors who had a prestigious family name or a large family patrimony, or both. In this respect, the adoption of paternalistic attitudes had caused only a superficial change in gender relations. Expectations for upper-class women continued to focus on their social role of being suitable candidates for a prestigious marriage, most likely one celebrating the alliance between two important families. However, it is also true that women were, nevertheless, far more likely to willingly accept their condition for the reason that they no longer had the impression that the patriarchal authority of the family simply imposed their fate upon them. Rather, they felt increasingly involved in the selection of their partner and, in a few cases, even conditioned their father's ultimate decision with their consent or denial.[95]

Illuminating, in this respect, is Agostino Serra's behavior toward his daughter, Giulia Brunas—the sister of Luciano Brunas—in regard to the subjects of marriage and choice of a suitable partner. In 1837, Serra had not yet formally adopted Giulia. Yet, he treated her as a part of his family—a clear indication that she was his natural daughter—and, in fact, he was ready to give her a considerable dowry of 40,000 ducats, provided that she married a person who met his approval. Giulia had already received a marriage proposal

---

94. On the use of the informal pronoun *tu*, see Barbagli, *Sotto lo stesso tetto*, 308–309.
95. See Montroni, *Gli uomini del Re*, 40.

by a civil servant whose name was de Biase; Serra found him agreeable and had already discussed with him matters related to the dowry. However, Luciano was uncomfortable with the idea of de Biase marrying his sister and entertained a correspondence with his father on the reasons why Serra supported Giulia's choice. Writing in his typical colloquial style, Serra told Luciano that he had "no reason other than making Giulia happy." Furthermore, he wrote that, although de Biase did not belong to a prominent family, he was certainly the best candidate if Giulia liked him, especially given the fact that the only prestigious individuals who had proposed to her were impoverished noblemen who were after her dowry.[96]

A few months before this exchange, Luciano had told his father that he did not believe de Biase really loved his sister. Serra's answer to his son's doubts revealed a great deal about his ideas on father-daughter relations. Serra replied to Luciano that he had never thought that a marriage could originate from romance, since matters of convenience, social prestige, and wealth prevailed for the most part. Therefore, even if de Biase did not love Giulia, the fact that he wished to marry her was enough; in time she would grow attached to him and she would learn to love him, regardless of what he felt for her. With his letter, Serra clarified to Luciano that Giulia was no different from any other daughter of a prominent family. Despite their professed attachment to their daughters, landowners such as Agostino Serra, who clearly adopted paternalistic attitudes in family relations, still influenced their behavior in matters related to spousal choice and asked them to take into account matters of convenience, rather than to think exclusively about their happiness.[97]

In fact, Serra had clear ideas about the nature of his relation of reciprocity with his daughter. In a subsequent letter to Luciano, he wrote that "for a girl, the choice and decision [regarding the partner] must have to do with sympathy, look, and behavior." On the other hand, "what then is a matter of marriage convenience in terms of the amount of land owned, and even more in regard to the moral qualities of the groom and his family, is something that a girl is unable . . . to detect so to decide on her own." Therefore, Serra went

96. Agostino Serra to Luciano Brunas Serra, 24 February 1838, quoted in Montroni, *Gli uomini del Re,* 38; see also 38–42.

97. Agostino Serra to Luciano Brunas Serra, 2 December 1837, quoted in Montroni, *Gli uomini del Re,* 39.

on, "it is the duty of the family to whom she belongs to take on this responsibility in the most delicate manner: this is what I have been trying to do."[98]

In other words, according Serra, the process through which a daughter married clearly divided between the part which related to the emotional sphere—where women were in charge—and the part related to business—where men were in charge. As a consequence, Giulia had the power to make a decision only as long as the reasons for her choice related to what she felt about her partner's "sympathy, look, and behavior." Her father would handle business matters, such as "the amount of land owned." To Serra, the tie of reciprocal obligations implied that he should give Giulia his unconditional emotional support. However, contrary to William and Susan Gaston's case, in return for his support, Serra insisted that Giulia conform not only to her gender role, but also to her social role, acting as an instrument for the conduction of family business and the construction of family alliances. Regardless of whether she loved him or not, Giulia never married de Biase. In 1838, soon after officially becoming Serra's adoptive daughter, Giulia married Ferdinando Lucchesi Palli, a member of one of the Bourbon kingdom's most prestigious aristocratic families. Like planters with paternalistic attitudes in the American South, landowners with paternalistic attitudes in the *Mezzogiorno* tended to give more attention to their daughters' wishes and to look for their approval. However, they were careful to not upset the gender-based asymmetry of power within the family. Especially in matters of business, the head of the household still had the final word.[99]

Paternalistic Masters and Their Laborers

In the American South, planters who privileged the paternalistic ethos broadened the practice of reciprocity—which provided the basis for egalitarian family relations—so as to extend it to their dependents both within the household and on the plantation. They talked of "our family, white and black" and they discussed their duties and obligations toward the members of what they perceived as an extended household that included both children and slaves. In turn, paternalistic ideas on the need to extend relations of

98. Agostino Serra to Luciano Brunas Serra, 6 December 1837, Serra di Gerace Family Papers, ASN.

99. See Montroni, *Gli uomini del Re,* 41–42. See also Fiume, "Making Women Visible," 5.

reciprocity to the treatment of slaves formed the core of an articulated justification of slavery—the proslavery argument—according to which masters felt an obligation to look after their unfree laborers, similar to the way they looked after their family dependents within the household.[100]

Planters who supported this paternalistic view of slavery usually belonged to the progressive section of the elite and were well aware of the applicability of capitalist values to plantation management. As a consequence, they sought to achieve the concurrent objectives of maximizing the profits of their agricultural enterprises and establishing a more efficient relationship with their workforce—which they accomplished by emphasizing the importance of reciprocal rights and duties between masters and laborers, rather than resorting to an unproductive policy of violent dehumanization. In doing so, progressive slaveholders followed principles comparable to the ones that guided other progressive landed elites in Europe and in the Americas— principles that related to the spread of liberalism and capitalist values on a global scale.[101]

Recently, a handful of scholars have attempted to reconcile Eugene Genovese's Marxist interpretation of the planters' paternalistic ideology as antimodern and antithetic to capitalism with the opposite view by James Oakes and other historians who have demonstrated the existence of a clear capitalist behavior among the majority of slaveholders. In his recent study on time and plantation management in the antebellum South, Mark Smith has shown that "planters could embrace very modern, even capitalistic methods for managing slave labor in an effort to modernize the Old South on their own terms—to embrace capitalism without its democratic connotations"; according to Smith, the capitalist and precapitalist features of southern society

100. See Eugene D. Genovese, "'Our Family, White and Black': Family and Household in the Southern Slaveholders' World View," in Carol Bleser, ed., *In Joy and in Sorrow*, 69–87; David Herbert Donald, "The Proslavery Argument Reconsidered," *JSH* 37 (1971): 3–18; Drew G. Faust, "Introduction: The Pro-Slavery Argument in History," in Drew G. Faust, ed., *The Ideology of Slavery: Proslavery Thought in the Antebellum South, 1830–1860* (Baton Rouge, La., 1981), 1–20; Bertram Wyatt-Brown, "Modernizing Southern Slavery: The Proslavery Argument Reinterpreted," in James Mourgan Kousser and James MacPherson, eds., *Region, Race, and Reconstruction: Essays in Honor of C. Van Woodward* (New York, 1982), 27–49; and Larry E. Tise, *Proslavery: A History of the Defense of Slavery in America, 1701–1840* (Athens, Ga., 1988).

101. For comparisons, see Clifford Griffin, *Their Brothers' Keepers: Moral Stewardship in the United States, 1800–1865* (New Brunswick, N.J., 1960); and Marta Petrusewicz, "Agromania: innovatori agrari nelle periferie europee dell'Ottocento," in Piero Bevilacqua, ed., *Storia dell'agricoltura italiana in età contemporanea*, vol. 3, *Mercati e Istituzioni* (Venice, 1991), 295–343.

were not mutually exclusive, but rather coexisted side by side. In his work focusing on the ideology of the "sugar masters" in Louisiana, Richard Follett has reached a comparable conclusion. At the same time, in his analysis of the rise of the master class in South Carolina and Georgia, Jeffrey Robert Young has argued that paternalism and capitalism coexisted in a hybrid ideology of "corporate individualism," one in which planters combined "their modern defense of a hierarchical slaveowning society with fundamentally bourgeois domestic conceptions of the loving family." Incidentally, both Smith and Young have also pointed out how, in their latest works, both Eugene Genovese and James Oakes have distanced themselves from their once irreconcilable positions and have acknowledged each other's merit in the understanding of the slave system of the antebellum South.[102]

There is much to learn from an analysis of planter ideology that gives equal weight to modern/capitalist and premodern/precapitalist features. In fact, the importance of this analysis transcends the boundaries of studies on the American South and shows the way to considering the planters' combination of paternalistic attitudes and capitalist values as a fairly common—rather than exceptional—case in comparative perspective with other nineteenth-century landed elites. Yet, in order to move from this analysis to an appreciation of those features that make the antebellum planters' ideology comparable to the worldviews of other nineteenth-century elites, one must first acknowledge the fact that—similar to what happened in other areas of the world—in the American South the spread of paternalism related

102. Smith, *Debating Slavery*, 93; Jeffrey R. Young, *Domesticating Slavery: The Master Class in Georgia and South Carolina, 1670–1837* (Chapel Hill, N.C., 1999), 9. See also Mark Smith, *Mastered by the Clock: Time, Slavery, and Freedom in the American South* (Chapel Hill, N.C., 1996); Richard J. Follett, "On the Edge of Modernity: Louisiana's Landed Elites in the Nineteenth-Century Sugar Country," in Dal Lago and Halpern, eds., *American South and Italian Mezzogiorno*, 73–94; Eugene D. Genovese, *The Slaveholders' Dilemma: Freedom and Progress in Southern Conservative Thought, 1820–1860* (Columbia, S.C., 1992); and James Oakes, *Slavery and Freedom: An Interpretation of the Old South* (New York, 1990). On the Marxist view, see especially Genovese, *Roll, Jordan, Roll*, 661–663; and Elizabeth Fox-Genovese and Eugene D. Genovese, *The Fruits of Merchant Capital: Slavery and Bourgeois Property in the Rise and Expansion of Capitalism* (New York, 1983), 114–115. On the opposite view, see James Oakes, *The Ruling Race: A History of American Slaveholders* (New York, 1982) 193–224; and Fogel and Engerman, *Time on the Cross*, 73–77. See also Laurence Shore, *Southern Capitalist: The Ideological Leadership of an Elite, 1832–1855* (Chapel Hill, N.C., 1986), 200–205; Scarborough, *Masters of the Big House*, 407–411; and Shearer Davis Bowman, *Masters and Lords; Mid-19th-Century U.S. Planters and Prussian Junkers* (New York, 1993), 182–183.

to the effort of the progressive section of the propertied class to embrace modernization. In fact, far from being a relic of antimodern attitudes—as patriarchalism was—paternalism provided progressive planters with the ideological tools to reconcile capitalist values and ideas of reciprocity with the justification of the inequalities that dominated social relations within the extended household and on the plantation. These particular features of paternalism provide us with a great deal of material for comparison with the worldviews of other nineteenth-century landed elites, and specifically with the worldview of progressive landowners in the Italian *Mezzogiorno*.[103]

Unlike American planters, who felt the need to concoct a proslavery argument—especially given the abolitionist movement's increasingly strong influence on American public opinion—articulate members of the southern Italian landed elite had little incentive to relate paternalism to a specific ideological justification of the social system. Southern Italian progressive landowners adopted paternalistic attitudes in their daily behavior toward members of the family and workers on their landed estates, yet only rarely did they reflect upon the significance of their behavior or speculate over the nature of a system in which they were long accustomed to taking their economic and social power for granted. When they did articulate their opinions and thoughts, it was mostly in private documents in which they showed that—even though they never went as far as explicitly considering their workforce to be part of an extended family—they were certainly conscious of their duties and obligations toward members of their household and laborers and they were also prepared to implicitly recognize that both of them had some rights. Yet, what compels a case for comparison between progressive southern Italian landowners and progressive American planters—and, ideally, other progressive landed elites—is the fact that both combined paternalistic attitudes with capitalist aims. Both sought to achieve the aim of managing rationally organized profit-making enterprises through a policy of productive collaboration with the workforce on their landed estates.[104]

103. See Enrico Dal Lago and Rick Halpern, "Two Case-Studies in Comparative History: The American South and the Italian Mezzogiorno," in Dal Lago and Halpern, eds., *American South and Italian Mezzogiorno*, 7–10; Mark M. Smith, "Old South Time in Comparative Perspective," *AHR* 101 (1996): 1432–1469; and Lacy K. Ford, *Origins of Southern Radicalism: The South Carolina Upcountry, 1800–1860* (New York, 1988), 358–359.

104. See Dal Lago and Halpern, "Two Case-Studies," 9–10. See also Montroni, *Gli uomini del Re*, 85–93.

Recently, Marta Petrusewicz has contended that the increasing interest that several progressive southern Italian landowners showed for the rationalization of production on the *latifondi* was part of a general move toward modernization among nineteenth-century European landed elites. Interestingly, those members of the southern Italian landed elite who showed an interest in capitalist practices and ways to modernize agricultural production also made a particular effort at guaranteeing stability in the management of their landed estates; typically, they did this through paternalistic practices that emphasized the reciprocal and contractual character of the relationship between master and workforce. Yet, both recalling Mark Smith's point on the mixed capitalist-noncapitalist character of American plantations and echoing Elizabeth Fox-Genovese and Eugene Genovese's description of the "Janus face" of slaveholders' capitalism, Petrusewicz has concluded that "*latifondismo* [the *latifondo*'s agricultural system] was neither feudal nor capitalist; it was a mixture . . . of subsistence and market-oriented production . . . of modern management combined with sharecropping and land assignments."[105]

To be sure, in both cases, the difference between the paternalistic ideal of efficient and fair management and the harsh reality of workers' lives on plantations and *latifondi* was striking. American slaves and southern Italian peasants benefited only in a few cases from the planters' and landowners' adoption of paternalistic attitudes. Most commonly, their exploitation continued in different ways and in different degrees, only in a less open and outspoken fashion. Although within the confines of the paternalistic ethos slaves and peasants had more room for bargaining with their masters over reciprocal rights and duties, the planters' and landowners' unquestionable force and authority routinely frustrated the workers' attempts to benefit from paternalism's implicit recognition of their needs. In fact, notwithstanding their adoption of capitalist values and practices in matters of management and labor relations, the progressive sections of the landed elites of the American South and the Italian *Mezzogiorno* enjoyed a higher degree of

---

105. Marta Petrusewicz, "The Demise of Latifondismo," in Robert Lumley and Jonathan Morris, eds., *The New History of the Italian South: The* Mezzogiorno *Revisited* (Exeter, 1997), 21. See also Marta Petrusewicz, "Land Based Modernization and the Culture of Landed Elites in the Nineteenth-Century Mezzogiorno," in Dal Lago and Halpern, eds., *American South and Italian Mezzogiorno*, 95–111; Petrusewicz, *Latifundium*, 10–16; Salvatore Lupo, "I proprietari terrieri del Mezzogiorno," in Piero Bevilacqua, ed., *Storia dell'agricoltura italiana in età moderna e contemporanea*, vol. 2, *Uomini e Classi* (Venice, 1990), 112–119; and Fox-Genovese and Genovese, *Fruits of Merchant Capital*.

power on their landed estates than any contemporary capitalist businessman had in his factories and they used this power to extract surplus labor
from their workers, while actively, and often violently, discouraging labor
resistance and protest.[106]

In the antebellum American South, planters who privileged the paternalistic
ethos extended the practice of reciprocal relations between members of the
family to relations between masters and laborers. Slaves became part of an
ideal extended household within which planters considered it their moral
obligation and duty to take personal interest in the lives of all their dependents. Planters who endorsed this paternalistic view of slavery often knew
their slaves by name, worried about their health (also for obvious economic
concerns), and interfered frequently in their lives. Indeed, they justified the
entire slave system by claiming that they took charge of helpless children
who needed guidance and who benefited from working under their direction. Transferring the model of family relations to the plantation, planters
who adopted paternalistic attitudes understood reciprocity as the implicit
obligation to take care of the slaves and feed them in return for the work
that they performed. As a consequence, according to Peter Kolchin, "masters
saw their slaves not just as their laborers, but also as their 'people,' inferior
members of their extended households from whom they expected work and
obedience, but to whom they owed guidance and protection."[107]

The idea that the planters' extended households included slaves as inferior members of their families was one of the pillars of the proslavery
argument, the justification of slavery that was at the heart of paternalistic
ideology. According to Willie Lee Rose, "proslavery philosophers intended
to suggest a benign institution that encouraged between masters and slaves
the qualities so much admired in the Victorian family: cheerful obedience
and gratitude on the part of the children (read slaves), and paternalistic
wisdom, protection, and discipline on the part of the father (read master)."
Yet, Eugene Genovese has pointed out that, despite these ideal qualities, "the
master-slave relationship, viewed as family matter, did not require special

106. See Genovese, *Roll, Jordan, Roll,* 661–663; Petrusewicz, *Latifundium,* 15–16; and Wallerstein, *Capitalist World-Economy,* 120–121. See also Howard Newby, "Paternalism and Capitalism," in Richard Scase, ed., *Industrial Society: Class, Cleavage, and Control* (New York, 1977),
59–73; Edward P. Thompson, *The Making of the English Working Class* (London, 1965); and Alan
Dawley, *Class and Community: The Industrial Revolution in Lynn* (Cambridge, Mass., 1976).

107. Kolchin, *American Slavery,* 112.

kindness or leniency; it required only a strong sense of duty and responsibility" for the welfare of the slaves. Therefore, paternalism did not necessarily lead to a less harsh or less violent master-slave relationship; in fact, in most cases, the master's care for his slaves was little more than a rhetorical fiction that planters used to fend off criticism.[108]

Yet, as time passed, the paternalistic justification of slavery became an increasingly complex rhetorical exercise. Within the parameters of this exercise, different elements—such as racism and religion—combined to provide planters with a refined ideological tool for their defense of the economic and social system that gave them absolute power over their agrarian laborers. In this respect, a particularly important part of the proslavery argument rested on the assumption that both the racial inferiority of African American slaves and the labor system that related to slavery were divinely sanctioned—as a supposedly correct interpretation of the Bible testified.[109]

Particularly significant were the sermons that South Carolinian preacher James Henry Thornwell, the most famous religious advocate of slavery, delivered on the subject. In an 1850 sermon entitled "The Rights and Duties of Masters," Thornwell wrote that slavery was "the obligation to labor for another, determined by the Providence of God, independently of the provisions of a contract." Therefore, Thornwell considered the slaves' obligation to work for their master a result of God's will and the system of reciprocal relations of rights and duties between masters and laborers which stemmed out of this obligation a consequence of the Providence's design. Religious arguments in support of slavery—such as the one by James Henry Thornwell—contributed a great deal to transforming the model of reciprocal relations at the heart of paternalism into a mainstream social practice among progressive planters. At the same time, religious justifications also provided a benign and cultivated explanation for the existence of an enslaved and racially exploited class of workers in the American South. Yet, even more important was the fact that religious reasons justified and encouraged a close contact

108. Rose, "Domestication of Domestic Slavery," 127; Genovese, *World the Slaveholders Made,* 199. See also Genovese, "Our Family," 72–73.

109. See George Fredrickson, *The Black Image in the White Mind: The Debate on Afro-American Character and Destiny, 1817–1914* (New York, 1971), 59–66; Stephen R. Haynes, *Noah's Curse: The Biblical Justification of American Slavery* (New York, 2002); Anne C. Loveland, *Southern Evangelicals and the Social Order, 1820–1860* (Baton Rouge, La., 1980); and Mitchell Snay, *Gospel of Disunion: Religion and Separatism in the Antebellum South* (New York, 1993).

between master and slaves, given that proslavery preachers argued that the master's Christian duties included both taking care of the material needs of the slaves and educating them through the teachings of the true religion.[110]

Whether with or without the support of religious justifications, in its essence, planters' paternalism implied the existence of continuous interaction and personal contact between masters and slaves, a contact that led to reciprocal knowledge to an extent previously unknown. Therefore, only a planter who was mostly resident on his plantation—as opposed to absentee—could adopt paternalistic practices, directly managing his workforce and becoming acquainted as much as possible with its strengths and weaknesses. A planter who adopted paternalistic practices typically attempted to enforce his decisions acting personally as the ultimate source of authority on the plantation. Even when he hired an overseer, he closely supervised the work routine and instructed him on how to treat the slaves so that they understood and followed his rules. Yet, the close contact between the planter and his workforce also allowed the slaves to take advantage of the system of reciprocal relations that was at the heart of paternalistic ideology. Through their daily resistance to their master's attempts at controlling their lives and enforcing his rules, slaves forced him to acknowledge that they had particular needs and to recognize that there had to be some substance to his pretensions to look after their well-being. In Genovese's definition of paternalism, the reciprocal relation between master and slaves rested on the concept of "the involuntary labor of the slaves as a legitimate return to their master for protection and direction"; and yet, in practice, as a result of slave resistance, "paternalism's insistence upon mutual obligations—duties, responsibilities, and ultimately even rights—implicitly recognized the slaves' humanity."[111]

An interesting nineteenth-century document linked the idea of the master's duties and responsibilities to the notion of slaves' rights; the document is an article which O. Lee published with the significant title "The Laborer: His Rights and Duties" in *De Bow's Review* in 1857. Lee characterized the

---

110. James H. Thornwell, *The Rights and Duties of Masters: A Sermon Preached at the Dedication of a Church, Erected in Charleston, S.C., for the Benefit and Instruction of the Colored Population* (Charleston, S.C., 1850), 24. See also Michael J. Westerkamp, "James Henry Thornwell, Pro-Slavery Spokesman within a Calvinist Faith," *South Carolina Historical Magazine* 87 (1986); William W. Freehling, *The Reintegration of American History: Slavery and the Civil War* (New York, 1994), 59–81; and Genovese, *Slaveholders' Dilemma*, 28–29.

111. Genovese, *Roll, Jordan, Roll*, 5.

master in paternalistic terms as the one "who feeds, clothes, and protects them [the slaves] alike in infancy, sickness, and old age, and who is bound by State laws to provide for all their wants through life." What Lee's piece shows is that, in practice, the planters' paternalistic behavior—a behavior that the state laws supported and encouraged as the proper duty of masters toward their slaves—led to constant interference in their bondsmen's lives. Slaves, in turn, resisted the attempts to interfere in their lives and control them by deliberately slowing the pace of work, feigning illness, breaking tools, stealing property, and generally causing incidents on the plantation, if not running away, as often happened. In doing this, slaves asserted their own idea of moral economy as a guiding principle of their actions, regardless of and in defiance of their master's authority and his impositions.[112]

One of the best-known examples of planters' paternalism and slave resistance is in the private papers of South Carolinian planter James Henry Hammond. Born the son of a New Englander and a South Carolinian, Hammond studied law and practiced it in Columbia, South Carolina, where he was also briefly editor of a newspaper. His marriage with Charleston heiress Catherine Fitzsimmons in 1831 transformed his life and introduced him to the restricted circle of South Carolina's planter elite. From the 1830s onward, Hammond's political career was almost a continuous string of successes. In 1836 he won a seat in the U.S. House of Representatives, in 1841 he became general of the South Carolina state militia, and in 1842 he won the governor's chair over Robert Allston. In 1857, Hammond gained a seat in the U.S. Senate and moved to Washington, where he staunchly defended southern slavery with his speeches; yet, he kept a moderate position on the issue of southern secession until 1861, when he finally embraced the Confederate cause. Aside from his political activity, Hammond gained wide notoriety as a progressive southern intellectual, a refined proslavery ideologue, and an enthusiastic advocate of agricultural modernization.[113]

---

112. O. Lee, "The Laborer: His Rights and Duties," *DBR* 22 (1857): 490. See also Kolchin, *American Slavery*, 118–127; Genovese, *Roll, Jordan, Roll*, 285–324, 597–657; Alex Lichtenstein, "'That Disposition to Theft, with Which They Have Been Branded': Moral Economy, Slave Management, and the Law," *JSoH* 21 (1988): 413–439; and Walter Johnson, *Soul by Soul: Life Inside the Antebellum Slave Market* (Cambridge, Mass., 1999), 19–30.

113. On Hammond, see Drew G. Faust, *James Henry Hammond and the Old South: A Design for Mastery* (Baton Rouge, La., 1982); Carol Bleser, *The Hammonds of Redcliffe* (New York, 1981); and Clement Eaton, *The Mind of the Old South* (Baton Rouge, La., 1964), 44–68.

Arguably, Hammond was a sort of nouveau riche within the southern planter elite. Through his marriage with Catherine Fitzsimmons, he acquired a ten thousand–acre cotton plantation—Silver Bluff—with 147 slaves in the South Carolina upcountry. Soon after, he started his career as resident planter and dedicated his efforts to improving agricultural production and managing his workforce with the help of an overseer. Following the advice of his friend Edmund Ruffin on scientific experimentation, Hammond obtained significant results with the use of marl and successfully transformed Silver Bluff into an extremely profitable agricultural enterprise. Seeking to achieve a similar success in the management of his workforce, Hammond wrote detailed instructions to his overseer in which he stressed the importance of being not too severe with the slaves, since excessive resort to violence signaled a failure at establishing authority. He wrote that "too much whipping indicates a bad tempered or inattentive manager and will not be allowed." Yet, as Drew Faust has noticed, posing as the "benevolent father" who rejected the outright use of violence, Hammond really aimed at "establishing a system of domination in which he could extract willing obedience from compliant slaves." Embracing the paternalistic ethos, he felt that his duty was to implement a fair code of practices in the management of his workforce, and he expected the slaves to fulfill their reciprocal obligations, willingly complying with his wishes.[114]

In his secret diary—which he kept between 1841 and 1864—Hammond reported his personal views on his life as resident planter at Silver Bluff and his efforts to manage and control his slaves through the use of paternalistic ideology. Hammond's diary clearly shows that he strove to strike a balance between the paternalistic ideal of reciprocal relations between master and slaves and the need to efficiently manage his plantation, whatever the cost. On one hand, he worried a great deal about the health of his slaves, who suffered from a high death rate throughout the twenty-three years covered in the diary. Doubtless, as Faust has pointed out, Hammond's preoccupations related to clear economic reasons. Yet, it is difficult not to see also a genuine humanitarian concern—which had to do with the master's duty to look after his workers—in diary entries such as the one in which he complained about

114. James Henry Hammond, "Governor Hammond's Instructions to His Overseer," in Rose, ed., *A Documentary History,* 354; Faust, *James Henry Hammond,* 101. See also James Henry Hammond, "Recent and Extensive Marling in South Carolina," *FR* 10 (1842).

4 September 1841 as being "the most painful day" among "several days of
anxiety and fatigue among my sick people." What made this day particularly
painful for Hammond was the loss of "a valuable [slave] woman," who was
taken in labor and died, despite the efforts of two different doctors and the
draining of three pounds of blood. Significantly, Hammond felt the need to
close the entry with the words "she was a good creature as ever lived."[115]

On the other hand, since his arrival at Silver Bluff in 1831, Hammond
had attempted to impose upon his slaves the practice of working in gangs.
He believed that the gang system was a particularly efficient labor regime,
particularly because, under the constant supervision of the overseer, slaves
were "not so apt to strain themselves" as they did with the less demanding task system. Yet, the gang system exhausted the slaves and required the
implementation of a harsh discipline. Through its enforcement, Hammond
clearly sought equally to assert his power, creating a docile labor force, and
to increase the efficiency of cotton production on the plantation. Yet, despite
his plans, the slaves reacted to his impositions by deliberately slowing the
pace of work, frequently feigning illness, and creating constant incidents
that prevented labor operations from proceeding smoothly and efficiently.
By 1850, years of poor work performance had convinced Hammond to abandon the gang system in favor of the task system. Resisting Hammond's repeated attempts at interfering in their lives, the slaves at Silver Bluff refused
to comply with his design of total control and redefined the boundaries of
the paternalistic master-slave relationship in such a way that both master
and slaves understood and acted upon their reciprocal rights and duties.
Hammond's slaves even led him to reward them for particularly efficient
work performances. Significantly, he complained that his slaves were "too
well fed and otherwise well treated."[116]

Episodes such as the bargaining over labor systems at Silver Bluff show
that, behind the paternalistic ideal, planters and slaves held different ideas
about the meaning of reciprocity and had different expectations of one another. In fact, in the words of Drew Faust, paternalism provided the ideological context in which the "dialectic of oppression, challenge, and concession

115. Hammond's secret diary, 4 September 1841, in Carol Bleser, ed., *Secret and Sacred: The
Diaries of James Henry Hammond, a Southern Slaveholder* (New York, 1988), 72–73; see also Faust,
James Henry Hammond, 75–77.

116. Hammond plantation diary, 16 May 1838 and 22 October 1843, both quoted in Faust,
James Henry Hammond, 75, 90. See also Genovese, *Roll, Jordan, Roll*, 285–324; and Charles
Joyner, *Down by the Riverside: A South Carolina Slave Community* (Urbana, Ill., 1984), 50–57.

produce[d] the interdependence of lord and bondsman that Eugene Genovese has so arrestingly described." In particular, Faust considers the study of the relationship between Hammond and his slaves at Silver Bluff as "an opportunity to supplement and refine some of Genovese's insights about the sources of that 'reciprocity' he has urged as a defining feature of the slave system."[117]

Particularly insightful in this respect is the study of Hammond's design to achieve total control over the minds of his slaves—what Genovese, borrowing the expression from Italian Marxist intellectual Antonio Gramsci, has termed "hegemony." Following his design, Hammond sought to impose upon his slaves the use of western religious and medical practices. Yet, the slaves managed to maintain a degree of religious autonomy and continued the practice of worship through their distinctive cultural tradition of African American Christianity, rather than passively agreeing to worship in Hammond's church and welcoming his white preachers' message of submission. At the same time, the slaves also continued to rely on African folk beliefs, occasionally even resorting to witchcraft rather than submitting to scientific medical practices. Ultimately, the impressive number of runaways—which reached an average of two per year between 1831 and 1855—testifies to the slaves' constant challenges to both Hammond's design for total control of their minds and his imposition of the exhausting gang system at Silver Bluff.[118]

James Henry Hammond's ambition to be the owner of a model plantation, one in which efficient production and paternalistic management of the slaves went hand in hand, was in tune with the interest that a substantial number of southern planters manifested toward capitalist ideas and practices. The activities and interests of cotton planters such as Hammond, who belonged to the most recent and progressive section of the southern slaveholding elite, epitomized especially—though not exclusively—the characteristics of a peculiar type of entrepreneurial spirit that combined ideas of capitalist efficiency and rationality with a paternalistic treatment of the workforce. In its essence, the paternalistic ethos suited the ideological needs of a progressive planter elite whose commitment to the modernization of southern

117. Drew G. Faust, "Culture, Conflict, and Community: The Meaning of Power on an Antebellum Plantation," *JSoH* 14 (1980): 84.

118. See also Faust, *James Henry Hammond,* 69–104; John Hope Franklin and Loren Schweninger, *Runaway Slaves: Rebels on the Plantation* (New York, 1999), 292–293. On "reciprocity" and "hegemony," see Genovese, *Roll, Jordan, Roll,* 145–149; and Christopher Morris, "The Articulation of Two Worlds: The Master-Slave Relationship Reconsidered," *Journal of American History* 85 (1998): 982–1007.

agriculture was equal to its commitment to the preservation of slavery as its central feature. In this respect, the proslavery argument, as a central feature of paternalistic ideology, doubtless was related—as Bertram Wyatt-Brown has argued—to "the desire to modernize, to improve the 'home system' [of slavery], so that its foundations were no less secure, no less progressive than those on which free labor rested."[119]

The progressive planters' great effort to modernize southern agricultural production while keeping the slave system intact ultimately led to their enthusiastic acceptance of the practices of efficient management of industrial capitalism. In fact, in his recent study on plantation capitalism, Mark Smith has argued that "those planters most devoted to the cause of progress mimicked northern factory-owning moderns to the extreme" in their wish "to regulate the productivity and rate of labor as well." Yet, progressive planters who sought to reform southern agriculture added to the capitalist practices of factory management their own distinctive view of paternalistic ideology as the basis of a reciprocal relation that bound both masters and slaves to the observance of specific rights and duties. As a consequence, in the antebellum South, adoption of paternalistic attitudes and respect for reciprocity became distinctive signs of behavior of those progressive members of the planter elite who believed in the conciliation of the slave labor system with the modern capitalist management of their landed estates.[120]

Significantly, in Virginia and in the areas of tobacco production, planters who embraced the paternalistic ethos were typically progressive members of the elite who advocated agricultural reform and crop diversification. In the 1830s, Virginia's tobacco agriculture and slave system were both in deep crisis. In January 1832, in the aftermath of Nat Turner's 1831 rebellion, the Virginian legislature held a debate over the possibility of gradual abolition of slavery. While the debate ultimately did not lead to any legal provision against slavery, it demonstrated the fragility of the state's economy and social system. The fact that in Virginia slavery was a decaying institution certainly caused particularly progressive planters to feel increasingly uncomfortable

119. Wyatt-Brown, "Modernizing Southern Slavery," 28. See also Steven G. Collins, "System, Organization, and Agricultural Reform in the Antebellum South, 1840–1860," *AH* 75 (2001): 1–27.

120. Mark M. Smith, "Time, Slavery, and Plantation Capitalism in the Ante-Bellum American South," *P&P* 150 (1996): 154. See also Follett, "Edge of Modernity," 74–75; Scarborough, *Masters of the Big House,* 176–206; and Newby, "Paternalism and Capitalism," 70–73.

with the contradiction of the coexistence of agricultural modernization and paternalistic attitudes with the enslavement of African American laborers.[121]

Particularly interesting in this respect is the case of John Hartwell Cocke of Bremo, the Virginian planter who was a renowned agricultural reformer and a staunch opponent of the tyranny of tobacco monoculture. On his plantation at Bremo, Cocke devised a program of total control of the activities of his slaves which had several points in common with the one James Henry Hammond sought to implement at Silver Bluff. Between 1801 and 1860, Cocke's strict supervision of the slaves' work, his enforcement of discipline, and his calculated employment of punishments and rewards created what M. Boyd Coyner Jr. has termed a "para-military regimen" at Bremo. Assuming a rather authoritarian pose, Cocke called the supervision of his slaves "my government." Yet, he was especially concerned with the efficiency of his agricultural enterprise and seriously believed that strict discipline enabled the slaves to improve their work performance. At the same time, Cocke showed that he fully embraced the paternalistic ethos and did not hesitate to discharge what he believed were his duties and obligations as master; in accordance with the unwritten law of reciprocity, he provided his slaves with comfortable cabins, plenty of clothes and food, and even opportunities to acquire the rudiments of education.[122]

In fact, Cocke combined his paternalistic attitudes with the zeal of a moral reformer, a result of his leadership in the temperance movement. Rather uniquely, he linked his efforts to achieve total control over the slaves' life with his aspirations to morally elevate their souls. By 1831, Cocke believed that, similar to the way reliance on tobacco had ruined southern agriculture, reliance on slavery had corrupted southern morality. Consequently, his fight for agricultural modernization became a fight against the evil of slavery. His plans coincided largely with the ideas of the founders of the Colonization Society, which promoted the manumission of slaves and their return to

121. See Alison G. Freehling, *Drift toward Dissolution: The Virginia Slavery Debate of 1831–1832* (Baton Rouge, La., 1982); and Kenneth S. Greenberg, "Introduction: The Confessions of Nat Turner: Text and Context," in Kenneth S. Greenberg, ed., *The Confessions of Nat Turner and Related Documents* (New York, 1995), 1–36. See also Frederick F. Siegel, *The Roots of Southern Distinctiveness: Tobacco and Society in Danville, Virginia, 1780–1865* (Chapel Hill, N.C., 1987).

122. John Hartwell Cocke diary, April 6, 1817, quoted in M. Boyd Coyner Jr., "John Hartwell Cocke of Bremo: Agriculture and Slavery in the Ante-Bellum South" (Ph.D. diss., University of Virginia, 1961), 120. See also Eaton, *Mind of the Old South,* 3–20.

Africa. However, Cocke also believed that the slaves needed an extensive training, mainly focusing on religious indoctrination, in order to be able to be free; in fact, he believed it was the master's duty to provide the slaves with this training while they were still in bondage. Since slavery was a sin that corrupted the slave no less than the master, slaves needed to purify their souls by receiving the teachings of Christianity; only then, Cocke thought, would the slaves be prepared to receive the full burden of freedom.[123]

Between 1820 and 1860, Cocke and his second wife, Louisa, a devout believer, implemented a massive program of religious indoctrination of their slaves at Bremo. While clergymen preached to the slaves every Saturday and Sunday in the plantation chapel, Louisa Cocke taught slave children the rudiments of reading and writing. The private papers that John and Louisa Cocke have left show that both considered their effort to morally uplift and educate their slaves to be part of their duties as slaveholders. In particular, in 1863, reflecting over his past deeds, Cocke wrote in his journal that "as soon as I determined to be a slaveholder I became sensible of the responsibility I assumed for the Beings over whom I assumed the Control." Such responsibilities went beyond the duties of a paternalistic relation of reciprocity and included the obligation "to increase the intelligence and improve the moral character" of the slaves. Yet, in order to provide the slaves with a complete program of moral education, Cocke also enforced "a system of police designed to increase cleanliness and comfort in their persons and houses" together with strict regulations that he had devised in order to eradicate the slaves' use of alcohol. Significantly, regarding his temperance program on the plantation, Cocke received the praise of his friend Edmund Ruffin, who himself fought against "drunkenness among slaves" and who, similarly, became a member of a temperance society.[124]

Among Cocke's many intrusions in the slaves' lives, including the prohibition against consuming alcohol, was also his attempt to regulate their marriages. In fact, a substantial part of the religious indoctrination that Cocke

123. See Eaton, *Mind of the Old South*, 9–14; and Randall M. Miller, "Introduction," in Randall M. Miller, ed., *"Dear Master": Letters of a Slave Family* (Ithaca, N.Y., 1986), 27–31.

124. John Hartwell Cocke journal, 1863–1864; John Hartwell Cocke to Rev. Henry Smith, 1 October 1833; John Hartwell Cocke to Rev. Henry Smith, 1 October 1831, and Edmund Ruffin to John Hartwell Cocke, 20 October 1834, all quoted in Coyner, "John Hartwell Cocke," 323–324, 340. See also John C. Willis, "From the Dictates of Pride to the Paths of Righteousness: Slave Honor and Christianity in Antebellum Virginia," in Edward C. Ayers and John C. Willis, eds., *The Edge of the South: Life in Nineteenth-Century Virginia* (Charlottesville, Va., 1991), 37–55.

imposed upon his slaves focused on his concern that they might live in sin. Consequently, Cocke encouraged his slaves' legal unions and manifested his approval of them by making personal gifts. In particular, Cocke was in the habit of giving personal items of his clothing to the slaves who united in marriage. At the same time, he often made sure that the wedding of a slave—especially a household slave—became an occasion for proper celebration among all the members of what he considered his extended family, acting in truly paternalistic fashion.[125]

Yet, despite Cocke's best intentions, his efforts to forcefully instill ideas of Christian morality in his slaves' minds encountered constant opposition. Neither thievery nor adultery stopped. The frequent floggings that Cocke and his overseers gave the slaves for acts of immorality and their threats to sell them to other masters did nothing to prevent the slaves' resistance to his attempts at achieving total control over their minds and souls. A typical story is that of foreman George, a slave who ran away from Bremo several times in order to be able to drink whiskey and wine in defiance of Cocke's temperance rules. Clearly, slaves understood and despised the fact that, despite Cocke's rhetoric, their status as enslaved laborers could improve only if they submitted to their master's will and they agreed to undertake the rigorous moral training that he demanded from them. However, given the powerful influence that Cocke exercised over their minds through education and religious indoctrination, relatively few slaves continued to openly oppose him, while an increasing number of them found the prospect of a promised freedom immensely attractive. Cocke's paternalistic program achieved its greatest success in 1833, when he freed Peyton Skipwith, a slave whom he considered "prepared for the change" because of his commitment to temperance and his devotion to Christianity. Skipwith showed that he had fully accepted his master's religious and moral teachings, since he performed his daily duties with little sign of resistance; in return, Cocke gave him the reward he long sought. In Cocke's thought, if the slaves worked hard enough to deserve it, the master would provide for their material and spiritual welfare, would teach them the blessings of Christianity, and, eventually, would grant them the gift of freedom.[126]

Still, behind the rhetoric of his idea of preparing his slaves for their future manumission, Cocke's chief objective was the creation of a docile

125. See both Willis, "From the Dictates of Pride"; and Coyner, "John Hartwell Cocke."
126. On the Skipwith slave family, see Miller, "Introduction," 34–36.

workforce, one that ought to feel wholly committed to the master for as long as he deemed necessary. In this respect, Cocke took the paternalistic idea of reciprocity in the master-slave relationship a step further than Hammond. In fact, it was hardly a coincidence that Cocke, a progressive planter and convinced agricultural reformer, attempted to perfect the paternalistic system, stretching the concept of reciprocity almost to the point of abolishing slavery. While engaging in the attempt to morally uplift his slaves, Cocke was also busy trying to improve the agricultural performance of his plantation. To this end, he made several experiments, following the example of advocates of scientific agriculture such as his friend Edmund Ruffin. In particular, Cocke made extensive use of marling, application of animal manure, crop rotation, and several different techniques for preparing the ground for cultivation. He raised his last tobacco crop in 1839; thereafter, he only grew wheat and corn, even though he obtained mixed results. Clearly, Cocke's commitment to scientific agriculture related to his attempts to reform slavery. In the same way he wished the earth to respond positively to his agricultural experiments, Cocke also wished his slaves to give a positive response to his experiments in paternalism and reciprocity—experiments that led him to treat them more humanely and motivate them with the prospective of their future manumission, even if he still kept them under strict control. In this respect, Cocke's example shows better than any other the simultaneous advantages and limitations of the type of paternalistic attitudes that a number of progressive planters adopted in the antebellum American South.[127]

Unlike progressive planters in the American South, progressive landowners in the *Mezzogiorno* did not have to come to terms with the contradiction of the coexistence of agricultural modernization with a system of unfree labor. Still, other factors—such as the backwardness of agricultural techniques and the structural constraints of an underdeveloped market—conditioned the southern Italian landowners' attempts to improve the agricultural economy to no less extent than slavery conditioned comparable attempts by American planters. In southern Italy, as in the American South, ideas focusing on rational management of both land and labor characterized the behavior of those members of the elite who showed their commitment to both agricultural modernization and liberal principles. Southern Italian landowners who adopted entrepreneurial attitudes in the management of their landed

127. See Charles W. Turner, "Virginia Agricultural Reform, 1815–1860," *AH* 26 (1952): 80–89.

estates were, typically, either progressive noblemen or landed bourgeois who had benefited from the abolition of feudalism. Their ethos had a great deal in common with the paternalistic ethos that characterized the ideology of a substantial number of progressive planters in the American South. Yet, an important difference lay in the fact, that, while combining ideas about rational management of the landed estates with paternalistic ideas about reciprocal relations between masters and laborers, southern Italian progressive landowners maintained a fairly flexible approach to the use of their free workforce and experimented with different contractual agreements and forms of tenancy—which was impossible for American planters under the constraints of slavery. At the same time, southern Italian progressive landowners tended to be equally strong advocates of direct—as opposed to absentee— land management, while they often adopted particular paternalistic practices in their actual treatment of the laborers.[128]

The analysis of the documents concerning Agostino Serra's landed estate at Cannavà is a particularly revealing case study in southern Italian paternalism. In her study, Mariarosaria Giorgio has related "the paternalistic model on which the nineteenth-century landed aristocracy built its link with the poorest peasant classes" to Serra's use of a particular type of contractual practice (*ingabellazioni a dettaglio*). This specific sort of contract allowed the sale of a limited portion of the harvest to the poorest tenants on the *latifondo* and made available to them a temporary form of employment that guaranteed their subsistence. Even though Giorgio seems to consider paternalistic practices as antimodern, we cannot help but notice that the documents show that the practice of the *ingabellazioni a dettaglio* was only one of a number of repeated manifestations of Serra's interest for the lot of his tenants. Consequently, it is entirely possible that his gradual adoption of different paternalistic practices—practices that, incidentally, also went in the direction of improving the agricultural output of the estate—had led him to believe in the importance of reciprocal relations between master and laborers and that, thus, he was prepared to respect his obligations toward them. Interestingly, in her analysis of the correspondence between Serra and his son, Luciano, in regard to the administration of the estate, Giorgio has emphasized the importance of Serra's modern "ideal of a present and attentive landowner"; at the same time, she has also concluded that Serra's particular concept of

128. See Renata De Lorenzo, *Società economiche e istruzione agraria nell'Ottocento meridionale* (Milan, 1998), 92–108; and Petrusewicz, "Land-Based Modernization," 95–96

labor relations—which she has characterized, reminding us of Genovese, as "still strongly personalized and paternalistic"—showed specifically in "the reciprocity of the obligations in [Serra's] relations with the personnel ... and with the [various types of] rural laborers."[129]

While they adopted paternalistic attitudes in the treatment of their laborers, southern Italian progressive landowners such as Agostino Serra identified the key to efficient land and work management in the direct conduction of their landed estates and in the direct supervision of their workforce. Landowners who advocated these principles usually engaged to different degrees in the production and sale of valuable agricultural products, such as citrus fruits, olive oil, and wine. The efficiency of their own agricultural enterprises and the success of their own agricultural business made their attempts to promote agricultural reform all the more credible. Like progressive planters in the American South, progressive landowners in the *Mezzogiorno* sought to maximize the profit of their agricultural enterprises by combining efficiency in the production of cash crops with the direct management of their landed estates. Yet, unlike American planters, southern Italian landowners had to come to terms with the structural constraints of an underdeveloped market, one in which merchants operated in extremely precarious conditions and with a low degree of organization. Given the frequent oscillations in the market demand for particular products, southern Italian landowners had to rely on diversification in economic activities and flexibility in labor relations in order to be able to invest in swift financial operations that gave them high returns in the short-term.[130]

Whereas American planters were utterly dependent on the global demand for one commercial crop, which they produced using the majority of arable land on their plantations, on the *latifondi* southern Italian progressive landowners implemented a different type of economic rationality and concentrated their efforts on the combined production of different crops with

129. Giorgio, "L'azienda calabrese," 46, 48. See also Montroni, *Gli uomini del Re,* 85–93; Sinisi, "Le aziende calabresi," 91–116. For other case studies, see Ruggero Moscati, *Una famiglia 'borghese' nel* Mezzogiorno *e altri saggi* (Naples, 1964); Biagio Salvemini, *L'innovazione precaria. Spazi, mercati e società nel* Mezzogiorno *tra Sette e Ottocento* (Catanzaro, 1995), 21–22; and Maria L. Storchi, "Un'azienda agricola della Piana del Sele tra il 1842 e il 1843," in Massafra, ed., *Problemi di storia,* 117–139.

130. See Salvemini, *L'innovazione precaria,* 22–24; and Alberto Banti, "Gli imprenditori meridionali: razionalità e contesto," *Meridiana* 6 (1989): 63–89.

oscillating market value. In fact, according to Salvatore Lupo, "the mixed agricultural enterprise, partially transformed by the cultivation of commercial crops, represent[ed] a real model of agrarian progress for several proprietors, both noble and non-noble." Lupo relates the idea of "agrarian progress" to the "enlightened vanguard" of southern Italian landowners, a group that included those who actively engaged in entrepreneurial activities. It was precisely this type of landed estate, with combined cultivation of different crops—which entrepreneurial landowners regarded as a model of agrarian progress—that was particularly adaptable to the fluctuations of market demand in the *Mezzogiorno*.[131]

Southern Italian progressive landowners who embraced the paternalistic ethos adapted the idea of reciprocal relations to the particular conditions of the nineteenth-century *Mezzogiorno*, a society in which—unlike American planters—they did not dominate as masters over an enslaved and racially exploited working class. Consistent with the behavior of other progressive agrarian elites, southern Italian landowners intended reciprocity as an obligation to "guarantee" their workers with subsistence and protection from abuse and violence in return for loyalty. The "guarantee system" struck a balance between the landowners' need to keep to a minimum the degree of labor conflict and achieve the maximum degree of efficient production and the workers' need to achieve a certain degree of stability and security in their employment. In her analysis of the nineteenth-century *latifondo*, Marta Petrusewicz has shown how the employees who worked at fixed salaries—the "provisionees" (*provvisionati*)—were the cornerstone of the guarantee system of reciprocal relations between landowner and workers, a system in which both understood the implications of each other's rights and duties. In the words of Petrusewicz, "it was the *provvisionati*'s duty to work well, respect the owners, and be disciplined, obedient, and loyal; it was the master's duty to treat them well and protect them." The entire "workability of the *latifondo* system depended primarily on the masters' and workers' recognition of reciprocity in their relations."[132]

In practice, the guarantee system was the key factor that prevented the *latifondo* from becoming a full-blown capitalist enterprise and preserved its

131. Lupo, "I proprietari," 112–113. See also Montroni, "Introduzione," 1–14; and De Lorenzo, *Società economiche e istruzione agraria*, 46–92.

132. Petrusewicz, *Latifundium*, 185.

hybrid character through the persistence of highly personalized relations between masters and workers and their widespread use of rewards in kind, rather than in cash. At the same time, according to Petrusewicz, the guarantee system allowed peasants to access the lands of the *latifondo* and grow crops as a supplement to their subsistence wage. This, in turn, prevented the proletarianization of the workforce—which lived only partly off its wage—and provided landowners with an unlimited supply of cheap labor. Despite her claim of a hybrid capitalist/noncapitalist character of the *latifondo*, Petrusewicz has insisted that her interpretation of the guarantee system differs from Genovese's interpretation of planters' paternalism, since in "the paternalism of the American slave system . . . the relationship between master and slave was essentially personal and links of control and subordination led from the individuals within one class to individuals within another." These particular features of American slaveholders' paternalism contributed to undermine solidarity among the plantation slaves. In contrast, the collective character of the social agreement at the heart of the guarantee system reduced the level of alienation of the *latifondo*'s agrarian laborers from their community and kept the level of social conflict to a minimum.[133]

Yet, notwithstanding Petrusewicz's claims, the ideologies at the heart of the guarantee system and of slaveholders' paternalism had an impressive number of characteristics in common. The most important common characteristic was the idea that reciprocal rights and duties bound in a sort of tacit agreement masters and laborers. In both cases, masters claimed that they provided their laborers with some sort of service—protection, or food and shelter—in return for the work that the laborers performed for them. However, while in the American South paternalism was really an ideological system that planters used to justify slavery and to which slaves had to adjust, trying to mold it to their own advantage, in the *Mezzogiorno* the absence of slavery worked in favor of the guarantee system, which was closer to a real labor contract binding an employer to his free employees. Still, the exploitation that both of these types of masters' paternalism masked showed particularly in the lack of workers' power and in the strict control that American planters and southern Italian landowners exercised over the lives and work activities of slaves and peasants.[134]

133. Petrusewicz, *Latifundium*, 17. See also Marta Petrusewicz, "Wage-Earners but Not Proletarians: Wage Labor and Social Relations in the Nineteenth-Century Calabrian Latifondo," *Review* 10 (1987): 471–503; and Petrusewicz, "Demise of Latifondismo," 33–39.

134. See, on some of these issues, the debate between Giancarlo De Vivo, John Davis, and

An illuminating case of a southern Italian progressive landowner who sought to achieve a high degree of control over the lives and work activities of the peasants who lived on his estate is that of Vito Nunziante Sr. Born to a family that belonged to the landed bourgeoisie of the region around Naples, Nunziante made his military career during the convulsed years of the 1799 Neapolitan Revolution and the Napoleonic occupation of southern Italy, always remaining loyal to the Bourbons. In 1816, acknowledging his loyalty to the crown, Ferdinand I granted Nunziante the noble title of marquis; subsequently, Ferdinand II made him commander-in-chief of the Bourbon army in the continental *Mezzogiorno*. Besides being an important public figure, Nunziante was also a complex personality with diverse interests and with specific ideas about economic improvement and agricultural reform. He was a member of the Economic Society of Calabria Ultra I and was in contact with important economic reformers and statesmen, such as Carlo Afan De Rivera and Ludovico Bianchini. Throughout his life, Nunziante engaged in several attempts at land reclamation and economic development in different areas of the Bourbon kingdom. At heart, he was a landed entrepreneur and a member of the progressive section of the southern landed elite close to the Bourbon administration; he epitomized the entrepreneurial spirit of those progressive landowners who belonged to the most recently formed aristocracy and to the landed bourgeoisie.[135]

In 1817, Nunziante set out to reclaim land on the plain of Rosarno, in Calabria, an area that was heavily infested by malaria. Five years later, in 1822, having completed the process of land reclamation, he proceeded to lay the foundations of a new village, San Ferdinando; the village was to be the exclusive property of Nunziante. Writing in 1839, Francesco Palermo described Nunziante's plan for the village as characterized by "two aligned rows of houses, with a spacious street in between; at one end [of the street] a church, at the other end a palace for himself." According to Palermo, "he [Nunziante] called this village San Ferdinando, and placed there a priest, then a doctor, and the necessary craftsmen, taking them, with the King's permission, from His Majesty's convicts, who were in great numbers in those times." Palermo

---

Piero Bevilacqua in the *TLS*, 8 November 1991, 29 November 1991, 6 December 1991, and 27 December 1991. Also, on paternalism among the Neapolitan aristocracy, see Macry, *Ottocento*, 63–74.

135. See Giuseppe Civile and Giovanni Montroni, *Tra il nobile e il borghese. Storia e memoria di una famiglia di notabili meridionali* (Naples, 1996), 31–37. See also Ferdinando Nunziante, "Il generale Vito Nunziante (1775–1836)," *ASPN* 23 (1964).

referred to the fact that Nunziante used convicts (*servi di pena*) to perform most of the work in the construction of the village and in the laying out of agricultural fields.[136]

Later, in order to attract inhabitants to his village, Nunziante allowed peasants to work on his estate without the obligation to pay any rent for the first two years. As a consequence, the population of San Ferdinando steadily increased until in 1850 it reached one thousand inhabitants. This figure included two different categories of peasants, both of whom were tenants on the Nunziante estate: the *coloni* and the *massari*. As the village rose in size, the *coloni* gradually replaced the *servi di pena* as the largest part of the working population; by 1850, they numbered almost six hundred. The *coloni* were the poorest category of workers at San Ferdinando; most of them could only afford to rent small portions of land and work as day field hands (*bracciali*), either directly for Nunziante or for the *massari*. The *massari* were richer tenants who typically owned cattle, if not land, of their own; they rented large tracts of the Nunziante estate and supervised the work that the *coloni* performed for them under exploitative conditions. Doubtless, the two hundred *massari* formed a sort of upper class in San Ferdinando; significantly, they lived in brick houses in the village, while the *coloni* lived in miserable dwellings made of straw (*pagliaie*). Nunziante duly acknowledged the *massari*'s privileged position, using a careful attitude in dealing with them, an attitude that was in marked contrast to his exploitation of both *coloni* and *servi di pena*.[137]

Despite its exploitative characteristics, the relationship between Nunziante and his workers at San Ferdinando was a model of reciprocity and of the particular type of paternalism that characterized southern Italian progressive landowners. In exchange for the work that they performed on his estate at San Ferdinando, Nunziante provided the *coloni* with dwellings to live in and land to work on and, above all, "guaranteed" their protection from abuse by the *massari*. According to Aurelio Lepre, the Nunziante family's paternalistic attitude related to their exclusive rights to property over the land and houses of San Ferdinando; as a result of these rights, the Nunziantes' position in the village was one of potentially absolute power, while the laborers' position was one of dependence. Lepre calls the relationship between

136. Francesco Palermo, *Vita e fatti di Vito Nunziante* (Florence, 1839), quoted in Civile and Montroni, *Tra il nobile e il borghese,* 40; see also 37–38. See also Salvatore Lupo, *Il giardino degli aranci. Il mondo degli agrumi nella storia del Mezzogiorno* (Venice, 1990), 44.

137. See Civile and Montroni, *Tra il nobile e il borghese,* 42–43.

the Nunziante family and the peasants of San Ferdinando "a father/master [*padre/padrone*] relationship" and he claims that it "did not diminish in time, but rather became stronger because of the Nunziantes' direct intervention in the management of all the services that the community needed."[138]

The concept at the heart of the *padre/padrone* relationship between southern Italian landowners and peasants resembled the American planters' paternalistic idea of the master-slave relationship, with its emphasis on the master's fictive extended family as one which included the laborers as well; yet, the link with an older feudal past provided the southern Italian version of paternalism with very distinctive features. In the case of the Nunziantes, as Civile and Montroni have noticed, "the ownership of all the village houses, the almost exclusive control of all the available land, the general [Vito Nunziante]'s position in the high hierarchies of Bourbon power" contributed to make their relationship with the peasant community at San Ferdinando similar to the one of feudal lords with their vassals. Moreover, the Nunziantes considered San Ferdinando to be the original and most important nucleus of their family property, similar to the way noblemen used to consider their fiefdom. Therefore, it is not exaggerated to imply that the Nunziantes had a *padre/padrone* relationship with the laborers on their estate that was potentially comparable to the one that former feudal lords had with their servants. Yet, the Nunziantes' management of San Ferdinando was hardly a relic of feudalism. Ever since Vito Nunziante's foundation of the village, agricultural experimentation, cash crop production, and organized administration distinguished the San Ferdinando estate and contributed to maintaining the family reputation of being agricultural entrepreneurs and innovators. Accordingly, in practice, the Nunziantes' *padre/padrone* relationship with their laborers—though rooted in the southern Italian feudal past—was not a repetition of old feudal practices, but rather the result of their transformation of it into a modern southern Italian version of paternalism, one in which reciprocity and the guarantee system loomed large.[139]

It is not difficult to imagine that the Nunziantes considered the laborers at San Ferdinando a sort of extended family, comparable to the way paternalistic planters saw the slaves on their plantations as part of their own

---

138. Aurelio Lepre, *Storia del Mezzogiorno d'Italia*, vol. 2, *Dall'Antico Regime alla società borghese (1657–1860)* (Naples, 1986), 143.

139. Civile and Montroni, *Tra il nobile e il borghese*, 40; see also 42–43.

extended household. More important still is the fact that, besides providing the inhabitants of San Ferdinando with a church, Vito Nunziante put
a priest, Father Pietro Arecchi, in charge of the general administration of
the landed estate and of the management of the workforce. Though this was
a fairly common practice among southern Italian landowners, we cannot
help but notice the parallel with John Hartwell Cocke of Bremo's designs
for control over his slaves' minds through religious education. In both cases,
taking the paternalistic idea of reciprocity a step further, the master provided
for both the physical and the spiritual well-being of his laborers in return for
the work that they performed for him, keeping a particularly close eye on
their religious indoctrination. Yet, it is clear that in both cases the master's
concern for the well-being of his laborers aimed primarily, if not exclusively,
at guaranteeing social peace on the landed estate. In fact, referring to the activities of southern Italian progressive landowners such as Luciano Serra—
and, doubtless, also Vito Nunziante—Giovanni Montroni has written that
"the numerous initiatives which were an expression of the master's paternalism aimed at guaranteeing the preservation of a social balance which was . . .
essential to both master and peasants."[140]

Interestingly, comparable to what happened in Cocke's case, Nunziante's
paternalistic project went hand-in-hand with a parallel project of economic
improvement and agricultural modernization. At San Ferdinando, commercial agriculture was the most important economic activity from the early
years of the village's existence. After Vito Nunziante's death, his sons and
nephews continued to engage in agricultural experimentation and in the
improvement of cash crop production, focusing on the cultivation of olives,
wine grapes, and citrus, until these became the strongest sector in the economy of San Ferdinando. By the 1850s, the Nunziante estate was a complex
and rationally managed agricultural enterprise in which diversification of
sectors of production and commercialization of agricultural products such as
olive oil, wine, and silk coexisted in harmony. By then, the Nunziantes were
the most successful example of ennobled bourgeois entrepreneurs, together
with the Barraccos. Both of them had successfully asserted their entrepreneurial spirit within the ranks of the southern Italian landed elite, maintaining a careful equilibrium between their landed bourgeois origins and their
recent cooptation into the progressive section of the aristocracy.[141]

140. Montroni, *Gli uomini del Re*, 91. See also Civile e Montroni, *Tra il nobile e il borghese*, 42–43.
141. Civile and Montroni, *Tra il nobile e il borghese*, 49–146. See also Giuseppe Civile and

A similar and equally emblematic example of an ennobled landed bour-geois who was both an entrepreneurial landowner and an agricultural re-former with paternalistic attitudes is that of Neapolitan Giacomo Savarese. In 1832, Savarese published an essay on the largest natural plain in the *Mezzo-giorno* (the *Tavoliere* in Apulia) in which he advocated the need to adopt a liberal policy so as to allow the agro-pastoral economy of the region to flourish without legal constraints. Subsequently, he took part in several gov-ernmental committees for land reclamation in the area around the Volturno River, where he owned property, and he gained the trust of the Bourbon administration. A convinced advocate of the primacy of agriculture, Savarese vigorously criticized industrialization because of the social disruption that accompanied it, while he believed in the importance of traditional social relationships. This belief led him to mature paternalistic convictions and to stress the importance of the elite's moral obligation to "improve soci-ety, modifying its individuals through education,"[142] as he wrote in an 1842 speech on Neapolitan kindergartens. Forty years later, Savarese would ex-tend his paternalistic approach also to the factories, writing an essay on the contribution of the upper classes to mitigating the effects of the exploitation of the industrial working class. In 1855, Ferdinand II appointed Savarese president of the Land Reclaim Commission, a post that renowned agri-cultural reformer Carlo Afan De Rivera had occupied before him. Soon after, the king granted Savarese the noble title of baron in recognition of his outstanding work. Throughout his career, Savarese advocated the necessity of strengthening the power of the landowning class with a liberal economic policy, and as a representative of the landowning bourgeoisie, he believed that his class, rather than the aristocracy, ought to lead the movement for agricultural reform in the Bourbon kingdom.[143]

Giovanni Montroni, "L'azienda agraria dei Nunziante di San Ferdinando nella seconda metà del XIX secolo," in Massafra, ed., *Problemi di storia*, 141–156; and Salvemini, *L'innovazione pre-caria*, 22–23.

142. Giacomo Savarese, *Discorso recitato all'Adunanza Generale degli Asili Infantili il 27 Feb-braio 1842 da Giacomo Savarese* (Naples 1842), 10. See also Giacomo Savarese, *Memoria sul Tavo-gliere di Puglia di Giacomo Savarese* (Naples, 1832), 10–14.

143. See Giacomo Savarese, *Delle cause del malessere delle classi operaie e del concorso delle classi agiate per attenuarne gli effetti* (Naples, 1883). See also Giovanni Aliberti, *Un oppositore agrario del Mezzogiorno: Giacomo Savarese* (Naples, 1967), 12–24; Antonio Anzilotti, *Movimenti e contrasti per l'unità italiana* (Milan, 1964), 257–303; and Costanza D'Elia, *Stato Padre, Stato Demiurgo. I lavori pubblici nel Mezzogiorno* (Bari, 1996), 84–85.

In his own landed estates, located on the Neapolitan coast and in the exceptionally prosperous region of Terra di Lavoro, Savarese engaged in different types of activities that related to commercial agriculture. Far from being an absentee landowner, he spent considerable time in the management of his land even though in his diary he complained that he was only able to attend to his fields when he left time aside from his other occupations. Savarese was especially fond of his estate at Carmiano, near Castellammare, which also included a villa and on which he engaged in the cultivation of grain and in the production of wine. Yet, the most important cash crop that Savarese produced at Carmiano was citrus; in his diary, he took careful notes on the number and types of orange and lemon trees he planted in his fields. The care that Savarese showed in his land management related closely both to his advocacy of agricultural reform and to the fact that, as a landed bourgeois, he considered landed property to be "the natural foundation of society," in the words of Giovanni Aliberti. In this respect, Savarese's belief that the propertied classes held a key role in guiding the process of agricultural modernization in the *Mezzogiorno* had a great deal in common with the ideology of foremost economic reformers both in the Kingdom of the Two Sicilies and in other European peripheries.[144]

In the most interesting part of his private diary—which he wrote in 1854—Savarese explained his ideas about relations with the workforce and elaborated further on the paternalistic character of his worldview that had characterized his earlier work. Similar to other southern Italian landowners, Savarese rented sections of his land to local peasants and did not hesitate to exploit tenants for the benefit of his agricultural enterprise. He also opposed ideas about the workers' social advancement. For these reasons, though he embraced the paternalistic ethos, in his diary he was particularly careful at outlining the concept of reciprocity, maintaining a clear distinction between upper and lower classes. Interestingly, though, Savarese linked the idea of reciprocal relations between master and laborers with the idea of rational land management in a way reminiscent of the paternalistic attitudes of progressive American planters, such as John Hartwell Cocke or James Henry Hammond. In fact, in a section of his diary entitled "On Personal Politics," Savarese wrote that "in the *proprietary* system . . . the idea of the master is

---

144. Giacomo Savarese's diary, 22 May 1854, Savarese Family Papers, ASN; Aliberti, *Un oppositore*, 30.

a *given* (*un'idea sine qua non*)," because "in the proprietary system, the . . . master is the reason for the good administration of the house."[145]

Later in the same section, Savarese further explained that "the good of the things we own, in the government of the family, is the consequence of the interest of the master . . . unless a landowner is lunatic, or ignorant, his interest leads him to make the best out of the things he manages. The vineyard will be well-pruned, the tree well-cared, the land well-manured, the flock fat, the *colono* rich, the tenant satisfied." Therefore, in his most personal and private document, Savarese reiterated the primacy of landed property and, at the same time, provided a powerful argument for the existence of social inequalities and for the landowners' need to look simultaneously after their interests and after the well-being of their tenants.[146]

The reading of Savarese's diary shows that he considered the difference between landowners and tenants as equally fixed and permanent as the difference between slaveholders and slaves was for James Henry Hammond. To Savarese, the master's duty was to look after his interests and his landed property; he believed that the master's rational management of his estate would automatically lead to improvement in the laborers' conditions. Savarese's belief in the advocacy of agricultural reform combined with his adoption of paternalistic attitudes and led him to interpret the meaning of reciprocity as the master's obligation to provide for the well-being of his tenants exclusively through good administration. To Savarese, the master, acting for his own good, implicitly acted for the workers' good as well. As long as the tenants did not aspire to social advancement and were content with what the master provided them with—rented land and protection—he enjoyed a minimum level of class-conflict on his landed estate.[147]

Therefore, Savarese's rhetoric of reciprocity was impressively close to the characteristics of the guarantee system that Marta Petrusewicz has studied on the Barracco estate. In both cases, the crucial point in the master-laborers relationship was the masters' awareness of the necessity of concessions to the workforce as a key to maintaining the minimum level of class conflict. Like

145. Giacomo Savarese's diary, 9 June 1854, Savarese Family Papers, ASN (original text underlined).

146. Giacomo Savarese's diary, 9 June 1854, Savarese Family Papers, ASN. See also Aliberti, *Un oppositore*, 25–31, and *Potere e società locale nel Mezzogiorno dell'800* (Rome-Bari, 1987), 80–81; and Lepre, *Storia del Mezzogiorno*, 2:154–155.

147. See Aliberti, *Un oppositore*, 25–30.

the Barraccos and the Nunziantes, Savarese was a progressive bourgeois landowner who privileged the paternalistic ethos and sought to follow the idea of reciprocity that was at its core when dealing with labor relations. Comparable to progressive planters in the antebellum American South, progressive landowners in nineteenth-century southern Italy were often, though far from exclusively, particularly successful individuals who had risen within the ranks of the most recently formed sections of the landed elite—individuals who had in common, together with a commitment to paternalism and reciprocity, an equally strong commitment to the advocacy of progressive ideas on agricultural reform and economic modernization.

In both the antebellum American South and the nineteenth-century Italian *Mezzogiorno*, paternalism was an ethos particularly privileged by progressive elites. Though adopted by both old and recent slaveholding and landowning families, its appearance related closely to the rise of new classes of landed proprietors. As a nineteenth-century ideology, paternalism differed radically from the eighteenth-century patriarchal ethos in regard to both family relations and treatment of rural laborers. In paternalistic family relations, reciprocity characterized parents' attitudes toward their children and functioned also as a model for relations between masters and laborers. Due to the presence of slavery in the American South, paternalistic planters differed substantially from paternalistic landowners in the *Mezzogiorno*, especially in the way they established reciprocal relations with their laborers. Still, both elite groups stressed the importance of rights and duties that masters and workers were obliged to respect. In both cases, reciprocity gave a new meaning to the ideological justification of inequalities between landed proprietors and workers. In both cases, the masters' search for consensus, rather than the brutal application of power, allowed laborers room for bargaining and a better chance of gaining recognition of some rights. Also, in comparable ways, progressive planters and progressive landowners used paternalistic ideology to achieve more effectively the objective of higher returns in cash crop production, while masking with their search for consensus the presence of an undiminished exploitation of the laborers.

As specific ideological elements of the two worldviews of the ruling classes of the antebellum American South and of the nineteenth-century Italian *Mezzogiorno*, patriarchalism and paternalism had the potential to combine into powerful political creeds that could provide, in different forms, the ideological material for the foundation of two nation-states. Indeed, in both regions and at different points in time, the two patriarchal-paternalistic worldviews formed the core of political ideologies that, within particular national programs of reform, assumed the characteristics of specific sets of values. These values provided both an explanation for the existence of social inequalities and a justification of the importance of truly nationalist and elitist cultures. The different attempts to transform the two patriarchal-paternalistic worldviews into the cores of political ideologies that appealed to the majority of the people were true operations of social engineering that cut across race and class divisions in the American South and cut across class divisions in southern Italy. Born in the two social settings—the elites' families and their landed estates—that provided the model for power relations at the local level, the constituent elements of the two patriarchal-paternalistic worldviews moved to a higher plane when they combined to create political ideologies for the construction of nation-states in the two southern regions.[148]

148. On social engineering and nationalist ideology, see Eric J. Hobsbawm, "Introduction: Inventing Traditions," in Eric J. Hobsbawm and Terence Ranger, eds., *The Invention of Tradition* (Cambridge, 1983).

CHAPTER 3

Elites, Politics, and National Programs in the American South and in the Italian *Mezzogiorno*

The landed elites of the American South and of the Italian *Mezzo-giorno* were firmly in control of the economic and social life of their respective regions. Through the profits that they derived from the production and sale of commercial crops on plantations, farms, and *latifondi*, American slaveholders and southern Italian landowners dominated the agricultural sectors of the two southern regional economies and controlled their relationships with the world market. At the same time, comparable—though different—patriarchal-paternalistic worldviews provided the two elites with complex ideological justifications for their privileged economic and social position and for their exploitation of the workforce on their landed estates.

Yet, despite their undisputed economic and social prominence, the two elites' political supremacy was far from uncontested. In fact, in both the American South and the Italian *Mezzogiorno*, the landed elite engaged in protracted ideological and political struggle with the central government in order to either retain or assert its right to local autonomy. The struggle developed in different ways and occurred in different degrees of intensity in the two southern regions; however, in both cases, at its heart was a comparable contrast between either feared or real national government attempts to implement centralizing measures and the southern peripheral elite's response to them, or between core and periphery. In the United States, even though until the 1850s the southern minority mostly succeeded in controlling the politics of a weak federal government and in turning the latter's policies to its own advantage, American slaveholders voiced their fears and their opposition to the possibility of increasing governmental power, and consequently of stronger centralization, through the doctrine of states' rights. Conversely, in the Kingdom of the Two Sicilies, from as early as 1815, the absolutist Bourbon monarchy did manage to impose a strongly centralized bureaucratic system, and for their part southern Italian landowners and local power-holders not only resisted the actual administrative centralization, but also voiced other, equally important, demands for constitutional liberties, especially at times of revolutionary upheaval.

Initially, in an attempt to resolve the issues at stake, the two southern elites either joined or led different programs of reform of the socioeconomic and political systems—programs that were the ideological nucleuses of formal political parties in the United States and of informal political movements in southern Italy. Furthermore, in both the antebellum American South and the nineteenth-century Italian *Mezzogiorno,* repeated political and institutional crises—the most important of which occurred in 1850 and in 1848— led to different types of compromises over the extent of local autonomy in the southern peripheral regions. Then, during the 1850s, the two southern regional paths shared some important similarities in their developments, even though within very different contexts. On one hand, in the United States, the federal government progressively increased its strength and, with the rise of the Republican Party, became the heart of a political program of centralization focused on antislavery measures and, therefore, strongly opposed by southern slaveholders. On the other hand, in southern Italy, the Bourbon monarchy accelerated the steps toward its transformation into a tyrannically absolutist and heavily centralized kingdom, with a consequent rapid increase in the disaffection and outright opposition of liberal landowners, especially in the peripheral areas. From the point of view of the analysis of these later phases in the two ideological and political struggles between either feared or attempted core governmental centralization and the peripheral elites' resistance to it, the break-up of the American Union and the collapse of the Kingdom of the Two Sicilies ultimately appear as two comparable outcomes, with crucial similarities and differences in both their premises and their results.

To be sure, the dynamics of the two processes of opposition to central governmental policies and the roles that the southern elites played in the ultimate collapse of American and southern Italian governmental institutions are topics that have received a great deal of scholarly attention. On one hand, in the United States, historians have analyzed the collapse of the American Union, maintaining the idea of the centrality of slavery as the primary cause of sectional conflicts and, ultimately, of the Civil War. On

the other hand, in Italy, historians have analyzed the collapse of the Kingdom of the Two Sicilies, maintaining the idea that the loss of legitimacy of
the Bourbon administrative monarchy was crucial for the success of Italian
unification.[1]

There is much to learn by comparing these two case studies, since the
process of collapse of governmental institutions in the two regions was related to a combination of different factors, among which sectional contro-
versies over slavery in the United States and the loss of legitimacy of the
Bourbon monarchy in southern Italy were only the two most important.
Equally relevant and tightly linked factors were the changes in the composition of the southern landed elites, the demands of political representation by
new propertied classes in both the American South and the Italian *Mezzogiorno,* and the increasingly irreconcilable relationship between these new
sections of the landed elites—which dominated political life in the southern
peripheral regions—and the governments' policies of centralization. Therefore, in both the United States and southern Italy, the long-term causes of
the events of 1860–1861 stretched as far back as the early 1800s and related
to the economic and social changes that we have described in the previous
chapters and to their influences on the increasing radicalization of political
regionalism in the two southern peripheries.

In the southern periphery of the United States, the formation of a new
large class of slaveholders—which related to the boom in cotton production—did not just change the internal composition of the southern landed
elite; it also altered dramatically the balance of national politics. In fact, the
course of sectional conflicts over slavery highlighted the struggle between
the federal government's weak and then progressively stronger attempts to
assert its centralizing authority and the resistance to centralization staged
by a powerful, determined, and increasingly larger slaveholding elite based
in the southern region, an elite that effectively had the means to control the
outcome of federal governmental policies for a number of decades. Yet, as
the federal government grew stronger, the power of southern slaveholders
became progressively marginalized and peripheral, until when, in a final attempt to regain its central status, the southern elite threw all its efforts in the
creation of its own slaveholding Confederate nation.

1. See Eric Foner, "Slavery, the Civil War, and Reconstruction," in Eric Foner, ed., *The New
American History* (Philadelphia, Pa., 2002), 26–59; and Lucy Riall, "Garibaldi and the South," in
John A. Davis, ed., *Italy in the Nineteenth Century, 1796–1900* (Oxford, 2000), 132–153.

On the other hand, in the southern Italian periphery, the creation of a new class of landowners—which related to the consequences of the abolition of feudalism—was the source of a great deal of conflict between recent and established sections of the elite at both the local and national levels. In the long term, the process also triggered the end of Bourbon absolutist practices, when the new landowners' increasing demands for the adoption of liberal institutions and for effective means to defend private property first led to their confrontation with the core Neapolitan administration and then caused its final collapse. This, in turn, came largely as a result of the increasingly central role that southern Italian landowners, especially those who were forced to leave in exile for the Piedmontese kingdom, played in the political and military process that led to the creation of the Italian nation through the defeat of the Bourbon monarchy.

In the period leading to 1860, therefore, polarization between the governmental core and the southern periphery increasingly radicalized and became the dominant political theme in both the American South and the Italian *Mezzogiorno*. As political confrontation between core and periphery intensified and governmental institutions progressively lost their legitimacy in the eyes of the two southern elites, their members increasingly concentrated their efforts on the creation of new national institutions that would effectively substitute the old ones, guaranteeing the defense of both established rights and local autonomy. It is, therefore, in this context that we have to see the formation of the Confederate States of America and of the Kingdom of Italy.

In principle, the ideologies that informed the elites' programs of creation of new national institutions in the American South and in the Italian *Mezzogiorno* had a great deal in common with the ones of contemporary nationalist movements across the western world. Yet, the conservatism that characterized nationalist ideologies in the two southern regions was the source of a sharp distinction from European nationalisms. Both American slaveholders and southern Italian landowners, in fact, treated nationalism as an ideological device to exploit for their own exclusive benefit and used it in the context of their struggle against a type of governmental centralization that harmed their economic and sociopolitical interests. For this particular reason, though internally divided in both regional and ideological terms, the two southern elites chose the option of collaborating to the realization of programs of nation-building. And yet, they did this only after they exhausted all other means of confrontation with the federal and the Bourbon governments. In this sense, theirs was in both cases a negative type of nationalism, rather than being the type of positive, active nationalism that characterized popular revolutions in other regions of Europe. With their support for nationalist projects, American slaveholders and southern Italian landowners sought to achieve the two comparable aims of defending slavery and property rights by causing the collapse of the central governments whose policies threatened them. In this perspective, therefore, the elites' participation in the creation of new nations played an important part in masking behind the fiction of high ideals their hidden conservative agendas.

Core and Periphery in the American South and in the Italian Mezzogiorno

The concept of a dialectical relationship between core and periphery is particularly useful to describe the complex set of factors involved in the process of state-building in the United States—and in the American South in particular—and in the Kingdom of the Two Sicilies during the early decades of the nineteenth century. According to Donald Meinig, "center-periphery, heartland-hinterland, core-domain relationships—and tensions—are part of the generic structure of every nation of considerable size." Within this structure, the core is "the geographical nucleus . . . the principal seat of its [the nation's] leadership, the intelligence center and main focus of the communication network"; in contrast, the area outside the core—the domain, or periphery—is hierarchically subordinate to it in both socioeconomic and geopolitical terms, since it is "less densely settled, less intensely developed, less closely bound to the power and influence of the center."[2] In the early nineteenth-century United States, the South—though of central importance in political terms—was part of the American domain, a large peripheral region that, in both economic and social terms, gravitated around the nuclear area formed by the axis that included the highly commercialized and cultured urban centers of New York and Philadelphia, together with the incipient national political capital, Washington, D.C. Conversely, in the Italian *Mezzogiorno,* Naples and the region around it gathered all the functions of

2. Donald W. Meinig, *The Shaping of America: A Geographical Perspective on 500 Years of History,* vol. 1, *Atlantic America, 1492–1800* (New Haven, Conn., 1986), 370.

a commercial, sociocultural, and political core at whose center was a large capital city, while the entire territory beyond it effectively gravitated around the core region and depended on it as the domain of a single, large, southern Italian periphery.

In the early nineteenth century, therefore, two very different types of dialectics characterized relations between the core region and the southern periphery in the United States and in the Kingdom of the Two Sicilies. In the United States, the southern slaveholding elite belonged to a peripheral region in geographical and socioeconomic terms, and yet one which held such a degree of political power that southerners had filled the presidential office almost uninterruptedly since the foundation of the American Republic. As a consequence, for the most part, the southern periphery controlled the politics of the national government located in Washington, D.C.—the political center of the core region—while southern interests, especially slavery, faced relatively little direct threat. Conversely, in the Kingdom of the Two Sicilies, the southern Italian landowning elite located in the provinces did not just reside in regions that were peripheral in both geographical and socioeconomic terms, but it also held a minimal degree of political power, since the latter rested firmly in the hands of the Bourbon administration. As a consequence, from the perspective of the Bourbon government located in the core capital Naples, most of the *Mezzogiorno* was—unlike the American South—a peripheral region especially in political terms.

These differences related also to the existence of particularly distinguishing characteristics between the recent histories of the United States and of the Kingdom of the Two Sicilies. In the early nineteenth century, the United States was still a relatively recent and experimental political institution. The foundation of the American republic had stemmed from the concurrent will of the different states to participate in the establishment of a highly decentralized and federal administrative and governmental system; these features left a great deal of room for local autonomy by nineteenth-century standards, so that, effectively, the main political action usually took place at the state level. Conversely, after the Restoration, the Bourbon monarchy that ruled over the Kingdom of the Two Sicilies inherited the Napoleonic tradition of rigid centralization of bureaucratic and administrative structures, which left little room for local autonomy, and combined it with its peculiar tradition of eighteenth-century enlightened monarchical absolutism. Whereas most Americans would have considered the small degree of local autonomy that characterized nineteenth-century southern Italy as little more than a byproduct of an intolerably despotic regime, most southern Italians would have considered the high degree of local autonomy that characterized the United States as part of a far too radical political system.

In both cases, though, momentous social and economic changes in the peripheral regions resulted in the rise to power of local elites that demanded a higher degree of participation in the political arena at both the regional and the national levels. However, in the American case, the southern peripheral elite that controlled the federal government attempted to take the protection of its interests a step further through the territorial expansion of slavery, and it was northern opposition to these plans that led to the first sectional conflict and provoked the Missouri Crisis of 1819–1820. Conversely, in the southern Italian case, specific legal provisions that emanated from the Neapolitan core to the periphery in an attempt to provide normative standards of institutional uniformity aroused a great deal of opposition from the local elites of the *Mezzogiorno*—an opposition that reached its peak during the Revolution of 1820–1821.

According to Donald Meinig, in the 1850s, "in spite of enormous expansion in territory, population, and geographic development, the United States remained firmly anchored on the same nuclear area . . . the basic New York-Philadelphia axis, with its extensions to Baltimore and Boston on either side, a pattern that had been clearly evident by 1800." This nuclear area— or core—represented the economic and social heart of the nation, and its connecting axis extended also to the emergent national capital, Washington, D.C., which—as the seat of federal governmental institutions—effectively provided the political center of the American Union. Therefore, from a geographical perspective, from as early as 1800 the entire southern region was an economic and social periphery that gravitated around a core area, an area that mostly included large commercial urban centers located in the North. As a result, according to Meinig, the South developed a strong "regional self-consciousness" based on slavery, mainly because its peripheral location in economic and social terms gave a major contribution in creating a distinctively regional "domain" culture both far and different from the culture that characterized the core.[3]

3. Donald W. Meinig, *The Shaping of America: A Geographical Perspective on 500 Years of History*, vol. 2, *Continental America, 1800–1867* (New Haven, Conn., 1993), 418, 424–425.

And yet, in political terms, Washington, D.C., functioned as a rather weak center; in fact, until the 1850s it was still in its embryonic stages of development as a political capital. Also, even though a minority, southerners dominated federal politics; they often succeeded in having either southern or pro-southern presidents elected and, equally often, could count on the votes of a majority of pro-southern senators in Congress in order to have specifically proslavery legislation passed. It was only with the rise of the Republican Party in the mid-1850s that the federal government located in the capital began to become the heart of a political program that included the implementation of a number of centralizing policies directed against the slaveholders' domination of Congress and against their designs of western expansion. In turn, this process—a process that was well on its way by 1860—led to the increasing strengthening of the central institutions of the federal government located in Washington, D.C., which progressively became the true political core of the Union; at the same time, the process led to the increasing relegation of southern slaveholders to a less powerful and more marginal political role and to the consequent rapid transformation of the South—already a peripheral area in both geographic and socioeconomic terms—into a political periphery (see map 3).[4]

In general, from the socioeconomic point of view, within the very large southern peripheral area there were regions that were closer to the core—such as Virginia and Maryland—and which both strongly influenced it and received its influence. At the same time, there were relatively large regional centers—such as Charleston in South Carolina, Natchez in Mississippi, and New Orleans in Louisiana—that gathered the wealth of powerful local slaveholding elites. Throughout the period 1800–1860, the southern periphery was on the move as the frontier of expansion of cotton production continuously shifted and redrew the boundaries of the American domain. As cotton penetrated the entire area of the Old Southwest and transformed it into a Cotton Kingdom with planters, farmers, and slaves as its inhabitants, regional centers rose in number and importance, and so did the power and influence of the local elites in control of the wealth of the different southern regions. At the same time, the geographical structure of core and periphery that characterized the entire United States was replicated on a smaller scale in an infinite number of cases within the boundaries of the southern

4. See Richard Franklin Bensel, *Yankee Leviathan: The Origins of Central State Authority in America, 1859–1877* (New York, 1990), 18–19.

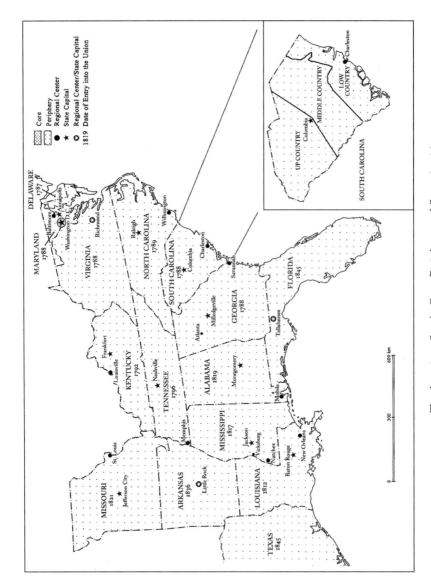

MAP 3. The American South: Core, Periphery, and States in 1860

peripheral area, while different counties and local communities increased or decreased in importance according to their proximity to the regional centers of economic, social, and political life.[5]

The territory of Mississippi—which became a state in 1817—was at the very heart of the frontier of expansion of cotton production. Between 1812 and 1820, this expansion caused the total figure of the South's cotton production to rise from three hundred thousand bales per year to more than double that number. Due to its enormous rate of agricultural growth, between the 1820s and the 1830s Mississippi became the largest recipient of slaves removed by the internal slave trade from their original location in the Atlantic Seaboard states. If in the 1820s the total number of slaves imported by Mississippi was less than twenty thousand, by the 1830s it had become more than one hundred thousand. By then, the average Mississippi plantation on which the majority of the imported slaves worked produced as much as 63,200 pounds of cotton per annum—which guaranteed most Mississippi planters handsome profits in their agricultural business.[6]

Within Mississippi, Natchez was the largest city and the most important regional center located on the southwestern cotton frontier. Founded as early as 1776 in a convenient location on the Mississippi River, from the 1790s onward the city rapidly rose in importance as farmers and planters in the Natchez district profited from the cultivation of cotton in the fertile alluvial soil on the river's banks. Though it never grew as much as other southern cities in population, barely reaching two thousand inhabitants in 1818, by the 1810s Natchez was already a center of fabulous wealth related to cotton production. Since cotton plantations located on alluvial soils—such as the ones around Natchez—were particularly productive and required large numbers of

5. See Thomas D. Clark and John D. W. Guice, *Frontiers in Conflict: The Old Southwest, 1795–1830* (Albuquerque, N.Mex., 1989); James D. Miller, *South by Southwest: Planter Emigration and Elite Ideology in the Deep South, 1815–1861* (Charlottesville, Va., 2002); Edward E. Baptist, *Creating an Old South: Middle Florida Plantation Frontier before the Civil War* (Chapel Hill, N.C., 2002); John Hebron Moore, *The Emergence of the Cotton Kingdom in the Old Southwest: Mississippi, 1770–1860* (Baton Rouge, La., 1988); Daniel S. Dupre, *Transforming the Cotton Frontier: Madison County, Alabama, 1800–1840* (Baton Rouge, La., 1997); and Donald McNeilly, *The Old South Frontier: Cotton Plantations and the Formation of Arkansas Society, 1819–1860* (Fayetteville, Ark., 2000).

6. The figures are in Michael Tadman, *Speculators and Slaves: Masters, Traders, and Slaves in the Old South* (Madison, Wisc., 1989), 12. See also Moore, *Emergence of the Cotton Kingdom,* 285–286; Charles Sydnor, *Slavery in Mississippi* (New York, 1933); and Mark M. Smith, *Debating Slavery: Economy and Society in the Antebellum South* (New York, 1998), 67–68.

slaves, in the Natchez district planter status was conferred upon individuals who owned no less than thirty slaves, rather than twenty slaves as in most of the South. The planter elite that controlled cotton production in Adams County, where Natchez was located, included invariably the same families from the 1790s onward. According to D. Clayton James, "throughout the [antebellum] era such clans as the Ellises, Dunbars, Hutchinses, Farrars, Bislands, and Brandons stood pre-eminent in landholdings, slave ownership, and social prestige." In Natchez itself, in the early 1810s the elite included both planters and professionals from no more than twenty families, all of whom engaged in the business of cotton planting; already by 1812, Natchez's wealthiest planter—Winthrop Sargent—owned "11,802 acres and 342 slaves in Adams County, as well as 20,000 acres in Ohio and Virginia."[7]

In fact, most of the members of Natchez's elite had ties with other areas of the South, since they often owned property and slaves elsewhere, especially in neighboring Louisiana, but also in faraway Virginia, as the example of Winthrop Sargent shows. Since the early 1800s, many planter families had relocated from the Atlantic Seaboard states to the southern frontier in the hope of reviving their agricultural business in new fertile lands. Similar to what happened in the other states of the Old Southwest, in Mississippi planters who fled the agricultural crisis that hit the Chesapeake and the Carolinas settled in different counties and made fortunes through cotton planting, all the while keeping their family ties with the East. As a consequence, some of the wealthiest slaveholders in Mississippi and in other frontier regions were absentee owners of extensive holdings in three or four different southern states, comparable to the majority of landowners of the *Mezzogiorno*, who resided in Naples and owned land throughout southern Italy.[8]

In the 1810s, if Natchez was the regional center—akin to a core with Adams County as its periphery—of a powerful rising elite of cotton planters, the entire state of Mississippi contributed in a major way to the formation

---

7. D. Clayton James, *Antebellum Natchez* (Baton Rouge, La., 1968), 149–150; and William K. Scarborough, "Lords or Capitalists? The Natchez Nabobs in Comparative Perspective," *JMH* 54 (1992): 229–267. See also Moore, *Emergence of the Cotton Kingdom*, 188–191.

8. See William K. Scarborough, *Masters of the Big House: Elite Slaveholders in the Mid-Nineteenth-Century South* (Baton Rouge, La., 2003), 24–25; Joan E. Cashin, *A Family Venture: Men and Women on the Southern Frontier* (Baltimore, Md., 1991); Jane Turner Censer, "Southwestern Migration among North Carolina Planter Families: 'The Disposition to Emigrate,'" *JSH* 57 (1991): 407–426; and Edward E. Baptist, "The Migration of Planters to Antebellum Florida: Kinship and Power," *JSH* 62 (1996): 526–554.

of a slaveholding class that based its fortunes on cotton production. A recent study of Warren County—which was settled by several Virginian and South Carolinian planters and was to become home to future Confederate president Jefferson Davis—shows that from the time of its formal establishment in 1810, the county developed as part of an area of cotton plantations that included a large section of the state of Mississippi. By the time of the foundation of the capital Vicksburg in 1819, the population of Warren County included already 1,400 whites, all of them either planters or farmers engaged in the production of cotton, and 1,280 enslaved blacks. Ten years later, Vicksburg was competing in size and wealth with Natchez as a regional center and the seat of a powerful planter elite, even though Vicksburg's planters could hardly count their slaves in hundreds as Natchez cotton "nabobs" did.[9]

As Warren County developed even before the foundation of its capital, Vicksburg, two different but related phenomena occurred. First, according to Christopher Morris, "population growth and eventual transition to staple agriculture enlarged households, changed their racial composition, and altered relations between their members." The overwhelming growth in the economic importance of slavery—because of its inextricable link with cotton production—mirrored its increasing pervasiveness as a model of relations both within the household and in society. Patriarchal-paternalistic attitudes soon became normative behaviors among cotton planters and farmers in their relations with family dependents and slaves.[10]

Second, the growing influence of slavery and cotton production, in dictating the changes in the geographical and economic landscape of the county, precluded the formation of large urban areas and at the same time subordinated the existence of the few small towns to the cotton planters' needs of ties with the national and international markets. As a consequence, until the beginning of the Civil War, Warren County remained an overwhelmingly agricultural area with few signs of either complex urban life or industrial production of any kind. A similar process accompanied the formation of large and small regional centers in the other frontier southern states whose settlement occurred from the 1790s onward. Recent studies of frontier communities in Alabama, Arkansas, and Florida have yielded abundant

9. See Christopher Morris, *Becoming Southern: The Evolution of a Way of Life, Warren County and Vicksburg, Mississippi, 1770–1860* (New York, 1995), 63–82; and James, *Antebellum Natchez*, 193–194.

10. Morris, *Becoming Southern*, 43. See also Janet Sharp Hermann, *The Pursuit of a Dream* (New York, 1981), 3–36.

evidence of the rapid rise in wealth of a powerful slaveholding elite that took advantage of the growth in cotton production and of the concurrent growth in the pervasiveness of slavery in the economic and social life of both town and countryside.[11]

Slavery was the reason behind the formation of states in the Old Southwest. Attracted by prospects of easy enrichment through cotton planting, thousands of settlers moved to the frontier regions of the South. As a result, in less than a generation, two frontier territories—Mississippi and Alabama—reached the number of people required to apply for statehood; Mississippi joined the American Union in 1817, followed by Alabama two years later. The speed of this development was, perhaps, the main sign that the slaveholding elites that dominated the cotton economy of the southwestern frontier wished to put forward an immediate claim to participation in national politics through the states' official inclusion in the Union. Though in Alabama the 1819 state constitution was exceptionally democratic, since all white males could vote and hold office, in Mississippi, as in most of the South except for Georgia and Maryland, until the 1830s there were clear restrictions on the electorate based on property and tax payment—besides the omnipresent requirement of having a white skin.[12]

At the same time, in the Atlantic Seaboard states, even though taxpayers could vote for both the lower House and the state Senate, the election of governors occurred strictly through the legislature. Also, property requirements regulated the elections of judges and county court officials throughout the South. Therefore, well into the 1820s, a slaveholding and landowning elite, which in the frontier states included some of the wealthiest cotton planters, ruled over the majority of the southern states, East and West. Since the United States was a federal union with a highly decentralized governmental system, by controlling the election of state officials the slaveholding elite effectively held the control of the local government. Though land was cheap and abundant throughout the South, the system of property quali-

---

11. See Morris, *Becoming Southern*, 103–113; Dupre, *Transforming the Cotton Frontier*, 11–48; McNeilly, *Old South Frontier*, 53–92; and Baptist, *Creating an Old South*, 18–19. See also Don H. Doyle, *Faulkner's County: The Historical Roots of Yoknapatawpha* (Chapel Hill, N.C., 1998), 53–86.

12. See William W. Freehling, *The Road to Disunion: Secessionist at Bay, 1776–1854* (New York, 1990), 163–164; and John Mills Thornton III, *Politics and Power in a Slave Society: Alabama, 1800–1860* (Baton Rouge, La., 1978), 97–98.

fications still created a situation by which in Virginia, in 1816—according to Thomas Jefferson—the members of the counties' governing bodies were "self-appointed, self-continued, holding their authorities for life, and with an impossibility of breaking in on the perpetual succession of any faction once possessed of the bench."[13]

Although Virginia's situation was somewhat extreme, the county courts had enormous power over local affairs and tended to be dominated by the wealthiest and most influential slaveholding families. In fact, in frontier southern states such as Mississippi, according to Christopher Morris, "local government mirrored informal structures of authority," privileging kinship ties and neighborhood leadership. In Warren County, as in countless places throughout the South, the local officeholders were not just part of the economic elite, they were often linked to one another through family connections. A similar importance in kinship ties characterized also the Florida communities studied by Edward Baptist. Significantly, this turned out to be a particularly important factor in the formation of political factions among members of the slaveholding elite at later times.[14]

Throughout the first two decades of the nineteenth century, if slavery formed the basis of the economic and social power of the rising elites in the southern periphery, the preservation of slavery was a matter that in turn related to national political debates over the extent of local autonomy. Since the early days of the republic, the vexing question of centralization or decentralization of political power had divided Americans between two different parties—Federalists and Jeffersonian Republicans—which expressed radically opposite political views in regard to the relation between the federal government and the individual states of the Union, or between core and periphery. In synthesis, Federalists advocated a strong national government with a much higher degree of legislative and executive powers than those of the individual states. Jeffersonian Republicans, instead, supported the view that, ultimately, sovereignty resided in the states' governments that had willingly joined the Union as a loose federation of regional political entities.[15]

13. Thomas Jefferson is quoted in Charles Sydnor, *The Development of Southern Sectionalism, 1819–1848* (Baton Rouge, La., 1948), 40.

14. Morris, *Becoming Southern*, 147. See also Dupre, *Cotton Frontier*, 47–48; and Baptist, *Creating an Old South*, 252–253.

15. See Stanley Elkins and Eric McKitrick, *The Age of Federalism: The Early Republic, 1788–1800* (New York, 1993), 553–555. See also Richard Hofstadter, *The Idea of a Party System: The Rise of*

The two views had a particular importance in relation to the southern states, where the preservation of slavery—an economic and social institution increasingly at odds with the rest of the country—was conditioned by two related factors: the federal government's determination to preserve it and its guarantee that no federal law would ever trespass the right of a state to regulate its internal institutions. The first factor depended on the balance between northern and southern states in Congress. In the Senate, balance was related to the presence of an equal number of senators—fixed at two for each state—for northern and southern states. In the House of Representatives, however—where the number of congressmen depended on the population of each state—the matter was regulated by the Constitution's three-fifths clause, according to which, purely for reasons of congressional balance, states counted each slave as three-fifths of a vote. Yet, in both houses, the balance was subject to continuous readjustment each time a new state joined the Union.[16]

After the 1787 Northwest Ordinance excluded slavery from the territories around the Great Lakes, the free states of Ohio, Illinois, and Indiana joined the American Union in the years between 1800 and 1819. Contemporarily, Louisiana, Mississippi, and Alabama joined the Union as slave states, so that, by 1819, twenty-two representatives of eleven northern free states and twenty-two representatives of eleven southern slave states balanced each other in the Senate. The same was not the case in the House of Representatives, where, despite the three-fifths clause, the difference between northern and southern seats increased from eleven in 1800 to thirty-three in 1820. Southern interests in the House would retain this minority status until the Civil War. It is true that, through the control of both the presidency and the Senate, the South mostly dominated national politics. However, from the perspective of southern politicians, the election of a number of southern presidents was an indispensable guarantee for the respect of the interests of

---

Legitimate Opposition in the United States, 1780–1840 (New York, 1970); Lance Banning, The Jeffersonian Persuasion: Evolution of a Party Ideology (Ithaca, N.Y., 1978); and Noble E. Cunningham Jr., The Jeffersonian Republicans: The Formation of Party Organization (Chapel Hill, N.C., 1957).

16. Roger Ransom, Conflict and Compromise: The Political Economy of Slavery, Emancipation, and the American Civil War (New York, 1989), 101. See also Paul Finkelman, "Slavery and the Constitutional Convention: Making a Covenant with Death," in Richard Beeman, Stephen Botein, and Edward C. Carter II, eds., Beyond Confederation: Origins of the Constitution and American National Identity (Chapel Hill, N.C., 1987), 188–225; Forrest McDonald, E Pluribus Unum: The Formation of the American Republic, 1776–1790 (Indianapolis, Ind., 1979); and Gordon Wood, The Creation of the American Republic, 1776–1789 (Chapel Hill, N.C., 1969).

the southern minority, and especially for "the protection of the most important property right in the South: the ownership of slaves."[17]

Besides the North-South balance in Congress, the other factor that conditioned the preservation of slavery in the southern periphery was the federal government's guarantee that the individual states maintained their rights to sovereignty and their prerogatives over local government. In the early years of the republic, a substantial number of southern slaveholders became Jeffersonian Republicans and enthusiastic advocates of the doctrine of states' rights. In broad terms, the ideology of Jeffersonian Republicanism combined the defense of state sovereignty with elements of egalitarianism—the belief in individual liberty and equality—and agrarianism—the idea that the perfectly virtuous republic was a republic of self-sufficient farmers. Consequently, southern slaveholders embraced Jeffersonian Republicanism as a way to advance their own interests as part of a republic of sovereign states and white property-owning—read "slave-owning"—farmers. As for state sovereignty, Thomas Jefferson and James Madison first elaborated the doctrine of states' rights in their protest resolutions—the Kentucky and Virginia Resolutions—against the antilibertarian 1798 Alien and Sedition Acts. In particular, in the Kentucky Resolution, Jefferson argued that the states retained the "right to their own self-government." Similarly, in the Virginia Resolution, Madison argued that "the powers of the federal government" derived "from the compact to which the states are parties." Both resolutions became pillars of the doctrine of states' rights. Based on the Tenth Amendment to the Constitution and born in response to Federalist pressures, the doctrine advocated the right of state legislatures to judge the constitutionality of federal actions and protect the liberties of their citizens, but it practically provided slaveholders with the legal means to defend their privileged positions in southern local affairs from possible federal governmental interference.[18]

17. Ransom, *Conflict and Compromise*, 101. See also Jesse T. Carpenter, *The South as a Conscious Minority, 1789–1861* (New York, 1930), 21–27. See also Thomas P. Abernathy, *The South in the New Nation, 1789–1819* (Baton Rouge, La., 1961); Peter Onuf and Leonard J. Sadofsky, *Jeffersonian America* (Malden, Mass., 2002), 52–66; and Charles A. Kromkowski, *Recreating the American Republic: Rules of Apportionment, Constitutional Change, and American Political Development, 1700–1870* (New York, 2002).

18. James Madison and Thomas Jefferson are quoted in Onuf and Sadofsky, *Jeffersonian America*, 199. See also John Ashworth, *Slavery, Capitalism, and Politics in the Antebellum American Republic*, vol. 1, *Commerce and Compromise, 1820–1850* (New York, 1995), 47–50; Forrest McDonald, *States' Rights and the Union: Imperium in Imperio, 1776–1876* (Lawrence, Kans., 2000),

Remarkably, once they became presidents, Jefferson and Madison adopted nationalist policies in tune with the country's drive toward westward
expansion and military assertion, with the 1803 Louisiana Purchase and with
the War of 1812 with Britain. Between 1812 and 1816, during his second presidential term, Madison was even instrumental in the creation of the second
Federal Bank of the United States—after Alexander Hamilton's first Federal Bank had encountered staunch opposition from Thomas Jefferson—and
in the federal government's adoption of protective tariffs in the interest of
northern textile and iron manufacturing centers. Madison also suggested a
far-reaching federal program of internal economic improvements. Little more
than a decade later, at the time of Jackson's presidency, each of these provisions was to become a harsh matter of contention between core and periphery, and a matter that strictly related to the federal government's policy on
states' rights. Yet, for the moment, given the country's outburst in nationalist
feeling, Madison's measures encountered little opposition in Congress and
found particularly strong support among politicians such as South Carolina
representative John C. Calhoun—the future ideologue of the extreme states'
rights doctrine of nullification. Still, even though Jefferson's and Madison's nationalist policies were clearly in conflict with their 1798 stance, for a majority
of Jeffersonian Republicans the doctrine of states' rights "remained the true
and unfulfilled credo of the party." Eventually, these contradictory attitudes
would lead to an ideological division between National Republicans and
Democratic Republicans, or between those Jeffersonian Republicans who
had a more conciliatory position toward the federal government and those
who were staunch supporters of the doctrine of states' rights.[19]

By 1819, the period of nationalist euphoria had passed and the United
States plunged into its first national economic depression—which triggered
the resurgence of the earlier "extreme democratic and agrarian rhetoric"
and renewed calls for an increase in the powers of the states' governments.
Among the areas that the 1819 depression hit particularly hard were the frontier regions of cotton production from upcountry South Carolina all the way

---

41–43; and William Watkins Jr., "The Kentucky and Virginia Resolutions: Guideposts of a
Limited Government," *IR* 3 (1999): 385–405.

19. See McDonald, *States' Rights*, 73–76; George Dangerfield, *The Awakening of American
Nationalism, 1815–1828* (New York, 1965), 46–51; Roger G. Kennedy, *Mr. Jefferson's Lost Cause:
Land, Farmers, and the Louisiana Purchase* (New York, 2003); Robert Allen Rutland, *The Presi-
dency of James Madison* (Lawrence, Kans., 1990); and Drew McCoy, *The Last of the Fathers: James
Madison and the Republican Legacy* (New York, 1989).

to Arkansas, and especially the newly formed states of Mississippi and Alabama, where cotton was the main economic asset and where speculations on land purchase had been high. In the wake of the economic depression and of Chief Justice John Marshall's Supreme Court ruling in the *M'Culloch* case that individual states had no constitutional right to tax the Bank of the United States, the rising slaveholding elites of the western territories embraced for the first time an extreme states' rights stance. They joined ranks with the older slaveholding elites of the Atlantic Seaboard states in the defense of self-government and slavery. Together, they fought against what they perceived as a northern-induced federal plan to block their projects of expansion during the first major political confrontation between America's core and southern periphery—the Missouri Crisis of 1819–1820.[20]

The crisis erupted in 1819, when the Missouri territory, at the border of the frontier cotton producing regions of the southern periphery, applied for statehood. Several northern congressmen objected to the Missouri state constitution's protection of slavery and proposed—with the Tallmadge Amendments—a plan for its gradual abolition. Among other consequences, the admission of Missouri as a slave state into the Union would have upset the congressional balance between North and South, tipping it in favor of the latter. In response to the proposed Tallmadge Amendments, southern congressmen such as South Carolinian planter Charles Pinckney upheld the states' rights card and advocated Missouri's constitutional right to self-government. In his 1820 speech to the House of Representatives, Pinckney argued that the American Constitution was a monument of "rational liberty," since it protected the right of each state to decide over the existence of slavery within its borders, and accused "the majority of this House" of a "wish to dissolve the Union and separate themselves from the slaveholding states."[21]

Slaveholders throughout the South shared Pinckney's opinion; fearing the consequences of congressional prohibition of slavery in the western territories, they joined in protest against the northern congressmen's reaction to their attempt to take the customary governmental protection of slaveholding interests a step further. Even though in Missouri slavery was hardly an important part of the economy and society in comparison with other regions

20. Richard Ellis, *The Union at Risk: Jacksonian Democracy, States' Rights, and the Nullification Crisis* (New York, 1987), 5–6. See also McDonald, *States' Rights*, 80–84; and David Brion Davis, *Challenging the Boundaries of Slavery* (Cambridge, Mass., 2003), 44–50.

21. Charles Pinckney is quoted in Bowman, *Masters and Lords*, 142; see also Frances Leigh Williams, *A Founding Family: The Pinckneys of South Carolina* (New York, 1978), 282–283.

deep inside the southern frontier, the rising slaveholding elites of Alabama and Mississippi saw the northern congressmen's proposal as a direct attack by the federal government on their cotton planting- and slaveholding-based power in the southwestern periphery. For their part, the established slave-holding elites of the Atlantic Seaboard states saw the entire matter as a first step toward the imposition by a future northern-dominated core of a cen-tralizing policy that would lead to the eventual abolition of slavery in the entire territory of the southern periphery. It took ten months of negotiation to reach a compromise, according to which Maine would join the Union as a free state, while Missouri would join it as a slave state in 1821. The Missouri Compromise of 1820 also confined the formation of future slave states to the territory acquired with the Louisiana Purchase under the latitude of 36° 30´.[22]

Though the 1820 Missouri Compromise was to guarantee thirty years of relative peace to the Union, several southerners—including Jefferson—highly criticized it. Some went as far as arguing that the territorial restriction of slavery resulted from the northern congressmen's determination to use the federal government's centralizing powers to act against the peculiar institu-tion and therefore harm the source of influence of the southern peripheral elite. And to be sure, the Missouri controversy had the effect of shaking the power of the peripheral slaveholding elite and of showing the real extent of their political influence over the core, since—according to North Carolina senator Nathaniel Macon—the Compromise did "acknowledge the right of Congress to interfere" with the issue of slavery in the western territories. In fact, even with southern presidents in the White House, the defense of the southern periphery's minority interests depended primarily on the delicate issue of congressional balance—i.e., on the number of southern representa-tives and senators in Congress—a factor that was bound to change repeat-edly with the Union's acquisition of new territories in the western frontier.[23]

* * *

22. See Glover Moore, *The Missouri Controversy, 1819–1821* (Lexington, Ky., 1966); Freehling, *Road to Disunion*, 144–161; Sydnor, *Southern Sectionalism*, 104–133; Andrew C. Lenner, *The Fed-eral Principle in American Politics, 1790–1833* (New York, 2001), 124–141; Leonard L. Richards, *The Slave Power: The Free North and Southern Domination, 1790–1860* (Baton Rouge, La., 2000), 52–82; and Ransom, *Conflict and Compromise*, 33–40.

23. Nathaniel Macon is quoted in Bruce Levine, *Half Slave and Half Free: The Roots of the Civil War* (New York, 1992), 160. See also Onuf and Sadofsky, *Jeffersonian America*, 216–217; Ash-worth, *Slavery, Capitalism, and Politics*, 68–79; Meinig, *Continental America*, 449–454; Don Feh-renbacher, *The South and Three Sectional Crises* (Baton Rouge, La., 1980), 10–20; and Kenneth M. Stampp, *The Imperiled Union: Essays on the Background of the Civil War* (New York, 1980), 26–28.

In the United States, the existence of an expanding western frontier played a determinant part in the rise to power of new elites and in the shaping of political relations between the federal governmental core and the southern periphery, relations in which the latter usually held the upper hand over the former. Conversely, in the Kingdom of the Two Sicilies, it was the absence of a frontier that had important—and in many ways opposite—effects on the formation of peripheral elites and on the shaping of political relations between a much stronger Neapolitan core and a much weaker southern periphery. In general, contrary to what happened in the American South, the expansion of commercial agriculture in the Italian *Mezzogiorno* did not lead to the settlement of previously unexploited land that was both abundant and cheap. Apart from a few cases, the cultivation of cash crops usually took place in areas that were parts of former feudal estates. Therefore, unlike the rising slaveholding elites in the southern frontier of the United States, the rising landowning elites in the peripheral areas of the Kingdom of the Two Sicilies competed both legally and politically with the older aristocracy for the ownership and exploitation of the same land—a competition that created an element of conflict with important political repercussions. At the same time, the absence of an expanding frontier also simplified relations between core and periphery, since none of the issues involved in the acquisition of new territories in the United States—issues such as the passing of specific legal provisions and the relationship between congressional balance and migration in frontier areas—troubled the Kingdom of the Two Sicilies. As early as 1817, and even before then, from the perspective of Naples—the administrative capital of the Bourbon government and effectively the center of the economic, social, and political core area—kings and ministers saw the entire *Mezzogiorno* as one large periphery framed by the geographical limits of seas and mountains (see map 4).[24]

In the continental part of the *Mezzogiorno,* core and periphery had stood in uneasy balance ever since the Napoleonic government of Joseph Bonaparte had decreed the abolition of feudalism in 1806 and had created a new system of administration based on the French model. The key aspect of the system was twofold: on one hand, it provided for the first time the provinces of the kingdom with limited means of local government; on the other hand, it created a bureaucratic network that increased a great deal the dependence

---

24. See Maria Grazia Maiorini, "The Capital and the Provinces," in Girolamo Imbruglia, ed., *Naples in the Eighteenth Century: The Birth and Death of a Nation State* (New York, 2000), 4–21.

Teramo
ABRUZZO
ULTRA I
Aquila
Chieti
ABRUZZO
ULTRA II
ABRUZZO
CITRA
MOLISE
CAPITANATA
Campobasso
Foggia
Barletta
TERRA DI LAVORA
Andria
Bari
Gaeta
Capua
PRINCIPATO
ULTRA
Caserta
Avellino
TERRA DI BARI
Naples
Salerno
Potenza
Brindisi
PRINCIPATO
CITRA
BASILICATA
TERRA D'OTRANTO
Taranto
Lecce
Sapri
CALABRIA
CITRA
Cosenza
Catanzaro
CALABRIA
ULTRA II
CALABRIA
ULTRA I
Messina
Reggio
Trapani
Palermo
Marsala
Caltanissetta
Catania
Girgenti
Sirucusa

0   100   200 km

MAP 4. The Italian *Mezzogiorno*: Core, Periphery, and Administrative Regions in 1817

of the administration of the southern periphery on the core capital, Naples. After 1815, the restored Bourbon king, Ferdinand I, kept the administrative apparatus built by the French and combined it with absolutist rule. Doubtless, the Bourbons aimed at a tighter control of the southern Italian periphery by the Neapolitan core. Yet, they could not avoid the fact that the instruments of local government provided by the administrative system soon led to the rise in political importance of provincial regional centers.[25]

In rising cities such as Bari, Foggia, Potenza, and Avellino, the elites also profited from the new opportunities that the nineteenth-century world market offered to the agricultural economy of the *Mezzogiorno*. According to Biagio Salvemini, the active participation of several southern Italian regions in the nineteenth-century international market led to the disruption of the dual character of the *Mezzogiorno*'s eighteenth-century economy—which was divided between the core market of Naples and a host of parasitic peripheral cities—and to the rise in economic power of a number of regional urban centers. Operating from these centers, the landowning and merchant elites of several southern Italian regions successfully inserted particular types of agricultural products into specific commercial circuits of the European and world economy.[26]

The nineteenth-century commercial revolution led to particularly significant changes in the region of Terra di Bari—in present-day Apulia—where the world market's demand for olive oil transformed the coastal area into what Angelantonio Spagnoletti has described as "an uninterrupted forest of olive trees, which filled 42% of the available surface." From the early years of the Restoration, Terra di Bari rapidly emerged as the region that produced the greatest quantity of olive oil in the entire Kingdom of the Two Sicilies, with a growth of 337 percent in the total volume of exports for the period between 1781–1794 and 1835–1839. By the 1820s, Terra di Bari's olive oil reached long-distance markets as far away as Marseille and other great European cities, producing widespread regional wealth. Olive oil's success,

25. See Angelantonio Spagnoletti, *Storia del Regno delle Due Sicilie* (Bologna, 1997), 38–42, 159–169; and "Centri e periferie nello stato napoletano del primo Ottocento," in Angelo Massafra, ed., *Il Mezzogiorno Preunitario. Economia, società, istituzioni* (Bari, 1988), 379–391; Giovanni Aliberti, *Potere e società locale nel Mezzogiorno dell'800* (Bari-Rome, 1987), 3–46; and Giuseppe Civile, "Appunti per una ricerca sulla amministrazione civile nelle province napoletane," *QS* 37 (1978): 228–263.

26. See Biagio Salvemini, *L'innovazione precaria. Spazi, mercati e società nel Mezzogiorno tra Sette e Ottocento* (Catanzaro, 1995), 12–17.

in turn, encouraged the production of other cash crops, such as wine grapes. By 1830, foremost southern Italian economist Luigi Granata could write that "in the provinces of Bari, oil is plentiful, and so are almonds ... [while] fruits of all kinds, and especially wine, are delicious."[27]

The city of Bari benefited a great deal from the commercial revolution that transformed the countryside around it. Between 1815 and 1828, Bari's population rose from eighteen thousand to more than twenty-one thousand inhabitants, while the city became the most important regional center of the continental *Mezzogiorno* and the second largest urban concentration after Naples. As Bari grew in size and importance, it became the focal point of a large web of commercial networks, upon which the activities of both landed proprietors and merchants—often the same individuals—converged. There they found their privileged market for the sale and export of the highly prized olive oil produced in the countryside. After 1815, when the restored Bourbon monarchy confirmed the abolition of feudalism, a growing class of large and small landed proprietors gradually came in possession of many former feudal estates and soon started raising commercial crops, engaging in the production of both olive oil and wine. By the 1820s, this landed bourgeoisie shared the control of Bari's booming economy with a rising merchant elite that included both natives and foreigners, notably Frenchmen such as Pietro Ravanas, who introduced the use of the mechanical press. Both landed bourgeois and merchants competed with the titled nobility—which included aristocratic entrepreneurs such as the marquis of Canneto—for the control of Bari's political power through participation in the provincial elective organs of the Kingdom of the Two Sicilies.[28]

If Bari was the largest regional urban center in the continental *Mezzogiorno*, it was far from being the only one rapidly rising in importance. The restored Bourbon kingdom kept the 1806 Napoleonic administrative division

27. Spagnoletti, *Storia del Regno delle Due Sicilie,* 260; Luigi Granata, *Economia rustica per lo Regno di Napoli,* vol. 1 (Naples, 1830), 227. The data are in Biagio Salvemini, "Prima della Puglia. Terra di Bari e il sistema regionale in età moderna," in Luigi Masella and Biagio Salvemini, eds., *La Puglia* (Turin, 1989), 153, 154–161; and Aurelio Lepre, *Storia del Mezzogiorno d'Italia,* vol. 2, *Dall'Antico Regime alla società borghese (1657–1860)* (Naples, 1986), 112–113.

28. See Salvemini, *L'innovazione precaria,* 33–34; Enrica Di Ciommo, *Bari 1806–1940. Evoluzione del territorio e sviluppo urbanistico* (Milan, 1985), 59–60, 67–68; Angelantonio Spagnoletti, "La formazione di una nuova classe dirigente in provincia di Bari. Sindaci e decurioni tra 1806 e 1830," *ASPu* 36 (1983): 117–165; and Nicola Antonacci, *Dalla Repubblica napoletana alla monarchia italiana. Politica e società in Terra di Bari (1799–1860)* (Bari, 2000), 7–20.

of the southern territory into thirteen provinces, only adding an additional one in Calabria. The law of 12 December 1816 also provided for their further subdivision into smaller units called districts. As a consequence, those cities that the Bourbon administration chose as district capitals rose in importance, often at the expense of older noble-dominated urban centers, while those cities that became both district and provincial capitals—as Bari did at the expense of Trani—acquired a great deal of power as provincial seats of the Bourbon government. In Terra di Bari, as in every other province, the provincial capital was a regional urban center of national stature at the top of an administrative hierarchy of subregional urban centers—a hierarchy that reflected the difference in economic importance among the landowning and merchant elites that inhabited the different cities.[29]

Among the urban centers in subordinate position to Bari's status as provincial capital was the important town of Andria. Located in the inner part of Terra di Bari, Andria was an *agrotown*—one of the urban centers that supplied the *latifondi* with their workforce—at the border of the largest area of grain production in the Bourbon kingdom, the *Tavoliere*. In a recent study of the town's nineteenth-century elite, Nicola Antonacci has demonstrated that the impact of the commercial revolution altered the traditional relations of power in *agrotowns* such as Andria. At the center of this process of change was the provincial landed bourgeoisie, the class that profited the most from the end of the feudal system. In Andria, as in most other peripheral centers of the *Mezzogiorno,* the landed bourgeoisie engaged in an aggressive policy of land acquisition, taking advantage of the enclosure and sale of common land and of the suppression of customary rights that followed the abolition of feudalism, mostly at the expense of the peasantry. According to Antonacci, in Andria the new class of landed proprietors succeeded in taking control of the "factors of production and [in] monopolizing the control of the commercial fluxes which ended in Naples and in other Italian cities."[30]

At the same time, the landed bourgeoisie also used the economic and social structure of *agrotowns* such as Andria for the construction of a complex web of family and kin relations. Through this informal network, families of the most recent section of the landed elite entered the ranks of a provincial

29. See Spagnoletti, "Centri e periferie," 381–382; Salvemini, *L'innovazione precaria,* 34–49; and Di Ciommo, *Bari,* 56–58.

30. Nicola Antonacci, "Le città rurali dell'Italia meridionale nel XIX e XX secolo. Rassegna critica e prospettive di ricerca," *S&S* 71 (1996): 131. See also Nicola Antonacci, *Terra e potere in una città rurale del Mezzogiorno. Le elites di Andria nell'Ottocento* (Bari, 1996), 52–68.

ruling class whose identity no longer related to the possession of noble titles or to identification with an urban aristocracy, but to the ownership of land. Similar to the planter elite in the American South, the southern Italian landed elite of important peripheral cities such as Andria often included lawyers or merchants who had tight family and business relations with the most prominent individuals among both recent and established landed proprietors. In general, the rising elite in the Bourbon provinces included different, but equally influential, social groups, among which the most important —but by no means the only one—was the landowning class.[31]

Recent studies conducted by scholars in the continental *Mezzogiorno* have shed light on the particular form the rise of the new class of landed proprietors took in different cities and provinces. Though most scholars agree on the fact that there was potential opposition between the old and new sections of the provincial elites, especially in regard to the crucial issue of control of the common land, their studies also document the actual existence of different degrees—from extremely low to very high—of kin alliance and cooperation in local politics as a means to diffuse class conflict. In some cases—as in Andria—the relatively open character of the local elite and the cooptation of members of the landed bourgeoisie into the local urban aristocracy provided the basis for the formation of a unified ruling class. In other cases, the conflict between old and new elites over the rights to own former feudal or common land proved irreconcilable and continued until unification. Yet, it is undeniable that it was with the rise in economic importance of the provincial landed bourgeoisie—whether in alliance with or in opposition to the feudal nobility and the local urban aristocracy—that a growing demand for more autonomous political representation emerged from the peripheral area of the continental *Mezzogiorno,* and especially from important urban regional centers such as Bari.[32]

Remarkably, even though instrumental in the very creation of the new landed elite, the Bourbon administration in the Neapolitan core proved ill

31. See Antonacci, *Terra e potere,* 156–157. See also Paolo Macry, "Le elites urbane: stratificazione e mobilità sociale, le forme del potere locale e la cultura dei ceti emergenti," in Massafra, ed., *Il Mezzogiorno preunitario,* 808–811.

32. See Antonacci, *Terra e potere.* See also, especially, Giuseppe Moricola, "Elite economica ed elite amministrativa nella città di Avellino dopo il Decennio napoleonico," and Enrica Di Ciommo, "Elites provinciali e potere borbonico: note per una ricerca comparata," both in Massafra, ed., *Il Mezzogiorno preunitario,* 831–845 and 965–1038; and Giuseppe Civile, *Il comune rustico. Storia sociale di un paese del Mezzogiorno nell'800* (Bologna, 1990).

equipped to respond effectively to this demand. As Marco Meriggi has recently noticed, the Napoleonic model of administration—a model in which state centralization loomed large—proved particularly resilient in the *Mezzogiorno* in comparison with other preunification Italian states. Between 1815 and 1820, Prime Minister Luigi De' Medici and Minister of Internal Affairs Donato Tommasi attempted to modernize from above the restored Bourbon kingdom through a policy of amalgamation that blended the administrative structure inherited from the period of French occupation with the tradition of Bourbon absolutism. In the process, they created the hybrid institution of the administrative monarchy (*monarchia amministrativa*), "a state where"—according to Lucy Riall—"power was shared between the monarch and the bureaucracy, thus obviating the need for representative government."[33]

From the core capital Naples, King Ferdinand I presided over the country's policy through the ministers' council (*consiglio di stato*) and ruled over the kingdom's peripheral provinces through a complex bureaucratic system whose officers depended on the Ministry of Internal Affairs. The 1816 Law on Civilian Administration gave particular relevance to the intendants (*intendenti*), who effectively acted as provincial governors—with the help of a council formed by members of the local elite—and supervised the activity of the subintendants (*sottointendenti*), the district officials. The fact that the king nominated the provincial intendants shows the degree of control that—in reverse pattern as compared with the American South—the core exercised over the southern periphery in the Kingdom of the Two Sicilies; and yet, as Angelantonio Spagnoletti has noted, the office of intendant provided the system with a particularly important element in regard to communication between the capital and the provinces.[34]

The municipal government (*comune*) of the several urban centers that formed the provincial districts provided another important element. The provincial intendant nominated the councils that governed the cities (*decurionati*)

33. Lucy Riall, *Sicily and the Unification of Italy: Liberal Policy and Local Power, 1859–1866* (Oxford, 1998), 30. On Napoleonic and early Restoration administration, see Marco Meriggi, *Gli stati italiani prima dell'Unità. Una storia istituzionale* (Bologna, 2002), 130–131; Michael Broers, "The Myth and Reality of Italian Regionalism: A Historical Geography of Napoleonic Italy," *AHR* 108 (2003): 688–709; and Rosario Romeo, *Mezzogiorno e Sicilia nel Risorgimento* (Naples, 1979), 51–114.

34. See Spagnoletti, *Storia del Regno*, 146–147; and Armando De Martino, *La nascita delle intendenze. Problemi dell'amministrazione periferica nel Regno di Napoli (1806–1815)* (Naples, 1984).

on the basis of lists of eligible officials (*liste degli eleggibili*) drawn from members of the local landed elite. In fact, consistent with the Bourbon government's policy of undermining the power of the provincial aristocracy, the main criterion for eligibility in the city councils was property ownership, rather than the noble title. For each city, the council suggested three names of local landowners among whom the provincial intendant chose the mayor (*sindaco*), the individual who was to rule the city with the help of two additional officers.[35]

The city council also suggested eligible names for another elective organ, equally important for the local elite: the general provincial council (*consiglio generale della provincia*). According to the original 1806 and 1808 laws—which the restored Bourbon kingdom confirmed in 1816—the provincial council, whose members were nominated by the king, had among its primary tasks gathering complaints, examining the state of the province, and suggesting ways to improve its conditions. In time, the provincial council became a preferential vehicle for the local elites' frustration at the rigid hierarchical structure of the Bourbon administration and at the intendant's inability to resolve positively the conflict of interests between the government's program of modernization from above and the elites' need for local autonomy.[36]

Thus, from the beginning, the complex Bourbon administrative system had several flaws, which already some of the most enlightened nineteenth-century southern Italian statesmen had noticed. Most of the problems had to do with the ambiguity of the relationship between the core and the periphery. On one hand, the Bourbon administrative monarchy provided the provinces with the first rudimentary instruments of local government at a time when the provincial elites, whose rise to power was linked to the commercial revolution and to the abolition of the feudal system, agitated for stronger political participation. On the other hand, the strict control that the king and the king's officers—according to the Bourbon tradition of absolutism—held over the provincial administration prevented elective councils, such as the

---

35. See Raffaele Romanelli, "La nazionalizzazione della periferia. Casi e prospettive di studio," *Meridiana* 4 (1988): 18–19; Civile, "Appunti per una ricerca," 228–231; and Paolo Pezzino, "Local Power in Southern Italy," in Robert Lumley and Jonathan Morris, eds., *The New History of the Italian South: The Mezzogiorno Revisited* (Exeter, 1997), 49–50.

36. See Alfonso Scirocco, "I corpi rappresentativi nel Mezzogiorno dal 'Decennio' alla Restaurazione: il personale dei consigli provinciali," *QS* 37 (1978): 104–105; and Di Ciommo, "Elites provinciali," 969–971.

decurionato and the *consiglio generale della provincia,* from becoming effective channels for the elites' participation in the decisional process in regard to matters of local policy. By the late 1810s, the Bourbon administrative system encountered opposition not only from the former feudal aristocracy—whose power had been greatly reduced by Bourbon reforms—but also from the provincial landed bourgeoisie, the very social class whose creation the Bourbon government had buttressed with the progressive legal dismantlement of the feudal system in an effort to check the power of the aristocracy.[37]

Weary of the limited amount of decisional power allowed to them by Bourbon absolutism, many members of the provincial landed elite joined secret societies—among which was the famous *Carboneria*—and participated in a vast conspiracy whose aim was the democratization of the kingdom. By 1820, despite the harsh policy of repression carried out by the reactionary chief of police prince of Canosa, the *carbonari's* secret meeting places (*vendite*) had spread throughout the territory of the Bourbon kingdom. The *carbonari* included provincial landed proprietors, merchants, professionals, and lower-rank administrators of bourgeois origins who supported provincial administrative autonomy and devolution of power in favor of the peripheral propertied classes. Equally important were the so-called *murattiani,* who were mostly high-ranking officers who had made their career during the period of Napoleonic occupation (*decennio*) and now felt excluded despite Medici's efforts to keep many of them in the administration through the policy of amalgamation.[38]

Both *carbonari* and *murattiani* sought to create a constitutional monarchy in which a parliament would check the king's absolute power, according to the model of the Spanish Constitution of Cadiz of 1812, and in which a more decentralized administrative system would substitute the Bourbons' rigidly centralized bureaucracy. In July 1820, when the *murattiani* officers in the army rebelled against the king's authority and took control of Naples, the provincial elites organized in the *vendite* joined them at once. At the same time, overwhelming support came also from the majority of the people, who had grown disaffected with the king ever since a disastrous famine had hit the

37. See Orazio Abbamonte, *Potere pubblico e privata autonomia. Giovanni Manna e la scienza amministrativa nel Mezzogiorno* (Naples, 1991), 182–184; and Raffaele Feola, "Accentramento e giurisdizione. Il progetto amministrativo nell'Ottocento napoletano," *ASPN* 93 (1985): 451–474.

38. See R. J. Rath, "The Carbonari: Their Origins, Initiation Rites and Aims," *AHR* 69 (1964): 353–370; and Alfonso Scirocco, *L'Italia del Risorgimento* (Bologna, 1990), 81–84.

countryside in 1816–1817 and the subsequent governmental decision to import grain from Russia had resulted in acute recession and economic crisis.[39]

The victory of the revolutionary movement led to the Neapolitan government's adoption of the Cadiz Constitution and to the formation of a national parliament, which, during its nine months of existence (*nonimestre costituzionale*)—from July 1820 to March 1821—provided the kingdom with basic legislation on civil liberties and functioned as a representative assembly for the provincial elites. In the words of Angelantonio Spagnoletti, the parliament "was the instrument used by the provincial bourgeoisie to even their relationship with the capital." In other words, with the Revolution of 1820–1821, the elites at the periphery of the kingdom asserted the right of the provinces to self-government in such a way that it is possible to speak of a tendency toward a sort of federalism, as Nicola Antonacci has recently suggested. In this respect, a significant example is provided by the revolutionary government of Daunia—a subregion of Apulia—which, in July 1820, proclaimed "its essential and exclusive right to self-government and to regulation of its entire administration, with a solely federal right left to the other regions which, together and through their Deputies in the Parliament presided by the King, represent the entire Nation."[40]

To be sure, during the entire period of the *nonimestre*, the provincial elites voiced petitions—which for the most part accused the intendants of despotism and corruption—or sent provincial representatives to the national parliament; and among the latter, particularly active were the representatives from Terra di Bari. Arguably, throughout the Revolution of 1820–1821, the issue of the provinces' self-government—an issue comparable to the doctrine of states' rights in the American South—loomed large among the peripheral elites of the Kingdom of the Two Sicilies and provided the basis for a policy of experimental changes in the administrative system. Related to this issue—as in the United States—was the issue of respect for individual liberties, which the constitution approved in 1820 guaranteed. However, the extent to which the elites were prepared to provide the population of the kingdom with libertarian institutions was an object of contention. Provincial representatives held discordant positions, ranging from relatively conserva-

39. See Aurelio Lepre, *Storia del Mezzogiorno d'Italia*, vol. 2, *Dall'Antico Regime alla società borghese (1657–1860)* (Naples, 1986), 231–233.

40. Spagnoletti, *Storia del Regno*, 49; the Daunia Proclamation is quoted in Antonacci, *Dalla repubblica napoletana*, 100.

tive to outright democratic, and fought bitterly in Parliament over the crucial issue of representation. The main conflict was between the *murattiani*, who, after initially taking the lead of the revolution, supported a moderate version of the constitution, and the most extreme fringes of the *carbonari*, whose radicalism went as far as proposing universal suffrage.[41]

And yet, at the practical level, both *carbonari* and *murattiani* failed to provide the revolutionary government with a consistent policy that addressed specific problems related to the existence of a largely landless southern peasantry. Ever since the start of the revolution, peasants had occupied property in several regions, demanding a halt to the process of enclosure and sale of common land and the restoration of customary rights. The response of the representatives of the provincial landed bourgeoisie in the revolutionary government was to urge the formation of a National Guard for the defense of private property. Moreover, as Giorgio Candeloro has noted, even the supposed "ultra-democratic" character of the universal suffrage guaranteed by the Cadiz Constitution was severely hampered by an electoral system in three subsequent steps, which was likely to privilege candidates who belonged to the elite in the competition for public offices. Aside from these severe limitations, the difference between moderate *murattiani* and democratic *carbonari* weakened a great deal the revolutionaries' ability to resist internal and external pressures and contributed significantly to their ultimate defeat. Yet, even after the revolutionary government fell in 1821, the experience of the *nonimestre* continued to provide the provincial elites of the continental *Mezzogiorno* with an important model of balance between core and periphery in matters of political representation and local power. At the same time, the division between moderate and democratic positions continued to influence the activities of those progressive members of the provincial elites who continued—openly or secretly—to work to transform the Bourbon kingdom into a constitutional monarchy devoid of bureaucratic despotism.[42]

41. See Antonacci, *Dalla repubblica napoletana,* 99–107; Alfonso Scirocco, "Il problema dell'autonomia locale nel Mezzogiorno durante la rivoluzione del 1820–21," in *Studi in memoria di Nino Cortese* (Rome, 1976), 485–528; Di Ciommo, "Elites provinciali," 971–975; and Antonino De Francesco, "Ideologie e movimenti politici," in Giovanni Sabbatucci and Vittorio Vidotto, eds., *Storia d'Italia,* vol. 1, *Le premesse dell'Unità* (Bari-Rome, 1994), 258–261.

42. See Giorgio Candeloro, *Storia dell'Italia moderna,* vol. 2, *Dalla Restaurazione alla rivoluzione nazionale (1815–1847)* (Milan, 1958), 79–84; and Aurelio Lepre, *La rivoluzione napoletana del 1820–21* (Rome, 1967), 108–133.

* * *

There are both similarities and differences between the trajectories that the peripheral elites of the American South and the Kingdom of the Two Sicilies followed in the period leading to 1820. In particular, in both cases, even though within the context of very different governmental and political systems, the need for a balance between central and local powers in matters of political representation and governmental policy was a central issue of debate among the rising social classes that dominated the economy of peripheral areas such as Mississippi and Terra di Bari. And yet, Natchez did not share with Bari the characteristics of a southwestern frontier's regional center, especially since, unlike Bari's growth, Natchez's rise resulted from the migration of a slaveholding class in search of fertile new land in the unsettled regions of the country. Still, as peripheral centers in their respective regions, Bari and Natchez shared other characteristics. Among them, the most important was the fact that both rose in size and wealth as a result of the impact of world market changes on peripheral economies and of the increasing demand for particular agricultural products at both the national and international levels.

However, on one hand, Natchez's rise in economic importance added an important chapter in the story of the formation of an increasingly more powerful southern peripheral slaveholding elite—an elite that, after securing control of local politics, could and did attempt to influence the decisions taken by the American government over the issue of slavery's expansion in the nation's western territories. On the other hand, Bari's rise in economic importance soon became related to the rise in political influence of a peripheral landowning elite that grew increasingly disappointed at the fact that the Bourbon government did not grant it a more incisive role in the control of local power in the provincial regions. These very different issues found their first dramatic expressions in two political crises that, remarkably, occurred in the years around 1820 in both the American South and the Italian *Mezzogiorno*.

In the American South, the Missouri Crisis of 1819–1820 served the purpose of clarifying that the issue of local rule in the southern periphery was strictly related to the southern elite's continuing influence on the federal government and on its policy vis-à-vis the protection of slaveholding interests in Congress and the expansion of slavery in the western territories. In the *Mezzogiorno*, the Revolution of 1820–1821 made manifestly clear that both provincial government and local power depended on the possibility of political representation of the peripheral elites in the kingdom's administration outside the rigid mechanisms of Bourbon bureaucratic centralization. To paraphrase Jefferson, in both cases, 1820 proved "a fire-bell in the night," a warning on the shape of future events. In fact, the opposing issues that the Missouri Crisis and the 1820–1821 Revolution had raised in regard to the relation between core and periphery in the American South and the Italian *Mezzogiorno* continued to be central concerns among both American slaveholders and southern Italian landowners, even though the evolution of political life complicated the picture and added new dimensions to those issues in both regions.

Reforming the Systems: Conflicting Programs

In both the American South and the Italian *Mezzogiorno*, the period between the 1820s and the 1840s witnessed radical transformations in the public sphere, transformations due to the fact that political debates over core-periphery relations and over conflicts between different interest groups assumed increasingly militant and factional tones. There are both similarities and differences between the political legacies of the Missouri Crisis of 1819–1820 in the American South and of the Revolution of 1820–1821 in the Italian *Mezzogiorno*. Both the similarities and the differences show clearly in the particular ways in which American slaveholders and southern Italian landowners approached the twin issues of maintaining the social structures that guaranteed their regional power and of reforming the economic systems reinforcing that power through political means.

In the American South, as everywhere else in the United States, the transformation of republican politics led to the gradual formation of two parties—the Democrats and the Whigs—which dominated political life; slaveholders used either one or the other to promote their different views of social empowerment and economic reform at the local and national level, while maintaining a hegemonic role in the key institutions of the federal government. Conversely, in the Italian *Mezzogiorno*, monarchical absolutism did not allow the formation of real political parties; however, landed proprietors gathered around two predominant political movements—the democrats and the moderate liberals—which represented different interests and promoted different ideas about reforming the monarchical system, to demand both the formation of local representative organs and the respect of constitutional liberties. Though in very different settings and under opposite conditions—one of virtually unchallenged hegemony over the political core and one of almost complete lack of power in front of it—the two southern peripheral elites comparably embraced or led nascent political movements and made use of their ideologies. In doing so, American slaveholders and southern Italian landowners manifested in clear political terms their will to either maintain or assert their regional hegemonic positions by conditioning the policies of the central governments so that the latter granted a higher degree of power to peripheral power-holders.

In the 1820s and 1830s, the American South witnessed a movement toward democratization of political life. Issues that related to the reform of the political system through changes in the electoral process and through more equitable distribution of political power became highly popular and hotly debated topics. Though these were widespread concerns among the American people, in the South they acquired distinctive features because of the planters' commitment to both republicanism and slavery. The growth of the southern population and the economic opportunities brought by the market revolution and by the spread of cotton agriculture in the Southwest soon led to a higher political awareness among both slaveholding and non-slaveholding yeomen. Planters, therefore, confronted the increasing demand of yeomen both for wider participation in the political system and, at the same time, for reaffirmation of their social and political privileges over enslaved African Americans.[43]

At the state level, the consequences of the movement toward democratization were momentous. By 1830, every southern state except South Carolina had its presidential nominees chosen by the people, rather than by the legislature, and by the mid-1830s every southern state except Louisiana and Virginia had universal white male suffrage. Equally, by the same time, local offices were open to popular elections everywhere aside from South Carolina. The most radical changes occurred in the western states of Alabama, Mississippi, Tennessee, and Arkansas—the last of which joined the United States in 1836. "In each of these states"—Charles Sydnor has noted—"the

43. See William J. Cooper, *The South and the Politics of Slavery, 1828–1856* (Baton Rouge, La., 1978), 23–42; and William J. Cooper and Thomas E. Terrill, *The American South: A History* (New York, 1996), 161–163.

governor was popularly elected, there was universal manhood suffrage, legislative apportionment in both houses was based on white population . . . and
county government was democratic."[44]

Equally momentous were the changes brought by the movement toward democratization of the national political system. By 1824, Jeffersonian
Republicans were deeply divided over the issue of states' rights. The onset
of the Missouri Crisis of 1819–1820 and the passing of two new protective
tariffs in 1820 and 1824 by the Madison and Monroe administrations led
many southerners to rally around candidates other than the one traditionally
chosen by the congressional caucus for the presidential election. In fact, the
1824 presidential election—in which for the first time presidential nominees
were chosen by popular vote in eighteen out of twenty-four states—saw
the first affirmation of Andrew Jackson, a Tennessee planter, former Indian
fighter, and war hero, as the quintessential people's candidate in a dawning
age of mass politics throughout the South.[45]

Though Jackson did not become president in 1824, by the next presidential election, in 1828, he had fully mustered the art of political persuasion of
the masses. In 1828, Jackson's supporters organized committees throughout
the South and mobilized electors through parades, rallies, and barbecues.
Jackson's figure had a strong appeal, especially to southern slaveholding and
nonslaveholding yeomen, who saw in him the self-made frontiersman. At
the same time, in his political program, Jackson vied to stand for limited
governmental interference in local affairs and for states' rights. And to be
sure, Jackson's election was a major step in the continuation of the pattern
of southern domination of the federal government. Also, southerners of all
classes believed that he would defend southern interests against the possible
expansion of northern interests and federal government's prerogatives. As
Richard Ellis has written, commenting on the alternation between two periods dominated by southern presidents, "Jackson's [1828] victory brought to
an end the era of Jeffersonian democracy. The era of Jacksonian democracy
had now begun."[46]

44. Sydnor, *Southern Sectionalism*, 284. See also Richard P. McCormick, *The Second American
Party System: Party Formation in the Jacksonian Era* (Chapel Hill, N.C., 1964), 175–254, 287–320.

45. See Lenner, *Federal Principle*, 151–176; and Joel H. Silbey, *The American Political Nation,
1838–1893* (Stanford, Calif., 1991), 16–20.

46. Richard E. Ellis, "The Market Revolution and the Transformation of American Politics,
1800–1830," in Melvyn Stokes and Stephen Conway, eds., *The Market Revolution in America:
Social, Political, and Religious Expressions, 1800–1880* (Charlottesville, Va., 1996), 170. See also

In fact, Jackson became the unchallenged leader of the Democratic Party, whose ideology he helped to create and which, in turn, allowed him to become president for two consecutive terms, 1829–1833 and 1833–1837. During this period and during Van Buren's 1837–1841 presidency, the Democratic Party consolidated its position as majority party in the South, a fact which shows better than any other that a number of southerners firmly identified with Jackson's and the Jacksonians' vision of economic, social, and political reform. Scholars have alternatively seen support for Jackson as coming from the people against a business aristocracy or from a rising entrepreneurial middle class struggling to gain power, or else as a result of different views over cultural issues, rather than of socioeconomic class divisions. More recently, several historians have maintained that, in the South, the Democratic Party found strong support among the yeoman majority that rejected the transformations brought by the market revolution and held on to the Jeffersonian ideal of an agrarian republic of small farmers.[47]

Yet, this recent view does not account for the evidence stemming from those highly commercial southern counties that consistently produced a Democratic majority or for the fact that—in the words of Donald Ratcliffe —"what lay at the root of the South's dissatisfaction was not so much antagonism toward the market revolution as the reluctance of thoroughly commercialized planters to contribute to the commercial development of other parts of the country." In other words, the Democrats' support in the South had a lot to do with the planter elite's attempt to keep its economic and social power through a reform program that aimed at maintaining a minimal amount of governmental interference and, at the same time, attracted the yeomanry through the glorification of Jeffersonian agrarian republicanism.[48]

Robert Remini, *Andrew Jackson and the Course of American Freedom, 1822–1832* (New York, 1981).

47. See Arthur Schlesinger, *The Age of Jackson* (Cambridge, Mass., 1945); Richard Hofstadter, *The American Political Tradition and the Men Who Made It* (New York, 1948), 56–85; Marvin Meyers, *The Jacksonian Persuasion: Politics and Belief* (Stanford, Calif., 1957); Thornton, *Politics and Power,* 20–57; Harry L. Watson, *Liberty and Power: The Politics of Jacksonian America* (New York, 1990); Michael P. Holt, *Political Parties and American Political Development: From the Age of Jackson to the Age of Lincoln* (Baton Rouge, La., 1992), 33–87; and Ronald P. Formisano, "The Invention of the Ethnocultural Interpretation," *AHR* 99 (1994): 453–477.

48. Donald J. Ratcliffe, "The Crisis of Commercialization: National Political Alignments and the Market Revolution, 1819–1844," in Stokes and Conway, eds., *Market Revolution in America,* 183. See also Charles Sellers, *The Market Revolution: Jacksonian America, 1815–1846* (New York, 1991), 332–363; and Ashworth, *Slavery, Capitalism, and Politics,* 289–314.

In regard to the crucial issues of states' rights and relations between core and periphery, Jackson's reform program of reduced governmental interference in local affairs succeeded only in part. His support for the removal of Native American tribes appealed especially to slaveholders who lived in the states of the southern periphery's cotton frontier. Even more important was Jackson's opposition to the Federal Bank. Even though it was at the origins of the disastrous economic depression of 1837, to most southerners Jackson's policy confirmed his designs to dismantle what they perceived as unnecessary and dangerous governmental institutions. However, during the nullification crisis of 1832–1833, Jackson sided with the federal government and supported the enforcement of protective tariffs passed by Congress in 1828 and 1832, against the protests of John C. Calhoun and South Carolinian states' rights extremists.[49]

Doubtless, many southerners, though not openly siding with South Carolina, thought along the same lines of convinced nullifier Robert Allston, who wrote to his wife, Adele Petigru, about "the proscription and tyranny of President Jackson." Still, by supporting the Union even at the risk of provoking South Carolina's secession, Jackson made clear that his program of reform in regard to relations between the federal core and the southern periphery aimed at keeping the upper hand firmly in favor of the latter by working within the existing governmental structure, rather than by threatening the federal government's destruction. Like Jefferson before him, Jackson truly believed that the federal government's "true strength consists in leaving individuals and States as much as possible to themselves." Such a constitutional view of the doctrine of states' rights allowed Jackson to attempt to reform the federal government in such a way that slavery and the economic and social power of the southern peripheral elites did not have to face the possibility of any unwanted interference.[50]

While he took care of the issue of core-periphery relations, Jackson also set out to implement a particular program of reform that was strictly related to his ideas about "democratic" government. He aimed at transforming the

49. See Anthony F. Wallace, *The Long, Bitter Trail: Andrew Jackson and the Indians* (New York, 1993); Robert V. Remini, *Andrew Jackson and the Bank War: A Study in the Growth of Presidential Power* (New York, 1967); William W. Freehling, *Prelude to Civil War: The Nullification Crisis in South Carolina, 1816–1836* (New York, 1966); Lenner, *Federal Principle,* 177–212; and Ellis, *Union at Risk,* 178–198. For more details on the nullification crisis, see chapter four.

50. Robert F. W. Allston to Adele Petigru Allston, 6 December 1833, Robert F. W. Allston Papers, SCL; Andrew Jackson's quotation in McDonald, *States' Rights,* 110.

patriarchal-paternalistic worldview of those southern planters whom he epitomized into the national ideology of a unified slaveholding class—a class whose power was firmly rooted in racial and gender inequalities. In fact, despite its democratic rhetoric and egalitarian ideal, the nation that Jackson and the Jacksonians had in mind was essentially a nation of producers. Jacksonian democracy applied to what Missouri senator Thomas Hart called the "productive and burthen[*sic*]-bearing classes." Planters figured prominently, but so did farmers and mechanics. African American slaves, Native Americans, and women were excluded.[51]

The truly brilliant innovation of Jacksonian democracy lay in its potentially egalitarian implications for all white males and in its special appeal to white yeomen. According to James Oakes, Jacksonians believed that "the only privileges recognized at birth were male gender and white skin, but among white men no laws recognized an artificial social hierarchy. The only legitimate distinctions were those of talent and merit." Jacksonian rhetoric never tired of reminding the Democratic Party electors of its egalitarianism. For example, Edward Baptist has pointed out how in Florida's Jackson and Leon counties, "Democrats appropriated the word 'people' . . . and substituted it as a word of praise where others might have inserted the more ambiguous 'countrymen.'"[52]

Yet, even given this egalitarian potential, Jacksonian democracy was also the ideology of an emerging planter elite that wholly embraced the patriarchal values of class and gender subordination and the paternalistic values of contractual reciprocity in social and political terms. Masked by egalitarian rhetoric, Jacksonian democracy—according to Alexander Saxton—merely "advocated [in principle] the equal opportunity of all white male citizens to engage in the pursuit of happiness," without real consequences at the practical level. Jackson's paternalism simply softened the terms of class inequalities by giving a token of appreciation to all southern white males in return for their social and political support of the planter class. With this unspoken

51. Thomas Hart's quotation is in Alexander Saxton, *The Rise and Fall of the White Republic: Class Politics and Mass Culture in Nineteenth-Century America* (New York, 1997), 144. See also John Ashworth, *"Agrarians" and "Aristocrats": Party and Political Ideology in the United States, 1837–1846* (London, 1983), 21–33.

52. James Oakes, *Slavery and Freedom: An Interpretation of the Old South* (New York, 1990), 121–122; Baptist, *Creating an Old South*, 164. See also Lacy K. Ford, "Popular Ideology of the Old South's Plain Folk: The Limits of Egalitarianism in a Slaveholding Society," in Samuel C. Hyde Jr., ed., *Plain Folk of the South Revisited* (Baton Rouge, La., 1997), 205–227.

agreement between him and his electors, Jackson managed to raise paternalism to the level of a southern national ideology that cut across class and regional differences. At the same time, Jacksonian democracy retained more than a few patriarchal elements, not least a fairly rigid attitude toward issues of class and gender discrimination.[53]

In Mississippi's Warren County, Christopher Morris has found that Democrats held a firm "belief in a hierarchical society in which the deference of the lower orders balanced the patriarchal responsibilities of elites." Still, one of Jacksonian democracy's most important characteristics remained the fact that it had an especially strong appeal for the large majority of southern slaveholders, particularly those "one-generation aristocrats" who—like Jackson —had made their fortunes riding the waves of the cotton boom. In fact, these found themselves particularly at ease with Jackson's resentment and rejection of the unparallel degree of power and influence held by the older planter aristocracy of the Atlantic Seaboard states in southern politics.[54]

Jackson's paternalism and its relationship with the political ethos of the more recent sections of the South's slaveholding elite were particularly evident in his approach toward slavery and race. The fact that he was a cotton planter with a recently acquired fortune in land and slaves gave Jackson a particularly sophisticated understanding of the workings of paternalism and contractual reciprocity and of how it applied to labor relations on plantations. Therefore, he was particularly well-suited to the task of transforming slaveholders' patriarchal-paternalistic worldview into a political ideology of defense of the southern slave system. Jackson's egalitarian paternalism toward white common men could only coexist with an equally racist paternalism that justified the exploitation of racially discriminated slaves.[55]

In the words of William Freehling, Jackson "epitomized the Herrenvolk South," since he "assumed that Great White Fathers must forever guide childish blacks." The slaveholders' patriarchal-paternalistic worldview could

---

53. Saxton, *Rise and Fall of the White Republic,* 142–143. See also Wallace Hettle, *The Peculiar Democracy: Southern Democrats in Peace and War* (Athens, Ga., 2001), 3–5; and Harry L. Watson, *Jacksonian Politics and Community Conflict: The Emergence of the Second Party System in Cumberland County, North Carolina* (Baton Rouge, La., 1984), 198–245.

54. Morris, *Becoming Southern,* 152. On "one-generation aristocrats," see Hofstadter, *American Political Tradition,* 58.

55. See Lacy K. Ford, "Making the 'White Man's Country' White: Race, Slavery, and State-Building in the Jacksonian South," *JER* 19 (1999): 713–737; and Robert V. Remini, *The Legacy of Andrew Jackson: Essays on Democracy, Indian Removal, and Slavery* (Baton Rouge, La., 1988), 83–112.

not receive a clearer blessing than this. By borrowing from proslavery writers the idea that the planters he represented acted as fathers who took care of "childish blacks," Jackson managed to raise one of the fundamental assumptions at the heart of the patriarchal-paternalistic ethos to the level of complexity of a national political ideology which justified both the existence of slavery and the exploitation of African Americans as an inferior race.[56]

Despite Jackson's and the Democratic Party's considerable achievements in terms of providing a unifying ideology for the southern slaveholding elite, Jackson's program of reform had only a mixed record of success and failure in terms of its appeal to the planter elite. Though most planters resented the federal government's sporadic intrusion in local affairs, especially if it affected their economic and social privileges, they also sought the government's active support in regulating the market economy and providing the necessary infrastructures for their daily transactions. The Democrats' record, in this respect, especially in the aftermath of the 1837 economic crisis, which hit particularly harshly the cotton-producing states of the southwestern frontier, was rather poor. On the other hand, after Jackson's demonstration of federal strength against South Carolina's nullifiers—mostly rice and cotton planters—even the most ardent supporters of the Democratic Party for the sake of states' rights were left with more than one doubt as to the president's loyalty to the cause.[57]

Already by 1834, in the aftermath of the nullification crisis, a national coalition of opponents to Jackson had formed and had given origin to the Whig Party. Significantly, in the South the Whig Party stood initially on a platform of advocacy of states' rights against the unexpected and unwelcome autocratic pretensions of Andrew Jackson and the Democrats. In 1835, Virginia's prominent Whig politician William Ballard Preston wrote to his friend James Coles Bruce, leaving no doubt as to the reasons why he had joined the party: "I . . . hope a great deal for a cause so morally and intellectually right as that of the Southern rights." The following year, the Whigs contended with the Democrats in the first presidential election in which white male suffrage prevailed in every southern state except for two. The Second Party System was born.[58]

56. William W. Freeling, *The Reintegration of American History: Slavery and the Civil War* (New York, 1994), 115. See also George Fredrickson, *The Black Image in the White Mind: The Debate on Afro-American Character and Destiny, 1815–1914* (New York, 1971), 25–27, 90–92.

57. See Ellis, "Market Revolution," 171–172.

58. Willliam Ballard Preston to James Cole Bruce, 3 December 1835, Bruce Family Papers,

As the Whig Party grew in numbers and influence, its issues became more defined and its constituency more homogenous, especially in the South. By the late 1830s, the party had moved from its rather undefined program of opposition to Jackson's policy in the name of states' rights to a program of reform with a clear platform and a precise vision of the type of policy that a future Whig president was to implement. Doubtless, the merit of this transformation rested in the hands of the most influential member of the party, Henry Clay. Though moderately critical of slavery, Clay was— like Jackson—a planter who had built his fortune taking the opportunities offered by the market revolution in the South. In Kentucky, where he had established himself, Clay had enjoyed the fruits and seen the possibilities of what Harry Watson has called a "uniquely hybridized economy built jointly on the profits of manufacturing, interstate commerce, and plantation slavery alike." It was this experience that first pushed him in the direction of reconciling manufacturing and agrarian interests in a coherent and regulated economic system.[59]

As early as 1832, Clay had elaborated a complex body of reforms which he had called the "American System" and which ran against Jackson's fundamental tenets of limited governmental interference by advocating a national bank, federal protection of manufactures through high tariffs, and an ambitious program of construction of infrastructures on a national scale—what he called "internal improvements," mainly canals, railroads, and roads. At the time that Clay's American System became the core of the Whig Party's official program in the early 1840s, only a few enlightened southern planters and entrepreneurs were engaged in discussing the benefits of a similar far-reaching project of economic improvement for the South. Yet, it was already clear to a number of them that it had potential advantages.[60]

The key factor in the Whig Party's appeal to southern planters was its outright support of the market revolution, which in the South identified primarily with the continuous expansion of cotton production on the

UVA, in RASP. See also Michael F. Holt, *The Political Crisis of the 1850s* (New York, 1978), 17–38; and Silbey, *American Political Nation*, 46–71.

59. Harry L. Watson, "Introduction," in Harry L. Watson, ed., *Andrew Jackson vs. Henry Clay: Democracy and Development in Antebellum America* (New York, 1998), 44. See also Stephen Aaron, *How the West Was Lost: The Transformation of Kentucky from Daniel Boone to Henry Clay* (Baltimore, Md., 1996).

60. See Robert V. Remini, *Henry Clay: Statesman for the Union* (New York, 1991); and Merrill D. Peterson, *The Great Triumvirate: Webster, Clay, and Calhoun* (New York, 1987).

southwestern frontier. The rapidly increasing importance of internal improvements and economic regulation—which in turn produced commercial
progress—convinced many planters that with the help of both they could
reap more thoroughly the benefits of the South's agricultural expansion than
if they were left without any governmental support. As a consequence, Whig
supporters included—in the words of Harry Watson—"far-sighted planters
who saw no way to sustain the slave-based economy without the advantages
of commercial institutions, and also a reasonable number of ambitious farmers who felt that the advantages of commercial progress were worth the risk."
Moreover, the Whigs' support first for a system of chartered banks and then
for a national bank and financial regulation appealed to both merchants and
businessmen in southern cities. Since planters and merchants were engaged
in the same business of producing and selling staple crops in the world market, it is no surprise that many of them shared similar views on the economic
needs of the South. Particularly "in the 'black belts' of the lower South,"
where—according to Charles Sellers—"the great cotton capitalists . . . were
especially dependent on commercial and credit facilities for financing and
carrying on their extensive planting operations," large planters and urban
businessmen voted consistently for the Whigs.[61]

In those counties of frontier states (such as Mississippi, Alabama, and
Louisiana) that had particularly large slave populations concentrated on
large plantations, the Whigs were the majority party throughout the 1830s
and 1840s. In Warren County, Mississippi, "merchants and lawyers made up
half of the group of active Whigs" in the towns, while "planters dominated
the countryside Whigs, each of whom owned an average of thirty slaves."
Whigs were a majority also in those regions of Atlantic Seaboard states, such
as Virginia, North Carolina, and Georgia, where planters and businessmen
desperately longed for internal improvements, infrastructures, and transportation facilities. In Virginia, in particular, the Whigs prevailed in towns and
in those areas that were more closely connected to the market. Similarly, in
Georgia—according to J. William Harris—the Whigs "attracted merchants
and commercially oriented planters, and its members were more likely to favor government intervention to spur economic development." For this reason,

---

61. Watson, "Slavery and Development," 59; Charles G. Sellers, "Who Were the Southern
Whigs?" *AHR* 59 (1954): 342. See also Ratcliffe, "Crisis of Commercialization," 177–178; and
Arthur Charles Cole, *The Whig Party in the South* (Gloucester, Mass., 1962; orig. pub. in 1912).

the Whig Party was particularly strong in Augusta County, an area of large cotton plantations, among which was "Liberty Hall," future Confederate vice president Alexander Stephens's estate.[62]

Unlike southern Democrats, southern Whigs wholeheartedly supported programs for agricultural reform and sought to reconcile changes in transportation and technology with the slave system. According to Steven G. Collins, "many southern Whigs heeded the new 'Industrial Gospel' of systemization, uniformity, and organization in agriculture, education, and industry, which appealed to their view of a progressive and orderly society." In fact, anticipating issues that in the 1840s and 1850s gathered widespread interest thanks to the regular publication of *De Bow's Review* and to the regular meetings of the Southern Commercial Conventions, southern Whigs were at the forefront of organic programs of southern economic reform that aimed at the collaboration of slaveholding agrarian interests with manufacturing entrepreneurship.[63]

Significantly, according to James Oakes, at the heart of the southern Whigs' "central theme" of reconciliation between industry and agriculture lay the fact that "they defended economic development among whites while insisting that agricultural labor be maintained as the special preserve for blacks." And, to be sure, the Whigs' program for reform had as much patriarchal-paternalistic ideology in it as that of the Democrats. While committed to economic modernization, Whigs respected social hierarchies and acknowledged the existence of inequalities. Politically conservative, they were deeply troubled by the Democrats' populist message and its egalitarian appeal to farmers and mechanics. Whigs wanted a competent elite—and in the South a competent planter elite—to run the economy and promote commercial development. Theirs was what John Ashworth has called a "merchant-capital-based elitism" with several elements of paternalism in it.[64]

62. Morris, *Becoming Southern*, 151; J. William Harris, *Plain Folk and Gentry in a Slave Society: White Liberty and Black Slavery in Augusta's Hinterlands* (Middletown, Conn., 1985), 114. See also Thornton, *Politics and Power*, 39–53; and William G. Shade, *Democratizing the Old Dominion: Virginia and the Second Party System, 1824–1861* (Charlottesville, Va., 2000), 9–11.

63. Steven G. Collins, "System, Organization, and Agricultural Reform in the Antebellum South, 1840–1860," *AH* 75 (2001): 1–2. See also Watson, *Jacksonian Politics*, 151–197; and Thomas Brown, "The Southern Whigs and Economic Development," *SoSt* 20 (1981): 20–38.

64. James Oakes, "From Republicanism to Liberalism: Ideological Change and the Crisis of the Old South," *AQ* 37 (1985): 563; Ashworth, *Slavery, Capitalism, and Politics*, 365.

Particularly illuminating is the comparison that Daniel Walker Howe has drawn between prominent Whig politician and southern planter/businessman Henry Clay and northern Whig industrialist Nathan Appleton, who ran the Lowell mills in Massachusetts. "In both cases"—Howe has pointed out—"capitalist economic enterprises served the owner's patriarchal social values . . . plantation slaves, like Lowell 'mill girls,' were thought to benefit from the benevolent discipline of paternalism." Being the ethos of a rising elite of capitalist-oriented businessmen and planters, paternalism was also the prominent ethos of the Whig Party. Economic reform and modern efficiency were the same fundamental tenets at the heart of the paternalistic ideology of businessmen and merchants, and especially of large cotton planters in frontier states such as Mississippi, where throughout the 1830s and 1840s Whiggery was synonymous with the slaveholding aristocracy.[65]

After 1840 and the Whig Party's official adoption of Clay's American System, the way to advocate a political conciliation of slaveholding paternalism with business capitalism and economic reform was open to planters. In Georgia, in particular, according to Anthony Gene Carey, "the idea of harmony of interest (between capital and labor, agriculture and commerce, North and South), a notion much propounded in Whig literature, jibed well with the emerging paternalistic slaveholding ideology." At the same time, the Whigs' elitism and their propensity to respect the hierarchy of social order fit well with the patriarchal values that many planter families privileged throughout the South. In fact, like the Democrats, the Whigs attempted to transform the patriarchal-paternalistic worldview of southern planters into the core ideology of a national political program. Yet, they were less successful than Jackson's followers precisely because of their stronger emphasis on elitism and their outright advocacy of the patriarchal ideal of a hierarchically ordered society and, therefore, remained the South's largest minority party until their demise in the 1850s.[66]

At the same time, after an initial period in which they drew support from southern states' rights advocates angry at Jackson's supposed betrayal of the Democratic Party's cause, the Whigs quickly became a party committed

65. Daniel Walker Howe, *The Political Culture of the American Whigs* (Chicago, 1979), 135. See also Morris, *Becoming Southern*, 149–153; and Bradley G. Bond, *Political Culture in the Nineteenth-Century South: Mississippi, 1830–1900* (Baton Rouge, La., 1995), 86–89.

66. Anthony Gene Carey, *Politics, Slavery, and the Union in Antebellum Georgia* (Athens, Ga., 2001), 110. See also Saxton, *Rise and Fall of the White Republic*, 53–76.

to strong governmental intervention in the economy—a commitment that contributed a great deal to their unpopularity among many southerners. In fact, it was the fear of the dangerous combination of elitism and support for a strong government—both features that had characterized the ideology of the previous Federalist Party—that led southern Democrat James Henry Hammond to write in his secret diary that leading Whig statesman Henry Clay was "a man for a monarchy where there are but two sides and everything conducted on the highest national principles, regardless of constitutional scruples, of state rights, and money."[67]

By 1841, when Hammond wrote his diary entry, the Whigs' program of reform in regard to relations between the federal governmental core and the southern periphery left already little doubt as to the fact that it implied a degree of sacrifice in terms of both states' rights and local power—which most southern slaveholders were hardly prepared to accept. Worse still was the fact that, while the Whigs were no less racist than the Democrats toward African Americans, there were, doubtless, more antislavery advocates among the Whigs than among the Democrats. Unlike the Democrats, the northern Whigs were strongly influenced by the rise of militant abolitionism after 1830. In turn, both the growth of a politically moderate antislavery attitude and the rise of a radical abolitionist movement were to bear particularly important consequences in the increasingly sectional atmosphere of the 1840s and 1850s, when the tensions arising from the different political interpretations of the relationship between the federal governmental core and the southern periphery led first to the crisis of the Second Party System and then to its demise in the United States.[68]

Unlike the influential regional elite of the southern periphery of the United States, which succeeded in maintaining its control of key governmental institutions throughout the 1830s and the 1840s, the regional elite of the *Mezzogiorno* only benefited from a relative increase of power in its relationship with the Neapolitan government during the brief period of the Revolution of 1820–1821. And still, the post-revolutionary return to absolutist monarchical practices ensured the obliteration of the innovative ideas of

67. James Henry Hammond's secret diary, 20 February 1841, in Carol Bleser, ed., *Secret and Sacred: The Diaries of James Henry Hammond, a Southern Slaveholder* (New York, 1988), 36. See also Ashworth, *Slavery, Capitalism, and Politics*, 350–360.

68. See Michael F. Holt, *The Rise and Fall of the American Whig Party: Jacksonian Politics and the Onset of the Civil War* (New York, 1999), 95–101.

the Neapolitan Revolution's "federal" experiment. In Prime Minister Luigi De' Medici's mind, the problem was mainly in the relationship between the revolutionary experience of devolution of power and the work of the constitutional assembly. Medici opposed devolution on the grounds that it would have been the first step toward the transformation of the Bourbon kingdom into a constitutional monarchy—a concession to "the impudence of the so-called ideas of the century," as he stated in 1823, which he was not prepared to accept.[69]

Despite Medici's opinion, in the first half of the 1820s, the Bourbon government embarked on a limited program of reform through the creation of the organs of a restricted representative monarchy (*monarchia consultiva*). It was an attempt to partially acquiesce to the peripheral elites' demand for devolution and parliamentary institutions by providing instead a constitutional model of government granted by the king in agreement with his absolutist powers. As a result, a law issued in 1824 created a restricted representative council (*consulta*) of twenty-four members, who were to be chosen from among the most prominent landed proprietors and public figures of the different provinces. Though it gathered representatives from all the provinces of the kingdom, the council differed from the former revolutionary parliament in two important respects: first, its members were relatively few and were all chosen by the king; second, its role was confined to offering advice to the Bourbon administration on exclusively technical matters. The significance of the council lay more in its example of a limited attempt at reform than in its effective work. And yet, by the time of Francis I's brief kingdom (1825–1830) the council had already fallen under Medici's influence and become just one more example of what Andrea Genoino has termed "ministerial despotism."[70]

The Revolution of 1820–1821 had left behind an even more important legacy than the ideas of representative government and balance of power between core and periphery. The main cause of the failure of the revolution had been the difference of opinion between the *murattiani*—who sought to

69. Luigi De' Medici's quotation is in Giovanni Aliberti, *Lo Stato postfeudale. Un secolo di potere pubblico nel Mezzogiorno italiano (1806–1910)* (Naples, 1990), 59.

70. Andrea Genoino's quotation is in Gaetano Cingari, *Mezzogiorno e Risorgimento. La Restaurazione a Napoli dal 1821 al 1830* (Bari, 1970), 202. See also Raffaele Feola, "Le Consulte di Stato nelle Sicilie," *Clio* 22 (1986): 23–49; Meriggi, *Gli stati italiani*, 170–171; Marco Meriggi, "Società, istituzioni e ceti dirigenti," in Sabattucci and Vidotto, eds., *Le premesse dell'Unità*, 159; and Spagnoletti, *Storia del Regno*, 52–53.

implement a moderate version of the constitution—and the *carbonari*—who envisioned a democratic form of government. In the 1820s, while the *murattiani* gradually disappeared, the *carbonari* continued to form *vendite* and organize popular revolts—such as the 1828 uprising in Cilento—but they never recovered the strength that they had had in the Revolution of 1820–1821. Despite the *murattiani*'s and *carbonari*'s loss of importance, the opposition between a moderate program of constitutional liberalism and a democratic program based on radical ideas continued to be a source of division among peripheral elites until the 1860s. Through subsequent transformations, the two political creeds gradually crystallized into the central ideologies of two different political movements: the democrats and the moderate liberals.[71]

Though the Bourbon monarchy did not allow the existence of real political parties, the debate between these two "different political orientations"—as Alberto Banti has called them—inflamed southern Italian public opinion. By the 1830s, the debate was ever more lively as a result of the increasing number of pamphlets and journals that addressed both economic and sociopolitical issues. Most of the voices expressing dissatisfaction over existing governmental institutions and enthusiasm for different programs of reform clearly grouped around publications that supported one or the other of the major political ideologies. These, in turn, became the means through which—in the words of Enrica Di Ciommo—"the new political ideal of the *nation* found specific expression." And within the contours of the political debate on the ideal nation, the issue of institutional reform in regard to the relationship between core and periphery was as central as the one of governmental reform according to more democratic or more elitist ideas.[72]

By the late 1820s, the *Carboneria* and the other secret societies were in deep crisis as a result of their repeated failure to achieve meaningful political changes. Yet, at the beginning of the 1830s, the democratic movement underwent a profound transformation that culminated in Giuseppe Mazzini's foundation of Young Italy in 1831. From Marseilles, Mazzini and several other Italian democratic exiles launched a program for an association— Young Italy—that rejected the secrecy that had characterized the *Carboneria*

---

71. See Giuseppe Galasso, "Le forme del potere, classi e gerarchie sociali," in Ruggero Romano and Corrado Vivanti, eds., *Storia d'Italia*, vol. 1, *I caratteri originari* (Turin, 1972), 527–534.

72. Alberto M. Banti, *La nazione del Risorgimento. Parentela, santità e onore alle origini dell'Italia unita* (Turin, 2000), 201; Enrica Di Ciommo, *La nazione possibile. Mezzogiorno e questione nazionale nel 1848* (Milan, 1993), 29.

and was committed to the formation of a unified Italian nation-state with a republican form of government. "In practice"—as Denis Mack Smith has remarked—"it [Young Italy] became the first organized Italian political party." Thanks to Mazzini's able use of propaganda and considerable journalistic skills—with which he directed his own clandestine paper, *La Giovine Italia*—Young Italy's network spread rapidly, covering the entire peninsula. Despite the tight police control that characterized Italy's Restoration governments, by 1833 the society's members already numbered well over fifty thousand. Mazzini had become the uncontested leader of the democratic movement in Italy.[73]

Yet, Mazzini and his followers had an extremely tormented relationship with the *Mezzogiorno*. In their mind, the exploited and impoverished southern peasantry—under the guidance of democratic leaders trained in northern Italy—had the potential to start the revolutionary insurrection that was to cause the downfall of the reactionary Bourbon government and ultimately lead to the formation of an Italian republic. This basic idea was at the root of elaborate plans for the training of guerrilla cells—such as Nicola Fabrizi's *Legione italica*, a clandestine revolutionary structure active in Malta between the late 1830s and the early 1840s—and of several ill-conceived expeditions—such as the famous one by the Bandiera brothers in 1844. Both activities aimed at providing southern peasants with the leadership and organization that they supposedly needed in order to start the revolution.[74]

There is little doubt that Mazzini's ideas suffered from poor knowledge of the social and political conditions of the *Mezzogiorno* and from a patronizing attitude toward the southern peasantry. The proof was not only in the repeated failure that Mazzinian initiatives encountered, but also in Mazzini's lack of awareness regarding land redistribution, a vital element in guaranteeing

73. Denis Mack Smith, *Mazzini* (New Haven, Conn., 1994), 7. See also Roland Sarti, "Giuseppe Mazzini and his Opponents," in John A. Davis, ed., *Italy in the Nineteenth Century* (New York, 2000), 82–84; Franco Della Peruta, *Mazzini e i rivoluzionari italiani. Il "partito d'azione," 1830–1845* (Milan, 1974), 69–160; and Stuart Woolf, *A History of Italy, 1700–1860: The Social Constraints of Political Change* (London, 1979), 303–309.

74. See De Francesco, "Ideologie," 293–294; Giuseppe Galasso, *La democrazia da Cattaneo a Rosselli* (Firenze, 1982), 20–23; Della Peruta, *Mazzini e i rivoluzionari italiani*, 278–314; and Enrico Dal Lago, "Radicalism and Nationalism: Northern 'Liberators' and Southern Laborers in the United States and Italy, 1830–1860," in Enrico Dal Lago and Rick Halpern, eds., *The American South and Italian Mezzogiorno: Essays in Comparative History* (New York, 2002), 197–214.

the southern peasants' participation in democratic activities and possibly—if one were to follow Antonio Gramsci's thought—the main reason for the failure of the Risorgimento's social revolution. In fact, notwithstanding Mazzini's misunderstandings about the *Mezzogiorno,* scholars have long established not only that the southern Italian democratic movement was both different and mostly detached from its Mazzinian counterparts in northern and central Italy, but also that it assumed characteristics which adapted it to the particularity of southern Italy's social and political conditions. For one thing, the southern Italian democratic movement was extremely diverse and regionally based. And yet, common to all the different democratic groups was the fact that their activities followed the earlier conspiratorial model of the *Carboneria;* even after Mazzini's foundation of Young Italy, little changed in this respect in the *Mezzogiorno.* Also, equally important was the fact that even those democratic groups—such as Benedetto Musolino's Calabrian association *I figliuoli della Giovine Italia*—that took inspiration directly from Mazzini claimed a substantial difference from the details of his message, only embracing the general idea of a unified republic while clearly working within the boundaries of a local tradition of radicalism.[75]

Yet, the most peculiar characteristic of the southern Italian democratic movement was the particularly high percentage of noblemen who joined in conspiratorial activities that aimed at overthrowing the Bourbon regime and establishing a republic. As far as we know, the majority of the articulated spokesmen on democratic reform programs in the *Mezzogiorno* belonged to the provincial liberal aristocracy, and regions such as Terra di Bari and the Calabrie hosted a particularly high percentage of them. The fact that these spokesmen belonged to the aristocracy did not necessarily mean that they aimed to provide an exclusively conservative interpretation of the democratic creed. In general, within the boundaries of republican ideology, their positions ranged from conservative to radical, according to the degree of their commitment to democratic institutions and initiatives—particularly in regard to the issue of land distribution.[76]

75. See De Francesco, "Ideologie," 281–282; and Candeloro, *Dalla Restaurazione,* 232–233. The most thorough analysis of the distinctive features of the southern Italian democratic movement is in Giuseppe Berti, *I democratici e l'iniziativa meridionale nel Risorgimento* (Milan, 1962), especially 196–199; for a critique, see Franco Della Peruta, "Mazzinianesimo e democrazia nel Mezzogiorno (1831–1847)," in A.A.V.V., *Democrazia e mazzinianesimo nel Mezzogiorno d'Italia, 1831–1872* (Geneve, 1975), 6–27.

76. See Candeloro, *Dalla Restaurazione,* 171–172.

Still, it is particularly significant that, whether they advanced a conservative or a radical interpretation of the democratic creed in their pamphlets, a number of southern Italian democratic noblemen shared a fierce critique of the Bourbon government's program of modernization and of its consequences on the southern countryside. The critique focused on the fact that, embarking on its program of modernization, the Bourbon government had followed its French predecessor in building a centralized bureaucratic administration—both corrupt and authoritarian—with the almost exclusive aim of curbing the power of traditional elites, and especially of the provincial aristocracy. Therefore, for many southern Italian democratic noblemen, the central issue was the alteration in the balance of power between the Neapolitan core and the southern Italian periphery that had arisen as a consequence of the Bourbon reforms, while their solution to the problem envisioned the creation of a democratic Italian nation that would restore the balance of power in the *Mezzogiorno* through a republican form of government. In fact, as foremost Apulian democratic nobleman and Italian nationalist Domenico Nicolai wrote in his 1830 pamphlet *Considerazioni sull'Italia* (Considerations on Italy), the Bourbon reforms had succeeded in abolishing throughout the territory of the Kingdom of the Two Sicilies "both the residual liberties and the features of self-government," especially in the aftermath of the Revolution of 1820–1821.[77]

Worse still was the fact that, with the confirmation of the abolition of feudalism and the sale of church and noble lands, the Bourbon government had created a new class of bourgeois landed proprietors (*galantuomini*), which had effectively replaced the aristocracy. In many democratic noblemen's view, the *galantuomini* were just a group of nouveaux riches who used their power and influence in the Bourbon institutions of local government to exploit the people. As one of Basilicata's foremost democratic noblemen— Ferdinando Petruccelli Della Gattina—put it, the landed bourgeoisie that dominated municipal and provincial councils in the southern peripheries was made of "sad men, men who were subservient to a tyrannical system." Consequently, even though they advanced their critique against the despotism of Bourbon governmental centralization in the name of the republican ideals of liberty for the individual and for the people, many democratic

---

77. Domenico Nicolai, "Considerazioni sull'Italia," in Franco Della Peruta, ed., *Scrittori politici dell'Ottocento. Giuseppe Mazzini e i democratici* (Milan, 1969), 354. See also Di Ciommo, *La nazione possibile*, 146–151.

noblemen also set out to show, with their programs of reform, that the aristocracy—as opposed to the bourgeoisie—was the real progressive class and
the one which could effectively rule southern Italy as part of an Italian nation. Therefore, different factors were at the root of the large number of
southern Italian noblemen's commitment to the democratic program. As
Enrica Di Ciommo has pointed out, ultimately it was in a sort of ideological
melting, which put together the liberal idea of "limitation of governmental
power, the well-rooted aspirations to local autonomy, the need to self-af-
firmation against the new bourgeois order, and the need for self-defense
against government centralization," that the southern Italian aristocracy—or,
at least, a large part of its liberal section—ended up embracing a democratic
model of society.[78]

But there was more than this to the picture. Even though they were
theoretically committed to republican ideas, moderate democrats such as
the followers of both Ferdinando Petruccelli and Giuseppe Ricciardi sought
the abolition of privileges, and yet they accepted social inequalities and class
divisions as "a permanent feature of Italian life"—a feature that reminds
us of the patriarchal view of the immutability of social order. In particular,
Giuseppe Ricciardi, a foremost democratic leader who descended from a
Neapolitan aristocratic family, went as far as theorizing a program of nation-building that maintained the concept of popular sovereignty at its
core, specifically in opposition to Bourbon despotism. However, despite his
radical openings toward both liberty and democracy, Ricciardi was afraid of
the possible consequences of economic equality, and during their illustrious
revolutionary careers both he and Petruccelli Della Gattina defended more
than once the right to private property against peasant activities of land occupation. At one point, Ricciardi even wrote with a certain amount of satisfac-
tion of how "in our country the masses are very docile toward the voice of
the most enlightened classes"—a sentence that illustrates particularly well
what Clara Lovett has called the Democrats' "paternalistic definition of the
relationship between the educated elite and the masses."[79]

78. Ferdinando Petruccelli Della Gattina's quotation is in Di Ciommo, *La nazione possi-
bile*, 156; see also 158–159. See also Clara Lovett, *The Democratic Movement in Italy, 1830–1870*
(Cambridge, Mass., 1982), 152–153; Woolf, *History of Italy*, 422–423; and V. Valinoti-La Torraca,
Ferdinando Petruccelli (Naples, 1915).

79. Giuseppe Ricciardi's quotation is in Berti, *I democratici*, 178; Lovett, *Democratic Movement*, 52, 55. See also Carlo Gentile, "Spunti democratici e mazziniani nella Daunia dell'epoca
risorgimentale," in A.A.V.V., *Democrazia e mazzinianesimo*, 44–62; Lepre, *Storia del Mezzo-*

The truth was that Ricciardi and other southern Italian democratic noblemen were, as Marta Petrusewicz has remarked, "more populist than socialist . . . suspicious of class struggle" and with a rather generic "faith in the people, about which, however, they knew very little." In other words, their democratic vision was highly paternalistic and combined ideas of civil progress and people's rule under the watchful eye of the liberal aristoc-racy, the class which alone possessed the necessary intellectual abilities and commitment to libertarian ideology to guide the masses in the process of construction of a republican nation, though not exactly of a perfectly equal society. In the democratic noblemen's mind, following the end of the landed bourgeoisie's power, the aristocracy was to become the dominant class of a future nation characterized by the paternalistic extension of political, rather than social and economic, benefits to the southern Italian peasantry. There-fore, in ways comparable to the democratic planters' program of reform in the American South, the southern Italian democratic noblemen's reform program was committed first and foremost to the elimination of possible problems arising from the interference of the central government in periph-eral affairs; in particular, in the *Mezzogiorno*, the central government's inter-ference showed specifically in the Bourbons' outright support for the landed bourgeoisie. Also comparable to the democratic planters' egalitarianism was the substantially populist message of moderate democrats, such as Petruccelli and Ricciardi, whose ambiguous relationship with ideas and practices of social and economic equality allowed them to maintain the patriarchal view of an immutably ordered society while supporting a project according to which, paternalistically, an intellectual elite would be in charge of guiding the masses on the path to national revolution.[80]

In 1830—the same year in which Domenico Nicolai published his demo-cratic pamphlet—Prime Minister Medici died and twenty-year-old Ferdi-nand II was crowned King of the Two Sicilies. Medici's replacement with Donato Tommasi, together with the young age of the new sovereign, created

giorno, 256–257; and Franco Della Peruta, *Politica e società nell'Italia dell'Ottocento. Problemi, vicende e personaggi* (Milan, 1999), 274–298.

80. Marta Petrusewicz, "Giuseppe Ricciardi, ribelle, romantico, europeo," *ASPN* iii (1999): 238. See also Di Ciommo, *La nazione possibile*, 184–187; and Banti, *La nazione del Risorgimento*, 32–36. This analysis is restricted to the 1830s and 1840s and, therefore, does not take into account Neapolitan nobleman Luigi Pisacane's truly socialist 1851 manifesto—*La guerra combattuta in Italia negli anni 1848–49* (War Fought in Italy in the Years 1848–49); see Woolf, *History of Italy*, 423–24.

an impression of change in Bourbon absolutism. Contributing to this was the fact that, as commander-in-chief of the army, Ferdinand II had shown already his wish to fight corruption and make the administration more efficient. In fact, from the outset, the new king adopted a policy of moderate reformism, cutting expenditures, decreasing onerous taxes, and increasing governmental intervention through the construction of public works. He also encouraged governmental support for reform programs and allowed progressive liberal economists, such as Ludovico Bianchini, to enter the kingdom's administration.[81]

It was in the first years of Ferdinand II's reign that the journal *Annali Civili del Regno delle Due Sicilie* started its publication with the twin objectives of promoting projects of land reclamation and agricultural improvement and putting in contact the multiform activities of the different Economic Societies of the Provinces. During the 1830s, as the landed bourgeoisie consolidated its power in the peripheral centers of the *Mezzogiorno*, the Economic Societies of the Provinces lived a sort of golden age, enjoying enormous prestige and gathering the most progressive members of the propertied classes. Indeed, it seemed that Ferdinand II sought to collaborate with the provincial landed bourgeoisie—whose interests were mainly in commercial agriculture and whose political creed was mostly moderate liberal—in the administration of the peripheries of the kingdom. As a consequence, as Alfonso Scirocco has remarked, liberals thought that they would soon be granted "representative institutions, or at least the strengthening of the existing council system," which still allowed only limited freedom of action.[82]

Arguably, the attempt to gain the support of the landed bourgeoisie by implementing moderate economic and liberal reforms and paying particular attention to the relationship between the Neapolitan core and the southern periphery was, in fact, a central part of Ferdinand II's policy. To this end, he embarked on frequent and systematic trips to the kingdom's provinces, trips during which he held private meetings with local administrators and

---

81. See Alfonso Scirocco, "Dalla seconda restaurazione alla fine del Regno," in Giuseppe Galasso and Rosario Romeo, eds., *Storia del Mezzogiorno*, vol. 4 (Rome, 1986), 683–734; Marta Petrusewicz, *Come il Meridione divenne una Questione. Rappresentazioni del Sud prima e dopo il Quarantotto* (Soveria Mannelli, Catanzaro, 1998), 70–71; Benedetto Croce, *Storia del Regno di Napoli* (Bari, 1925), 225–226; and Elena Croce, *La patria napoletana* (Milan, 1999), 83–110.

82. Scirocco, "Dalla seconda restaurazione," 700. See also Di Ciommo, "Elites provinciali," 1017–1024; Antonacci, *Terra e potere*, 31–34; and Renata De Lorenzo, *Società economiche e istruzione agraria nell'Ottocento meridionale* (Milan, 1998), 74–78.

members of the provincial elites, praising their work and gathering their complaints. He also took part in highly spectacular ceremonies in which he visited public offices, gave speeches, and promised the government's help to those who needed it. Ferdinand II actually planned carefully his behavior during his trips so as to appear like a benevolent father whose main concern was the welfare of his country—in comparable terms to the metaphor of parenthood in paternalistic relations. In similar fashion, governmental rhetoric presented the king's trips to the provinces as visits that a father owed to his numerous children.[83]

Commenting on an 1834 issue of the *Annali Civili,* Angelantonio Spagnoletti has noticed how "the king's family itself was the metaphor of the nation." And yet, the fact that it was clearly only a metaphor showed in the undiminished degree of suffering and exploitation of the southern peasantry and in the continuation of absolutist monarchical practices, such as the constant employment of police forces. Even the "development and support of the southern bourgeoisie"—Silvio De Majo has noted—"were sought . . . as long as they did not imply any change in the absolutist and personal administration of power." In this perspective, it was highly significant that one of Ferdinand II's first acts as king was the 1831 creation of a special royal secretariat, an act that gave him almost absolute control over the activities of all his ministries.[84]

Yet, notwithstanding Ferdinand II's ambiguous attitude toward reformism, during the 1830s, liberal intellectuals confronted each other in a debate that focused on the best way to provide the Bourbon kingdom with new and efficient institutions, so as to resolve the crucial problems of economic development and political representation of the provincial landed bourgeoisie. A crucial area of the debate regarded specifically juridical reforms. Moderate liberals advocated the rationalization of the administrative system, whose complexity resulted in the governmental authorities' abuses and corruption, and the legal protection of individual rights against absolutist monarchical pretensions. A central figure in the legal debate was Matteo De Augustiniis, the most active and prolific in a group of Neapolitan lawyers who advanced

83. See Alfonso Scirocco, "Ferdinando II Re delle Due Sicilie: La gestione del potere," *RSR* 86 (1999): 487–500; and Spagnoletti, *Storia del Regno,* 84–89.

84. Spagnoletti, *Storia del Regno,* 87; Silvio De Majo, *Breve storia del Regno di Napoli. Da Carlo di Borbone all'Unità d'Italia (1734–1860)* (Rome, 1996), 47. See also Di Ciommo, *La nazione possibile,* 21–22; Scirocco, *L'Italia del Risorgimento,* 153–157; and Candeloro, *Dalla Restaurazione,* 232–233.

a coherent program of reforms and supported it with a complex theory of juridical liberalism. In particular, in an important article entitled "Della Proprietà e delle sue leggi" (Of Property and Its Laws)—which he published in his journal *Il Progresso delle Lettere, Scienze, Arti* (The Progress of Letters, Sciences, and Arts) in 1840—De Augustiniis argued that, together with the protection of individual rights, the reform of the legal system ought to guarantee the right to own private property, which he called "the first and principal instrument of civilization." And, doubtless, by "civilization," De Augustiniis meant the ordered, legalistic, and progressive bourgeois world to which he belonged.[85]

In De Augustiniis's and in the liberal intellectuals' minds, legal reforms were instruments for a much broader program of economic and social reforms. The program, which they termed "Social Economy" (*Economia sociale*), was to lay the foundations of an economically strong and politically moderate liberal bourgeois nation, a nation in which individual rights and collective interests combined harmoniously. In this view, progress identified firmly with the preeminence of the provincial landed bourgeoisie, which was eager to abandon the two equal scourges of Bourbon protectionism and absolutism and to restore the balance of power in core-periphery relations.[86]

Initially, the doctrine of social economy was part of De Augustiniis's and Giuseppe De Thomasis's program of modernization and collaboration with the monarchy. Yet, when Ferdinand II's moderate reformist overtures ceased in the second half of the 1830s, it became an important part of the moderate liberals' political program in opposition to the king's increasingly absolutist practices. After Ferdinand II failed in his attempt to enforce protectionism over the kingdom's industries—and especially over Sicilian sulfur extraction—against foreign interference, the Bourbon administrative absolutism tightened its grip once more. As it did, opposition from liberal intellectuals and articulate members of the landed bourgeoisie became more vocal and

85. Matteo De Augustiniis, "Della proprietà e delle sue leggi. Primo discorso. Della natura della proprietà e de' suoi principi fondamentali," *PSLA* 25 (1840): 40. See also Matteo De Augustiniis, *Della condizione economica del Regno di Napoli* (Naples, 1833); Di Ciommo, *La nazione possibile,* 70–84; Luigi Parente, "Ideologia politica e realta sociale nell'attività pubblicistica di Matteo De Augustiniis," *ASPN* 90 (1972): 29–137; and Aurelio Lepre, *Il Mezzogiorno dal feudalesimo al capitalismo* (Naples, 1979), 110–111.

86. See Gaetano Cingari, *Problemi del Risorgimento meridionale* (Messina, 1965), 40–56; Francesco Di Battista, *L'emergenza ottocentesca dell'economia politica a Napoli* (Bari, 1983), 97–111; and Abbamonte, *Potere pubblico,* 41–42.

the doctrine of social economy increasingly focused its critique on the role
of the protectionist system in core-periphery relations. The reason, according to De Augustiniis, was that the system privileged only a few, mostly
Neapolitan, industrial entrepreneurs and factory owners, whose plans were
sponsored by the government against the interests of the majority of provincial landowners, many of whom practiced commercial agriculture. And in
fact, there is little doubt that the latter was the most important sector of the
kingdom's economy and its true natural resource—especially judging from
the steady growth of olive oil and wine production and export in areas such
as Terra di Bari and Terra di Lavoro during the 1830s.[87]

Yet, even though all liberal intellectuals agreed on the need to abandon
economic protectionism, their views on the role of the state in economic
matters differed substantially. While De Augustiniis thought to restrict the
state's intervention, Antonio Scialoja—author of an important treatise on
social economy—advocated its strong role in resolving conflicts between
different interest groups. According to Scialoja, the political and economic
unification of the different sectors of production would have strengthened
the landed bourgeoisie's power a great deal. Even more radical was economist Silvio Spaventa, who went as far as identifying nation and state and
attributing to the latter the role of regulating the different aspects of social
life. According to Spaventa, state regulation was to have important repercussions on core-periphery relations through the creation of a decentralized
system of government and the resolution of the crucial issue of the provincial elites' political representation.[88]

Yet, Spaventa's main concern was the fact that the landed bourgeoisie,
due to its recent origins and the Bourbon government's limited support,
"had little authority on the people to make them accept its political beliefs

87. See Matteo De Augustiniis, *Istituzioni di economia sociale* (Naples, 1837). See also Di Ciommo, *La nazione possibile*, 85–98; Petrusewicz, *Come il Meridone*, 82–83; Lepre, *Storia del Mezzogiorno*, 148–149; Spagnoletti, *Storia del Regno*, 229–234; John A. Davis, *Imprenditori e societa
nel regno borbonico (1815–1860)* (Bari, 1979), 225–245; Salvemini, *L'innovazione precaria*, 152–157;
Antonacci, *Terra e potere*, 18–19; and Pietro Tino, *Campania Felice? Territorio e agricolture prima
della "grande trasformazione"* (Catanzaro, 1997), 36–37.

88. See Antonio Scialoja, *I principi della Economia sociale esposti in ordine ideologico* (Turin,
1846); Di Ciommo, *La nazione possibile*, 124–142, Di Ciommo, "Elites provinciali," 1019–1020;
Lepre, *Storia del Mezzogiorno*, 259–260; Petrusewicz, *Come il Meridione*, 74–75; P. Roggi, "Antonio Scialoja, fra A. Smith ed A. Genovesi," *RE* 46 (1977): 1485–1524; Elena Croce, *Silvio Spaventa* (Milan, 1969); and Carlo Ghisalberti, "Silvio Spaventa teorico dello stato liberale," *Clio* 7
(1971): 541–606.

and induce them to defend them." Significantly, he thought that the state played a fundamental role in helping the bourgeoisie to establish its hegemony on the lower classes and guide the march toward progress. In retrospect, it seems fair to say that, in the 1830s and 1840s, Spaventa and his fellow liberal thinkers gave a decisive contribution to advancing what Marta Petrusewicz has called a "civilizing project," a project according to which the landowning elite—and especially the provincial landed bourgeoisie—was to lead paternalistically the rural masses on the path to modernization after having established its hegemonic position in both social and political terms. And yet, this was a conservative type of modernization, one that was equally "based on rural harmony, and implicitly, on the preservation of the old hierarchical order," in clear agreement with the fundamental tenets of the patriarchal ethos.[89]

Remarkably, in the 1830s and 1840s, the increasing politicization of the issue of relations between core and periphery led to comparable, even though somewhat different, developments in the American South and in the Italian *Mezzogiorno*. In each case, the peripheral landed elite used two different types of political ideologies to condition the central government's decisions on the need to reform the socioeconomic and representative systems. On one hand, similar to southern Jacksonian Democrats in America, southern Italian democrats sought to enlarge the electoral basis and include peripheral classes and interest groups that were overlooked by traditionally center-dominated politics. Yet, behind the democratic rhetoric lay also a truth of social privileges enjoyed by two powerful regional classes—planters and noblemen—and an attempt by both to claim their right to guide the development of future reformed societies in patriarchal-paternalistic fashion. On the other hand, while they demanded more opportunities of political representation, many southern Italian liberal landowners specifically sought the central government's strong intervention to help them maintain their economic and social privileges in the peripheral regions, much like Whig slaveholders did. Also comparable is the fact that, similar to the southern Whigs, southern Italian moderate liberals were a substantially elitist political

89. Silvio Spaventa, *Dal 1848 al 1861. Lettere, scritti, documenti pubblicati da Benedetto Croce* (Naples, 1898), 137; Marta Petrusewicz, "Land-Based Modernization and the Culture of Landed Elites in the Nineteenth-Century Mezzogiorno," in Dal Lago and Halpern, eds., *American South and the Italian Mezzogiorno*, 108–109.

coalition, whose proponents combined a patriarchal commitment to the preservation of the social order with a paternalistic belief in the need to guide the rural masses on the path to modernization.

However, behind these comparable features lay particularly striking differences that resulted from the existence and absence of slavery, the great distinguishing characteristic between mid-nineteenth-century politics in the American South and in the Italian *Mezzogiorno*. Already in the 1830s and early 1840s, southern politics showed signs of a predominance of slavery in both the Democratic and the Whig programs of reforms, as a consequence both of the slave system's ties to the socioeconomic privileges of the planter class and of its importance in discourses connected to political representation and relations between core and periphery. Though the white antebellum American South was incomparably more democratic in its political life than the nineteenth-century Italian *Mezzogiorno*, in the former the overpowering influence of slavery ensured that even the most radical southern political programs of reform always aimed at preserving the inequality of the racial status quo. On the other hand, free from the constraints resulting from the need to maintain white supremacy, southern Italian political radicalism could contemplate, at its best, the creation of a truly democratic society. And yet, precisely because in the *Mezzogiorno* there was no clear dividing color line between privileged and unprivileged, several articulate members of the southern Italian elite who subscribed to either the democratic or the moderate liberal programs of reform were more forthright than politicians in the American South in advancing ideas that advocated maintaining a certain degree of social status quo.

Slavery, Landed Property, and Nationalism

In the second half of the 1840s and in the 1850s, as debates over different ways of reforming the socioeconomic and governmental systems continued to rage among different political groups within the two southern elites, the issues that had characterized core-periphery relations in the American South and in the Italian *Mezzogiorno* since 1820 reached a point of no return. The occurrence, at slightly different times, of two equally important "transformational crises"—the Crisis of 1850 in the American South and the Revolution of 1848 in the *Mezzogiorno*—had major effects on the evolving nature of political relations between the southern peripheral elites and the central governments in the two regions. As a consequence, in the course of the 1850s, the two southern elites underwent comparable changes in terms of increasing the radical aspects of their oppositional policies and of rejecting political expression through institutional means, favoring instead more decisive extra-institutional activity. However, while in the American case the changes were related to the fact that southern regional politics became progressively isolated and peripheral vis-à-vis the federal government, in the Italian case the changes were linked to the unfolding of a reverse process—a process in which southern politics increasingly occupied a central place in the different plans for the unification of Italy.[90]

In the United States, from the mid-1850s on, the increasing isolation of southern interests in the national political arena derived primarily from the growing influence and power of the Republican Party, the first major political party to embrace a clear antislavery position in its presidential platform. As the Republican Party grew, the political course of the previous fifty years reversed and turned against the southern minority, which, until the 1850s, had enjoyed an almost unchallenged hegemony over the federal government. The process reached its climax with the 1860 presidential election and the victory of Republican candidate Abraham Lincoln, an event that signaled the de facto end of the influence of the southern Slave Power over federal institutions and ultimately triggered southern secession from the Union. Conversely, in the Italian *Mezzogiorno* the 1850s saw the Bourbon monarchy's return to the most intransigent practices of absolutism, a fact that led a growing number of representatives of the southern Italian peripheral elite to join the ranks of the opposition and become political exiles in the liberal Piedmontese kingdom. From there, the southern exiles publicly voiced their discontent and contributed in a major way to make the problem of despotism in the *Mezzogiorno* a central concern of the northern Italian public opinion. At the same time, southern exiles in contact with the northern Italian democratic circles vigorously advocated a central role for revolutionary actions in the South—which ultimately led Giuseppe Garibaldi to head his Red Shirts in the conquest of Sicily, in 1860.

Within these concurrent, and in some ways opposite, contexts, nationalism —intended as an ideology that sparked characteristically extra-institutional activity—found particularly fertile ground in both southern regions. Though

90. On the concept of transformational crisis, see Geoffrey W. Conrad and Arthur A. Demarest, *Religion and Empire: The Dynamics of Aztec and Inca Expansionism* (New York, 1984).

according to different patterns, in both cases, and in comparable terms, nationalism filled the political vacuum left by the end of the organic, and at times particularly tense, relationship between the central government and the southern periphery that had characterized political life in the previous decades. In the American case, southern nationalism arose specifically from the increasing political isolation of the southern elite and from its need to break the isolation by seceding from the Union and creating a conservative Confederate nation that protected the elite's interests against governmental interference. Comparably, in the southern Italian case the *Mezzogiorno*'s elite joined the movement that ultimately led to the annexation of the South to the Italian kingdom in order to create an equally conservative nation that would substitute Bourbon absolutism with Piedmontese moderate liberalism and would protect those interests that the Bourbon government harmed.

Therefore, even though—in the course of opposite processes—southern nationalism in America ultimately led to secession, while Italian liberal nationalism in the *Mezzogiorno* ultimately led to unification, there are striking similarities between the two nationalist movements. Both southern nationalism in America, with its combination of defense of slaveholding privileges and its advocacy of states' rights, and Italian liberal nationalism in the *Mezzogiorno*, with its protection of socioeconomic privileges and its fulfillment of the elite's demand for political representation, became increasingly the ideological creeds of consistently large and powerful interest groups within the two southern peripheries. And in both cases, in a relatively short time, the southern nationalist ideology in the United States and the Italian nationalist ideology in the *Mezzogiorno* succeeded in providing the backgrounds for the revolts of the two southern elites against the central governments—revolts that resulted in the two different, but comparable, outcomes of secession from the Union and formation of a Confederate nation in the American South and of Bourbon defeat and annexation to the Italian nation in the *Mezzogiorno*.

In the American South, the second half of the 1840s witnessed the planter elite's return to a confrontational attitude in its relation with northern interests in the federal government. For the previous twenty years, while southerners mostly controlled federal institutions, the Missouri Compromise held as an equitable solution to the difficult issue of distribution of power between core and periphery—an issue that inevitably related to slavery's constant expansion in the western territories. Moreover, as Don Fehrenbacher has pointed out, "the redevelopment of a two-party system in the decades that followed the Missouri crisis served to calm passions over the slavery issue, at least temporarily." Whigs and Democrats attracted different constituencies within the southern elites with their substantially different programs of reform. Still, both parties vied to defend southern interests, protecting the existence of slavery and upholding the southern tradition of states' rights against any unwelcome intrusion from the federal government. Therefore, southerners channeled their concerns for core-periphery issues and for the economic and social development of their region in the different political visions of two parties equally committed to southern interests. As a result of southern hegemony over federal institutions, of agreement over the Missouri Compromise, and of what William Cooper has called "the politics of slavery," direct confrontation between the southern elites and the federal government on the issue of relations between core and periphery was postponed for several decades.[91]

Yet, in the later part of the 1840s, a new wave of American expansion heralded by the doctrine of Manifest Destiny and prompted by the problem of the existence of a Texan slaveholding republic seeking annexation to the United States led to the Mexican War of 1846–1848 and to the acquisition of five hundred thousand square miles of land, half of it in the Southwest. The fact that the president who conducted the war—James K. Polk—was a southern Democrat and a large planter contributed in confirming the idea that slaveholders had used their power in the federal government to launch a war in which they had a lot to gain from new territorial acquisitions. In fact, the southern elite—especially the slaveholders in the frontier states—considered as a given the fact that the new territories were open to slavery. As far as they were concerned, the Missouri Compromise had provided clear guidelines on the issue of slavery's expansion in the frontier areas of the southern periphery. Therefore, to southerners, northern Democrat David Wilmot's 1846 proposal to ban slavery from the new territories came as a shock.[92]

91. Don E. Fehrenbacher, *The Slaveholding Republic: An Account of the United States Government Relations with Slavery* (New York, 2001), 266. See also, Cooper, *South and the Politics of Slavery*, xi–xv; Richard E. Brown, "The Missouri Crisis, Slavery, and the Politics of Jacksonianism," *SAQ* 65 (1966): 69–70; and Michael F. Holt, "From Center to Periphery: The Market Revolution and Major Party Conflict, 1835–1860," in Stokes and Conway, eds., *Market Revolution in America*, 224–258.

92. See Fehrenbacher, *Slaveholding Republic*, 67–71. See also John H. Schroeder, *Mr. Polk's War: American Opposition and Dissent, 1846–1848* (Madison, Wisc., 1973).

Though the Wilmot Proviso passed in the House, it found strong opposition in the pro-southern Senate, where South Carolinian John C. Calhoun
argued in the 1847 *Calhoun Resolutions* that the property rights of the citizens
—which included slavery—applied to the new territories as well. President
Polk himself called the Proviso "a mischievous and foolish amendment,"
even though—like Jackson before him—he was no friend of South Carolinian states' rights extremists. Though in 1848 Democratic presidential nominee
Lewis Cass publicly repudiated the Wilmot Proviso and advocated popular
sovereignty in the western territories, northern Whigs and members of the
newly born Free-Soil Party now supported the Proviso in Congress. As in
1819–1820, the southern peripheral elite had attempted to use its control
of the federal core to accelerate the process of slavery's expansion and the
northern congressmen's protests had led to a new and even more difficult
political crisis.[93]

After the election of Zachary Taylor, a Whig president who opposed the
expansion of slavery and supported California's admission into the Union as
a free state, tensions ran high among the southern slaveholding elite. Southern Democrats took the lead in defending southern states' rights and in what
they perceived as resistance to northern aggression, while the elite became
convinced once more that the current course of affairs would eventually lead
to the federal government's actual interference in the issue of slavery. Building on the background created by South Carolinian John C. Calhoun's in-
cessant call for southern unity, in October 1849 the Mississippi Slaveholders'
Convention met at the state capital, Jackson, and issued a call for a formal
meeting to be held in Nashville on 3 June 1850; delegates from all southern
states were to join the Nashville Convention "to counsel together for their
common safety."[94]

Though South Carolinian states' rights extremists were still a minority,
the magnitude of the crisis was such that the call for the Nashville Convention found enthusiastic supporters throughout the South. Indeed, according
to Thelma Jennings, "the Nashville Convention was a landmark in regional
cooperation" and in many ways "a watershed." In fact, the Crisis of 1850,

93. James K. Polk's quotation is in Ashworth, *Slavery, Capitalism, and Politics,* 433. See also
Michael P. Morrison, *Slavery and the American West: The Eclipse of Manifest Destiny and the Coming of the Civil War* (Chapel Hill, N.C., 1997).

94. *Jackson Weekly Mississippian,* 5 October 1849, quoted in Freehling, *Road to Disunion,* 481.
See also John McCardell, *The Idea of a Southern Nation: Southern Nationalists and Southern
Nationalism, 1830–1860* (New York, 1979), 296–298.

which prompted the Nashville Convention, was truly a transformational crisis in the relationship between the federal government and the South and the initial stage of a course that eventually led to the end of political balance between Whig and Democratic programs of reform on core-periphery issues. At the same time, the significance of the Nashville Convention lay in the fact that it gave for the first time a political dimension to the preeminently economic and cultural phenomenon of southern nationalism and, in so doing, paved the way for the construction of a southern confederacy committed to the defense of both states' rights and slavery.[95]

Soon after the Mississippian slaveholders' call, state legislatures all over the South elected delegates to send to the Nashville Convention. First South Carolina, then Georgia, Texas, Virginia, and Mississippi voted to participate and sent official delegations. Four other states—Florida, Alabama, Arkansas, and Tennessee—were unofficially represented. The most radical states— South Carolina, Georgia, and Mississippi, which hosted several ardent secessionists, or "fire-eaters"—were also the ones with most representatives. Among the most vocal of the fire-eaters was newly elected Mississippi governor and large planter John A. Quitman, the man who had masterminded the Mississippi Slaveholders' Convention. However, secessionists such as Quitman were still a minority; most southerners continued to support programs of reform within the boundaries of the existing political system. In fact, the division between a majority of Unionists and a minority of secessionists severely impeded plans for southern unity at the Nashville Convention—a fact also highlighted by the absence of six slaveholding states.[96]

Still, in writing the Convention's "Address to the People of the Southern States," South Carolinian fire-eater Robert Barnwell Rhett kept much of the original radical and secessionist content. Besides advocating support for the extension of the Missouri Compromise, the address called for southern opposition to "any law imposing onerous conditions or restraint upon the rights of masters to remove their property into the Territories of the United States." Rhett clearly linked the "rights of masters" in the American territories to the protection of the "institution of slavery," which "sets apart the

---

95. Thelma Jennings, *The Nashville Convention: Southern Movement for Unity, 1848–1851* (Memphis, Tenn., 1980), 12. See also Avery O. Craven, *The Growth of Southern Nationalism, 1848–1861* (Baton Rouge, La., 1953), 83–85; and Scarborough, *Masters of the Big House,* 261–274.

96. See David M. Potter, *The Impending Crisis, 1848–1861* (New York, 1976), 104–105; Eric H. Walther, *The Fire-Eaters* (Baton Rouge, La., 1992), 99–100; and McCardell, *Southern Nation,* 298–299.

Southern States as a peculiar people." In retrospect, though the Nashville Convention failed to unite the South in a movement for secession, its fundamental document—Rhett's address—already contained the basic elements of Confederate nationalism.[97]

As the June 1850 Nashville Convention drew to a close with the vow to meet again, prominent Whig politician Henry Clay succeeded in devising a compromise between slaveholding and nonslaveholding interests in Congress that gave a temporary respite to the vexing problem of slavery's expansion in the newly acquired western areas. The compromise allowed the two new territories of New Mexico and Utah to be open to slavery and placed a new Fugitive Slave Law under federal jurisdiction, while, on the other hand, providing for the admission of California into the Union as a free state and for the abolition of the slave trade in the District of Columbia. The Compromise of 1850 deeply divided both Whigs and Democrats along sectional lines and passed in both houses mainly because of the sudden death of Zachary Taylor. Yet, it succeeded in resolving temporarily the issues that had caused the Crisis of 1850, and most members of the southern slaveholding elite accepted the Compromise of 1850 as an equitable deal.[98]

However, as David Potter has noted, by this time, the ongoing activity of a minority of radical leaders cast more than one doubt as to "whether the momentum for secession could be arrested by the rather limited concessions which the Compromise had offered." In fact, the crisis was still far from its conclusion when Governors George Towns of Georgia and John Quitman of Mississippi called special state conventions, while southern secessionists took control of the second Nashville Convention on 11 November 1850. However, despite Quitman's belief that if "Georgia or Mississippi take the lead and secede . . . gradually the other states will join," secessionists were divided between those who sought cooperation with other southern states and those who advocated separate state secession. Largely as a result of these divisions, the momentum for secession was lost.[99]

97. Robert Barnwell Rhett, "Address of the Southern Convention to the People of Delaware, Maryland, Virginia," *Mobile Advertiser*, 29 June 1850, quoted in Ashworth, *Slavery, Capitalism, and Politics*, 487.

98. See also Fehrenbacher, *Slaveholding Republic*, 83–87; and Holt, *Political Crisis*, 67–100.

99. Potter, *Impending Crisis*, 122; John A. Quitman is quoted in Jennings, *Nashville Convention*, 177. See also Robert E. May, *John A. Quitman: Old South Crusader* (Baton Rouge, La., 1996), 228–235.

Subsequently, between 1850 and 1852, Southern Rights' Associations—which sought to create a movement for southern unity—sprang up everywhere across the South, with a particularly high concentration in South Carolina. Yet, even in states such as Georgia, with its fame of radicalism, extreme southern nationalists were hardly in a position of strength. By December 1850, the Georgia Convention adopted the so-called Georgia Platform, which, even though opposed in principle to the Compromise of 1850, accepted it as a safeguard for the existence of the Union. Even though the Georgia Convention reserved for itself the right to oppose any congressional interference on slavery in the name of southern states' rights, its adoption of the Georgia Platform was substantially a compromise to avoid secession. By 1851, secessionists had lost ground not only in Georgia, but also in Mississippi. In November 1852, following the defeat of the Southern Rights' Party's candidate, Jefferson Davis, in the race for the governorship, the Mississippi State Convention voted to accept the Compromise of 1850; a little later, the South Carolina State Convention adopted a similar resolution.[100]

The 1852 presidential elections sanctioned the beginning of the decline of the Whig Party and the beginning of the unchallenged hegemony of the Democratic Party in the South. While southern Whigs felt increasingly isolated as sectional tensions over slavery escalated, southern Democrats—who called themselves National Democrats—continued to work for the benefit of southern states' rights within the boundaries of the party's political program of reform. The leader of the southern Democrats was Mississippi planter and congressman Jefferson Davis. Leaving behind his former extremist positions, Davis vowed to defend the states' rights cause by working within the federal government, especially given his close relationship with newly elected Democratic president, Franklin Pierce.[101]

In fact, the Democratic program for reform in regard to relations between the federal government and the southern periphery—a program that advocated strong decentralization and devolution of power in favor of southern slaveholders in all the areas under slavery's present and potential influence—enjoyed unprecedented success under the 1853–1857 Pierce administration and, for the last time before the Civil War, the southern

100. See Craven, *Southern Nationalism*, 103–115; Freehling, *Road to Disunion*, 553–554; and Holt, *Political Crisis*, 127–130.

101. See McCardell, *Southern Nation*, 295–306.

periphery held an unchallenged hegemony over federal governmental policies and institutions. The new president clearly looked favorably on southern
slaveholders and also encouraged their ill-conceived plans for the creation of
what an 1856 issue of the *New York Times* called a "Southern Slave Empire"
in Cuba—plans at whose center was ubiquitous fire-eater John Quitman.
And yet, notwithstanding this rather bizarre initiative, even Quitman and
his fellow fire-eaters put a momentary halt to talks of secession and returned
within the ranks of conventional Democratic policies, given Pierce's outright
protection of slavery and states' rights.[102]

To be sure, Pierce even supported, together with both southern Democrats and southern Whigs, the passage of the 1854 Kansas-Nebraska Act,
which allowed two new territories above the Missouri Compromise line
to decide the issue of slavery on the basis of popular sovereignty. Predict-
ably, northern politicians saw—correctly—the Kansas-Nebraska Act as one
more proof of the influence of the Slave Power in Congress, while, to the
dismay of both northerners and southerners, a miniature civil war exploded
in Kansas between proslavery and antislavery forces. More important was
the fact that sectional conflict over the Kansas-Nebraska Act led to the
final demise of the Whig Party, which had virtually disappeared by the time
that Democrat James Buchanan was elected president in 1856. While in the
South Democrats became the unchallenged hegemonic political force, the
truly revolutionary change occurred in the North, where the Republican
Party—a new antislavery coalition that gathered a number of former northern Whigs—sought to reverse the course of core-periphery relations in favor of a stronger federal government and against the slaveholders' abuse
of local power and unchecked expansionism. In fact, as William Freehling
has remarked, "in 1856, the new northern Republican Party almost won the
Presidency with an anti-Slave Power agenda," one that focused on fighting
both against the imposition of the southern minority's proslavery laws in
Congress and against the plans for slavery's expansion in the West. As a
result, the rise of the Republican Party signaled the beginning of the end
of the southern periphery's hegemony over the federal government and the
progressive transformation of southern politics into a peripheral issue.[103]

102. *NYT,* 25 November 1856, quoted in McCardell, *Southern Nation,* 269. See also McDonald, *States' Rights,* 167–170; and James McPherson, *Battle Cry of Freedom: The Civil War Era*
(New York, 1988), 78–169.

103. William W. Freehling, *The South vs. the South: How Anti-Confederate Southerners Shaped

Both in concurrence with and as a consequence of these important changes in the relations between the federal core and the southern periphery, the real novelty of the 1850s in the South was the growth of southern nationalist feelings. The beginnings of southern political nationalism occurred in the aftermath of the Crisis of 1850, at a time when, even though southern nationalists were allowed little room in conventional party politics, "the idea of a Southern nation"—according to John McCardell—"began to permeate activities outside the political process." In fact, the rise of support for a southern nationalist movement, which built upon the ideas expressed at the 1850 Nashville Convention and which found avenues of expression with little in common with the reform programs advocated by the established parties, was a visible phenomenon in the 1850s. Together with the activity of fire-eaters—who were ready to accelerate their plans for secession as soon as the federal government turned actively against slaveholding interests—and the hegemonic political position of the Democratic Party and its policy of supporting southern states' rights, the rise of a southern nationalist culture provided the indispensable background for the creation of the southern Confederacy in 1861.[104]

In fact, the question of the causes of southern nationalism is tightly linked to the question of the origins of Confederate nationalism, even though recent scholarship has often analyzed the two as if they were discrete entities. Recent scholarship has also broken important ground in relating the study of nationalism in the American South to the most recent work on nationalist ideology in nineteenth-century Europe. Even though there is still only a handful of studies which welcomes this approach—as opposed to older approaches that either focused on particular characteristics of southern culture as a background for nationalism, or simply considered southern nationalism as little more than a defense of slavery in political form—it is clear that there is much to learn from a comparison between southern and European nationalism. This is especially the case if one focuses on the analy-

---

the *Course of the Civil War* (New York, 2001), 35. See also Potter, *Impending Crisis*, 177–266; Richards, *Slave Power*, 162–189; Cooper, *South and the Politics of Slavery*, 322–369; Holt, *Rise and Fall of the Whig Party*, 836–985; and William E. Gienapp, *The Origins of the Republican Party, 1852–1856* (New York, 1987).

104. McCardell, *Southern Nation*, 308. See also Donald Ratcliffe, "The State of the Union, 1776–1860," in Susan-Mary Grant and Brian Holden Reid, eds., *The American Civil War: Explorations and Reconsiderations* (Harlow, 2000), 27–31.

sis of distinctive ideological features that the nineteenth-century elites used in the process of nation-building in the two regions.[105]

A number of studies have established a link between nationalism and modernization and have argued, in particular, that nationalist movements have occurred in connection with two phenomena: the construction of modern centralized states and the formation of public opinion through the spread of mass literacy. Therefore, without a concurrent process of state-building, nation-building could hardly occur. At the same time, nations became part of the everyday life of the people only through the spread of nationalist propaganda and rhetoric. However, as several nineteenth- and twentieth-century examples have documented, the process of state-building could work both ways: it could either lead to the positive construction of a nation-state or prompt a negative reaction that unleashed separatist movements.[106]

If the southern slaveholders' problem was the protection of slavery (the source of their local power) from the federal government's action—or, in other words, the problem of balance of power between core and periphery—then the unfolding and increasing radicalization of southern nationalism in the 1850s, especially in the aftermath of the rise of the Republican Party, was akin to other movements of resistance of peripheral elites to governmental centralization in the nineteenth-century world. In most cases in which a central government attempted to enforce modernization through

---

105. Older studies include Charles Sellers, *The Southerner as American* (Chapel Hill, N.C., 1960); Craven, *Southern Nationalism*; Carl N. Degler, *Place over Time: The Continuity of Southern Distinctiveness* (Baton Rouge, La., 1977); David Potter, *The South and Sectional Conflict* (Baton Rouge, La., 1978); McCardell, *Southern Nation*; Emory M. Thomas, *The Confederate Nation, 1861–1865* (New York, 1979); and Steven A. Channing, "Slavery and Confederate Nationalism," in Walter J. Fraser and Winifred B. Moore, eds., *From the Old South to the New: Essays on the Transitional South* (Westport, Conn., 1981). More recent studies include Drew G. Faust, *The Creation of Confederate Nationalism: Ideology and Identity in the Civil War South* (Baton Rouge, La., 1988); Carl Degler, "One Among Many? The Civil War and National Unifications," in Gabor Boritt, ed., *Lincoln, the War President* (New York, 1992), 89–120; James M. McPherson, *Is Blood Thicker than Water? Crises of Nationalism in the Modern World* (New York, 1998); Don H. Doyle, *Nations Divided: America, Italy, and the Southern Question* (Athens, Ga., 2002); Peter Kolchin, *A Sphinx on the American Land: The Nineteenth-Century South in Comparative Perspective* (Baton Rouge, La., 2003); and Susan-Mary Grant, "From Union to Nation? The Civil War and the Development of American Nationalism," in Grant and Reid, eds., *American Civil War*, 341–343.

106. See Michael Hechter, *Containing Nationalism* (Oxford, 2000), 28–29; Ernest Gellner, *Nations and Nationalism* (New York, 1983), 1–8; and Eric J. Hobsbawm, *Nations and Nationalism since 1780: Programme, Myth, Reality* (Cambridge, 1990), 80–100.

the spread of uniform social, economic, and political institutions throughout a country, it encountered resistance from peripheral elites that clung on
to their local power. This phenomenon occurred not just in states such as
the Bourbon kingdom, whose highly centralized administration was typical of nineteenth-century governmental practice, but also in states such as
nineteenth-century America, whose federal form of government with highly
decentralized institutions made it even more vulnerable to centrifugal forces
(not until Lincoln's 1860 election were the Republicans strong enough to
impose centralizing and anti-southern legislation). In fact, in comparable
terms to what occurred in the Bourbon kingdom and in other nineteenth-
century European states, issues of balance of power between core and periphery plagued the United States from the time of the Missouri Crisis on;
and yet, these issues—at the center of which were the slaveholders' worries
over the fate of slavery—only became a dangerous matter of contention in
the second half of the 1850s, when the southern periphery lost its grip over
the federal core.[107]

Also, if governmental centralization was part of the process of modernization of political institutions and nation-building, then the slaveholders'
reaction to it was a conservative movement that sought to maintain the
status quo in the face of increasing pressure. With the crisis and virtual
disappearance of the Whig Party, the southern elite lost its opportunity to
relate the system of slaveholding paternalism to the deep needs for economic reform—needs epitomized by the collaboration between agrarian and
industrial interests—generated by the market revolution. Yet, the elite lost
that opportunity because of the fundamental incompatibility between the
slaveholders' need to protect their local power and the link between economic modernization and political centralization that the Whigs increasingly emphasized in their reform program.[108]

As the Democratic Party remained the hegemonic political force in the
South, the forces of localism prevailed and sought to tip the balance of power
in favor of the southern periphery so as to protect slaveholding interests.
Together with the unconditional support for states' rights, the Democrats'

---

107. See Liah Greenfeld, *Nationalism: Five Roads to Modernity* (Cambridge, Mass., 1992),
472–480; McPherson, *Is Blood Thicker than Water?* 1–26; Kolchin, *Sphinx on the American Land*,
88–90; and Bensel, *Yankee Leviathan*, 10–11.

108. See Oakes, "From Republicanism to Liberalism," 565–571; Harry L. Watson, "Conflict
and Collaboration: Yeomen, Slaveholders, and Politics in the Antebellum South," *SH* 10 (1985):
290–298; Freehling, *Reintegration*, 105–137; and Howe, *Political Culture*, 180–209.

conservative and populist type of paternalism—the type that embraced economic reform but neither challenged the preeminence of agrarian interests nor embraced governmental centralization—became the unchallenged ideological creed of the majority, even though not of the totality, of the southern elite and the basis of a southern nationalist ideology. Southern nationalism in the 1850s was a movement that stemmed directly from the radical fringes of the Democratic Party, from fire-eaters such as John Quitman, but also from moderate states' rights supporters, such as Jefferson Davis. Significantly, both Quitman and Davis—who epitomized the two souls of southern nationalism—embraced paternalism and modernization on their own plantations, but never doubted the preeminence of the agrarian sector over the industrial sector in the economy of the South.[109]

As they set out to build a nationalist ideology for the South, slaveholders confronted two sets of problems. One was the fact that the very forces of localism that they had unleashed threatened to destroy the idea of a southern nation before it even came into being. More an aggregation of regions—each with its own distinctive culture—than a uniform nation, the South was continuously pulled apart by centrifugal forces, which asserted the rights of the individual states to govern themselves, rather than to be united in a novel suprastate political institution that represented their elites' interests. After all, narrow localism had been the main reason behind the debacle of the 1850 Nashville Conventions. As David Potter put it, "state loyalty no doubt gave ground to [southern] regional loyalty between the 1830s and the 1860s, but localism by no means ceased to compete with southernism."[110]

Even in 1865, after the fall of the Confederate nation, Alexander Stephens declared, "my native land, my country, the only one that is country to me is Georgia." Doubtless, many members of the southern slaveholding elite thought along similar lines in regard to their loyalty to their native state, as Robert E. Lee had a chance to prove in 1861, when he resigned from the U.S. Army on the ground that he could not fight against his family and his native Virginia. In this respect, South Carolina's elite—with its blend of peculiar regional culture and extreme support of slavery and states' rights—did a great deal to show the elites of other states how to merge state loyalty into loyalty for a southern nation. South Carolina's elite also embarked first on

109. See Hettle, *Peculiar Democracy*, 4–5; McCardell, *Southern Nation*, 318–319; May, *Quitman*, 130–146; and William J. Cooper, *Jefferson Davis, American* (New York, 2002), 223–237.

110. Potter, *Impending Crisis*, 463. See also Meinig, *Continental America*, 446–447; and Thomas, *Confederate Nation*, 32–33.

the course that led to the construction of the Confederate nation by prompt-ing the state's secession from the Union in 1860. For these particular reasons, South Carolina has a separate treatment in the present work.[111]

The other, equally crucial, problem that the slaveholding elite faced in the creation of a southern nation was the question of loyalty to the southern nationalist cause among different classes of southern whites. In the words of Drew Faust, "an elite of planters, clergy, politicians, and intellectuals led the movement to create a shared public culture and to produce consent to the terms of its rule," especially among nonslaveholding whites. In the 1850s, slaveholders played a hegemonic role in southern society, at least in those areas in which staple crop production was widespread, which covered the majority of the southern territory. By presenting themselves as the people's political representatives at the state and national level, but also by using ties of kinship and systems of patronage—which were of paramount importance in every southern county—slaveholders were able to "elicit the consent and cooperation of the masses of non-slaveholding whites," who mostly aspired to own slaves and feared the loss of privileges if slavery were to end.[112]

Yet, this was hardly enough to create a southern nationalist sentiment among the masses, especially at a time in which pamphlets such as North Carolinian Hinton Rowan Helper's *The Impending Crisis of the South* (1857)—which urged nonslaveholding yeomen to revolt against the exploitative planter aristocracy—circulated widely. Moreover, even though southern in-tellectuals had been successful at alerting the public opinion to the existence of a southern national culture through the spread of literary magazines and novels, the population of a region such as the antebellum South, with its high levels of illiteracy, could hardly think in terms of a nation's "imagined community" in the sense described by Benedict Anderson. For this reason, it was only after secession and the construction of the Confederate nation

111. Alexander Stephens's quotation is in Myrta Lockett Avery, ed., *Recollections of Alexander H. Stephens* (New York, 1910), 253. See also Emory M. Thomas, *Robert E. Lee* (New York, 1995), 188–189. On South Carolina's regionalism, see chapter four.

112. Faust, *Creation of Confederate Nationalism*, 15–16. See also T. J. Jackson Lears, "The Con-cept of Cultural Hegemony: Problems and Possibilities," *AHR* 90 (1985): 561–593; Ralph A. Wooster, *Politicians, Planters, and Plain Folk: Courthouse and Statehouse in the Upper South, 1850–1860* (Knoxville, Tenn., 1976); Ralph A. Wooster, *The People in Power: Courthouse and Statehouse in the Lower South, 1850–1860* (Knoxville, Tenn., 1975); Christopher J. Olsen, *Political Culture and Secession in Mississippi: Masculinity, Honor, and the Antiparty Tradition, 1830–1860* (New York, 2000), 116–119; and Robert C. Kenzer, *Kinship and Neighborhood in a North Carolina Community: Orange County, North Carolina, 1849–1881* (Knoxville, Tenn., 1987), 52–70.

that the process of nationalization of the southern masses really took place. Significantly, the process, then, focused on the commonality of Civil War experiences and Confederate symbols and relied a great deal on the idea of a shared Christian evangelicalism among white southerners.[113]

Yet, until 1861, southern nationalism was mainly—though far from exclusively—a slaveholders' affair, and the slaveholding elite's attempt to construct a southern nationalist ideology in the 1850s reminds us of what Eric Hobsbawm has called "invention of tradition." In Hobsbawm's thought, the invention of tradition is a process of social engineering focusing on the deliberate adoption of national paraphernalia and of a nationalist rhetoric, which the elites have constructed and used in response to external pressures and in order to legitimize the struggle to retain their power. In this connection, it is worth noticing that the rhetorical notion of a timeless, romantic South populated by gentlemen who, supposedly—in what James McPherson has called the "central myth of southern ethnic nationalism"—descended from seventeenth-century English Cavaliers, cared about their slaves, and valued the many benefits of traditional ways of life and personal relationships first appeared in the 1850s.[114]

Significantly, in the late 1850s, few elites were under more pressure than southern slaveholders. After the last southern political victory with the 1857 Dredd Scott decision—in which Chief Justice Roger Taney declared that the Missouri Compromise's ban of slavery in the territories north of the 36° 30′ line was illegal—the tide began to turn. The victory of the antislavery forces in Kansas, the rise of the Republican Party—the first major party to stand on a consistent platform of opposition to slavery's expansion—under the skillful leadership of Abraham Lincoln, and the growing radicalism of the militant fringes of the abolitionist movement, which led to John Brown's 1859 raid at Harpers Ferry, placed southern slaveholders on the defensive.

113. See David Brown, "Hinton Rowan Helper: The Logical Outcome of the Non-Slaveholders' Philosophy?" *HJ* 46 (2003): 39–58; Harris, *Plain Folk and Gentry,* 72–77; McCardell, *Southern Nation,* 141–176; James McPherson, *Drawn with the Sword: Reflections on the American Civil War* (New York, 1996), 37–54; Benedict Anderson, *Imagined Communities: Reflections on the Origin and Spread of Nationalism* (New York, 1983); and Faust, *Creation of Confederate Nationalism,* 22–33.

114. McPherson, *Is Blood Thicker than Water?* 45. See also Eric J. Hobsbawm, "Introduction: Inventing Traditions," in Eric J. Hobsbawm and Terence Ranger, eds., *The Invention of Tradition* (Cambridge, 1983), 1–14; William R. Taylor, *Cavalier and Yankee: The Old South and American National Character* (New York, 1961); Rollin G. Osterweis, *Romanticism and Nationalism in the Old South* (Baton Rouge, La., 1949).

Then, in 1860—as Don Fehrenbacher has noted—"southerners made no mistake in perceiving the election of Lincoln as a sharp break with the past." The federal government's protection of slavery was gone, together with the South's control of the presidency and the Senate, and a number of southerners concluded that it was time to create another "federal republic, with its constitution more closely bound to slavery."[115]

By the time Lincoln was elected, southern Democrats had become a party of their own with a southern nationalist and proslavery agenda. Yet, as a consequence of Lincoln's election, South Carolina seceded from the Union in December 1860. Subsequently, in the periods before and after the fall of the Union's garrison at Fort Sumter in April 1861, special "secession conventions," first in the Deep South's states and then in the Upper South's states—with the exception of the border slaveholding states of Missouri, Kentucky, Maryland, Delaware, and West Virginia—one by one declared the Union dissolved. Arguably, the relative speed with which the majority of the southern states joined the secession movement was also due to the efficiency of very active "secession commissioners" (see map 5).[116]

On 4 February 1861, delegates of all the seceding southern states met at Montgomery and declared the birth of the Confederate States of America, a southern nation committed to the defense of slaveholding and states' rights—both included in articles in the Confederate Constitution. The Confederate president was Mississippi Democrat Jefferson Davis, its vice president Georgia Whig Alexander Stephens. By the time the Confederacy was born, Italian nationalism was triumphant in the *Mezzogiorno*. In an attempt to link the Italian nationalist movement to the movement for southern independence in the United States, Confederate Secretary of State Robert Toombs could very well say that Confederate nationalism stemmed from "reasons no less grave and valid than those which actuated the people of Sicily and Naples."[117]

* * *

115. Fehrenbacher, *Slaveholding Republic*, 296–297. See also Potter, *Impending Crisis*, 267–297, 356–384, 405–447.

116. See Ralph A. Wooster, *The Secession Conventions of the South* (Princeton, N.J., 1962); Charles B. Dew, *Apostles of Disunion: Southern Secession Commissioners and the Causes of the Civil War* (Charlottesville, Va., 2001); Steven A. Channing, *Crisis of Fear: Secession in South Carolina* (New York, 1974); William Barney, *The Secessionist Impulse: Alabama and Mississippi in 1860* (Princeton, N.J., 1974); and Michael P. Johnson, *Toward a Patriarchal Republic: The Secession of Georgia* (Baton Rouge, La., 1977);

117. Robert Toombs is quoted in Faust, *Creation of Confederate Nationalism*, 13. See also

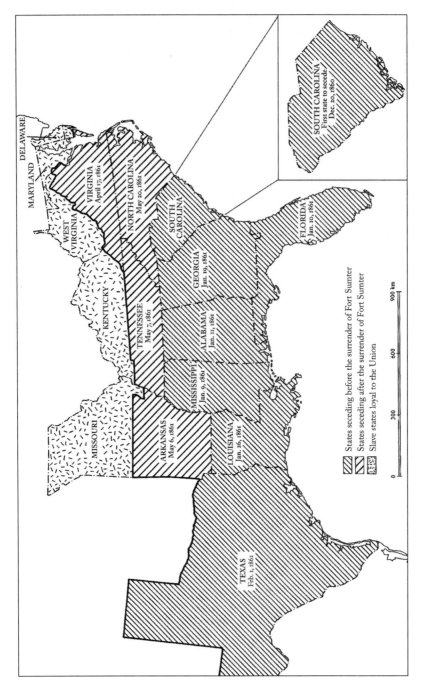

MAP 5. The Pattern of Secession in the American South

Arguably, during the 1840s and 1850s, politics in the Italian *Mezzogiorno* followed a trajectory partly comparable to the one followed by politics in the American South, with the noticeable progressive deterioration of relations between core and periphery. At the same time, thanks to the work of propaganda engaged in by southern Italian exiles in Piedmont, southern Italian politics became increasingly a central issue of debate and concern in public opinion and in the plans for national unification. Initially, the process of deterioration of relations between core and periphery in the *Mezzogiorno* triggered a major upheaval, the Revolution of 1848—a transformational crisis comparable to the Crisis of 1850 in the American South and a pivotal event whose causes related to the increase in political opposition and conspiratorial activity by both democrats and moderate liberals against the Bourbon monarchy. Already in 1847, a major conspiratorial plan masterminded by Calabrian democrats had involved the cities of Reggio Calabria and Messina. The revolutionaries rebelled against Bourbon rule at the beginning of September, but were defeated by General Vito Nunziante.[118]

A few months before, well-known liberal agitator Luigi Settembrini had published his famous pamphlet *Protesta del popolo delle Due Sicilie* (Protest of the People of the Two Sicilies), in which he had accused Ferdinand II's administration of arbitrary despotism and corruption. Settembrini's pamphlet had come at the end of a period in which the Bourbon monarchy had gradually retracted from its previous reformist program and at a time in which the other governments in the Italian peninsula had seemed to move steadily toward cautious reformism. Ferdinand II's involution, in turn, led to an increase in the opposition of the provincial landed bourgeoisie and of the liberal intellectuals to the monarchy. Particularly the latter radicalized their plans for the establishment of a constitutional kingdom and envisioned the participation of a Neapolitan nation in a federation of Italian states, following Vincenzo Gioberti's "neo-Guelf" program, with its focus on federalism.[119]

McPherson, *Battle Cry of Freedom*, 202–275; William C. Davis, *"A Government of Our Own": The Making of the Confederacy* (New York, 1996); and Freehling, *The South vs. the South*, 33–46.

118. See Giorgio Candeloro, *Storia dell'Italia moderna*, vol. 3, *La rivoluzione nazionale (1846–1849)* (Milan, 1970), 60–62; and Mack Smith, *Mazzini*, 41–42.

119. See Luigi Settembrini, *Protesta del popolo delle Due Sicilie* (Naples, 1847). See also Candeloro, *La rivoluzione nazionale*, 70–72; Alfonso Scirocco, "Il 1847 a Napoli: Ferdinando II e il movimento italiano per le riforme," *ASPN* 115 (1997): 431–465; Scirocco, "Ferdinando II," 506–509; and Raffaele Romanelli, "Nazione e costituzione nell'opinione liberale italiana prima del '48," *Pa&Pr* 46 (1999): 157–172.

On the eve of the revolution, the most interesting political proposal came from jurist Giovanni Manna, who, in two fundamental treatises, theorized a complete administrative reform of the Bourbon kingdom in liberal terms. In particular, Manna contemplated a program of modernization of the system through the incorporation of an "aristocracy of talent"—the professional bourgeoisie—in the governmental organs and envisioned a solution for the conflict of interests between core and periphery based on decentralization and on empowerment of municipal councils—the main organs of representation of the provincial landed bourgeoisie. To be sure, the liberals employed in the different regions of the Bourbon kingdom—such as subintendent Francesco Viti in Abruzzo Ultra I—still attempted to redefine the relation between core and periphery in favor of the provincial elites and provided the local government with examples of good administration. Yet, the truth was that by 1848 the rift between moderate liberal proprietors and intellectuals and the monarchy had led to the withdrawal of both groups' support for Ferdinand II—a dangerous situation that demanded an immediate solution.[120]

On 12 January 1848, revolution broke out in Sicily, and by the second half of January it had extended to the Cilento area. Meanwhile, in Naples popular demonstrations grew in number and size by the day, also stimulated by the news from Sicily. A privileged observer of these demonstrations was South Carolinan planter Charles Manigault, who happened to travel to Naples on 15 January 1848. In a letter to his friend Francis Corbin in Paris, Manigault confessed his deepest fears for the events, writing that "the storm volcano of political discord, social strife, is now seriously disturbing *the surface* of the earth *here.*" Though no major uprising had happened yet, Manigault witnessed an episode in which the crowd and the soldiers stood on two opposite side of a square, ready to attack each other. From this, he deducted that the tension was high and that the events "foreboded some virulent outbreak—of which there is no telling of *where,* of *how,* it will end."[121]

120. See Giovanni Manna, *Il diritto amministrativo nel Regno delle Due Sicilie* (Naples, 1840); and Giovanni Manna, *Il Diritto Costituzionale d'Europa dal 1791 sino a' nostri giorni* (Naples, 1848). See also Abbamonte, *Potere pubblico,* 120–146, 185–197; and Antonacci, *Dalla Repubblica napoletana,* 136–138.

121. Charles I. Manigault to Francis P. Corbin, 15 January 1848, Charles I. Manigault's letterbook, SCHS. See also Scirocco, "Dalla seconda restaurazione," 722–732; and Spagnoletti, *Storia del Regno,* 59–60.

In fact, demonstrations such as the one witnessed by Manigault multiplied and soon became unmanageable. Fearing the mounting of popular protest, Ferdinand II allowed the formation of a new government headed by Nicola Maresca, duke of Serracapriola, and announced the adoption of a liberal constitution by 10 February. The constitution—whose author was liberal lawyer and philosopher Francesco Paolo Bozzelli—gave political representation only to large landed proprietors and provided guidelines for the formation of a parliament with two Houses. In one the members were nominated by the king, while in the other one they were chosen through elections. Praised and supported by moderate liberals in the capital and in the provinces, the February Constitution was harshly criticized by the Neapolitan democrats—several of whom were noblemen—who organized popular protests in the streets of the city.[122]

In her work, Enrica Di Ciommo has reconstructed the different views of southern Italian democrats over the liberal program in the initial phases of the Revolution of 1848. A group of moderate democrats, close to the Neapolitan nobility and intellectual aristocracy, and headed by lawyer Aurelio Saliceti—who directed the periodical *Charivari de le Deux Siciles*—proposed a program of conciliation of republican principles with monarchical institutions through a radical reform from above, which was to guarantee civil liberties and the formation of a constituent assembly elected with universal suffrage. A more radical group, which included Giuseppe Ricciardi and Ferdinando Petruccelli, gathered around the periodical *Mondo Vecchio e Mondo Nuovo* (Old World and New World)—directed by nobleman Michele Pepe—and focused on criticism of the large landed proprietors' ruthless policy at the expense of both provincial nobility and petite bourgeoisie. The group envisioned the latter's leading role in a popular revolution and advocated its violent seizure of power. Clearly, the two groups reflected the peculiarities of the southern Italian democratic movement, which included within its ranks classes as different as the aristocracy and the petite bourgeoisie. Yet, interestingly, both democratic groups joined the southern Italian liberals in rejecting plans for the creation of a strongly centralized Italian nation-state headed by the Piedmontese-based Sardinian monarchy—whose

122. See Spagnoletti, *Storia del Regno,* 287–288; Luigi Parente, "Francesco Paolo Bozzelli e il dibattito sulla costituzione," *ASPN* 117 (1999): 75–101; and Carlo Ghisalberti, *Storia costituzionale d'Italia, 1848–1948* (Rome-Bari, 1989), 23–33.

king, Charles Albert, led an inconclusive war for Italian independence against Austria—and opting, instead, for the participation of a Neapolitan state in an Italian federation.[123]

In March 1848, as revolution spread to other states in the peninsula, the increase in popular protest orchestrated by the democrats forced the resignation of Serracapriola, while democratic newspapers diffused the details of the program for a new constitution. Among the most important points were the adoption of universal suffrage, the abolition of the higher House, and the democratic reform of local administration. The latter was an attempt to resolve the conflict between core and periphery through the empowerment of local governmental organs, substituting the municipal councils with popular assemblies and the intendants with special commissioners (*commissari ordinatori*). The program, masterminded by Saliceti, found a large group of followers among moderate democrats in Naples, while in the provinces only the cities and towns that had been penalized by Bourbon reforms supported it; flourishing regional urban centers such as Bari rejected it in favor of the liberal program.[124]

At the beginning of April, moderate liberals and democrats agreed on the formation of a new government headed by moderate liberal Carlo Troya, the most important advocate of neo-Guelf ideas in the *Mezzogiorno*. Troya transformed Saliceti's democratic program into a set of moderate liberal reforms. He extended suffrage to the professional bourgeoisie's aristocracy of talent and lowered the property requirements for voting; he also kept the two Houses in the parliament and instituted new provincial officers (*delegati ordinatori*) with unspecified inspecting tasks. Saliceti's program of revolution from above was defeated, while moderate liberals gained the upper hand. The new government's minister for agriculture and commerce was Antonio Scialoja, who immediately set out to implement moderate liberal policies, focusing especially on freedom of trade and the "growth of the agricultural, manufacturing, and commercial industries"—which clearly benefited the rising landed bourgeoisie the most.[125]

---

123. See Di Ciommo, *La nazione possibile*, 216–244; De Francesco, "Ideologie," 310–311; and Ferdinando Petruccelli, *La rivoluzione di Napoli nel 1848. Ricordi* (Genoa, 1850).

124. See Scirocco, *L'Italia del Risorgimento*, 284–286. See also Giuseppe Massari, *I casi di Napoli dal 29 gennaio 1848 in poi. Lettere politiche* (Turin, 1849).

125. Antonio Scialoja's quotation is in Di Ciommo, *La nazione possibile*, 285. See also Candeloro, *La Rivoluzione nazionale*, 221–225; and Petrusewicz, *Come il Meridione*, 106–107.

Yet, Troya also called some democrats to participate in his government. In particular, the minister of internal affairs was Raffaele Conforti, a democratic lawyer who gave clear indications that he intended to resolve the most pressing problem for the democratic leadership—the relation with the peasant masses. Ever since the start of the revolution, peasants in different regions had manifested their rage against the bourgeois landowners who expropriated common land and the Bourbon administration that supported them, attacking the authorities and occupying and destroying private property. In April 1848, Conforti directed the provincial intendants to reclaim the expropriated common land and divide it among the peasantry. On one hand, Conforti's initiative had the effect of increasing peasant violence in the countryside and preoccupying the moderate liberals who supported the Troya government and who had already created a National Guard for the defense of constitutional rights and bourgeois privileges.[126]

On the other hand, as Di Ciommo has noted, Conforti's action offered the democratic leadership the opportunity to forge the alliance with the agrarian masses that they had been unable to gain in the 1820–1821 Revolution. Yet, there is little doubt that the majority of the democrats had moderate ideas and, in any event, subordinated the resolution of social problems to the resolution of the political problem represented by the support of the monarchy for the liberal government. Both moderate and radical democrats encouraged the peasant masses to rebel in order to pressure the monarchy to yield to democratic requests. Yet, after facing the peasants' spontaneous occupations of expropriated land and fearing that they could not control the popular movement, they condemned the violation of private property, as Petrucelli himself did on the pages of the journal he edited.[127]

After the April elections, as the 15 May date for the first session of the parliament approached and representatives from all the provinces of the kingdom gathered in Naples, Ferdinand II demanded that the MPs swear allegiance to the February Constitution rather than to the April one. When the parliament resisted the imposition, people gathered in the streets of Naples in support. On 15 May, Ferdinand II asked the MPs to swear al-

126. See Tommaso Pedio, *Classi e popolo nel Mezzogiorno d'Italia alla vigilia del 15 Maggio 1848* (Bari, 1979), 322–329; and Daniela Luigia Caglioti, "False notizie, complotti e vociferazioni: gendarmi, intendenti e paure nel Regno delle Due Sicilie nel 1848," *S&S* 94 (2001): 725–741.

127. See Pedio, *Classi e popolo,* 322–329; Di Ciommo, *La nazione possibile,* 290–309; and Lovett, *Democratic Movement,* 162–164.

legiance to the constitution as it was to be "modified by the two Houses in agreement with the King." While the moderate liberals agreed and asked the people to leave the streets, the democrats rejected the proposal. Fighting broke out, and the Bourbon army killed several hundred people. Ferdinand II took the opportunity to close the two Houses and restore order with a coup. Yet the insurrection moved from the capital to the provinces, and throughout May and June the Calabrie remained at the center of revolutionary activities headed by Ricciardi and Musolino. Significantly, even in this occasion, tensions among the democrats over the primacy of political over social aims seriously hampered the insurrectionary movement, and while the most radical groups wished to proceed to tax the large landowners to finance the revolution, Ricciardi condemned any violation of the principle of private property, as Petruccelli had done before him.[128]

After the Calabrian revolutionaries were defeated, political persecution forced most of the democrats into exile. Meanwhile, the Neapolitan parliament resumed its activity in early July. By then, it was hopelessly compromised and dominated by the most conservative liberals and, therefore, played a subservient role to the king. Liberals continued to stage debates in the public opinion for about a year, while the threat of a social revolution contributed to the cohesion of the landed elite—which in several provinces succeeded in restoring order despite the lack of governmental authority. Yet, in March 1849, Ferdinand II abruptly decided to put an end to the liberal experiment. As he ruthlessly repressed the Sicilian revolution, he also closed the Houses, never to reopen them again, and persecuted liberal activists, who soon joined the democrats in exile. In the following years, Ferdinand II restored Bourbon absolutist rule, increased the power of the police, and held a number of political trials. By the early 1850s, Ferdinand II's absolutist practices had alienated both the moderate liberal intellectuals—who were mostly in exile—and the progressive economists of the kingdom. The latter were particularly weary of the fact that most of the government's expenditures went into the army, while public works and infrastructures were seriously

128. Ferdinand II is quoted in Enrica Di Ciommo, "Napoli, 15 Maggio 1848. Barricate in Via Toledo," *S&D* 4 (1989): 9. See also Giuseppe Ricciardi, *Storia documentata della sollevazione delle Calabrie del 1848* (Naples, 1873); Benedetto Musolino, *La rivoluzione del 1848 nelle Calabrie* (Naples, 1903); Lepre, *Storia del Mezzogiorno,* 263–265; Aurelio Lepre, *Il Mezzogiorno dal feudalesimo al capitalismo* (Naples, 1979), 98–101; Cingari, *Problemi del Risorgimento,* 155–161; and Spagnoletti, *Storia del Regno,* 61–63.

deficient in all the provinces and the commercial agricultural sector received little support.[129]

In 1851, the trial of the members of the secret society Italian Unity (*Unità italiana*) led to the subsequent arrest of liberal intellectuals Silvio Spaventa, Luigi Settembrini, and Carlo Poerio—an episode that caused international uproar and discredited the Bourbon monarchy. In the same year, British politician William Gladstone famously branded Bourbon absolutist practices as the "negation of God." Meanwhile, both southern Italian liberals and democrats in exile in Turin—the Piedmontese capital of the liberal Kingdom of Sardinia—stirred the northern Italian public opinion, further increasing the international disrepute of the Bourbon kingdom. Even though ideologically different, both groups of exiles contributed in a major way to place southern Italian problems firmly at the center of national political debates, while they also organized plans for destruction of the Bourbon regime. Among the liberals, the *murattisti* aimed at placing on the throne Luciano Murat, son of the former French king of Naples, Joachim Murat; yet, by 1856, the plan had fallen through because of French emperor Napoleon III's opposition. Most southern Italian moderate liberals looked at Piedmont's Prime Minister Camillo Cavour and King Victor Emmanuel II as the leaders of the liberal struggle against the Bourbons. At the same time, an increasing number of moderate democrats, having subordinated all other plans to the objective of Italian unification, also reluctantly agreed to achieve it under Piedmontese leadership.[130]

Only radical democrats rejected the so-called Piedmontese solution and still sought to create a republic through mass revolution. In fact, in the late 1850s the *Mezzogiorno* gained again a central place in plans for revolutionary upheavals, since several democrats were convinced that the conditions of exploitation of the southern masses were such that the time was ripe for them to provide the initial spark for a general national insurgence. Among these democrats was Neapolitan nobleman Carlo Pisacane, who in 1857 landed in Sapri—in the continental *Mezzogiorno*—with three hundred men, with the

129. See Scirocco, *L'Italia del Risorgimento,* 321–323; Di Ciommo, *La nazione possibile,* 321–346; Giorgio Candeloro, *Storia dell'Italia moderna,* vol. 4, *Dalla rivoluzione nazionale all'unità (1849–1860)* (Milan, 1964), 33–38; and Nelson Moe, *The View from Vesuvius: Italian Culture and the Southern Question* (Berkeley, Calif.), 131–134.

130. See Riall, "Garibaldi and the South," 139–141; Petrusewicz, *Come il Meridione,* 119–134; and Candeloro, *Dalla rivoluzione nazionale,* 224–231.

intent of sparking a peasant revolt and initiating a social revolution; they ended up dispersed by the Bourbon government's militias, while Pisacane himself committed suicide. Yet, despite Pisacane's failure and the democrats' and moderate liberals' internal divisions, by the late 1850s the Bourbon kingdom was in a very precarious position. It was increasingly marginalized abroad, while its administration had lost the crucial support of the elites and was unable to prevent social revolution in the countryside, if the right type of opportunity arose.[131]

Remarkably, during the 1850s, as the process of internal collapse of the Bourbon kingdom unfolded, the *Mezzogiorno* saw a steady growth of nationalist feelings among the elites—comparable to what happened in the American South, though with crucial differences. To be sure, until recently, little was available in terms of interpretation of the collapse of the Bourbon kingdom in its last decade of existence. Older studies regarded the course of events from the aftermath of the 1848 revolution to unification as the inevitable result of the Bourbon government's loss of legitimacy in the wake of its return to absolutism and of the irresistible march of Italian nationalist ideas and actions. As a consequence, scholars tended to focus their studies of the 1850s almost exclusively on the different national programs of southern Italian exiles, paying little attention to the analysis of the growth of Italian nationalist feelings in the *Mezzogiorno* itself. Both the Marxist and the liberal historiographic positions, though irreconcilable, added little to what Lucy Riall has termed a "teleological" view of the Risorgimento, especially in regard to the *Mezzogiorno*.[132]

In fact, liberal and Marxist historians differed mainly in the fact that the former praised the southern Italian bourgeoisie for its active role in the success of the liberal movement for Italian unification, while the latter condemned it for its weakness and passivity in front of it. Particularly according to Marxist intellectual Antonio Gramsci, the southern Italian bourgeoisie was a weak class that did not have either the ability or the will to guide the peasant masses in a social revolution. Through a process that Gramsci significantly termed "passive revolution," the southern Italian bourgeoisie had become subservient to the stronger northern Italian bourgeoisie. At the

131. See Candeloro, *Dalla rivoluzione nazionale,* 244–273; Berti, *I democratici,* 706–721; De Francesco, "Ideologie," 327–330; Dal Lago, "Radicalism and Nationalism," 208–209; and Roberto Martucci, *L'invenzione dell'Italia unita, 1855–1864* (Florence, 1999), 139–145.

132. See Lucy Riall, *The Italian Risorgimento: State, Society, and National Unification* (London, 1994), 1–5.

same time, the liberals had succeeded in imposing upon the democrats their moderate—i.e., conservative—program of national unification.[133]

Since the 1980s, revisionist historians have operated something akin to a paradigm shift, rejecting as irrelevant the assumptions behind the debate on the southern Italian bourgeoisie and placing firmly at the center of their analysis the issue of relations between core and periphery. Rather than seeing the process of Italian unification as the inevitable success of the moderate liberal program due to the weakness of southern Italian democrats, revisionist historians have focused their attention on the reasons for the internal collapse of the Bourbon kingdom and have claimed that it resulted from an increasing lack of support for the program of bureaucratic modernization that characterized the administrative monarchy. At the heart of this process was the relationship between central government and peripheral elites. Piecing together the picture presented in revisionist works, we have seen how the different sections of the elites in the peripheral regions of the *Mezzogiorno* had different reasons to be in conflicting terms with the Bourbon program of administrative centralization. Still, undoubtedly, both the landed aristocracy and the bourgeoisie aimed mainly at maintaining, restoring, or strengthening their local power and privileges. In this particular respect, their resistance to Bourbon centralization was a conservative movement comparable to the one through which American slaveholders intended to resist the federal government's imposition of antislavery legislation.[134]

Yet, it would be wrong to conclude that all southern Italian landowners opposed modernization because they opposed Bourbon administrative reforms. Unlike what happened in the American South, where the slaveholders' opportunity to embrace centralized modernization vanished with the collapse of the Whig Party, in the *Mezzogiorno* the liberal landed proprietors—who were the ones who advocated modernization and economic

133. See Antonio Gramsci, *Quaderno 19. Il Risorgimento* (Turin, 1949); Paul Ginsborg, "Gramsci and the Era of Bourgeois Revolution in Italy," in John A. Davis, ed., *Gramsci and Italy's Passive Revolution* (London, 1979), 31–66; and Rosario Romeo, *Risorgimento e capitalismo* (Bari, 1959).

134. See Riall, *Italian Risorgimento*, 6–10; Lucy Riall, "Elite Resistance to State Formation: The Case of Nineteenth-Century Italy," in Mary Fullbrook, ed., *National Histories and European History* (London, 1993), 56–65; Romanelli, "La nazionalizzazione della periferia," 13–24; Salvatore Lupo, "Tra centro e periferia. Sui modi dell'aggregazione politica nel Mezzogiorno contemporaneo," *Meridiana* 2 (1988): 13–50; and Paolo Pezzino, *Il paradiso abitato dai diavoli. Societa, elites, istituzioni nel Mezzogiorno contemporaneo* (Milan, 1992), 27–94; and Pezzino, "Local Power in Southern Italy," 42–58.

reform, but also active governmental intervention in defense of their interests—succeeded in gaining the upper hand in the process of Italian unification. In their program of creation of the new Italian nation, southern
Italian moderate liberals combined economic modernization with a type
of administrative centralization that—unlike the Bourbon one—successfully protected local privileges, especially in regard to private property, and
guaranteed balanced representative institutions and the advancement of
agrarian over industrial interests. Therefore, if the defeat of the democrats in
1848 ensured that, afterward, politics in the *Mezzogiorno* followed a rather
conservative path, the moderate liberals' hegemony in the movement for
Italian unification ensured that modernization proceeded with an agenda
that privileged the interests of the provincial landed bourgeoisie, a class
that believed itself ready to guide—in paternalistic fashion—the peasant
masses on the road to progress, though not to social equality. In synthesis,
southern Italian landowners joined the moderate liberal movement because
it simultaneously represented the victory of conservative politics, restricted
representation (though balanced in terms of core-periphery relations), defense of local privileges and private property, economic modernization, and
antiprotectionist policies.[135]

Therefore, both the widespread opposition to Bourbon administrative
centralization and the particular characteristics of the content of the moderate liberal program provide an explanation for the moderate liberals' success
in building a consensus on the need to create an alternative nation-state to
the Bourbon monarchy in order to defend the interests of the propertied
classes. Yet, as they set out to build their bourgeois nation, southern Italian
moderate liberals encountered problems comparable to the ones that American planters faced in creating the Confederacy. Although in the southern
Italian case, regional allegiance was not nearly as strong as in the American
South—where loyalty to the state of birth was of paramount importance in
the federal system—it still provided an issue that the elites had to confront
in the construction of a national institution. The issue was especially strong
in the case of Sicily, where, comparable to what happened in South Carolina,
regionalism was long established and was not just a source of identity within

135. See Di Ciommo, *La nazione possibile*, 347–360; Petrusewicz, "Land-Based Modernization"; Antonacci, *Dalla repubblica*, 19–20; Ennio Corvaglia, *Prima del Meridionalismo. Tra cultura napoletana e istituzioni unitarie: Carlo De Cesare* (Naples, 2001), 138–161; and Galasso, "Le
forme del potere," 534–542.

the elite, but also the major reason behind opposition to Bourbon rule—an opposition that led to separation of the island from the continental South in 1848–1849 and in 1860 and was a crucial factor in the collapse of the Kingdom of the Two Sicilies. For these particular reasons, in the present work I have treated Sicilian regionalism in comparison with South Carolinian regionalism in a separate chapter.[136]

Aside from regionalism, particularly crucial in the process of nation-building was the issue of nationalization of the southern Italian masses. Notwithstanding the Marxist-Liberal debate on the southern Italian bourgeoisie, there is little doubt that both moderate liberals and a substantial number of democrats failed to win the southern Italian masses to their national political programs as a result of their negative attitude toward the peasants' demand for land. Largely as a consequence of this attitude, therefore, the level of nationalization of the southern Italian population was rather low. And yet it is interesting to notice that, paying rather little attention to this clear historical development, the most recent scholarship on nationalism has made ample use of the Italian case in the creation of theories of construction of modern nations. In fact, nearly all of the recent studies on nationalism consider Italian unification to be an emblematic example of how the existence of a shared culture and language functioned as a background and motive for the creation of a unified nation-state out of a fragmented political situation. This assumption, in turn, has reinforced the validity of the related ideas that the spread of national public opinion predated the existence of nations and that the educated elites were the driving force behind the creation of modern nations.[137]

Arguably, this was particularly true in the Italian peninsula in the 1850s, since only two percent of the population could read and write in Italian, while an even lower percentage could do the same in the Kingdom of the Two Sicilies. Yet, most scholars have ignored the fact that, precisely for this

136. See Galasso, *La democrazia da Cattaneo a Rosselli*, 20–43; Adrian Lyttelton, "Shifting Identities: Nation, Region, City," in Carl Levy, ed., *Italian Regionalism: History, Identity, and Politics* (Oxford, 1994), 33–53; and Nino Recupero, "La Sicilia all'opposizione, 1848–1876," in Maurice Aymard and Giuseppe Giarrizzo, eds., *La Sicilia* (Turin, 1986). On Sicilian regionalism in comparison with South Carolinian regionalism, see chapter four.

137. See Anderson, *Imagined Communities*, 118–119; Gellner, *Nations and Nationalism*, 98–100; Ernest Gellner, *Nationalism* (London, 1997), 52–53; and Hobsbawm, *Nations and Nationalism since 1780*, 60–61.

reason, the Italian language, or even simply literacy, was hardly an important factor compared to religion in the building of an Italian imagined community, especially in the *Mezzogiorno,* where the overwhelming majority of the population was both illiterate and devoutly Catholic. As recent scholarship has demonstrated, the employment of religious concepts in the nationalist propaganda and religious images of famous nationalist leaders, and especially of Giuseppe Garibaldi, was of fundamental value in winning the people to the cause of Italian nationalism. In this respect, there is more than one parallel with the crucial role of evangelical Christianity in the creation of Confederate national identity in the Civil War South.[138]

Yet, for the most part, the creation of an Italian national identity in the 1850s' *Mezzogiorno* was a business restricted to the articulated members of the elites—most of whom were in exile—who joined in and even guided, to a certain extent, the process of inventing the tradition of an Italian nation. Comparable to what happened in the late antebellum American South and compatible to Eric Hobsbawm's model, also in the late pre-unification *Mezzogiorno,* the process of invention of tradition occurred as a result of mounting political pressure. In the latter case, the pressure came mainly from the acceleration of activities directed to the creation of a unified Italian nation through the collapse of the Bourbon kingdom. By 1857, this common goal had succeeded in uniting moderate democrats and liberals in the support for the increasingly militant action of the Italian National Society—an important organization dedicated to the achievement of Italian unification under the leadership of the liberal Piedmontese monarchy.[139]

On 11 May 1860, with the support of the Italian National Society and in the name of the Piedmontese king, Victor Emmanuel II, Giuseppe Garibaldi landed with his "Thousand" in Sicily, where—with the substantial help of local landowners and peasant forces organized by democratic activists—in only two months he defeated the Bourbon army and declared the island's independence from Naples. After his landing in Calabria on 19 August,

138. See Alberto Banti, "Telling the Story of the Nation in Risorgimento Italy," in Gudmunour Halfdanarson and Ann Catherine Isaacs, eds., *Nations and Nationalities in Historical Perspective* (Pisa, 2001), 15–26; Alberto M. Banti, *La nazione nel Risorgimento,* 170–173; and Lucy Riall, "Hero, Saint, or Revolutionary? Nineteenth-Century Politics and the Cult of Garibaldi," *MI* 3 (1998): 191–204. For a comparison, see Faust, *Creation of Confederate Nationalism,* 82–83.

139. See Hobsbawm, "Introduction," 1–14; Candeloro, *Dalla rivoluzione nazionale,* 415–438; and Raymond Grew, *A Sterner Plan for Italian Unity: The National Society in the Risorgimento* (Princeton, N.J., 1963).

Garibaldi was welcomed by the majority of local landowners and by the peasant masses of the continental South, which revolted against Bourbon rule according to a pattern of events similar to the one that had occurred in Sicily. After a relatively short string of victorious military skirmishes, at the beginning of September 1860, Garibaldi triumphantly entered Naples. By then, the Bourbon king, Francis II—who had succeeded his father Ferdinand II in 1859—had fled the capital after granting the constitution in a late attempt to win liberal public opinion. After defeating the largest contingent of the Bourbon army at the battle of Volturno, in October Garibaldi handed over the *Mezzogiorno* to King Victor Emmanuel II, unknowingly fulfilling the plan masterminded by Cavour. On 21 October, plebiscites throughout the *Mezzogiorno* sanctioned the wish of the overwhelming majority of the voting population to join the Piedmontese Kingdom of Sardinia (see map 6).[140]

As it happened, in his brief period of rule in southern Italy, even though he had received substantial help from both moderate and radical democrats, Garibaldi proved to be no friend of peasant demands for land, but rather was willing to look for the support of liberal landowners. At the same time, despite his repeated attempts to keep law and order, he was unable to prevent the collapse of Bourbon governmental structure. Therefore, while in many municipal councils the provincial landed bourgeoisie simply established a de facto rule, peasant violence and attacks against private property became widespread. As a result, even those landed proprietors who had been less than inclined to join the liberal movement contributed to accelerating the process of Italian unification, so that the Piedmontese army could succeed where Garibaldi had failed, in restoring law and order. The official proclamation of the Kingdom of Italy occurred in March 1861. On one hand, the new nation represented the fulfillment of moderate liberal aspirations, since the hegemonic classes in a parliament elected with restricted representation were the landed proprietors and the professional bourgeoisie. On the other hand, the Italian kingdom was a strongly authoritarian and centralized state—a feature that forecast its administration's imminent encounter with a renewed movement of opposition to governmental policies by many southern Italian landowners.[141]

140. See Scirocco, *L'Italia del Risorgimento*, 399–415; Martucci, *L'invenzione dell'Italia unita*, 139–242; and Riall, *Sicily and the Unification of Italy*, 71–75.

141. See Riall, "Garibaldi and the South," 144–147; Riall, *Sicily and the Unification of Italy*; Alfonso Scirocco, *Il Mezzogiorno nella crisi dell'unificazione (1860–1861)* (Naples, 1975); John A. Davis, *Conflict and Control: Law and Order in Nineteenth-Century Italy* (London, 1988), 50–53;

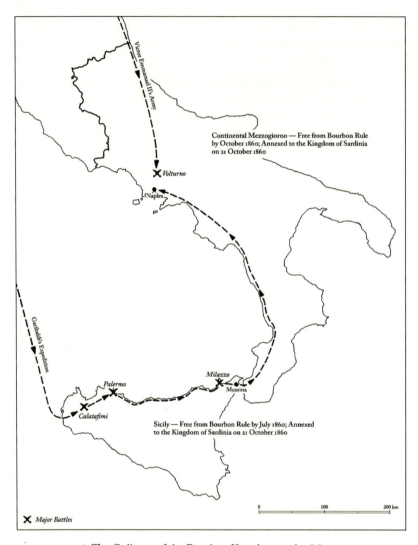

Continental Mezzogiorno — Free from Bourbon Rule by October 1860; Annexed to the Kingdom of Sardinia on 21 October 1860

Victor Emmanuel II's Army

Garibaldi's Expedition

✗ *Volturno*

Naples

Milazzo

Palermo

Messina

✗ *Calatafimi*

Sicily — Free from Bourbon Rule by July 1860; Annexed to the Kingdom of Sardinia on 21 October 1860

0	100	200 km

✗ *Major Battles*

MAP 6. The Collapse of the Bourbon Kingdom in the *Mezzogiorno*

*   *   *

Altogether, mid-nineteenth-century political developments in both the American South and the Italian *Mezzogiorno* are best understood as the results of either perceived or real tensions between a core—represented by the central government—and a periphery, and specifically a southern peripheral elite. In both cases, initially the peripheral elite channeled its dissatisfaction for the prospect of governmental centralization—which, in the American South, in reverse terms to the situation in the *Mezzogiorno*, appeared as a sudden break from a reassuring past hegemony of the periphery on the core government—into political movements of reform and attempted to ease the tensions through institutional means. Yet, when institutional politics failed to provide an assurance of protection of local interests, the tensions led to political crises during which the collapse of governmental institutions was narrowly avoided. In both cases, the elite considered as its ultimate option for retaining its degree of local power and privileges an open opposition to the central government followed by the formation of an alternative national institution clearly based on the principle of balance of power between core and periphery.

Seen from this perspective, both the American slaveholders' and the southern Italian landowners' engagements in experiments of nation-building seem to have been related to a particular type of nationalism—a "peripheral nationalism" that conservatively pursued the protection of peripheral interests against governmental centralization, rather than effectively claiming a cultural distinctiveness from a nation that already existed. In fact, southern cultural distinctiveness in the United States was no less an invented tradition than the supposed centuries-long linguistic and cultural distinctiveness of the Italian nation. Also, in both cases, the claim to distinctiveness served the purpose of reinforcing the validity of the propertied classes' call to the people to build a nation under the elite's guidance.[142]

Clearly, there were several differences between the two projects of nation-building. On one hand, the dissatisfaction of American slaveholders with the American federal system led a number of them to join the movement for

---

Alberto M. Banti, *Storia della borghesia italiana. L'età liberale* (Rome, 1996), 3–22; Claudio Pavone, *Amministrazione centrale e amministrazione periferica da Rattazzi a Ricasoli (1859–1866)* (Milan, 1964), 73–95; Martucci, *L'invenzione dell'Italia unita*, 375–418; and Raffaele Romanelli, *L'Italia liberale* (Bologna, 1990), 40–52.

142. See Hechter, *Containing Nationalism,* 70–83.

secession, leaving the Union and creating an alternative national federation of southern states. On the other hand, the southern Italian landowners' opposition to monarchical absolutism led them to join a program of national unification through which they wished the *Mezzogiorno* to become part of a federation of Italian states. In general, the difference between the two alternative courses of secession and unification stemmed from particular characteristics in the developments of the relationship between core and periphery in the two southern regions. In the United States, southern slaveholders were part of a highly decentralized national governmental system, which they considered very close to perfection and on which they exercised an almost uninterrupted political hegemony until the mid-1850s. Consequently, when they lost their political hegemony, slaveholders felt as if the only option they were left with was to secede from the American Union and create a new and similarly decentralized national governmental system—one that they could make perfect by exercising an unchallenged control over its institutions. Conversely, in the *Mezzogiorno,* southern Italian landowners were part of a highly centralized and absolutist administrative system that allowed them very little power and upon which they exercised increasingly less control, especially from the 1850s. Therefore, their most viable option to change the system was to bring about the collapse of the Bourbon kingdom and to substitute it with a constitutional Italian monarchy, building a new and different state whose governmental policy they could control through limited representative institutions.

It is important, though, to point out a particular difference in regard to the actual dynamics of the movements for secession and unification. In the American case, the support of slavery clearly prevented slaveholders from allying with other elites outside the South and, in turn, gave marked regional characteristics to their antigovernmental struggle for the creation of a southern Confederate nation. On the contrary, in the Italian case, southern Italian liberal and democratic landowners could count on the fact that both the liberal and the democratic movements were widespread throughout the peninsula, and as a consequence the elite's alliances with northern Italian politicians and activists transformed its anti-Bourbon struggle and made it assume the characteristics of a pivotal episode in the creation of the Italian nation.

At the same time, it is also true that in the American South the majority of the slaveholding elite in the secessionist states joined enthusiastically in the regional program of Confederate nation-building. Conversely, in the *Mezzogiorno* the constant conflict between different sections of the landowning elite ensured that even in 1860 the basis of consensus for the Italian nation was not nearly as widespread. As a number of studies has shown, the reasons for this particular difference have a lot to do with the fact that in the American South the elite built the consensus around slaveholding—effectively the economic and social basis of the southern nation—and the privileges it gave to the white population. In doing so, the elite created the impression of a democracy of the white race, making a particularly effective use of the powerful rhetorical image of the republic of white farmers living off the labor of the legally enslaved and racially discriminated African American population. Conversely, in the Italian *Mezzogiorno,* where the peasant masses were neither enslaved nor racially discriminated against, the elite could not employ republican rhetoric and defend its privileges at the same time. For this reason, aside from a few notable exceptions—the most famous of which is represented by Carlo Pisacane—those southern Italian democrats who happened to be either noblemen or large landowners were often prepared to support radical political programs only as long as they did not touch private property—the economic and social foundation of the type of Italian nation that they envisioned—and in so doing they alienated the masses of landless peasants and rural laborers.[143]

Ultimately, though, both American slaveholders and southern Italian landowners used the rhetoric of nineteenth-century nationalism as a means to either maintain or enhance their position of privilege over the masses. They both sought to create a new and alternative imagined community, a nation that theoretically was to embrace the elites and the people alike, but, first and foremost, was to guarantee the end of the threat of governmental interference in local affairs and the protection of established economic and social privileges. As a result, in both regions, nationalism showed the characteristics of a conservative ideology that aimed at justifying and perpetuating the power of the ruling classes over the masses through the creation of modern nations—nations, though, whose main socioeconomic features, slavery and large landholding, included both modern and antimodern elements, as we have seen. Yet, ultimately, even though unwilling to guide their regions on a path to modernization that contemplated radical social change, American slaveholders and southern Italian landowners opted to join and even guide the two radical movements for the creation of the Confederate States

143. See especially Freehling, *Road to Disunion,* 39–58; and Lovett, *Democratic Movement,* 152–153.

of America and of the Kingdom of Italy, either following or taking advantage of the situations provoked by South Carolina's and Sicily's extreme regionalisms. In doing so, the two elites put in motion a chain of events that altered forever the structure of the two southern societies and eventually led to the end of their economic, social, and political power.

CHAPTER 4

The Ideological Bases of Secession and Separatism

Regionalism in South Carolina and Sicily

The contrast between core and periphery, so central to the ideological and political activities of American slaveholders and southern Italian landowners, assumed a marked regional character in South Carolina and Sicily. Nineteenth-century South Carolina and Sicily were microcosms of the economic and social structures of the American South and of the Italian *Mezzogiorno.* While their economies relied on both old and new systems of agricultural production, their elites included both old and recently formed sections. In nineteenth-century South Carolina, rice and cotton production coexisted as the economic bases of wealth of both long and recently established planters, while in nineteenth-century Sicily, grain cultivation and citrus, wine grape, and olive cultivation coexisted as the economic bases of the social power of a landowning class that included both noblemen and bourgeois. Yet, specific social and cultural features combined with the ones mentioned above to provide the elites of the two regions with peculiar identities in social and political terms and gave origin in both cases to a very distinctive type of regionalism, one which played an important role in the success of nationalist programs among American slaveholders and southern Italian landowners.

Both South Carolina and Sicily were regions with features that set them apart from the rest of the American South and the Italian *Mezzogiorno.* In particular, the oldest sections of the two elites—South Carolina's rice planters and Sicily's aristocracy—were relatively small, homogenous, and extremely powerful groups of propertied individuals. Even after the drafting of two specific pieces of legislation—the Constitution of 1808 in South

Carolina and the Constitution of 1812 in Sicily—which contributed a great
deal to the social advancement of the newer sections of the landed elites,
South Carolina's rice planters and Sicily's noblemen retained a substantial
degree of control in matters of regional politics and used this control to
push forward programs that aimed at the secession/separation of their regions from their respective national governments. In both regions, in the
aftermath of the issue of the two constitutions, a process of amalgamation
between old and new took place; in general, it led to the creation of an increasingly homogenous propertied class in South Carolina, less so in Sicily.
The reasons for these divergent outcomes are related to the different contexts
and shapes of the particular processes of amalgamation in the two regions.
While in South Carolina there was little reason for antagonism between
old and recent slaveholders, in Sicily—as in the rest of the *Mezzogiorno*—a
bitter struggle over the ownership of common lands (*demani*) set the landed
aristocracy against the landed bourgeoisie.

However, it is also important to notice that, contrary to this general
feature, the liberal part of the Sicilian aristocracy acted in many ways as an
"open elite"—similar to South Carolina's planter class—successfully incor-
porating the wealthiest landed bourgeois within its ranks. For this reason,
comparison in the present work focuses particularly on South Carolinian
rice and cotton planters and Sicilian liberal noblemen and ennobled bourgeois. In comparable terms, South Carolina's planters and Sicily's liberal
noblemen and ennobled bourgeois agreed on the need to defend the economic and social privileges of the propertied classes and promoted regional
independence as the most effective means to defend these privileges. In fact,
in the period between 1820 and 1860, South Carolinian planters and Sicilian
noblemen actively supported an extreme type of regionalism that promoted
secession/separation from the United States and from the Bourbon kingdom. Doubtless, a degree of regional autonomy and power similar to the
one that South Carolinians enjoyed within the American Union would have
been an achievement in the minds of Sicilian separatists, who lived in the
shadow of the Bourbon absolute monarchy. Yet, despite this important difference, it is clear that the roots of the two regions' comparable and peculiar
separatist tendencies lay in both cases in particular social and political features that distinguished them from the rest of the American South and of
the Italian *Mezzogiorno* in a number of respects. Among these features, none
was more important than the characteristically dominant role of a highly

regionalized propertied class, a role that, in both South Carolina's and Sicily's cases, originated and developed as a result of the particular historical trajectory that the region followed from the seventeenth century onward.[1]

The Social Origins of Regionalism in South Carolina and Sicily

The particular type of regionalism that characterized nineteenth-century South Carolina and Sicily had its roots in long traditions of social and cultural distinctiveness and also of relative political autonomy. In the case of South Carolina, since the seventeenth-century foundation of the colony, the slave-holding elite had set out to create a distinctively aristocratic society whose political spokesmen upheld the right to retain a degree of local autonomy first, as a colonial government, from the British Crown and then, through the representative organs at both the state and federal levels, from the American Union. In the case of Sicily, since the Middle Ages, the political tradition of local autonomy was grounded in the presence of a noble representative assembly (*parlamento nobiliare*) through which the local aristocracy effectively administered the island under the formal supervision of a representative of the Neapolitan kingdom. In both cases, cultural and social distinctiveness and political autonomy combined as important elements in the history of relationships between peripheral elites and central governments and provided the background for the future explosions of regionalist tendencies.[2]

The economic power that derived from large slaveholding and landownership was the key to the two elites' social and cultural hegemony over South Carolina and Sicily. Since the early modern era, South Carolinian planters and Sicilian noblemen acquired wealth by producing and selling particular crops and agricultural products on the world market. Despite both being relatively small groups, they managed to control the political and social spheres of the two peripheral regions in conditions of relative autonomy from their respective central administrations. Yet, by no means were these two groups

1. On the concept of "open elite," see Lawrence Stone, *An Open Elite? England, 1540–1880* (New York, 1984).

2. On South Carolina's and Sicily's regional political culture, see James M. Banner, "The Problem of South Carolina," in Stanley Elkins and Eric McKitrick, eds., *The Hofstadter Aegis: A Memorial* (New York, 1974), 60–93; and Francesco Renda, *Storia della Sicilia dal 1860 al 1970*, vol. 1, *I caratteri originari e gli anni dell'unificazione italiana* (Palermo, 1984), 19–62.

akin to closed castes. Throughout the modern history of South Carolina and Sicily, newcomers mingled with established families and old and new sections of the elites together reshaped several times the social boundaries of power. While in South Carolina upcountry planters established ties with the older aristocratic families of the lowcountry, in Sicily—even though to a lesser degree—the wealthiest landed bourgeois mingled with aristocratic families and often even acquired noble titles.

In South Carolina, by the first half of the nineteenth century, established lowcountry aristocratic clans—such as the Manigault, the Izard, and the Heyward—fully recognized as part of the same ruling elite families such as the Hamptons, the Chesnuts, and the Hammonds, which belonged to the upcountry cotton gentry. The celebration of a number of marriages between members of different clans—as in the case of the famous matrimony between Rebecca Chesnut and James S. Deas, who belonged to a branch of the Izard family—helped to cement the alliance between upcountry gentry and lowcountry aristocracy. In fact, according to George Germany, "the intermarriage of important families on a local scale was one of the earliest and basic forms of alliance within the governing class"; as time passed, "by the second or third generation the practice resulted in marriage within one's near kin and the formation of a political dynasty within a close family group."[3]

In Sicily, a comparable phenomenon occurred, especially in the last four decades preceding the fall of the Bourbons. During that period, several of the wealthiest families of the landed bourgeoisie—families such as the Turrisi Colonnas, the Risos, and the Tascas—either bought or received from the Bourbon monarchy a noble title and joined a titled aristocracy that included prestigious noble clans, such as the Trabias, the Monteleones, and the Paternòs. Also, as in the case of South Carolina, several marriages sanctioned alliances between families of the old and new sections of the landed elite. For example, as a result of his marriage with "noble" Beatrice Lanza e Branciforte, princess of Trabia, "bourgeois" Lucio Mastrogiovanni Tasca became count of Almerita. In fact, according to Marcello Verga, the Sicilian aristocracy's open policy allowed it "to absorb among its ranks . . . the rising

3. George P. Germany, "The South Carolina Governing Elite, 1820–1860" (Ph.D. diss., University of California, Berkeley, 1972), 169. See also Robert H. Taylor, *Antebellum South Carolina: A Social and Cultural History* (Chapel Hill, N.C., 1942).

elements of the local bourgeoisie . . . well beyond the nineteenth century." This, in turn, contributed in a major way to the continuous exercise of the political, social, and cultural hegemony of the noble families over the island.[4]

The reasons for the strength and homogeneity of the South Carolinian planter elite and the Sicilian aristocracy have a lot to do with patterns of historical development and class formation. The process started in the sixteenth century in Sicily and in the seventeenth century in South Carolina, when the two elites began their rise to power through the production and sale of particular crops—rice and grain—on the world market. A similar process occurred again at the beginning of the nineteenth century, when new elites rose to power through the production and sale of other, more valuable products, such as cotton, citrus, and wine. In the midst of these parallel processes, South Carolina's planter elite and Sicily's aristocracy functioned as open elites. In both cases, the wealthiest members of the new propertied classes became part of the established upper class, reinvigorating the social and economic power of the latter with fresh blood—a process that received legal sanctioning with the drafting of the Constitutions of 1808 and 1812. In South Carolina, the Constitution of 1808 opened parliamentary representation to the upcountry gentry and balanced the political power of the lowcountry aristocracy in the administration of the state. In Sicily, the Constitution of 1812 abolished the feudal privileges of the landed aristocracy and recognized the right of the landed bourgeoisie to participate in the regional government.

From the time they settled the lowcountry, South Carolinian planters set out to create a frontier society that closely resembled seventeenth-century England and clearly distinguished the propertied aristocracy from the lower classes. In 1660, Charles II gave a substantial land grant in the territory of the Carolinas to eight of his major supporters, the so-called Lord Proprietors. A few years later, the Lord Proprietors planned to organize the new colony by implementing John Locke's 1669 *Fundamental Constitutions,* which guaranteed religious freedom but also provided guidelines for the creation of a stratified social system with a hereditary local nobility. According to the *Constitutions,* the colony of South Carolina was to include provinces,

4. Marcello Verga, "Il 'Settecento del baronaggio.' L'aristocrazia siciliana tra politica e cultura," in Franco Benigno and Claudio Torrisi, eds., *Elites e potere in Sicilia dal medioevo ad oggi* (Catanzaro, 1995), 88. See also Orazio Cancila, *Palermo* (Rome-Bari, 1988), 9–21.

counties, seigneuries, baronies, and precincts; moreover, the document also prescribed the creation of two noble titles, the *landgrave* and the *cacique*. Though the plan never became reality, South Carolinian planters were likely influenced by the provisions laid out in Locke's *Constitutions* when they colonized the lowcountry, founding new villages and employing a model of social organization based on rigid class divisions. In the new settlements, thanks to the boom in rice production and the ensuing plantation revolution, planters immediately became the individuals who held power and authority over the entire community. Since most South Carolinian planters had been established slaveholders in the Barbados, where they had engaged in a luxurious lifestyle and had owned immense plantations with hundreds of slaves, they were particularly prone to create a distinctively aristocratic society. In fact, in South Carolina—unlike in the Chesapeake—planters declared slavery hereditary soon after their arrival and maintained the traditions of primogeniture and entail for a longer time. Already by 1696, special "slave codes" restricted the freedom of any person of color and sanctioned the enslavement of Africans for life.[5]

Together with dramatic social changes, South Carolina's plantation revolution and the boom in rice production also produced clear changes in the landscape. Almost everywhere in the lowcountry, South Carolinian planters transformed large swamps into plantations on which large numbers of African slaves grew rice. The plantation frontier stretched north and south on the coast of South Carolina and Georgia, and all its settlements had the same pattern: rows of rice fields along the two sides of the rivers alternated with large residential mansions and slave quarters. By the beginning of the eighteenth century, the scale of the agricultural enterprises and the luxury of the Big Houses were such that the rice aristocracy of South Carolina was, together with Virginia's tobacco planters, the richest and most refined plantation elite in the American South.[6]

5. See Robert Weir, *Colonial South Carolina: A History* (New York, 1983), 54–58; Jack P. Greene, "Colonial South Carolina and the Caribbean Connection," *South Carolina Historical Magazine* 88 (1987): 192–210; Peter A. Coclanis, *The Shadow of a Dream: Economic Life and Death in the South Carolina Low Country, 1670–1920* (New York, 1989), 13–26; and Peter Wood, *Black Majority: Negroes in Colonial South Carolina from 1670 through the Stono Rebellion* (New York, 1974), 144–147.

6. See Coclanis, *Shadow of a Dream*, 48–110; and Ira Berlin, *Many Thousands Gone: The First Two Centuries of Slavery in North America* (Cambridge, Mass., 1998), 142–176.

Within fifty years, South Carolinian planters had managed to create a distinctively aristocratic way of life, the economic basis of which lay in the agricultural business related to the planting of rice and to the particular environment of the lowcountry. Since swamplands were unhealthy during the hot summer months, planters spent more than half of each year in their urban houses in Charleston, acting as absentee landowners and slaveholders. Unlike other planter elites in the South, South Carolinian planters had a unique relationship with the largest city of their region; Charleston's refined urban activities complemented well the isolated life of the plantation realm. In turn, the time planters spent in the city contributed a great deal to creating a strong social cohesion within the elite; interaction and participation in the same cultural activities and political debates helped to forge a sense of identity and eased the road to promotion of the same economic interests. During the summer season—when malaria infested plantations in the lowcountry—planters flocked to Charleston, where they replicated their plantation lifestyle in the city. They lived surrounded by black servants in big white houses with porticos, houses which often faced the fashionable area of the "Battery," where ladies and gentlemen met during the evening walk. As the eighteenth century progressed, Charleston rapidly turned into a fashionable city and a cultural center with concerts, plays, exhibitions, and lectures at which members of the lowcountry aristocracy met and exchanged ideas on economy, society, and politics.[7]

In the second half of the eighteenth century, farmers colonized the inner part of South Carolina and began the cultivation of cotton with the help of African American slaves. With the invention of the cotton gin in 1793, cotton became a highly profitable business. Stimulated by foreign demand, cotton production increased exponentially and paved the way to the further colonization of the inner areas of the state and especially of the fertile soils of the upcountry. As lowcountry planters had done with rice almost 150 years before, a number of slaveholders seized the opportunities provided by the

---

7. See Joyce E. Chaplin, *An Anxious Pursuit: Agricultural Innovation and Modernity in the Lower South, 1730–1815* (Chapel Hill, N.C., 1993), 92–107, 227–276; Roger Waterhouse, *A New World Gentry: The Making of a Merchant and Planter Class in South Carolina, 1670–1770* (New York, 1989); Robert Olwell, *Masters, Slaves, and Subjects: The Culture of Power in the South Carolina Low Country, 1740–1790* (Ithaca, N.Y., 1998), 17–56; George C. Rogers, *Charleston in the Age of the Pinckneys* (Norman, Okla., 1965); and Enrico Dal Lago, "The City as Social Display: Landed Elites and Urban Images in Charleston and Palermo," *JHS* 14 (2001): 372–396.

expansion of the market and by the increase in global demand for cotton. Also, as rice planters had done with the lowcountry, upcountry planters and slaveholders transformed large areas of inner South Carolina, founding a number of settlements with plantations and farms on which bondsmen cultivated cotton.[8]

Despite the planters' attempts to create an upcountry aristocracy that resembled the one in the lowcountry, a society in which cotton plantations were the centers of economic and social power, by 1820 the number of planters was still relatively small compared to the total number of slaveholders. And yet, in only twenty years, cotton planters had increased from one hundred to six hundred; also, they were only the wealthiest representatives of a rapidly rising upcountry slaveholding elite. However, with the possible exception of Columbia, no town in the inner part of the state performed the function of cultural center for cotton planters to the same degree that Charleston did for the lowcountry rice aristocracy. Therefore, despite the fact that the civilization and habits of the upcountry were very different from those of the lowcountry, Charleston provided a focal point for the entire slaveholding population of South Carolina. In time, the differences subsumed, the upcountry and lowcountry elites mingled, and Charleston became a sort of social and cultural capital of South Carolina for both cotton and rice planters, while Columbia became the political capital of the state in 1816.[9]

According to Rollin Osterweis, during the antebellum period, "socially, there was no wall between the rice, indigo, and later on the cotton planters who came in Charleston for some city life." Charleston was a city with a busy social and cultural life and with traditions, a city in which slaveholders from both lowcountry and upcountry areas of South Carolina could meet and exchange their ideas while enjoying many recreational activities. The habit of using Charleston as a meeting point and a forum for debate was instrumental in creating a strong bond among several individuals who be-

---

8. See Joyce E. Chaplin, "Creating a Cotton South in Georgia and South Carolina, 1760–1815," *JSH* 57 (1991): 171–200; Alfred G. Smith, *Economic Readjustment of an Old Cotton State: South Carolina, 1820–1860* (Columbia, S.C., 1958), 2–6; and Lacy K. Ford, *The Origins of Southern Radicalism: The South Carolina Upcountry, 1800–1860* (New York, 1988), 5–13.

9. See John Roberson, "The Foundations of Southern Nationalism: Charleston and the Lowcountry, 1847–1860" (Ph.D. diss., University of South Carolina, Columbia, 1991), 38–43; and William W. Freehling, *Prelude to Civil War: The Nullification Controversy in South Carolina, 1816–1836* (New York, 1966), 19–22.

longed to the lowcountry and upcountry slaveholding elites. It also helped them to become convinced of the peculiar regional character of a homogenous South Carolinian elite, one whose characteristics set it apart from other plantation aristocracies of the South and made it fit to rule the state in its own right.[10]

The key moment in the interaction between lowcountry and upcountry slaveholders occurred with the Compromise of 1808. Throughout the colonial and revolutionary period, lowcountry rice barons had sought to limit the political representation of upcountry representatives because they saw them as socially and culturally inferior. In fact, still in the nineteenth century there were a few cases of prejudice by members of the lowcountry aristocracy against members of the upcountry gentry. In her 1864 diary, Mary Chesnut tells the story of a lady from the lowcountry, who remarked that "the upcountry are a new people, it seems. The blood of the cavalier stays near the salt water." This attitude had informed the drafting of three consecutive constitutions, the last of which dated to 1790. At that time, there were no planters and very few slaves in the upcountry. However, the situation changed dramatically a few years later; the post-1790 boom in cotton production led to the rise in wealth of a number of planters and smaller slaveholders and in a significant increase in the slave population. Soon, upcountry slaveholders held enough power to require an amendment to the Constitution of 1790.[11]

Therefore, the expansion of cotton production not only had led to the formation of a new slaveholding elite in the upcountry, but it had also altered significantly the balance of power within the state. Thanks to the boom in cotton production, within a few decades upcountry slaveholders had managed to accumulate large amounts of wealth and had become a serious political threat

---

10. Rollin G. Osterweis, *Romanticism and Nationalism in the Old South* (New Haven, 1949), 113. See also William Gillmore Simms, "Charleston, the Palmetto City," *HM* 85 (1857): 1–22; David Moltke-Hansen, "The Expansion of Intellectual Life: A Prospectus," in Michael O'Brien and David Moltke-Hansen, eds., *Intellectual Life in Antebellum Charleston* (Knoxville, Tenn. 1986), 3–44; and Dal Lago, "City as Social Display," 363–365.

11. Entry for October 1861, Mary Chesnut's diary in C. Van Woodward, ed., *Mary Chesnut's Civil War* (New Haven, Conn., 1981), 217. See also Rachel N. Klein, *Unification of a Slave State: The Rise of the Planter Class in the South Carolina Backcountry, 1760–1808* (Chapel Hill, N.C., 1990), 214–246; Jeffrey Robert Young, *Domesticating Slavery: The Master Class in Georgia and South Carolina, 1670–1837* (Chapel Hill, N.C., 1999), 91–122; and Rebecca Starr, *A School for Politics: Commercial Lobbying and Political Culture in Early South Carolina* (Baltimore, Md., 1998), 126–135.

to the hegemony of lowcountry rice planters in the South Carolina legislature. By the early nineteenth century, the cotton gentry dominated the economic and social life of the upcountry—whose population, in the meantime, had expanded exponentially—and controlled local politics in the increasingly important city of Columbia. And yet, in the words of David Moltke-Hansen, "as planter interests and leadership came to dominate the Upcountry . . . the Lowcountry planters found it easier to compromise . . . on renewed Upcountry demands for representation." The lowcountry planters' open policy, in turn, led to a major compromise and to the amendment of the state constitution along the principle of allowing upcountry slaveholders an equal share of power in both the legislature and the state politics of South Carolina.[12]

The amendment led to the drafting of a second version of the constitution, eighteen years after the previous one. The 1808 Constitution provided the guidelines for the creation of a Senate with 45 seats and of a House of Representatives with 124 seats. The rice aristocracy held the control of the Senate, where the number of representatives was equal to the number of election districts, traditionally more numerous in the lowcountry; on the other hand, the cotton gentry held the control of the House, where the number of representatives was set according to the number of people, which grew increasingly higher in the upcountry. According to Lacy K. Ford, "the Compromise of 1808 established a *de facto* balance of power between the Upcountry and the Lowcountry." The key to the compromise was precisely in the fact that "the Lowcountry, with the help of the senators from black-majority districts along the fall line, controlled the Senate, while the Upcountry enjoyed a comfortable majority in the House of Representatives." Therefore, the compromise that led to the drafting of the Constitution of 1808 established a new balance of power between the older and the newer sections of the slaveholding elite; from that moment on, they acted as part of the same governmental institutions and defended the same interests in times of social and political crisis.[13]

12. David Moltke-Hansen, "Protecting Interests, Maintaining Rights, Emulating Ancestors: U.S. Constitution Bicentennial Reflections on 'the Problem of South Carolina,' 1787–1860," *SCHM* 89 (1988): 177. See also Banner, "Problem of South Carolina," 60–65; Kenneth S. Greenberg, *Masters and Statesmen: The Political Culture of American Slavery* (Baltimore, Md., 1985), 65–84; and Manisha Sinha, *The Counterrevolution of Slavery: Politics and Ideology in Antebellum South Carolina* (Chapel Hill, N.C., 2000), 10–14.

13. See Ford, *Southern Radicalism*, 106. See also Klein, *Unification of a Slave State*, 247–256; and William W. Freehling, *The Road to Disunion: Secessionists at Bay, 1776–1854* (New York, 1990), 220–223.

In order to ensure that the governmental institutions stayed in the hands of the unified slaveholding elite, property qualifications continued to be necessary to sit in both the Senate and the House. Although by 1810 there was universal white male suffrage, it applied exclusively to the election of local officials. The legislature chose all the executive officials and all the other important state officials, and slaveholders effectively controlled membership in the legislature. These aristocratic features of South Carolina politics—features that isolated it from the other states of the South—were an important aspect of the state's regional elitist culture and the main characteristic that historians have pointed out when talking about "the problem of South Carolina." Yet, far from being an anomalous feature, the antidemocratic character of South Carolina's internal politics was the logical result of a process that had led to the establishment of a powerful regional slaveholding class, a class that had renewed itself with the Compromise of 1808 and that claimed to represent the people and their political will at both the local and national levels.[14]

Following the compromise, intermarriages between families that belonged to the lowcountry rice aristocracy and families that belonged to the upcountry cotton gentry helped to build a strong alliance between the two in relation to local politics. By the time the nullification crisis began in 1828, a few families dominated the local politics of every county and district of South Carolina; often, these were families with economic interests in both the lowcountry and the upcountry. The representatives of these families were the most likely to have access to the most prestigious political office of the state, the governorship. By 1842, upcountry nouveau riche James Henry Hammond could compete with lowcountry aristocrat Robert Allston for the office of governor. This fact is perhaps one of the clearest examples of the phenomenon which David Moltke-Hansen has called "the transition from a lowcountry to a statewide plantation economy and [political] leadership" in South Carolina—a process that was at the heart of South Carolina's particular regional politics of secession.[15]

14. See Banner, "Problem of South Carolina," 69–71; William A. Schaper, "Sectionalism and Representation in South Carolina," *Annual Report of the American Historical Association for the Year 1900* (Washington, D.C., 1901), 379–395; Samuel C. Boucher, "Sectionalism, Representation, and the Electoral Question in South Carolina," *WUS* 4 (1916): 1–62; Greenberg, *Masters and Statesmen*, 65–84; and Stephanie McCurry, *Masters of Small Worlds: Yeoman Households, Gender Relations and the Political Culture of the Antebellum South Carolina Low Country* (New York, 1995), 240–251.

15. Moltke-Hansen, "Protecting Interests," 177. See also Freehling, *Prelude to Civil War*, 19–21; Lacy K. Ford, "Republics and Democracy: The Parameters of Political Citizenship in Ante-

* * *

In comparison with South Carolinian slaveholders, Sicily's landed elite underwent a process of class formation that was substantially longer and included different phases. Between the sixteenth and the seventeenth centuries, Sicily's aristocracy underwent important changes. Several families that came from the ranks of the commercial and bureaucratic bourgeoisie acquired noble titles. Most of them had little land and even less power; however, they soon promoted a movement of internal colonization of the island that led to a reversal of fortunes. The new noblemen sought and obtained from the Spanish crown permission to found new villages (*licentia populandi*) in the inner parts of Sicily, where population density was low and they could implant extensive grain cultivation. Between 1583 and 1714, the movement toward internal colonization led to the foundation of almost a hundred new villages and towns, several of which were in the grain-growing areas of the western part of the island. In founding a village, a nobleman usually acquired the title of prince and absolute authority and power (*miro e mesto imperio*) over the land and the inhabitants. Soon, the names of several new villages became linked to new and prestigious noble titles of members of a rising grain-growing elite, as in the case of Trabia, a western Sicilian town for which the Lanza family obtained the title of prince in 1601.[16]

What triggered this massive internal colonization, which involved several thousand settlers, were the concurrent factors of the antagonistic attitude of the new feudal aristocracy toward the old nobility and of the expansion of the grain market in the world economy. According to Orazio Cancila, "four hundred feudal lords . . . all recently ennobled . . . led the movement for the colonization and foundation of new villages in the island"; therefore, the movement was "the response of the new feudal class to the old one and its privileges." All around the new villages, the princes had feudal estates with

bellum South Carolina," in David R. Chesnutt and Clyde N. Wilson, eds., *The Meaning of South Carolina History: Essays in Honor of George C. Rogers, Jr.* (Columbia, S.C., 1991), 121–145; Robert H. Taylor, "The Gentry of Ante-Bellum South Carolina," *NCHR* 17 (1940): 114–131; Charles D. Davidson, *The Last Foray: The South Carolina Planters of 1860, A Sociological Study* (Columbia, S.C., 1971), 1–17.

16. See Timothy Davies, "La colonizzazione feudale della Sicilia nella prima età moderna," and Maurice Aymard, "Le città di nuova fondazione in Sicilia," both in Ruggero Romano and Corrado Vivanti, eds., *Storia d'Italia,* Annali VIII, *Insediamenti e Territorio* (Turin, 1985), 407–414; and Franco Benigno, "Vecchio e nuovo nella Sicilia del Seicento. Il ruolo della colonizzazione feudale," *SS* 27 (1986): 93–107.

latifondi where peasants grew grain for commercial exchange. At the center of the feudal estate, there was a small settlement with a palace, a church, and a prison—the symbols of the authority and power of the feudal lord. By the beginning of the eighteenth century the noble families that had promoted internal colonization had been able to acquire such wealth through the production and sale of grain that they had obscured the power of the old nobility and had rapidly become the most powerful social and economic group in Sicily. In addition, they had become enormously influential in the crown's viceroyal administration.[17]

During this process, the feudal lords redefined their identity as Sicily's "national" aristocracy, a class with a unique way of life related to the agricultural system based on the grain-growing *latifondi* of the inner parts of the island. In the first half of the eighteenth century, noblemen began to neglect the management of their feudal estates, which they left in the hands of *amministratori* and *gabelloti*, preferring to live as *rentiers* in Palermo. Akin to the effect that Charleston had on South Carolinian planters, Palermo's urban environment, with its rich cultural life and lively political debates, helped to forge a sense of identity within the Sicilian aristocracy. Noblemen built magnificent villas in the city's environs, where they enjoyed a refined cultural life and met with other members of the elite at social occasions in which they often exchanged views on the social and political situation of the island. By the mid-eighteenth century, these views were often in opposition to the Neapolitan monarchy's policy of curbing the power of the Sicilian feudal aristocracy and of its centuries-old representative assembly. As a consequence, when, in the 1780s and 1790s, Viceroys Caracciolo and Caramanico fought Sicily's feudal power with a number of different provisions that hit the landed aristocracy particularly hard, they only succeeded in causing a stronger unity among Sicilian noblemen against the Bourbon government's interference in local affairs.[18]

17. Orazio Cancila, *Baroni e popolo nella Sicilia del grano* (Palermo, 1983), 163. See also Giuseppe Giarrizzo, "La Sicilia da viceregno a regno," in Rosario Romeo, ed., *Storia della Sicilia*, vol. 6 (Naples, 1977), 90–95; Marcello Verga, *La Sicilia dei grani. Gestione dei feudi e cultura economica fra sei e settecento* (Florence, 1993), 13–48; and Francesca Gallo, *L'alba dei Gattopardi. La formazione della classe dirigente nella Sicilia austriaca (1719–1734)* (Catanzaro, 1996), 159–162.

18. See Gallo, *L'alba dei Gattopardi*, 147–162, 222–227; Verga, "Il 'Settecento,'" 87–102; and Dal Lago, "City as Social Display," 386–387. See also Francesco Renda, *Baroni e riformatori in Sicilia sotto il ministero Caracciolo (1786–1789)* (Messina, 1974); and Giuseppe Giarrizzo, "La Sicilia dal Cinquecento all'Unità d'Italia," in Vincenzo D'Alessandro and Giuseppe Giarrizzo, *La Sicilia dal Vespro all'Unità d'Italia* (Turin, 1989), 557–608.

At the beginning of the nineteenth century, an economic revolution took place when sulfur, citrus, and wine became the primary Sicilian products for export, replacing grain. Some noblemen adapted quickly to the changes and became increasingly involved in the production of citrus and wine and in the extraction of sulfur in selected areas of their *latifondi*; many, though, continued to live as absentee landlords. Meanwhile, *amministratori* and *gabelloti* grew increasingly rich with their usurious practices on the rent that they collected from the peasants. In several instances, the capital that they accumulated through these practices allowed their children and grandchildren to enter a mercantile profession or become landed proprietors. Either way, the new generations were able to join the ranks of a rising bourgeois elite of merchants and landowners who effectively controlled the production and sale of commercial agricultural items, such as citrus, wine, and olive oil.[19]

In fact, the wealthiest members of the most recent landed aristocracy—men such as Baron Niccolò Turrisi Colonna—were usually landed bourgeois whose fathers or grandfathers had administered the feudal estate of a noble family. Often, after reaching a high social position through acquisition of wealth, they secured recognition of their family's status by purchasing a noble title. However, it would be wrong to infer from this phenomenon that those landed bourgeois who sought the noble title simply aped the decadent customs of the feudal aristocracy. Sicily's ennobled landed bourgeois were often at the forefront of agricultural innovation together with liberal noblemen. Often both showed marked entrepreneurial attitudes and actively encouraged direct land management and cultivation of cash crops. And yet, comparable to the difference between lowcountry and upcountry planters in South Carolina, there was also a genuine cultural difference between noblemen and ennobled bourgeois, and their mutual antagonism focused on both ideological and social issues.[20]

19. See Orazio Cancila, *Storia dell'industria in Sicilia* (Bari-Rome, 1995), 5–132; Renda, *Storia della Sicilia*, 1:99–111; Maurice Aymard, "Economia e società: uno sguardo d'insieme," in Maurice Aymard and Giuseppe Giarrizzo, eds., *La Sicilia* (Turin, 1987), 15–18; Salvatore Lupo, "Tra società locale e commercio a lunga distanza. La vicenda degli agrumi siciliani," *Meridiana* 1 (1987): 81–112; Enrico Iachello, *Il vino e il mare. Trafficanti siciliani tra '700 e '800 nella contea di Mascali* (Catania, 1990), 145–164; Alfio Signorelli, *Tra ceto e censo. Studi sulle élites urbane nella sicilia dell'Ottocento* (Milan, 1999), 147–183; and Alfio Signorelli, "Elites e classi sociali nella Sicilia preunitaria," in Franco Pillitteri, ed., *Contributi per un bilancio del regno borbonico* (Palermo, 1990), 43–58.

20. See Salvatore Lupo, *Il giardino degli aranci. Il mondo degli agrumi nella storia del Mezzogiorno* (Venice, 1990), 62–69; and Rosario Romeo, *Il Risorgimento in Sicilia* (Bari-Rome, 1950), 224–231.

An 1894 pamphlet on the social question in Sicily—a work whose author was close to the feudal aristocracy—described accurately, though with a certain disdain, the origins of the new noblemen, stating that "the richest proprietors in the island, called '*baroni*' and *clearly distinguished* from the inheritors of the ancient families of the Princes, come from the class of the *massarioti* [the managers of the *masserie*], who have then become rich acquiring the *latifondi*, where they used to keep their houses." Notwithstanding the tone of this observation, it was also thanks to the entrepreneurial activity of ennobled bourgeois such as Baron Turrisi Colonna and Count Tasca that Sicilian agriculture developed new techniques and reached high standards of productivity.[21]

A key event in the relationship between aristocracy and bourgeoisie occurred with the drafting of the Constitution of 1812. In the early nineteenth century, liberal noblemen—who were close to the landed bourgeoisie in economic matters—sought to abolish the feudal law and transform fiefs into private property. Between 1811 and 1815, when Palermo functioned as the headquarters of the Bourbon king Ferdinand IV in exile from French-occupied Naples, Britain established a protectorate on Sicily. Against the wishes of both the monarchy and the conservative aristocracy, British general William Bentinck was instrumental in the formation of a Sicilian government whose dominant representatives were liberal noblemen. Headed by renowned liberal Carlo Cottone, prince of Castelnuovo, in 1812 the Sicilian *parlamento* approved the project of a constitution similar to the English one. The constitution provided the guidelines for the formation of an independent Sicilian constitutional monarchy, with a parliament divided in an upper House and a commons' House, and abolished all feudal privileges. Practically, with the abolition of feudalism, the law recognized the primacy of landownership over possession of noble title and effectively opened the ranks of the island's ruling elite to the landed bourgeoisie.[22]

21. The 1894 quotation is in Salvatore Lupo, "I proprietari terrieri del Mezzogiorno," in Piero Bevilacqua, ed., *Storia dell'agricoltura italiana in età contemporanea*, vol. 2, *Uomini e Classi* (Venice, 1990), 118.

22. See Romeo, *Il Risorgimento in Sicilia*, 85–103, 132–154; Giarrizzo, "La Sicilia dal Cinquecento," 611–666; Francesco Renda, "Dalle riforme al periodo costituzionale, 1734–1816," in Romeo, ed., *Storia della Sicilia*, vol. 6; Antonino De Francesco, "La Sicilia negli anni rivoluzionari e napoleonici," in Enrico Iachello, ed., *I Borbone in Sicilia (1734–1860)* (Catania, 1998), 32–46; John Rosselli, *Lord William Bentinck and the British Occupation of Sicily (1811–1814)* (Cambridge, 1956); and Francesco Renda, *La Sicilia nel 1812* (Caltanissetta, 1962).

Even though the independent Kingdom of Sicily only lasted until 1815, the provisions on the abolition of feudalism never disappeared. The restored Bourbon government confirmed them in legislation passed between 1816 and 1818. With further legislation, the government promoted massive sales of lands that belonged to both the aristocracy and the church, while ordering the enclosure of common land and the abolition of customary rights. As in the continental *Mezzogiorno*, the main beneficiary of the sales was the landed bourgeoisie, which acquired most of the land and soon included some of the richest landed proprietors on the island. Furthermore, the administrative reforms related to the Royal Decree of 11 October 1817 gave the Sicilian elite—similar to other peripheral elites of the *Mezzogiorno*—new avenues of social and political expression, even though under the strict control of the Bourbon bureaucracy. In fact, also in Sicily, the creation of the *liste degli eleggibili,* through which the local intendant chose the mayor of each *comune,* contributed a great deal to even the differences between the aristocracy and the landed bourgeoisie, given the fact that the prerequisite to access the lists was landownership rather than the noble title. Effectively, the aristocracy and the bourgeoisie—whether it included landed proprietors or professionals—were the only classes that could vote and participate in the local and regional governments.[23]

To be sure, in several Sicilian *comuni* the rising bourgeoisie fought bitterly against the aristocracy over the control of local government and common land, making use of both patronage and kin alliances. In fact, between the 1810s and the 1840s, the *liste degli eleggibili* of many *comuni* expanded considerably to gather an emerging elite of local power holders and landowners (*notabili*), mostly of bourgeois origins. In the factional struggles between aristocracy and bourgeoisie, the peasantry supported either class purely according to its chances of recovering the often illegally expropriated common land. Occasionally, and especially during the revolutions of 1820

---

23. See Enrico Iachello, "Borbone e stato in Sicilia: la riforma amministrativa del 1817," in Iachello, ed., *I Borbone,* 47–51; Antonino De Francesco, "Cultura costituzionale e conflitto politico nell'età della Restaurazione," in Benigno and Torrisi, eds., *Elites e potere,* 103–120; Giarrizzo, "La Sicilia dal Cinquecento," 665–678; Orazio Cancila, "Vicende della proprietà fondiaria in Sicilia dopo l'abolizione della feudalità," in Pillitteri, ed., *Contributi,* 93–114; and Lucy Riall, "Ill-Contrived, Badly Executed [and] . . . of no Avail? Reform and Its Impact in the Sicilian *Latifondo,* c. 1770–1910," in Enrico Dal Lago and Rick Halpern, eds., *The American South and the Italian Mezzogiorno: Essays in Comparative History* (New York, 2002), 136–137.

and 1848, peasant anger at both land expropriation and abolition of customary rights resulted in a spiral of violent actions that forced both noble and
bourgeois proprietors to intensify the use of armed outlaw bands (*bande
armate*) to effectively defend their land—a practice that previously had characterized only the aristocracy.[24]

As of today, we still do not have enough data to make generalizations
over local politics in Bourbon Sicily. Yet, it is entirely possible that—similar
to what happened in some *comuni* of the continental *Mezzogiorno*—the aristocracy and the bourgeoisie found, at times, a common ground in defense of
propertied interests, against both peasant threats and Bourbon administrative policies. In fact, in summarizing the evidence from Naro, Paolo Pezzino
has noticed that, despite the inevitable competition for political power and
the control of local resources, in that *comune* the aristocracy and the bourgeoisie formed a compact alliance in defense of local autonomy. Looking at
the progressive enlargement of the *lista degli eleggibili* and at the alternation
of noble and bourgeois in the most influential posts of the local administration, it appears that the two classes agreed to share the instruments of local
government and use them to resist Bourbon centralization.[25]

If we, then, move from the local to the regional plane, an important factor to consider is the number and type of members of the highest echelons
of the Sicilian landed bourgeoisie who collaborated with the liberal aristocracy in programs of agricultural reform. As Giovanna Cianciullo has
pointed out, these individuals—such as ennobled bourgeois Niccolò Turrisi
Colonna—were the inheritors of a tradition of liberalism whose earlier supporters were noblemen Carlo Cottone and Ruggero Settimo. Sicily's liberal
noblemen and wealthiest landed bourgeois shared a common project of
modernization of the island which was part of a wider vision of achievement
of regional political independence under the guidance of the richest members of the propertied classes. The commonality of this project was possible

24. See Lucy Riall, "Nelson versus Bronte: Land, Litigation and Local Politics in Sicily,
1799–1860," *EHQ* 29 (1999): 39–73; Giovanna Fiume, "Cariche e parentela. La lotta politica
a Marineo (1819–1858)," *NE* 45 (1999): 37–46; Giuseppe Giarrizzo, *Un comune rurale della Sicilia etnea: Biancavilla* (Caltanissetta, 1965); and Giovanna Fiume, *Le bande armate in Sicilia
(1819–1849). Violenza e organizzazione del potere* (Palermo, 1984).

25. See Paolo Pezzino, "L'intendente e le scimmie. Autonomia e accentramento nella Sicilia
di primo Ottocento," *Meridiana* 4 (1988): 25–54; and Giuseppe Barone, "Dai nobili ai notabili,"
in Benigno and Torrisi, eds., *Elites e potere*, 167–175.

because of the particular open elite characteristics of the Sicilian nobility, a class that—according to Salvatore Lupo—during the preunification period, accepted "*gabelloti*, local proprietors, lesser noblemen, and rich bourgeois ... through the flexible channels of marriage policy." In this respect, the Constitution of 1812 and the Bourbon reform of 1817 functioned as indispensable legal prerequisites to the formation of a sort of "proprietary front" that united Sicily's largest noble and bourgeois landowners against both Bourbon centralization and peasant demands.[26]

Through the Constitutions of 1808 and 1812, South Carolinian planters and Sicilian noblemen managed to link the idea of regional identity to the idea of a unified ruling class. As pressure from the American federal government and the Bourbon administration mounted against the southern peripheries, South Carolinian and Sicilian regional traditions served as the bases of two increasingly definite political programs of resistance to centralization, programs within which the two elites played crucial roles. In fact, both political programs not only aimed at the achievement of regional independence, but also rested on equally important modernization projects— projects in which the old and new planter elite in South Carolina and the liberal aristocracy and the ennobled bourgeoisie in Sicily collaborated with the comparable aims of creating economically strong agricultural regions dominated by slaveholders and landowners.

Modernization, Paternalism, and Regionalism

Collaboration between the old and the new planter elite in South Carolina and between the liberal aristocracy and the ennobled bourgeoisie in Sicily in modernization projects led, in both cases, to the elites' adoption of a patriarchal-paternalistic worldview. In both cases, elements of patriarchalism and paternalism joined together in an organic elitist worldview, similar to what happened in other peripheral areas of the American South and the Italian *Mezzogiorno*. However, contrary to what happened in other parts of the American South and of the *Mezzogiorno*, in South Carolina and Sicily the

26. Lupo, *Il giardino degli aranci*, 74–75. See also Giovanna Cianciullo, "La nobiltà siciliana tra rivolte e restaurazione: il 'Partito Costituzionale' (1812–1860)," *SS* 37 (1996): 629–654; Pinella Di Gregorio, 'Nobiltà e nobilitazione in Sicilia nel lungo Ottocento,' *Meridiana* 19 (1994): 106–107; and Renda, *Storia della Sicilia*, 1:33–36.

ideological synthesis that resulted from this process showed characteristically regional features and effectively formed the foundation of a discourse of political regionalism. Numerous South Carolinian rice-growing planters and Sicilian liberal noblemen who supported patriarchal views in regard to social relations acted as enlightened entrepreneurs and embraced the values of reciprocity and efficiency which lay at the basis of the paternalistic ethos, while also supporting ideas of regional cultural, social, and political distinctiveness.

In both cases, social interaction and participation in debates and projects to improve regional agricultural performance favored combining patriarchal and paternalistic attitudes into a complex worldview with regional characteristics. In the debates over agricultural reform that took place in South Carolina and Sicily in the period between the 1820s and the 1850s, rice planters and cotton planters in one case, and liberal noblemen and ennobled bourgeois in the other, advocated the importance of patriarchal principles within the family and in society, and yet they often intervened side by side in support of the fundamental tenets of the paternalistic ethos. Related to the latter were support for crop diversification and improvement of agricultural techniques, rational management of both land and the workforce, and respect of reciprocity in the relationship between master and laborers.

In South Carolina, a striking example of a member of the older low-country aristocracy actively supporting paternalistic principles was that of Robert F. W. Allston, the great rice planter and premier political figure from the Georgetown district. Allston wrote several articles in *De Bow's Review* advocating the use of scientific methods in the cultivation of rice, and he repeatedly argued against the lowcountry planters' widespread practice of absenteeism. In Sicily, a comparable example was that of Carlo Cottone, prince of Castelnuovo, the main supporter of the Constitution of 1812 in the Sicilian noble assembly. A liberal nobleman, Cottone was the founder of the prestigious agricultural school *Istituto Agrario* (Agrarian Institute) and an advocate of agricultural improvement through crop diversification and direct management. Generally speaking, judging from the record of highly specialized periodicals available in the two regions, such as *The Southern Agriculturalist* and *Gli Annali di Agricoltura Siciliana* (Annals of Sicilian Agriculture), it is possible to say that issues related to agricultural reform catalyzed the attention of the wealthiest and most prestigious South Carolinian planters and Sicilian noblemen and served effectively as instruments for their collective action toward regional economic improvement. This action formed the basis for a program of regional political claims by the propertied classes against the central governments' interferences in local affairs.[27]

In South Carolina, several rice planters who supported a patriarchal view of society embraced the paternalistic ethos and engaged in entrepreneurial activities on their plantations in the lowcountry. Even though they belonged to a traditionally absentee elite, these entrepreneurial rice planters strove to either be physically present on their plantations or else have very close contact with their sons or the overseers whom they had placed in charge. When they did not directly supervise their plantations, they demanded periodic reports on the state of the crops and on the health and behavior of the slaves. Overall, they succeeded in adapting the paternalistic ideas of direct management and contractual reciprocity to their way of life. They took personal interest in their slaves, most of whom they often knew by name, and they interfered in their lives either directly or through their sons and their overseers. In frequent and very detailed letters, they guided their sons' and overseers' activities step by step, advising them on how to raise cash crops in the most profitable way and on how to manage the workforce in the most rational manner. In fact, as William Dusinberre has abundantly demonstrated, the rice planters' display of paternalism—intended as a "system of punishments, allowances, and privileges"—related specifically to their search for profit and to their attempt to realize as high a return as possible in their agricultural enterprises.[28]

An earlier example of this attitude is in the documents of the Ball family, a prestigious lowcountry aristocratic clan whose plantations were in the region around Charleston. The Balls' attitude toward social relations, and especially gender relations within the family, was clearly informed by patriarchal principles. The Ball family had been in the business of rice production since the seventeenth century and had accumulated immense fortunes thanks to a policy of aggressive capitalism that from the beginning had focused specifically on the search for agricultural profit. And yet, the family

27. On South Carolina, see Germany, "South Carolina Governing Elite," 98–100; Smith, *Economic Readjustment,* 90–94; and Charles G. Steffen, "In Search of the Good Overseer: The Failure of the Agricultural Reform Movement in Lowcountry South Carolina, 1821–1834," *JSH* 63 (1997): 752–793. On Sicily, see Cianciullo, "La nobiltà siciliana," 645–654; Lupo, *Il giardino degli aranci,* 63–64; and Cancila, *Palermo,* 37–38.

28. William Dusinberre, *Them Dark Days: Slavery in the American Rice Swamps* (New York, 1996), 202.

documents show that the Balls always combined aggressive capitalism with a paternalistic attitude toward their slaves. Among the documents that show early examples of paternalism in the family's attitudes, especially representative are two contracts, or "agreements," stipulated by Isaac Ball—the family patriarch—with two overseers, one with Benjamin Aims in 1820 and one with Daniel Pipkins in 1821. Significantly, in both contracts Isaac Ball recommended with special emphasis a humane treatment of the slaves on his rice plantation and the use of punishments only when necessary, similar to how James Henry Hammond would several years later in his instructions to his overseer at Silver Bluff.[29]

A particularly illuminating example of this type of entrepreneurial and paternalistic rice planter is Charles Manigault. A successful lowcountry planter and a renowned businessman, Manigault descended from one of the oldest and most prestigious families in South Carolina and had the habits and culture of the Charleston aristocracy. In 1833, when he was thirty-eight, Manigault purchased Gowrie, a rice plantation on the Georgia side of the Savannah River with a population of fifty slaves, and declared his intent to transform it into his most profitable enterprise. During the 1830s and 1840s, he bought and established facilities for the milling and processing of rice; then, in 1834, he built a Big House in the middle of the plantation. Gowrie's returns were such that Manigault quickly recovered the initial capital he had invested; by 1835 the rate of profit was already 15 percent, and it remained well over 9 percent until the 1850s.[30]

In his relationship with the workforce at Gowrie, Manigault relied heavily on his overseers since he was absent for most of the time. Interestingly, the terms outlined in the contracts Manigault wrote for his overseers were short and straightforward, presumably because he knew he would give his overseers very specific instructions by letter. In fact, Manigault exchanged literally hundreds of letters with his overseers at Gowrie between 1833 and 1860. Most of the replies from the overseers were more than two pages

29. See "Agreement between Isaac Ball and Benjamin Aims," 1820, and "Agreement between Isaac Ball and Daniel Pipkins," 1821, Ball Family Papers, SCL. On the Balls, see Lorry Glover, "An Education to Southern Masculinity: The Ball Family of South Carolina in the New Republic," *JSH* 69 (2003): 39–70; and M. S. Schantz, "A Very Serious Business: Managerial Relationships on the Ball Plantations, 1800–1835," *SCHM* 88 (1987): 1–22.

30. See Dusinberre, *Them Dark Days,* 27–47; and Daniel Kilbride, "Cultivation, Conservatism, and the Early National Gentry: The Manigault Family and Their Circle," *JER* 19 (1999): 220–256.

long and extremely specific in their reports on agricultural improvement, slave health, and slave management. The picture that emerges from these exchanges is one of a skillful businessman and a demanding landlord who did not hesitate to dismiss an overseer or a driver if he did not perform his duties properly. In the course of the years, Manigault replaced six overseers, either because they were unable to produce a satisfactory crop or because they failed to strike the right balance between discipline and familiarity with the slaves. Although most of the time he was not physically present in the Big House, Manigault strove to impose the master's authority on overseers, drivers, and slaves alike and, at the same time, control all aspects of life on his plantation.[31]

In particular, Manigault's adoption of the paternalistic ethos showed in his ideas and practice of contractual reciprocity. According to Manigault, the slaves' duty was to do their work and acknowledge the master's authority, while the master's duty and obligation was to ensure that his overseer treated them well and to take a personal interest in their health and living conditions. In fact, in January 1848, while he was on holiday in Naples, Manigault wrote to Jesse Cooper—his overseer at Gowrie—recommending that he both watch and take care of his slaves, so that they would continue to be obedient and would not have any reason to complain. "My Negroes"—Manigault asserted—"have the reputation of being *orderly and well disposed*—but like *all Negroes,* they are up to anything, if not watched and attended to. I expect the *kindest treatment* from you—for this has always been a principal *thing with me.*" Manigault's display of paternalistic attitudes led him to even boast that, unlike other masters, he took "the pride, and the expense, of clothing my Negroes in the substantial way I have always done."[32]

As Eugene Genovese has noticed, Manigault conceived the distribution of slave clothing as a paternalistic ritual, one in which the master called every slave by name and gave clothes and blankets to each of them individually. However, far from giving the same treatment to each and every slave, Manigault had a well-devised system of rewards, which created ranks of

31. See James D. Clifton, "Introduction," in James D. Clifton, ed., *Life and Labor on Argyle Island: Letters and Documents of a Savannah River Rice Plantation, 1833–1867* (Savannah, Ga., 1978); and James D. Clifton, "The Rice Driver: His Role in Slave Management" *SCHM* 82 (1981): 331–353.

32. Charles Manigault to Jesse T. Cooper, 10 January 1848, Charles Manigault to James Haynes, 1 November 1846, Charles I. Manigault's letterbook, SCHS (original text underlined).

privilege and drew divisions among the slaves. The typical rewards to "good Negroes"—several of whom were house servants and cooks—included two equally important items for the slaves' daily survival: extra rations of food and extra clothing. The habit of rewarding faithful or hard-working slaves was so important in Manigault's conception of contractual reciprocity that he mentioned it on several occasions. In particular, in his manuscript on his family history entitled "Souvenirs of Our Ancestors and of My Immediate Family," he returned to the subject and wrote of how he needed to be physically present on the plantation at least half a year in order to personally preside over the distribution of clothes among the slaves.[33]

To be sure, Manigault's adoption of the paternalistic ethos also led to his constant interference in the slaves' lives and to his attempt to control all their activities, even those related to the cultivation of their personal plots of land, a customary practice under the task system in use on rice plantations such as Gowrie. In fact, Manigault paid particular efforts to protect the slaves' rights to raise their crops and livestock. Clearly, by allowing slaves to take care of their own plots of land, he achieved simultaneously three aims: he diffused the tension within his workforce, he kept the slaves under the watchful eye of the overseer, and he let them take care of their own food. Yet, this controlled freedom was hardly enough for the slaves, especially because, in return for it, Manigault expected his workforce to be obedient at all times and abide by his overseer's instructions—following a rather patriarchal model of master-slave relationship—no matter how harsh the work and living conditions were.[34]

In turn, the slaves' rejection of Manigault's narrow concept of reciprocity and their resistance to the continuous exploitation they suffered under his patriarchal-paternalistic system resulted in an unusual number of runaways. Over the years, every overseer employed at Gowrie confronted the same problem and, in response, increased the frequency of punishments—such as whipping and confinement—but to no avail. According to Jeffrey Robert Young, among the most common causes of running away at Gowrie were the harsh discipline and the appalling sanitary conditions—the latter being the cause of many deaths and the proof that Charles Manigault's manage-

33. See Charles Manigault's "Souvenirs of Our Ancestors and of My Immediate Family," Charles Manigault Papers, SCL. See also Eugene D. Genovese, *Roll, Jordan, Roll: The World the Slaves Made* (New York, 1974), 554–555.

34. See Charles Manigault to James Haynes, 1 March 1847, Charles Manigault's letterbook, SCHS.

ment was as ill-equipped as James Henry Hammond's in dealing with problems related to the workforce.[35]

Despite Manigault's serious troubles in slave management, his attempt
to create a model plantation at Gowrie, where the production of a cash crop
such as rice was a highly rational and profitable business and where the
master adopted elements of the paternalistic ethos in his relations with the
workforce, showed the extent of the influence of progressive ideas on the
ideology of entrepreneurial rice planters in the lowcountry. The achievement
of high returns in the production of cash crops and the rational and paternalistic management of the workforce were the two most important topics
of debate among agricultural reformers who voiced their opinions in South
Carolina's specialized agricultural periodicals. These topics interested specifically lowcountry rice planters such as Manigault, who were committed
to implementing marked capitalistic practices in the management of both
plantations and slaves. In fact, according to William Dusinberre, "Charles
Manigault was among the leaders . . . of the vigorous agricultural capitalism
which dominated the antebellum lowcountry." In their active engagement
in profitable agricultural production and rational slave management and in
their position at the vanguard of the movement for agricultural reform and
the spread of agricultural education throughout the state, Charles Manigault
and other members of the lowcountry rice aristocracy shared more than one
interest with prestigious upcountry cotton planters, such as James Henry
Hammond. This fact is a particularly significant indication of the degree of
ideological homogeneity that the South Carolinian planter elite had reached
in the decades before the Civil War.[36]

Particularly influential among the elite's agricultural reformers was the
activity of the South Carolina Agricultural Society, which had its headquarters in Charleston and which gathered all the most important rice and
cotton planters in the state. Similar to the Royal Institute of Encouragement in the *Mezzogiorno,* the South Carolina Agricultural Society promoted
agricultural improvement through the activity of its local branches and established premiums for accomplished agriculturalists. From 1828, the society published a periodical—*The Southern Agriculturalist*—edited by John D.

35. See Jeffrey Robert Young, "Ideology and Death on a Savannah River Rice Plantation,
1833–1867: Paternalism amidst 'a Good Supply of Disease and Pain,'" *JSH* 59 (1993): 672–706.

36. Dusinberre, *Them Dark Days,* 203. See also James M. Clifton, "Charles Manigault's Essay
on the Economics of the Milling of Rice," *AH* 52 (1978): 104–110.

Legaré. The publication's mission was, according to Legaré, "to establish the SCIENCE OF AGRICULTURE on a surer foundation" through promotion of agricultural knowledge, crop rotation, and rational plantation management. To this aim, Legaré maintained contact with all the local branches of the South Carolina Agricultural Society and received periodic reports and articles from planters located in different districts; he thought that, in time, the publication's essays would form a sort of "agricultural library" for progressive planters.[37]

Under Legaré's editorship, *The Southern Agriculturalist* treated themes that emphasized the capitalist spirit of the entrepreneurial management of plantations and farms and focused on the achievement of profit through agricultural innovation. At the same time, the journal gave advice on slave management, following the paternalistic model of contractual reciprocity. Several articles in the journal encouraged planters to use specific rules in regard to the pace of work, the diet, and the hygiene of the slaves. At the same time, a number of articles advised planters to allow slaves to have free time on Saturdays or to give them a plot of land on which to grow their own crops in return for their work performance. Given its commitment to the paternalistic idea of reciprocal obligations between planter and workforce, "the journal"—according to Theodore Rosengarten—"gave the impression that master and slave always pulled the same end of the rope."[38]

Yet, when seen in comparison with the overall policy of the South Carolina Agricultural Society, *The Southern Agriculturalist*'s support of paternalistic ideas seems to have been only partly in tune with the society's attitude toward reform. Following the paternalistic ethos, the main aim of the society's policy was the improvement of the agricultural performance of plantations and farms both through rational slave management and through the creation of a competent group of overseers recruited from the yeomanry and educated at special agricultural schools. However, the society's founders set out to achieve their aim within the framework of a patriarchal logic, which viewed social relations as immutable and left very little room for change. As a result, their chief preoccupation was that the sources of planters' power and wealth—which distinguished them from members of the lower classes, black and white—remained intact even at the cost of setting boundaries to

37. John D. Legaré, "Introduction," *SA* 1 (1828): ii, vi (capital letters in the original text).
38. Theodore Rosengarten, "The *Southern Agriculturalist* in an Age of Reform," in O'Brien and Moltke-Hansen, eds., *Cultural Life in Antebellum Charleston*, 287.

the agricultural education of the overseers and containing its effects on slave supervision and plantation management within clear limits.[39]

In 1838, Legaré traveled extensively through the rice-growing coast of South Carolina and Georgia. He wished to gain firsthand knowledge of the achievements and setbacks of plantation agriculture in the lowcountry. His ultimate aim, though, was to find the ideal planter, an individual who made use of an extensive knowledge of scientific agriculture and was significantly successful in managing his enterprise while simultaneously employing a paternalistic attitude in the treatment of his slaves and succeeding in disciplining them, keeping a firm hand. Arguably, Legaré thought he had found his ideal planter when he met James Hamilton Couper. A respected businessman and the owner and manager of Hopeton Plantation, Couper had inherited the Georgia estate from his father, John Couper, in 1818 and had transformed it into a model plantation, experimenting with crop rotation and other agricultural techniques.[40]

At Hopeton, Legaré wrote, "all the valuable crops of the South are cultivated in rotation . . . [and] also prepared for the market on the place." The range of staple crops included rice—the plantation's main commercial agricultural product—and Sea Island cotton, both of which Couper grew for export in the world market. Yet, Couper also grew corn, peas, and sweet potatoes as subsistence crops, for the plantation's self-sufficiency and for the internal market. In addition, he also made experiments with the cultivation of sugar, but with little success, even though he went as far as purchasing a sugar mill in 1830.[41]

Aside from the scientific experiments in agriculture, Legaré clearly thought that Hopeton's most striking feature related to the way Couper handled plantation management. Highly competent overseers, who had extensive knowledge and long experience in supervising workers on rice, cotton, and sugar plantations, were in charge of his five hundred slaves. Couper also personally chose the drivers, selecting them on the grounds of their competence in directing work activities. At the same time, in his relation-

---

39. See Steffen, "In Search of the Good Overseer," 788–900.

40. See James E. Bagwell, *Rice Gold: James Hamilton Couper and Plantation Life on the Georgia Coast* (New York, 2000), 103–140; and James D. Clifton, "Hopeton, Model Plantation of the Antebellum South," *GHQ* 56 (1982): 331–337.

41. John D. Legaré, "Account of an Agricultural Excursion made into the South of Georgia in the Winter of 1832; by the Editor," *SA* 6 (1833): 359. See also Rosengarten, "*Southern Agriculturalist,*" 292–293.

ship with the slaves, Couper followed the paternalistic model of contractual reciprocity and took it to an unprecedented level. According to James D. Clifton, at Hopeton, the task system left slaves with "considerable leisure time in the afternoon to work in their gardens, look after their poultry and livestock, go hunting or fishing." Couper even allowed slaves to sell their products and have several holidays. Although the whip was still the symbol and the instrument of discipline—and not surprisingly, given the fact that Couper's was, effectively, a mixed patriarchal-paternalistic system—Legaré was under the impression that Couper made an exceptional effort in looking after his slaves, especially in regard to food, clothing, and shelter. Perhaps, the most striking proof of this was the presence of a hospital, where, according to Kenneth Stampp, "ailing slaves received the best medical attention that the South could provide."[42]

Unsurprisingly, in his enthusiastic report of the visit to Hopeton—which he published in the 1833 issue of *The Southern Agriculturalist*—Legaré wrote that "we hesitate not to say that '*Hopeton*' is decidedly the best regulated plantation we ever visited, and we doubt whether it can be equaled (certainly not surpassed) in the Southern States." He was so impressed that he thought that, in order to appreciate the importance of Hopeton, one needed to consider agricultural enterprises on a national scale. To this end, he wrote that "when we consider the extent of the operations, the variety of crops cultivated, and the number of operatives who have to be directed and managed, so that their work may be productive, it will not be presumptuous to say that it [Hopeton] may fairly challenge in comparison with any establishment in the United States."[43]

James Hamilton Couper's model plantation at Hopeton, with its productive efficiency, scientific agricultural techniques, crop rotation, competent management, and a master-slave relationship based primarily—though far from exclusively—on contractual reciprocity, served as inspiration and represented a sort of ideal for other planters. Legaré's description of Hopeton in *The Southern Agriculturalist* contributed a great deal to spreading the knowledge of Couper's achievement across South Carolina and among both rice and cotton planters. With its examples of profitable and rationally organized enterprises such as Hopeton, *The Southern Agriculturalist* functioned as an

42. Clifton, "Hopeton," 443; Kenneth M. Stampp, *The Peculiar Institution: Slavery in the Ante-Bellum South* (New York, 1956), 313.

43. Legaré, "Agricultural Excursion," 359 (italics in the original text).

important forum for the elite's debate on agriculture and slave management. In Legarè's articles, planters found useful advice on the best ways to make their own estates profitable enterprises. At the same time, South Carolina's planter elite found a common ground in the issues that the South Carolina Agricultural Society and its journal addressed. In time, the elite's common experience of participation in debates, experiments, and projects on agricultural reform provided an important background to the formation of a regional class consciousness in political terms.

In comparable terms to what happened in South Carolina—where the lowcountry rice aristocracy adopted elements of the paternalistic ethos—in Sicily several liberal noblemen and ennobled bourgeois adopted entrepreneurial attitudes and strove to achieve high profits through the cultivation of high-value cash crops. Also, they tended to directly manage their landed estates and to be aware of the necessity of relations of reciprocity with the workforce, even though they often continued to exploit the peasantry through usurious contracts. The liberal aristocracy's and ennobled bourgeoisie's adoption of capitalist attitudes influenced different fields of activity beyond the level of agricultural management. In fact, those liberal noblemen and ennobled bourgeois who implemented scientific agriculture and engaged in relations of reciprocity with the workforce on their landed estates were also at the forefront of movements that supported moderate economic and social progress and the improvement of the living conditions of the lower classes through paternalistic reforms. Typically, they were advocates of liberal economic policies—policies that featured prominently in pamphlets and articles written by progressive intellectuals—and of programs of political liberalism, the ideological driving force behind the adoption of the Constitution of 1812.[44]

A prominent bourgeois entrepreneur whose example had a profound influence over the progressive ideology of liberal noblemen and ennobled bourgeois alike was Vincenzo Florio. A man with a broad view of business, Florio emerged in the 1830s and 1840s as the most successful entrepreneur in Sicily. He was involved in commercial activities as diverse as cotton manufacturing, the tuna processing industry, the creation of several shipping companies, banking experiments, and the foundation of the Oretea iron works in Palermo. His most important business was the production of wine

44. See Michele Grillo, "L'economia politica nella Sicilia borbonica," in Iachello, ed., *I Borbone*, 54–61.

in Marsala, where in 1832 he founded a large establishment that by 1854 had grown to include more than one hundred workers. In the 1850s, many members of the elite regarded Florio's Marsala factory as a model of paternalistic management. Not only did Florio's workers live in better conditions than did workers at other factories, but also a fourth of them knew how to read and write, at a time in which the lower classes were mostly illiterate.[45]

One of the most striking examples of a nobleman who embraced the type of liberal ideology—with its fundamental tenets of economic reform and paternalistic reciprocity—that characterized the activities of entrepreneurs such as Vincenzo Florio is Pietro Lanza. A descendant of the aristocratic princes of Trabia, in 1832 Pietro Lanza married Eleonora Spinelli and became also prince of Scordìa, in Calabria. In addition to owning a number of large *latifondi*, the Trabias also showed a renowned interest in commercial agriculture and economic development. They were among the leading citrus producers in the *Conca d'oro* region, around Palermo, where they owned numerous landed estates on which they grew lemon trees. They were also involved in manufacturing and collaborated in several business activities with ennobled landed bourgeois, such as Niccolò Turrisi Colonna, Giovanni Chiaromonte Bordonaro, and Giuseppe Riso.[46]

Continuing the family tradition, Pietro Lanza became a leading liberal economist and intellectual and wrote several important treatises. In particular, in a treatise that he published in 1842—*Dello spirito di associazione in Inghilterra* (On the Spirit of Association in England)—he praised the entrepreneurial spirit of liberal England and exhorted the Sicilian elite to follow the English example. Lanza also actively participated in the debate over the Bourbon kingdom's adoption of liberal policies, versus protectionist ones, and wrote articles in support of the former for prestigious economic reviews such as Ferdinando Malvica's *Effemeridi*. As for his policy toward social progress, at heart Pietro Lanza was a patriarchal aristocrat with marked

45. On Florio, see Sergio Candela, *I Florio* (Palermo, 1986), 92–94; Alfio Signorelli, "Tra negozianti inglesi e traffici locali. I Florio e l'imprenditoria siciliana dell'Ottocento," and Rosario Lentini, "Una nuova cultura del vino," both in Federico Pillitteri, ed., *L'economia dei Florio. Una famiglia di imprenditori borghesi dell'800* (Palermo, 1990), 41–56, 71–86; and M. D'Angelo, "Vincenzo Florio, mercante-imprenditore," in Angelo Massafra, ed., *Il Mezzogiorno preunitario. Economia, società e istituzioni* (Bari, 1988), 257–269.

46. On the Trabias, see Salvatore Lupo, "Agricoltura ricca nel sottosviluppo. Storia e mito della Sicilia agrumaria (1860–1950)," *ASSO* 79 (1983): 43–44; and Cancila, *Storia dell'industria in Sicilia*, 74–75.

paternalistic attitudes, and his ideas represented at best a combination of elements of the two worldviews. He was willing to implement reforms for the benefit of the people, whom he felt obliged to care for, but only insofar as the reforms did not challenge the existing social order.[47]

In one of his most important works—*Sulla istruzione del popolo* (On the Education of the People), which he published in the *Effemeridi* in 1834—Lanza claimed that "primary, elementary, or popular instruction . . . should not have any other aim than refining the lowest class of society, [and] taming its habits . . . all the administrative and ecclesiastical authorities should watch over it." Lanza also wrote that the state had the obligation to fulfill "the main need" of the poor, "which is the one of becoming a man for the society." Therefore, Lanza supported educational reforms that favored the poor, but he also intended them as a vehicle to mold the character and the habits of the lower classes in such a way that they would no longer be a threat for the society in which they lived. In other words, Lanza thought that, in return for the attainment of peaceful social relations, the liberal aristocracy had the obligation to respect the relationship of reciprocity that bound the elite to the masses and to provide for their education. As a result, in his treatise on education, Lanza combined clear patriarchalistic principles, according to which social roles were fixed and immutable, with the paternalistic idea that the elite's duty was to help the poor and the indigent—those who could not be expected to take care of themselves, and yet were expected to be deferential toward higher authorities.[48]

Following the example set by prestigious liberal noblemen such as Pietro Lanza, several members of the liberal aristocracy and ennobled bourgeoisie gathered in the progressive circle of the *Istituto Agrario*—a Sicilian institution akin to the South Carolina Agricultural Society—which Carlo Cottone, prince of Castelnuovo, had devised in 1819. Aside from his public activity as the political leader of the liberal section of the aristocracy and the main advocate of the Constitution of 1812, Cottone also owned a large villa and the nucleus of an agricultural enterprise in Palermo's environs. After his death, in 1829, renowned liberal noblemen Ruggero Settimo, of the House of Fitalia, made a fundamental contribution in establishing the *Istituto Agrario* in Cottone's former villa. Together with the new director of the institute, Mario Inzenga, Settimo expanded Cottone's original orange grove, creating

47. See Romeo, *Il Risorgimento in Sicilia,* 271–273.
48. Pietro Lanza di Scordia, "Sulla istruzione del popolo," *ESLS* 2 (1834): 389.

a garden that included examples of all the most important Sicilian trees and leaving ample room for cash crops, such as olives and wine grapes.[49]

In 1847, the *Istituto Agrario* commenced its official activities. Its mission was to spread the knowledge of scientific agriculture and innovative techniques of cultivation among members of the elite and to spread agricultural education among the lower classes in a learning environment that emphasized paternalism and reciprocity. In fact, according to Salvatore Lupo, in the institute, "during the course of studies, which lasted six years, thirty children from peasant families of the surroundings learned both scientific agriculture and the love for the benefactors, who belonged to the noble House of Fitalia." Comparable to the way South Carolina's progressive planters set out to provide the state's plantations and farms with a reliable class of competent overseers and a well-trained enslaved workforce without upsetting the balance of power, Sicilian progressive noblemen set out to provide the region's *latifondi* and farms with a class of administrators and small peasant proprietors well-versed in agricultural knowledge but who did not question the existing social order. In both cases, patriarchal principles advocating the existence of fixed social roles combined with paternalistic views of obligation toward the less wealthy within the parameters of the regional vision of a process of agricultural modernization guided by the landed elite.[50]

Also comparable to the activity of the South Carolina Agricultural Society is the fact that, from 1853, the *Istituto Agrario* issued its own periodical—the prestigious *Annali di Agricoltura Siciliana*—whose editor was the institute's director and renowned agronomist Mario Inzenga. On its pages, the journal hosted reports on agricultural progress in different areas of Sicily and debates on the necessity of agricultural reform as a means to increase the productivity of the landed estates. Liberal noblemen and ennobled bourgeois alike wrote for the *Annali* and consistently stressed the same key points: the improvement of agricultural techniques, the rationalization of management, and the direct conduction of the estates. Several articles in the *Annali* showed examples of what agricultural reformers meant by direct conduction and rational management and what results the adoption of both led to. These articles profoundly influenced the Sicilian landowning elite and provided models of progressive agricultural enterprises—such as the Bonvicino and Regaliali estates—that both noble and ennobled bourgeois

49. See Cianciullo, "La nobiltà siciliana," 645–650.

50. Lupo, *Il giardino degli aranci*, 64.

landowners admired and attempted to imitate. As a result, rational management and direct conduction became the fundamental tenets of a Sicilian
regional agronomic culture that characterized both the liberal aristocracy
and the ennobled bourgeoisie. At the same time, the new agronomic culture
epitomized in practical examples of progressive agricultural enterprises was
strictly related to the liberal noblemen's and ennobled bourgeois' adoption
of paternalistic principles in the practice of workers' management.[51]

Commenting on the entrepreneurial attitudes of citrus growers in nineteenth-century Sicily, Salvatore Lupo has written that the Sicilian agronomic culture strictly related to the bourgeoisie's acquisition of former noble
land and mirrored "some of its fundamental tenets, among which the idea of
direct management of the estates as guarantee of technical progress." In the
1855 issue of the *Annali*, Inzenga translated a piece from French agronomist
L. De Lavergne on entrepreneurship in agriculture entitled *Delle agricole intrarprese* (On Agricultural Enterprises). In his preface, Inzenga argued that
De Lavergne's article fit the Sicilian case particularly well. Its main concept
was the idea that the agrarian entrepreneur was a capitalist businessman
ready to invest his capital for whatever was necessary for the improvement of
his agricultural enterprise. Aside from Inzenga's judgment, this description
applied to a number of representatives of the liberal aristocracy and of the
ennobled bourgeoisie who invested their capital in the cultivation of specific
cash crops on highly profitable agricultural enterprises, which they often
managed as resident landlords.[52]

One of the most interesting examples of Sicilian ennobled bourgeois
with progressive ideas in both land and work management is that of Lucio
Tasca, baron of Regaliali. A descendant of a family of *gabelloti*, Lucio Tasca
acquired the title of baron late in life, while his son, Lucio, became count
of Almerita in his famous marriage with Beatrice Lanza. Therefore, Tasca's
family represented particularly well the combination of old and new within
the Sicilian elite. Tasca had acquired a former feudal estate at Regaliali, in
the inner part of Sicily, where he had established a large farm for the cultivation of grain and olives and the production of wine. During the 1830s and

51. See Lupo, *Il giardino degli aranci*, 61–69. See also, on some of these issues in broader
perspective, Marta Petrusewicz, "Agromania: innovatori agrari nelle periferie dell'Ottocento,"
in Piero Bevilacqua, ed., *Storia dell'agricoltura italiana in età contemporanea*, vol. 3, *Mercati e
istituzioni* (Venice, 1991), 295–325.

52. Lupo, *Il giardino degli aranci*, 65. See also Mario Inzenga, "Prefazione a L. De Lavergne,
'Delle agricole intrarprese,'" *AAS* 3 (1855): 103–104.

1840s, Tasca transformed the estate's *latifondo*, which the former noble owner used to manage as an absentee landlord, into a model farm (*fattoria modello*) for his experiments in scientific agriculture. On a portion of his estate, Tasca employed direct management and placed agricultural implements—such as new prototypes of ploughs and particular types of hoes imported from England—which he encouraged the laborers to use for the cultivation of his land. With the help of this and other types of innovations, Tasca was able to achieve a consistently high profit in the production and sale of cash crops and became a highly regarded landed entrepreneur by both liberal noblemen and ennobled bourgeois.[53]

In a series of articles that he wrote for the 1854 issue of the *Annali di Agricoltura Siciliana*, Baron Niccolò Turrisi Colonna wrote about his visit to the Regaliali farm, shortly after Lucio Tasca's death. Similar to Lucio Tasca, Niccolò Turrisi Colonna, baron of Bonvicino, was among the most progressive members of the Sicilian ennobled bourgeoisie. A friend of both Mario Inzenga and Ruggero Settimo, Turrisi Colonna had taken over Settimo's activities in the *Istituto Agrario* after the latter had been exiled following the 1848 revolution and, since the 1850s, had been actively involved in continuing Cottone's long-term project of Sicilian agricultural modernization under the watchful eye of the island's landed elite. As Giovanna Cianciullo has noted, within the parameters of this project, Turrisi Colonna played a particularly important role, both as representative of the ennobled bourgeoisie with strong liberal views and as convinced advocate of the indispensable "connection between large landholding, capitalist enterprise, and agricultural innovation." Though he was also involved in manufacturing and owned a large paper factory at Castelbuono, Turrisi Colonna considered as his most important activity the management of his model farm at Bonvicino, where—together with his brother—he practiced crop rotation and made experiments in scientific agriculture.[54]

Being both a fellow landed entrepreneur and an agronomist, Turrisi Colonna was in excellent position to judge Lucio Tasca's work. He praised Tasca's courage and innovative spirit and wrote in his article that he managed to achieve "a better economic organization" and "a better administrative

53. See Cancila, *Storia dell'industria in Sicilia*, 118–119.

54. Cianciullo, "La nobiltà siciliana," 650. See also Cancila, *Storia dell'industria in Sicilia*, 79–81, 117–119; Niccolò Turrisi Colonna, "Sullo stato attuale dell'industria e dell'istruzione agraria in Sicilia," *AAS* 1 (1851); and Giuseppe Inzenga, "Una visita alla masseria di Bonvicino, proprietà dei fratelli Turrisi," *AAS* 1 (1853): 213–223, 303–314, and *AAS* 3 (1855): 117–149.

organization, which kept a sense of order ... among a thousand workers." In particular, according to Turrisi Colonna, Tasca managed to both rationalize and improve the production of cash crops by implementing a mixed system of direct land management and sharecropping. At the same time, in regard to his relation with the workforce, Tasca abolished the previous tenancy agreements (*colonie a terratico*), long-term leases according to which tenants paid a fixed rent for the land they cultivated. Fully embracing the paternalistic ethos, he drew exclusively sharecropping agreements (*colonie parziarie*) with his tenants. The *colonie parziarie* were short-term contracts according to which master and laborer agreed on the terms of a laborer's tenancy on particular tracts of land. The master provided the laborer with the agricultural implements, while the laborer contributed a share of the capital investment calculated on the basis of the product of the rented plot.[55]

Arguably, the *colonie parziarie* were the most advanced form of agricultural contract in Sicily and the closest equivalent to the sharecropping contracts practiced in the more advanced regions of northern and central Italy. In fact, according to Jane and Peter Schneider, "while [Sicilian] sharecroppers did not have the leverage of yeomen farmers, who owned their own land, they were not so constrained as slaves or serfs. They contributed a share of the capital investment in the holding, participated in the risks and profits, and to some extent worked on their own initiative." Therefore, Tasca's insistence on the drawing of sharecropping agreements with his workforce was in tune with his adoption of the paternalistic ethos and especially of the idea of contractual reciprocity, a concept that clearly provided an important model for the master-laborer relationship at Regaliali.[56]

Yet, Lucio Tasca's building policy at Regaliali betrayed his ideological combination of patriarchal and paternalistic elements. In his article, Turrisi Colonna wrote that Tasca believed that progress was impossible on the *latifondi* if the laborers did not have places to live and facilities in which to store the products; for this reason, Tasca invested a considerable amount of capital in the construction of dwellings and barracks. Turrisi Colonna, then, described in detail the main building on the Regaliali farm, a building that

55. Niccolò Turrisi Colonna, "La fattoria Regaliali," *AAS* 2 (1854): 169, 269–272. On agrarian contracts, see Augusto Placanica, "Il mondo agricolo meridionale: usure, caparre, contratti," in Bevilacqua, ed., *Storia dell'agricoltura*, 2:293–297.

56. Jane and Peter Schneider, *Culture and Political Economy of Western Sicily* (New York, 1976), 59. See also Sidney Sonnino, "I contadini in Sicilia," in Luigi Franchetti and Sidney Sonnino, *Inchiesta in Sicilia* (Florence, 1876), 153–180.

Tasca saw as an architectural representation of the patriarchal-paternalistic relationship between master and laborers. The ground plan—which Turrisi Colonna included in his article—showed a rectangular-shaped construction; at the center was "the master's house, which [provided] a comfortable residence to the landowner who wished to supervise the activities on his estate." Turrisi Colonna praised the rationality of the construction plan and noticed that it was "well-equipped with places suitable for the dwellings of workers and employees, for the conservation of products, and for the stables of the animals used for transportation." Tasca's adoption of the paternalistic ethos and his respect for the obligations of contractual reciprocity prompted him to provide his laborers with dwellings where they could live in return for the work that they performed on his estate. However, faithful to the patriarchal concept of fixed and clearly distinct social roles, in drawing his construction plan, Tasca ensured that the master's residence was immediately recognizable as the largest section of the main building of the farm, while he also placed it at a clear distance both from and above workers' houses and animals' stables.[57]

The particular features of the ground plan of the main building on the Regaliali farm reflected Lucio Tasca's incorporation of paternalistic and entrepreneurial elements into the elite's patriarchal view of social order. The constant presence of the master—both as supervisor of his workforce and as manager of his land—was an important feature of daily life on the Regaliali farm and the living emblem of the elite's patriarchal-paternalistic worldview. At Regaliali, the master's residence was at the center of the main compound, in a particularly detached and convenient position to watch over the property and the workers' activities. The same principle informed the ground plan of a number of main compounds on other landed estates that belonged to the liberal aristocracy and the ennobled bourgeoisie. In fact, similar to Niccolò Turrisi Colonna, Ruggero Settimo, and Carlo Cottone, Lucio Tasca was one of a number of liberal noblemen and ennobled bourgeois who were at the vanguard of the movement for agricultural reform in Sicily. They all participated, in different degrees and at different times, in the realization of a broad project of regional agricultural modernization, a project in which the elite played the two complementing roles of actively promoting agricultural progress through debates in scientific journals and guiding and instructing the lower classes through agricultural education. And yet, as happened in

57. Turrisi Colonna, "La fattoria Regaliali," 171, 275.

South Carolina, in Sicily the effects of the elite's participation in these important regional activities went beyond the economic realm and effectively
provided an important background for its involvement in political activities
that focused on regionalist claims against the central government's interference in local affairs.[58]

In general, in both South Carolina and Sicily, the highest echelons of
the landed elites found a common ground by participating in the debates
on scientific agriculture and work management that filled the pages of periodicals issued by particularly prestigious regional institutions, such as the
South Carolina Agricultural Society and the Sicilian *Istituto Agrario.* The
convergence of interests over agricultural issues contributed a great deal to
the eventual working out of ideological differences within the South Carolinian planter elite and within the Sicilian liberal aristocracy into coherent
worldviews. These worldviews formed the background for the creation of
regional political movements, movements that claimed the need to enhance
the regional distinctiveness of South Carolina and Sicily through their separation from their respective central governments. In the midst of these comparable political processes, as in the midst of the processes of agricultural
modernization, both South Carolina's planter elite and Sicily's liberal aristocracy constructed powerful ideological arguments to justify the need for
their guiding role, a role that was to prove especially crucial in the difficult
transition from regional to national politics.

Regionalism and Political Change

In South Carolina and Sicily, the emphasis on regionalism that characterized
the planter elite's and the liberal aristocracy's economic and social programs
of reform provided the basis of a type of political extremism that related to
wider movements of resistance of the peripheral propertied classes against
what they perceived as the national governments' efforts to centralize the
administration and to control the development of specific peripheral issues.
However, in the United States, South Carolina's regionalist aspirations related to the slaveholders' support of the doctrine of states' rights and to their
attempts to maintain their hegemonic position in the federal government
by bending to their own advantage federal policies vis-à-vis the expansion

58. See Cianciullo, "La nobiltà siciliana," 645–654.

of slavery in the southern periphery. Conversely, in southern Italy, the advocacy of Sicilian autonomy was part of a general oppositional stance of the peripheral landowning elites to the Bourbon monarchy's repeated efforts to enforce programs of administrative centralization in the provincial areas of the Kingdom of the Two Sicilies.

In both cases, the needs of a national policy of modernization—a policy that ultimately increased pressure on regional ruling classes and provoked changes in the distribution of power between core and periphery—accelerated South Carolina's and Sicily's move toward secessionist and separatist politics as protective measures against either perceived or real government interferences in local affairs. In both South Carolina and Sicily, as in the broader contexts of the American South and of the continental *Mezzogiorno,* a sequence of crises—nullification and the Revolution of 1820, the Crisis of 1850 and the Revolution of 1848, and finally secession/separation in 1860—defined the relationship between peripheral elites and core governmental administration. Through these crises, South Carolina's planter class and Sicily's nobility/ennobled bourgeoisie tested the strength of their political programs of regional independence against alternative visions of loyalty to the central governments and eventually opted to merge their regional projects with wider projects of nationalism that included the upper classes of the entire American South and Italian *Mezzogiorno.*[59]

In the United States, the nullification crisis highlighted the substantial difference between South Carolina's ruling class and the elites of other southern regions in regard to the possibility of the federal government's interference in southern peripheral matters. In the early 1830s, Andrew Jackson's support for the Tariff of 1828—the so-called Tariff of Abominations—provoked a major institutional crisis at whose center was the Palmetto State. South Carolinian planters assumed the vanguard position in the movement to protect the rights of the southern states against what they interpreted as the latest provision of a tariff policy devised at the exclusive advantage of northern manufactures and with little regard for southern agriculture. Significantly, no other southern state supported South Carolina during the nullification crisis, in part because, beyond the specific episode of the tariff, southern politicians actually enjoyed a virtually unchallenged hegemony in govern-

59. See James McPherson, *Drawn with the Sword: Reflections on the American Civil War* (New York, 1996), 37–54; and Renda, *Storia della Sicilia,* 19–62.

mental institutions. And yet, South Carolina's isolated and extreme regionalist stance gave origin to a situation by which, for the first time, the defense
of southern states' rights came close to provoking an armed confrontation
with the federal government.[60]

In 1829, South Carolinian politician John C. Calhoun published anony-
mously his *South Carolina Exposition and Protest,* in which he argued that
tariffs such as the 1828 one were "unconstitutional, unequal, and oppressive,"
since, according to the Constitution, Congress could tax citizens only to
raise revenues. Calhoun's theory justified South Carolina's veto of the Tariff
of 1828, claiming that the individual states retained their sovereignty and
allowed the federal government to exercise only the particular powers enu-
merated in the Constitution. A tyrannical northern majority had imposed
the tariff over the southern minority, allowing the federal government to
trespass its powers; therefore, individual states had the right to veto, or nul-
lify, a federal law that was unconstitutional. Supporters of the veto called
several state conventions in order to debate the possibility of nullifying the
tariff. Finally, in March 1833, South Carolina issued the Nullification Proclamation. By then, Jackson had denounced nullification as treason and stood
ready to send federal troops into Charleston. However, later that month,
Congress passed a compromise tariff, according to which by 1842 rates would
progressively drop to the level of 1816.[61]

Several historians have elaborated upon the reasons for South Carolina's
peculiar behavior during the nullification crisis. In general, they have seen
South Carolinian extremists as the first advocates of southern nationalism,
mostly because of their commitment to the twin issues of preservation of
slavery and southern states' rights. The short-term causes of South Carolinian extremism lay in the state's deep economic depression following the crisis
of 1819. Throughout the 1820s, the prices for staple crops were low; between
1818 and 1831 cotton prices fell from thirty-one cents a pound to eight cents
a pound. The depression hit cotton planters in the upcountry especially hard,

60. See Freehling, *Road to Disunion,* 253–288; Richard E. Ellis, *The Union at Risk: Jacksonian
Democracy, States' Rights, and the Nullification Crisis* (New York, 1987); and Forrest McDonald,
States' Rights and the Union: Imperium in Imperio, 1776–1876 (Lawrence, Kans., 2000), 97–120.

61. John C. Calhoun's quotation is in McDonald, *States' Rights,* 104. See also [John C. Cal-
houn], *Exposition and Protest, Repeated by the Special Committee of the House of Representatives on
the Tariff* (Columbia, S.C., 1829); Freehling, *Prelude to Civil War,* 260–300; Sinha, *Counterrevolution of Slavery,* 33–62; Ford, *Southern Radicalism,* 115–144; and Young, *Domesticating Slavery,*
197–229.

but rice planters faced hard times as well. Thousands left for the states of the Old Southwest, where they hoped to find new land to start afresh. The Tariff of 1828 dealt the final blow to South Carolina's faltering economy. To several members of the state's elite, it seemed as if the federal government not only abused its power but also increased pressure on impoverished cotton and rice planters.[62]

In 1832, the South Carolina legislature elected as governor Senator Robert Hayne, an intellectual and staunch supporter of southern states' rights whom Charleston poet William Grayson defined as a gentleman who "united integrity, frankness, cordial manners, and ardent zeal for the honor and safety of his native state." In his inaugural speech, Hayne captured the spirit of the struggle that free white South Carolinians conducted against the federal government's interference in regional matters. He called it the "great struggle in which we are engaged for the *preservation of our rights and liberties,*" a struggle related to the recognition of the "SOVEREIGN AUTHORITY OF THE STATE" and "HER SOVEREIGN WILL." In linking opposition to the tariff to the preservation of rights and liberties, Hayne implied that the nullification crisis was a struggle that the freeborn population of South Carolina conducted under the leadership of its planter class in order to preserve its privileges over the slaves. At the same time, Hayne linked the struggle for the preservation of these privileges to the recognition of state sovereignty and, in the process, provided South Carolina's extreme regionalism with the state government's official support.[63]

In the *Exposition and Protest* and in later writings, John C. Calhoun elaborated a coherent theory of explanation of South Carolina's extreme regionalism and of the planter elite's support of it. He argued that the southern minority should protect itself from the unconstitutional acts of a majority "which could pervert its powers to oppress and plunder" it. This argument

62. See McCardell, *Southern Nation,* 27–37; Sinha, *Counterrevolution of Slavery,* 36–38; Freehling, *Road to Disunion,* 213–228; and Greenberg, *Masters and Statesmen,* 65–84. On the economic crisis of the 1820s and planter emigration, see John G. Van Deusen, *Economic Bases of Disunion in South Carolina* (New York, 1928); Smith, *Economic Readjustment,* 47–53; Freehling, *Prelude to Civil War,* 25–48.

63. William J. Grayson's quotation is in Robert J. Calhoun, ed., *Witness to Sorrow: The Antebellum Diary of William J. Grayson* (Columbia. S.C., 1990), 117; "Governor Robert Y. Hayne's Inaugural Address, *Columbia Telescope Extra,* December 13, 1832," in David Brion Davis and Sidney Mintz, eds., *The Boisterous Sea of Liberty: A Documentary History of America from Discovery to the Civil War* (New York, 1999), 371 (capital letters and italics in the original text).

had a particular appeal for South Carolinian planters, who saw the federal government's fiscal measures as a real threat to the preservation of their regional slaveholding power. In later writings, Calhoun also justified the elite's rule over the masses, drawing from the tradition of eighteenth-century republicanism, and linked this justification to the regionalist struggle of a South Carolinian minority against the northern majority rule in Congress.[64]

In his last essay—*Disquisition on Government,* which was released post-humously—Calhoun argued that demagogic spoilsmen would use majority rule to practice political patronage, if "the poor and ignorant" did not rely on their "leaders and protectors" to make decisions for them against "the wealthy and ambitious." As William Freehling has noted, this theory linked the concept of restricted political representation to the justification of the elite's paternalistic control of the superior over the inferior. At the practical level, it justified the necessity of property qualifications to gain access to the state legislature. Doubtless, in justifying minority rule in the context of a complex theoretical argument of political science, Calhoun—a cotton planter from South Carolina's upcountry—had in mind the example of the unique features of his native state, where a minority of planters ruled over the majority of the population and regarded themselves as the legitimate elite of an aristocratic nation.[65]

To be sure, even though Calhoun's writings provided a theoretical basis for the doctrine of nullification and for the elite's support of extreme regionalism, it was the opposition to the 1828 tariff that unified South Carolina's planter elite around a common issue of concern. Some of the most outspoken nullifiers were planters whose fortunes in cotton production had been in-

---

64. John C. Calhoun to Virgil Maxcy, 6 August 1831, quoted in Freehling, *Prelude to Civil War,* 155. See also Freehling, *Road to Disunion,* 213–227; David Scribner, "A Study of the Antecedents, Argument, and Significance of John C. Calhoun's *Exposition*" (Ph.D. diss., University of Houston, 1957); Pauline Maier, "The Road Not Taken: Nullification, John C. Calhoun, and the Revolutionary Tradition in South Carolina," *SCHM* 82 (1981): 1–19; and Irving Bartlett, *John C. Calhoun: A Biography* (New York, 1988), 139–151.

65. See Richard K. Crallè, ed., *The Works of John C. Calhoun: A Disquisition on Government and a Discourse on the Constitution and Government of the United States* (Charleston, S.C., 1851); and William W. Freehling, *The Reintegration of American History: Slavery and the Civil War* (New York, 1994), 85–95. See also J. William Harris, "Last of the Classical Republicans: An Interpretation of John C. Calhoun," *CWH* 30 (1984): 255–267; and Lacy K. Ford, "Republican Ideology in a Slave Society: The Political Economy of John C. Calhoun," *JSH* 54 (1988): 405–424; Ford, *Southern Radicalism,* 120–145.

strumental in their recent cooptation in the ranks of the ruling class. According to James Brewer Stewart, leading nullifiers and "upcountry men with names like McDuffie, Hammond, Hampton, Miller forged alliances by marrying into tidewater [or lowcountry] fortunes." In taking the reins of the political movement for the defense of South Carolina's minority rights in the federal government, nullifiers achieved the vanguard position in the realization of a regionalist project that ultimately sought to ensure the hegemony of the planter elite over the population of an independent southern state. The nullification crisis effectively provided the occasion for the rise to prominence of a generation of articulate planters and intellectuals who belonged to different sections of South Carolina's ruling class. Aside from John C. Calhoun and Robert Hayne, personalities who emerged during nullification included Thomas Cooper, Langdon Cheves, A. P. Butler, and Francis Pickens, among others. All were convinced that South Carolina and the American South were separate cultural and social entities from the rest of the United States and all sought an acknowledgment of this difference in political terms.[66]

An incident reported by English traveler George Featherstonhaugh reveals a great deal about the general attitude of South Carolina's planter elite at the time of the nullification crisis. In 1835, Thomas Cooper, president of the South Carolina College, invited Featherstonhaugh to dinner, together with several professors and gentlemen from the area around Columbia. At the dinner, the Englishman heard one of the guests say the following words: "if you ask *me* if I am an American, my answer is *No, Sir*, I am a *South Carolinian*." The individual who pronounced this phrase was an upcountry gentleman, most likely a wealthy planter and, at one point, a convinced nullifier. The wording of his phrase suggests that South Carolinian planters regarded the nullification crisis as the first opportunity to express freely the strong regionalist feelings that they held about their state of birth.[67]

In this respect, equally interesting is a 1832 piece written by Henry Laurens Pinckney, a renowned planter and editor of the *Charleston Mercury*—a paper with the fame of being an extreme supporter of southern states' rights

66. James B. Stewart, "A Great Talking and Eating Machine: Patriarchy, Mobilization and the Dynamics of Nullification in South Carolina," *CWH* 27 (1981): 201. See also Osterweis, *Romanticism and Nationalism in the Old South* (New Haven, Conn., 1949), 137–139; and McCardell, *Southern Nation*, 57–64.

67. George Featherstonhaugh, *Excursion through the Slave States* (London, 1838), 341.

—at the start of the nullification crisis. Writing as if he spoke on behalf of South Carolina's planter class, Pinckney acknowledged the vital contribution of the people of the state in supporting the nullification struggle, a struggle in which they showed "that they only love and support liberty, but will support and uphold whatever constitutional measure may be adopted by the state to preserve it for themselves and transmit it to their children." Pinckney, then, continued with a call to prize loyalty to South Carolina and to "the inestimable birthrights as a citizen" of the state above all else and even prophesied that "if the people of South Carolina were thoroughly united, the American system would soon crumble into atoms."[68]

Doubtless, the opposition to the tariff during the nullification crisis succeeded in unifying large portions of South Carolina's population, and especially the planter elite, in the extreme defense of southern states' rights and against a perceived governmental interference in local affairs. However, the course of the crisis also proved that the advocates of South Carolinian regionalism needed the support of the majority of the free citizens of the state in order to achieve the aim of seceding from the Union. Notwithstanding Pinckney's rhetoric during the crisis, not all South Carolinians responded positively to the call to be loyal to their state of birth. Several pockets of support for the federal government remained in different areas of the state where unionists were strong and seriously threatened to compromise the outcome of the nullification struggle. Especially in the mountain regions, where slaveholding was less widespread, unionists were the majority. By the time Jackson was ready to march on Charleston, in January 1833, the prospect was as much that of a civil war between South Carolinians as one between Americans.[69]

After the issue of the 1833 compromise tariff, nullifiers politically persecuted unionists and in several instances forced them out of South Carolina. The struggle between the two groups divided the elite and the people of the state until the end of the 1830s. Yet, as Manisha Sinha has noted, "in the 1830s, the rise of the antislavery movement and emancipation in the British West Indies converted some unionist planter politicians into rabidly proslavery southern nationalists." Though unionism remained a feature of South Carolinian politics that—unsurprisingly, given the strength of south-

68. Henry Laurens Pinckney, "Editorial," *CM*, 4 January 1832.

69. See Stewart, "Great Talking and Eating Machine," 214–220; Freehling, *Prelude to Civil War*, 301–360; Ford, *Southern Radicalism*, 145–182; and Sinha, *Counterrevolution of Slavery*, 51–53.

ern interests in the Union—characterized some prestigious members of the elite, such as James Louis Petigru, its influence gradually waned as the state's planter class confronted the need to present a united slaveholding front against the mounting national and international pressure to abolish slavery, especially after the foundation of the American Antislavery Society in December 1833 and the subsequent increase in abolitionist activities. Besides providing the pretext for the elaboration of complex proslavery arguments by South Carolina's foremost intellectuals, the emergence of an aggressive abolitionist movement, which advocated an immediate end to slavery, provoked an outburst in the state's support for regionalist and secessionist politics—a factor on which the most ardently regionalist members of the planter class were ready to capitalize.[70]

As the nullification crisis had done with the United States, the Revolution of 1820 shook the foundations of the Kingdom of the Two Sicilies. Sicily played a major role in the institutional crisis that involved the entire apparatus of the Bourbon administrative monarchy in both Naples and the peripheries. The roots of the revolution in Sicily are complex and still the object of debate. Until recently, the historiography described the event as an exclusively separatist movement from the Neapolitan government, a movement that lay the foundation for the future Sicilian separatist experiences of 1848 and 1860. Yet, recent studies have demonstrated a substantial similarity between the Restoration period in Sicily and in the continental *Mezzogiorno* and have advanced a more complex interpretation of the Revolution of 1820, one in which the internal divisions within the landed elite—divisions comparable to the one between nullifiers and unionists in South Carolina—seem to have played a crucial role. In general terms, the Revolution of 1820 originated in the contradiction of Bourbon administrative reforms and the elite's response to them. Yet, in Sicily's case, the failure of the revolution—rather than its occurrence—had particularly momentous consequences on the development of the island's future separatist politics.[71]

70. Sinha, *Counterrevolution of Slavery,* 59. See also Young, *Domesticating Slavery,* 218–224; and William H. and Jane H. Pease, *James Louis Petigru: Southern Conservative, Southern Dissenter* (Athens, Ga., 1995).

71. See Antonino De Francesco, "Premessa," *RISN* 28 (1991): 11–20; Giovanni Cingari, "Gli ultimi Borboni," in Rosario Romeo, ed., *Storia della Sicilia,* vol. 8 (Naples, 1977), 11–17; and Nino Cortese, *La prima rivoluzione separatista siciliana (1820–1821)* (Naples, 1951).

As in other peripheries of the *Mezzogiorno,* in Sicily the Bourbon reforms of 1815–1820, which related to the creation of the "administrative
monarchy," provoked mixed reactions from different groups of the landed
elite. The Bourbon experiment of creating the structures of local government
within the parameters of a heavily centralized bureaucracy showed the possibilities and limits of the Neapolitan road to modernization. In 1816, with the
creation of the Kingdom of the Two Sicilies and the forced union of Sicily
to Naples, the island's administrative autonomy ceased to exist. Then, in 1817,
the restored Bourbon monarchy abolished the Constitution of 1812, and yet
it confirmed its provisions in regard to the abolition of feudalism.[72]

With the reforms, Sicily was also divided into seven new administrative
regions, in whose capitals the Bourbon intendants resided. As a consequence,
Palermo, the former residence of Sicilian viceroys and briefly the seat of an
autonomous Sicilian government, fell to the status of provincial capital—a
fact that had traumatizing effects on western Sicily's landed aristocracy. For
most of the Sicilian landed elite, however, the primary source of disappointment with the Bourbon administration related to the policy of protectionism that heavily favored Neapolitan products and industries over Sicilian
ones. Michele Palmieri di Miccichè—a liberal nobleman who was forced
into exile in France after the failure of the Revolution of 1820—remembered
in his memoirs how Bourbon restoration brought to Sicily "the end of trade,
which became an almost exclusively Neapolitan monopoly, [while] the heavy
provisions implemented by Neapolitan minister De' Medici to this end . . .
provoked a fall . . . in the prices of land and crops," and the consequent
"complete ruin of our proprietors."[73]

Yet, notwithstanding the opposition to protectionism, the Bourbon
monarchy's effort to involve the Sicilian upper class in its project of modernization of the island through bureaucratic centralization had far-reaching
consequences. As in the continental *Mezzogiorno,* in Sicily the intendant
connected the central government with the provincial government and the
municipal councils. He also chose the members of the local administration
through the *liste degli eleggibili.* These were all members of the proprietary

72. See Enrico Iachello, "Appunti sull'amministrazione locale in Sicilia tra la Costituzione
del 1812 e la riforma amministrativa del 1817," *RISN* 28 (1991): 125–165; and Giarrizzo, "La Sicilia
dal Cinquecento," 668–675.

73. Michele Palmieri di Miccichè, *Pensées et souvenirs historique et contemporaines* (Paris, 1830),
252–253. See also Rosario Romeo, *Mezzogiorno e Sicilia nel Risorgimento* (Naples, 1968), 51–114.

class and effectively formed the local Bourbon bureaucracy of the island. By coopting the Sicilian landed elite, and especially the aristocracy, which filled all the most prestigious offices in the administration, the Bourbon monarchy attempted to transform its members—in the words of Enrico Iachello—"into bureaucrats, in the hope of taking away all their political connotations, while calling them to manage local politics."[74]

Arguably, regardless of their aim, the Bourbon reforms succeeded in redefining the relationship between the peripheral power and the central government as a struggle between the local ruling classes and the state for the control of the bureaucratic apparatus and its provincial and municipal organs. Yet, given their contradictory aims, the reforms stirred a great deal of opposition, especially among the landed aristocracy based in Palermo, which was traditionally opposed to the central government's interference in local affairs. At the same time, the Bourbon reforms won to the government's cause those sections of the Sicilian landed elite—especially the bourgeoisie of the other cities of the island—that were previously underrepresented in governmental institutions.[75]

The Bourbon reforms also contributed in driving a deeper wedge between nobility and bourgeoisie at the local level. In several *comuni,* the two classes, deeply divided into factions and occasionally joining different political sides, fought for control of the new instruments of local government and of the common land, whose enclosure had been decreed in 1817. In political terms, in Sicily, as in the continental *Mezzogiorno,* the landed elite divided between "moderates"—who advocated political conservatism and were mostly, but not exclusively, liberal noblemen—and "democrats"—who belonged to radical organizations and secret societies, such as the *Carboneria,* and who were mostly bourgeois landowners, professionals, and artisans. Yet, while Sicilian moderates agitated for separatism, deeming the Bourbon government's policy of modernization through bureaucratic centralization to be irreconcilable with Sicilian self-government, Sicilian democrats agitated for the expansion of constitutional liberties and the establishment of a balance of power between core and periphery, similar to the Neapolitan *carbonari*

74. Iachello, "La trasformazione degli apparati," 108–109. See also Iachello, "Borbone e stato," 47–51; and Iachello, *Il vino e il mare,* 145–182.

75. See De Francesco, "Cultura costituzionale," 128–130; and Giuseppe Giarrizzo, "Borghesia e provincia nel Mezzogiorno durante la Restaurazione," in A.A.V.V., *L'Età della Restaurazione* (Bari, 1983), 21–33.

in the continental *Mezzogiorno*. This deep division manifested fully in the Revolution of 1820.[76]

In July 1820, after revolution in Naples led to the formation of a constitutional government, the western Sicilian aristocracy advocated separation from the Bourbon kingdom and a return to the Constitution of 1812. The aristocracy succeeded in taking control of the revolutionary movement after a popular insurrection caused by both economic depression and a tax increase and headed by Palermo's artisans' and workers' associations (*maestranze*) overtook Sicily's largest city and the countryside around it. To the aristocratic program of separatism—which appeared as little more than a narrow defense of noble privileges against bureaucratic centralization—the *carbonari* opposed an unconditional support for the Neapolitan constitutional government. As a number of recent studies have demonstrated, similar to what happened in the continental *Mezzogiorno*, in Sicily—especially in the cities of the eastern part of the island—the enlargement of the electoral basis practiced during the nine months of constitutional government led to a renewed and equal representation of the peripheral elites in the national assembly. As Antonino De Francesco has pointed out, the result was, effectively, the acceleration of the process of advancement of Sicily's provincial landed bourgeoisie—a process that had started under the Bourbons—and the completion of the cycle of administrative and constitutional reformism that had begun in 1817, with the extension of the French bureaucratic system to the island.[77]

The contrast between aristocratic separatism and bourgeois support for the Neapolitan constitutional government was also a conflict between the two parts of Sicily: the one dominated by *latifondi* and gravitating around Palermo and the one of the cities, especially those located on the eastern coast. As the revolution continued, the conflict became an internal civil war between moderate and democratic Sicilians and noble and bourgeois groups and factions. The war raged as much over different views on the

76. See Lucy Riall, "Elites in Search of Authority: Political Power and Social Order in Nineteenth-Century Sicily," *HWJ* 55 (2003): 25–46; De Francesco, "La Sicilia negli anni rivoluzionari," 32–47; and Giarrizzo, "La Sicilia dal Cinquecento," 667–683.

77. See De Francesco, "La Sicilia negli anni rivoluzionari," 43–45, Antonino De Francesco, "Anni inglesi, anni francesi, mesi spagnoli. Classi dirigenti e lotta politica a Catania dall'antico regime alla rivoluzione; 1812–1821," *RISN* 28 (1991): 167–223; G. Rota, "Società politica e rivoluzione nel Mezzogiorno: la carboneria palermitana, 1820–1822," *ASSO* 88 (1992): 195–214; and Francesco Renda, *Risorgimento e classi popolari in Sicilia (1820–1821)* (Milan, 1968).

relationship with Naples as over control of local government. Caught in the middle, peasants—often organized in guerrilla cells (*squadre*) headed by radical democratic leaders—gave vent to their rage against landowners, often devastating enclosed common land.[78]

To be sure, from the outset, peasant violence was one of two main problems—together with the Sicilian cities' opposition to the separatist program—that the Sicilian revolutionaries headed by the prince of Villafranca and based in Palermo had to face. To address the issue of peasant unrest, the Sicilian revolutionary government created a special "security guard" with the specific purposes of controlling the masses, restoring law and order, and defending private property. More difficult was the defeat of the centers of Neapolitan loyalty. To this end, the revolutionary government deployed forty-five hundred troops against the eastern cities of Messina, Caltanissetta, Catania, and Siracusa—a move that cost many lives and was instrumental in causing the end of the revolution. In fact, weakened by war and internal dissent, the Sicilian revolutionary government fell a few months later, when Palermo surrendered to Neapolitan general Florestano Pepe in October 1820.[79]

In 1821, after the failure of the revolution in both Sicily and Naples, the Bourbon monarchy abolished every trace of the constitutional experiment and reverted to a policy that combined modernization from above with despotic centralization. In Sicily, this policy had the result of legitimizing the separatist program initially advanced by the aristocracy. As in the continental *Mezzogiorno,* in Sicily radicals continued their conspiratorial activities in the *Carboneria* and in other secret societies that aimed at overthrowing Bourbon absolutism in favor of a constitutional monarchy. Yet, by the 1830s, secret societies had proven ineffectual, while southern Italian democrats had moved toward more complex and forthright forms of political organization, partly under the influence of Giuseppe Mazzini and his followers. At the same time, Ferdinand II's despotic centralization drove an increasing number of bourgeois toward the support for the landed aristocracy's separatist program and into a sort of alliance of moderate liberal forces. Recogniz-

78. See Antonino De Francesco, *La guerra di Sicilia. Il distretto di Caltagirone nella rivoluzione del 1820–1821* (Acireale, 1992), 140–170; and Giuseppe Berti, *I democratici e l'iniziativa meridionale nel Risorgimento* (Milan, 1962), 220–222.

79. See Paolo Pezzino, "Risorgimento e guerra civile. Alcune considerazioni preliminari," in Gabriele Ranzato, ed., *Guerre Fratricide. Le guerre civili in età contemporanea* (Turin, 1994), 66–67; and Giorgio Candeloro, *Storia dell'Italia moderna,* vol. 2, *Dalla Restaurazione alla rivoluzione nazionale (1815–1847)* (Milan, 1958), 86–88.

ing the possibility of transforming the aristocratic idea of autonomy from governmental interference into the nucleus of an ideology of freedom from Bourbon despotism, many Sicilian democrats gradually abandoned the idea of supporting a constitutional Neapolitan monarchy and advocated instead the separation of Sicily from Naples.[80]

In the 1830s, the debate on the Bourbon customs' system—which allowed freedom of trade (*cabotaggio*) within the kingdom and increased the movement of goods between the continental *Mezzogiorno* and the island—also contributed in sowing the seeds of Sicilian separatism. The Sicilian elite—especially its moderate liberal section formed by large noble and bourgeois landowners—was mostly against the Bourbon protectionist policy and its exclusive focus on Naples. In 1836, Ferdinando Malvica published an important essay—*Memoria sul cabotaggio tra Napoli e Sicilia* (Essay on Trade between Naples and Sicily)—in which he argued that the new system reduced Sicily to a market for Neapolitan products. Malvica linked the island's autonomy to its economic advancement through a protectionist policy aimed at Sicilian products and to the development of commercial agriculture. In a later pamphlet, he explained, "I was the author of the *Memoria* . . . in which a political problem was disguised under an economic argument." In fact, Sicily's commercial agricultural production was mostly in the hands of the liberal aristocracy and of the landed bourgeoisie. As Malvica—himself a member of the landed elite—was well aware, by the mid-1830s both classes sought political independence from Naples in order to control the island's agrarian economy.[81]

Then, in 1837, a cholera epidemic with thousands of victims triggered a new revolt against the Bourbon regime that involved all the major Sicilian cities. Significantly, in Catania, a number of former supporters of Neapolitan constitutionalism became convinced of the disastrous consequences of Bourbon administration and began to advocate separatism in marked demo-

80. See De Francesco, "Cultura costituzionale," 130–132; Rosario Romeo, *Il Risorgimento in Sicilia* (Bari, 1950), 308–311; Berti, *I democratici*, 240–242; Franco Della Peruta, "Mazzinianesimo e democrazia nel Mezzogiorno (1831–1847)," in A.A.V.V., *Democrazia e mazzinianesimo nel Mezzogiorno d'Italia, 1831–1872* (Geneva, 1975), 17–20; and Alfonso Scirocco, "Ferdinando II e la Sicilia: gli anni della speranza e della delusione (1830–1837)," *RSR* 74 (1987): 275–298.

81. Ferdinando Malvica, *Al Parlamento di Sicilia* (Palermo, 1848), 6; Ferdinando Malvica, "Sul cabotaggio fra Napoli e Sicilia," *ESLS* 5 (1836): 7–101. See also Giovanna Fiume, *La crisi sociale del 1848 in Sicilia* (Messina, 1982), 15–37, 53–66; and Grillo, "L'economia politica," 59–61.

cratic tones. The revolt failed largely because of divisions between moderate liberals and democrats over the shape of Sicily's future independent society. Yet, clearly by the late 1830s, even within the parameters of democratic interpretation, the model of Sicilian regionalism originally advanced by the landed aristocracy emerged as a hegemonic ideology in support of feelings of separatism that were widespread among different sections of the elite. And still, subsequently, the liberal aristocracy and a part of the bourgeoisie would attempt to guide Sicily's separatism away from the democratic positions and transform it into a conservative movement focusing on respect for private property within the limits of a narrow program of economic modernization.[82]

Important common traits and differences emerge from the comparative analysis of the nullification crisis and of the Revolution of 1820 and their aftermaths. In South Carolina, the nullification crisis highlighted the deep divisions between those members of the planter elite who supported an extreme regionalism and advocated secession and those who maintained their loyalty to the federal government. Only after the crisis subsumed did nullifiers and unionists, preoccupied with offering a united slaveholding front in the face of the threat presented by the abolitionist movement, reconcile their differences, with some notable exceptions. In comparable fashion, in Sicily, the Revolution of 1820 catalyzed the landed elite's deep divisions between aristocracy and bourgeoisie and between the moderate separatist program and the democratic support for a Neapolitan constitutional monarchy. Only the failure of the revolution and the subsequent return to Bourbon absolutism prompted the conciliation between a number of moderate liberal and democratic members of the landed elite in view of the common aim of resisting the government's despotic centralization with regional separatism. Yet, one major difference between the two case studies is the fact that in South Carolina the defense of slavery provided a much more powerful unifying factor for the planter elite than the defense of private property did for the landed elite in Sicily. As a consequence, South Carolina's planter elite was far less divided internally than Sicily's landed elite—a factor that provided the former with a much better chance to move united toward outright secessionist politics, when the time was ripe.

* * *

82. See Giarrizzo, "La Sicilia dal Cinquecento," 720–730; and Antonino De Francesco, "Ideologie e movimenti politici," in Giovanni Sabbatucci and Vittorio Vidotto, eds., *Storia d'Italia*, vol. 1, *Le premesse dell'Unità* (Rome-Bari, 1994), 277–278.

In South Carolina, by 1840 the politics of compromise prevailed over divisions between unionists and nullifiers. Though pockets of unionism continued to remain, under the skilled leadership of John C. Calhoun, South Carolina's commitment to the preservation of slavery—combined with the powerful influence of southern interests in the federal government—provided a safe key to reconciliation between the different factions of the elite. Calhoun led his followers—by then the majority of the state's politicians—on a path that took them from outright opposition to Jackson to a convenient alliance with the Democratic Party against Henry Clay's Whigs. And yet, until his death in 1850, Calhoun worked to form a party that, led by South Carolinian planters, would have represented a more organic view of southern minority interests in Congress. As a result, both of South Carolina's "aristocratic politics"—i.e., the election of high state officials by the legislature—and of the continuous hegemony of Calhounite Democrats, the state remained substantially removed from the Second Party System and from the struggle between Whigs and Democrats that took place in all the other southern states at local and national elections.[83]

Then, in 1846, at the time of the Mexican War, congressional discussion over the issue of the expansion of slavery into the new territories contributed a great deal to dividing internally the Democratic Party and to convincing many members of the South Carolinian elite of the need to protect slaveholding interests independently from party politics. In particular, Calhoun was largely instrumental in forging an extreme pro-southern interpretation of the Wilmot Proviso as a clear indication of the northern-dominated Congress's wish to take steps against the economic and social power of the southern elites. In the following years, South Carolinians' increasing hostility toward northern congressmen focused over both the Wilmot Proviso and the projected annexation of California into the Union. Calhoun was at the forefront of the protest, especially after the circulation of his 1849 "Southern Address," which invited southerners to unite "in defense of rights involving your all—your property, prosperity, equality, liberty, and safety."[84]

---

83. See Ford, *Southern Radicalism*, 145–182; Greenberg, *Masters and Statesmen*, 52–61; and William J. Cooper, *The South and the Politics of Slavery, 1828–1856* (Baton Rouge, La., 1978), 269–321.

84. John C. Calhoun, "Address of the Southern Delegates in Congress," in Richard K. Crallè, ed., *The Works of John C. Calhoun*, vol. 6 (New York, 1855), 295. See also Ford, *Southern Radicalism*, 184–189; and Ernest M. Lander, *Reluctant Imperialists: Calhoun, the South Carolinians, and the Mexican War* (Baton Rouge, La., 1980).

Yet, in March 1850, unexpectedly, Calhoun died. According to George P. Germany, "in mourning for Calhoun, the people of South Carolina mourned also for themselves," none the least because "their peculiar way of life . . . was threatened by political trends in the North." Calhoun's death had a cataclysmic effect on South Carolinian politics. Although he was the supreme theorist of southern states' rights and of the doctrine of nullification of federal laws, Calhoun intended both as essential parts of American politics and society. While defending southern—and especially South Carolina's—states' rights, Calhoun struggled to preserve the democratic character of the Union intact. Against Calhoun's wishes, the planters and politicians who dominated the politics of South Carolina after his death completed the transformation of the state's peculiar regionalism into an extreme political movement and advocated secession from the United States as the only viable way to defend a social and economic way of life based on slavery.[85]

In 1850, in South Carolina and in much of the South the atmosphere was tense as a result of the congressional debates that led to the last great compromise on sectional conflicts. The majority of the ruling elite of South Carolina—together with slaveholders throughout the South—rejected the Compromise of 1850. By summer, most planters and politicians in the state were ready to secede. At the June 1850 Nashville Convention, which had been inspired by Calhoun's vision of a movement for southern unity, South Carolina's delegates played a prominent role among the ones of the eight southern states that were formally represented. South Carolinian John Barnwell Rhett drafted the Convention's "Address to the People of the Southern States," which rejected the federal government's interference in the slaveholders' property rights and advocated the protection of slavery south of the 36° 30´ parallel. Both Rhett and James Henry Hammond left the convention convinced that South Carolina would lead the South to secede in a relatively short time.[86]

Yet, in November 1850, delegates at the second Nashville Convention failed to adopt any meaningful resolution and sharp divisions ensued be-

85. Germany, "South Carolina Governing Elite," 2–3. See also Freehling, *Road to Disunion,* 517–519, Sinha, *Counterrevolution of Slavery,* 76–86; and McCardell, *Southern Nation,* 295–296.

86. See John Barnwell, *Love of Order: South Carolina's First Secession Crisis* (Chapel Hill, N.C., 1982), 103–112; Freehling, *Road to Disunion,* 481–486; Sinha, *Counterrevolution of Slavery,* 96–104; Philip M. Hamer, *The Secession Movement in South Carolina, 1847–1852* (Allentown, Pa., 1918), 292–295; and Thelma Jennings, *The Nashville Convention: Southern Movement for Unity, 1848–1851* (Memphis, Tenn., 1980), 175–197.

tween a minority of southern secessionists led by South Carolina's, Georgia's, and Mississippi's fire-eaters and a majority of southern Unionists, who felt satisfied with the adoption of the Compromise of 1850. In the same autumn, South Carolinian governor James Seabrook's plan for secession—which involved Mississippi's Governor John Quitman—fell through. Since the elites of other southern states appeared unreliable, several South Carolinian political leaders called for action with or without the help of their fellow southerners. In May 1851, 450 planters and politicians met in Charleston and announced South Carolina's intention to secede; no representatives of other southern states joined them. As at the time of the nullification crisis, South Carolinians confronted the federal government alone.[87]

During the period from 1850 to 1852, South Carolina's elite divided between those—such as James Henry Hammond—who advocated cooperate state secession and those—such as fire-eater Robert Barnwell Rhett—who advocated separate state secession. As early as 1843, Hammond argued that South Carolinians ought to defend their state "not less by power of intellect than by force of arms"; yet he thought that, in order for the defense to be successful, South Carolina's ruling class ought to cooperate with the elites of other southern states. It was thanks to the efforts of cooperationists such as Hammond that, between 1850 and 1852, Southern Rights' Associations—which advocated the formation of a unified southern political movement—sprang up in every district of South Carolina and in every southern state. A contemporary editorial in the extremist *Charleston Mercury* reported a comment from the local *South Carolinian* paper that showed the eagerness of a part of the public opinion to create a southern nation through the activity of the Southern Rights' Associations: "we believe the formation of these associations would do much to unite the people of the South." And arguably, the Southern Rights' Associations did become a major factor in the promotion of the cause of southern nationalism.[88]

87. See Barnwell, *Love of Order,* 134–135; Freehling, *Road to Disunion,* 528–533; Sinha, *Counterrevolution of Slavery,* 105–113; and Cooper, *Politics of Slavery,* 304–310.

88. James Henry Hammond, "Message to the Senate and House of Representatives of the State of South Carolina, November 28, 1843," in *Selections from the Letters and Speeches of the Hon. James Henry Hammond of South Carolina* (New York, 1866), 71; *The South Carolinian,* quoted in *CM,* 13 November 1850. See also Faust, *James Henry Hammond,* 236–241; Chauncey S. Boucher, "The Secession and Cooperation Movements in South Carolina, 1848–1852," *WSS* 5 (1918): 67–138; N. W. Stephenson, "Southern Nationalism in South Carolina in 1851," *AHR* 36 (1931): 314–35; and Barnwell, *Love of Order,* 123–131.

On the other hand, Rhett, who was the editor of the *Charleston Mercury,* wrote several articles in the paper supporting the argument for South Carolina's separate state secession. In a particularly enlightening 1850 editorial, he compared South Carolina's past "secessions"—during the American Revolution and during the nullification crisis—with the one he thought imminent. Also, in a speech that he delivered in the same year and then reprinted a year later in the *Charleston Mercury,* Rhett argued that South Carolina's secession from the United States would have been the latest historical example of the success of a smaller state in its struggle for independence against a larger state. Yet, Rhett was adamant that South Carolina should secede first only in order to lead the other states to form a southern nation. In this respect, Rhett clarified his thoughts on the future of the entire southern nation when, in the same editorial, he wrote that "wealth, honor, and power, and one of the most glorious destinies which ever crowned a great and happy people await the South, if she but control her own fate."[89]

Despite Rhett's strength of commitment to southern nationalism, the idea of comparing small European states with what South Carolina might become was very popular among a small number of extreme advocates of South Carolinian regionalism. In 1851, William Denison Porter, president of the South Carolina Senate, published a pamphlet—*Separate State Secession*—in which he gathered a series of articles that he had previously written for *The Edgefield Advertiser.* Porter compared South Carolina's small size and her successful agricultural economy with the ones of small European states, past and present. He argued that small republics were characterized by greater liberty and higher intellectual achievements. He also argued that such a future South Carolinian republic would hold a distinctive political culture, while he hoped that the Union would not set as its objective to crush its independence. Though Porter was not alone in advocating an independent South Carolinian state, only a few of his fellow countrymen held the same view. The majority wished to achieve independence as part of a southern nation.[90]

89. Robert Barnwell Rhett, "Editorial," *CM,* July 11, 1851, and "Editorial," *CM,* July 20, 1850. See also Freehling, *Road to Disunion,* 521–526; Barnwell, *Love of Order,* 131–149; McCardell, *Southern Nation,* 304–306; and Eric H. Walther, *The Fire-Eaters* (Baton Rouge, La., 1992), 138–145.

90. William Denison Porter, *Separate State Secession, Practically Discussed in a Series of Articles published originally in the Edgefield Advertiser* (Edgefield, S.C., 1851), 8–10. See also L. M. Ayer, *An Address on the Question of Separate State Secession* (Charleston, 1851); George Fitzhugh, "Small Nations," *DBR* 29 (1860): 561–569; and Roberson, "Foundations of Southern Nationalism," 529–541.

Regardless of their differences, apart from a minority of extreme advocates of South Carolinian regionalism, both cooperationists and separatists shared the basic aim of preserving social order within the state and leading a southern nationalist counterrevolution. Both groups argued that their aim was the protection of southern states' rights and slavery through the creation of a southern nation led by South Carolina. South Carolinian planters and politicians were at the forefront of the southern nationalist movement because the majority of them were willing to take extreme measures—i.e., secession—in order to preserve the region's slaveholding regime and minority political rule against what they perceived as the federal government's interference and abuse. In fact, both cooperationists and separatists supported South Carolina's regionalism as part of a wider southern nationalist project; they only differed on the best way to achieve the aims of their political program. Still, cooperationists clearly outnumbered separatists. By 1852, the former, led by James L. Orr, had formed an alliance with the Unionist Democrats in a momentary truce from secessionist politics. As in the rest of the South, in South Carolina the post-1852 period signaled a return to the normality of party politics as a result of both the hegemonic position of southern minority interests in Congress and the election of pro-southern Democratic president Franklin Pierce.[91]

Interestingly, in 1853, only three years after Calhoun's death, the editor of the literary magazine *Southern Quarterly Review*—a publication whose writers staunchly supported southern nationalism—used Calhoun's ideas to justify the defense of minority rights against the tyranny of the majority, arguing that "such is the school of politics in which Carolina is reared. An equal abhorrence of absolute monarchy, and unbridled majorities . . . she would protect the citizen's property as well as his life." However, the editor then concluded with an extremist tone which would have displeased Calhoun and with the words "she [South Carolina] loved the Union well, but, more than all things, she loves her *liberty*; the liberty to obey no human laws but those she has consented to." Despite the momentary truce in secessionist politics, South Carolina's regionalism—now fully transformed into extremist southern nationalism—was ready to explode and cause the next crisis as soon as

---

91. See Boucher, "Secession and Cooperation"; Stephenson, "Southern Nationalism," 331–339; Harold S. Schultz, *Nationalism and Sectionalism in South Carolina, 1852–1860: A Study of the Movement for Southern Independence* (Durham, N.C., 1950), 27–37; Ford, *Southern Radicalism*, 211–214; and Carpenter, *South as a Conscious Minority*, 184–189.

the conditions were ripe. In fact, the tone of the *Southern Quarterly Review* anticipated the tone of the future *Declaration of the Immediate Causes of Secession* of 1860. The "liberty to obey no human laws" referred to the preservation of the social and economic privileges related to slaveholding. The defense of those privileges was to unite the majority of the South Carolinian elite in the common aim of leading the formation of a southern slaveholding nation.[92]

Comparable to the way the Crisis of 1850 marked the mid-century in South Carolina, the Revolution of 1848 was the defining event in the relationship between the Bourbon central government and Sicily's peripheral elite. The roots of the revolution can be clearly located in the transformations of the late 1830s and early 1840s, when the Bourbon monarchy accelerated the legal processes of extension of the administrative system to Sicily and of complete dismantlement of the island's feudal institutions. The subsequent enclosure and sale of common land led to an exacerbation of conflict in many *comuni,* while the tighter administrative grip caused dissatisfaction among many members of the local elites already unhappy with the Bourbon protectionist system. While the commercial sector of Sicilian agriculture underwent a major growth with little help from the state's protectionist favoritism to Naples, the extraction of sulfur—the island's premier industrial item—suffered a major setback after Ferdinand II's protectionist policy experienced a humiliating defeat in its attempt to break the English merchants' monopoly over the product's export.[93]

   The strengthening of antiprotectionist positions occurred at a time in which different sections of the elite debated the merits and possibilities of Sicilian autonomy. On one hand, moderate liberals found their manifesto in Jesuit Luigi Tapparelli D'Azeglio's 1840–1843 essay, in which he argued that the most important feature of a Sicilian "nation" and of every nation ought to be "always [the people's] observance of law and order"—a theory that practically justified the defense of private property and the social status quo along with several other features of the aristocratic tradition of regionalism. On the other hand, under the suggestion of northern European romantic nationalism, democrats explored the roots of Sicilian autonomy by focusing

92. E. H. B., "Political Philosophy of South Carolina," *SQR* 7 (1853): 140.
93. See Giarrizzo, "La Sicilia dal Cinquecento," 734–743; John A. Davis, "Palmerston and the Sicilian Sulfur Crisis of 1840: An Episode in the Imperialism of Free Trade," *Risorgimento* 1–2 (1982): 5–24; and Vincenzo Giura, *La questione degli zolfi siciliani, 1838–1841* (Naples, 1973).

on the island's medieval history. In particular, in 1843 Michele Amari wrote a fundamental historical treatise in which he argued that the 1242 war with which Sicilians rejected French rule was a people's war and formed an important precedent for the future popular revolution which was to give birth to a Sicilian nation. Even though they had little in common in terms of content, both the moderate liberal and the democratic views moved within the confines of Sicilian regionalism and both their influences were equally important in the movement for Sicilian autonomy that played a major role in the Revolution of 1848.[94]

To be sure, the Revolution of 1848 began as a genuine popular upheaval. In January of that year, peasants in different areas of the island protested against the appalling conditions of life in the Sicilian countryside and against the Bourbon government's support for the landowners' expropriation of common land. Peasants attacked and destroyed property, occupied land, and burned the documents that legalized the enclosures, forcing the Bourbon authorities to leave. From the very beginning of the revolution, the peasant guerrilla cells (*squadre*) emerged as a determinant force in the downfall of Bourbon rule on the island. Yet, the *squadre* were also the agents of a threatening type of popular violence that both democrats and moderate liberals attempted to control throughout the revolution with little success. Ultimately, it was the democrats' failure to channel the revolutionary potential of the *squadre* into a coherent radical political program and the moderate liberals' fear of social subversion that doomed the Sicilian revolution to failure.[95]

At the same time, from the very beginning of the revolution, on both sides of the political divide, noble and bourgeois landed proprietors felt equally unsafe in the hands of a sequence of revolutionary governments that were unable to keep law and order in the countryside. Particularly illuminating on this point is a letter that Prospero Colonna, prince of Roviano, wrote to Francesco Villanueva, the administrator of his lands in Sicily, in February 1849. In the letter, he referred to the effects of the Revolution of 1848 and, significantly, talked about the "misfortunes which hit the entire class of Propri-

94. Luigi Tapparelli D'Azeglio's quotation is in Giarrizzo, "La Sicilia dal Cinquecento," 738. See also Michele Amari, *La Guerra del Vespro* (Florence, 1851); Romeo, *Il Risorgimento in Sicilia*, 395–316; De Francesco, "Ideologie," 278–280; and Giuseppe De Rosa, *I Gesuiti in Sicilia e la rivoluzione del '48* (Rome, 1963).

95. See Fiume, *La crisi sociale*, 118–129; Paolo Pezzino, "La tradizione rivoluzionaria siciliana e l'invenzione della mafia," *Meridiana* 7–8 (1989–90): 45–71; and Cingari, "Gli ultimi Borboni," 48–50.

etors in Sicily," without distinguishing between aristocracy and landed bourgeoisie. It is highly probable that, similar to other noblemen, Colonna felt
close to the many bourgeois landowners who had experienced comparable
fears and devastations of property as a result of widespread peasant violence.[96]

There is little doubt that at the start of the revolution, thanks to the
activity of the *squadre* and to the presence of a number of prestigious democrats who were personally acquainted with their leaders, the potential for
social change was particularly high. The first revolutionary government,
which began its works on 14 January 1848, was presided by renowned Sicilian
nationalist Ruggero Settimo and included both noblemen and bourgeois,
among whom were democrats Pasquale Calvi and Francesco Crispi. Perhaps the most significant moment in the early phases of the revolution was
when—on 25 January—the revolutionary government in Palermo issued a
call to form revolutionary committees in every Sicilian town. What followed
was a flourishing of the municipal localism that the Bourbon administration
had strongly repressed.[97]

The spirit of the call was in the encouragement to provide the Sicilian
comuni with democratic institutions, so as to have truly representative forms
of local government. According to Calvi, the changes were such that "in
some *comuni* . . . the old municipal authorities disappeared; in others, they
were preserved in subordinate conditions to the committees." In the following months, ensuing decrees further clarified the terms of representative institutions. Yet, despite the best intentions, in most of the cases the formation
of the new municipal governments served mostly to sanction the hegemonic
position of the bourgeoisie in local politics—a position that it had reached
through either struggle or cooptation into the landed aristocracy—rather
than to signal a time for genuine social change.[98]

Though often on opposite political sides, during the Revolution of 1848
the aristocracy and the landed bourgeoisie developed a functional alliance on

96. Prospero Colonna to Francesco Villanueva, Pisa, 12 February 1849, Riario Sforza Family
Papers, ASN. See also Romeo, *Il Risorgimento in Sicilia*, 317–320.

97. See Giarrizzo, "La Sicilia dal Cinquecento," 749–754; Christopher Duggan, *Francesco
Crispi, 1819–1901: Nation and Nationalism* (Oxford, 2002), 56–75; and Giovanni Candeloro, *Storia
dell'Italia Moderna*, vol. 3, *La rivoluzione nazionale (1847–1849)* (Milan, 1970), 118–124.

98. Pasquale Calvi, *Memorie storiche e critiche della rivoluzione siciliana del 1848*, vol. 1 (London, 1851), 159. See also Giuseppe La Farina, *Storia della rivoluzione siciliana* (Capolago, 1851);
and Giovanni La Masa, *Documenti sulla rivoluzione siciliana del 1848–1849 in rapporto all'Italia*
(Turin, 1850).

the common terrain of defense of private property from peasant violence—
which eventually played a large role in the causes of the Sicilian revolutionary government's conservative involution. Already on 28 January, with the
consent of the revolutionary government, ennobled bourgeois Baron Pietro
Riso formed a private militia—the National Guard (*Guardia Nazionale*)—
whose task was "protecting the property and the people" from popular violence. In practice, the Sicilian landed elite used the National Guard as an
instrument of control of possible popular insurrections. The Guard served
mainly to check and dissolve the *squadre*, which threatened the social order with their disrespect for private property, noble and bourgeois alike—as
Prospero Colonna's letter shows. In this respect, the National Guard was
truly the living emblem of the alliance between aristocracy and bourgeoisie
in the name of preservation of social privileges.[99]

In the following months, the National Guard acted as the strong arm
of the liberal party, which, with the excuse of restoring law and order, often
prosecuted and imprisoned democratic activists. At the same time, in May
1848, with the expulsion of Pasquale Calvi from the revolutionary government, the democrats lost their most prestigious leader and soon divided
amongst themselves between a radical-socialist and a conservative current.
In view of this, it is remarkable that, in the summer of 1848, when the revolution had already lost most of its democratic content, democrats Francesco
Crispi and Giuseppe La Farina could still organize a people's army to fight
against the incoming Bourbon forces.[100]

To be sure, from the outset, moderate liberals and democrats had agreed
that Sicily should have adopted the Constitution of 1812 with important
modifications. The program of the revolutionary government was, in fact,
"the Constitution of 1812 updated." Yet, if for both political groups this was
a reference to the importance of Sicily's regionalist tradition, for democrats
the updating regarded the creation of democratic institutions, while for
moderate liberals it meant no more than the extension of political privileges
to the propertied classes. According to the Constitution of 1812, the Sicilian Parliament included two Houses—an upper House based on hereditary
noble titles and a lower House based on property qualifications. Yet, during
the works to update the Constitution, the bourgeois elements of the revolu-

99. See Salvatore Francesco Romano, *Momenti del Risorgimento in Sicilia* (Florence, 1952),
84–87; Romeo, *Il Risorgimento*, 320–322; and Cingari, "Gli ultimi Borboni," 52–53.

100. See Giarrizzo, "La Sicilia dal Cinquecento," 753–754; and R. Composto, "Francesco
Crispi da moderato a democratico," *ASS* 6 (1980): 302–392.

tionary government—who far outnumbered the aristocratic elements—succeeded in eliminating the hereditary noble title qualification for the upper House from the final version of the document and in extending the right to vote to the intellectual and mercantile bourgeoisie. Therefore, the Constitution of 1848 fully recognized the bourgeoisie's preeminent role in society. Propertied men—regardless of their affiliation to either aristocracy or bourgeoisie—dominated both Houses in the Sicilian Parliament. The new Constitution cemented with the written word of the law the conservative character of the revolution and was particularly instrumental in building a temporary alliance between the two dominant propertied classes of the island—an alliance that was instrumental to both the preservation of social and economic privileges and the political struggle against the Neapolitan government.[101]

An important feature of the operation of updating the Constitution of 1812 was the reassertion of Sicilian regionalism through the creation of an independent government. This was a main source of contrast with the Neapolitan constitutional government that took control of the Bourbon capital from February 1848. In general, Sicilian liberals and democrats agreed on the fact that Sicily and the continental *Mezzogiorno* ought to have different and separate institutions. Yet, they disagreed on the relationship between the island's government and the rest of Italy. Democrats were by far less regionalist than moderate liberals and were in contact with their political peers dispersed throughout the peninsula. On the other hand, moderate liberals were the true inheritors of the landed aristocracy's separatist tradition, and yet, during the first few months of the Revolution, they realized that they needed the help of other Italians if they were to engage in successful struggle against the Bourbon monarchy. Summarizing both points of views, on 25 March 1848, Ruggero Settimo opened the first session of the Sicilian Parliament with the wish that Sicily would join the "great fate of the Italian Nation, free, independent, and unified."[102]

It is possible to follow the entire trajectory of Sicilian moderate liberals, from the dream of autonomy to the realization of the need for collaboration, in Vincenzo Fardella of Torrearsa's 1887 *Ricordi sulla Rivoluzione siciliana degli anni 1848 e 1849* (Memoirs of the Sicilian Revolution of the Years 1848

101. See De Francesco, "Ideologie," 307–309; Romeo, *Il Risorgimento*, 323–325; and Francesco Brancato, *L'Assemblea siciliana del 1848–1849* (Florence, 1945).

102. Settimo's quotation is in Romano, *Momenti del Risorgimento*, 92. See also Romeo, *Il Risorgimento*, 338–343; and Cingari, "Gli ultimi Borboni," 48–61.

and 1849). A liberal nobleman who briefly led the revolutionary government, Fardella wrote an analysis of the events from a conservative perspective. His aim was to explain the reasons for the failure of the revolution, blaming democratic and radical elements. He thought and argued that democrats such as Pasquale Calvi had weakened the revolutionary government by making constant pressures on the constituent assembly to adopt a demagogic policy of "popular sovereignty" and by stirring the masses into revolt against the elite.[103]

At the same time, Fardella wished to point out that Sicily's revolution could hardly succeed without the help of other Italian states. Even though he subscribed to the 1848 motto "Sicily independent and Italian," Fardella gradually realized that Sicily could have a real chance to separate from the Bourbon kingdom only if its elite actively sought an alliance with the liberal elite of the Kingdom of Sardinia—a state whose plans of expansion in the name of Italian unification were a cause of distress among Sicilian regionalists. Yet, Fardella believed that Sicilian revolutionaries needed to address the issue of preservation of Sicilian political autonomy before proceeding to participate to an Italian alliance against the Bourbons. Writing almost forty years after the Revolution of 1848, Fardella saw how failure to address this fundamental issue had led to the postponement of Sicilian independence from the Bourbon kingdom.[104]

In retrospect, the path that the Sicilian landed elite followed during the Revolution of 1848 resembles the one of the South Carolinian slaveholding elite during the Crisis of 1850. In both cases, the institutional crisis that occurred at mid-century caused the elite to confront the contradictions of its regionalist program and to face the existence of alternative views on the region's future. The nature of both Sicilian and South Carolinian extreme regionalisms was an object of confrontation between different sections of the elites. In turn, ensuing divisions within the elites proved fatal for the success of both regionalist programs.

Yet, the nature of the divisions within the elite was profoundly different in the two cases. In South Carolina, by 1850, the planter class was mostly

103. See Vincenzo Fardella of Torrearsa, *Ricordi sulla Rivoluzione siciliana degli anni 1848 e 1849* (Palermo, 1988; orig. pub. in 1887), 87–88. See also Luigi Becchina, "La rivoluzione siciliana del 1848–1849 nel giudizio degli storici contemporanei," *NQM* 15 (1966).

104. See Fardella of Torrearsa, *Ricordi sulla Rivoluzione,* 67–68, 123–130. See also Nino Recupero, "La fine del Regno," in Iachello, ed., *I Borbone,* 62–67.

united in the defense of its privileges and in considering secession as an ultimate, and yet very close, option at its disposal. The elite's internal divisions
between cooperationists and separatists were limited to the implications of
the ensuing struggle with the federal government. The issue at stake was
the relationship between South Carolinian planters and the elites of other
southern states, for most of whom, in the early 1850s, the defense of slaveholding privileges hardly justified such an extreme move as secession, given
the power and influence of the southern elite in the federal government. On
the other hand, in Sicily, still in 1848, deep and often overlapping divisions
between the aristocracy and the bourgeoisie and between moderate liberals
and democrats characterized the region's elite. If for a brief period noblemen
and bourgeois found a common ground in the creation of a revolutionary
government committed to the defense of social privileges, moderate liberals
and democrats continued to hold radically different views both over social
issues and over the necessity of joining other Italian revolutionaries in the
struggle against the Bourbons.

Ultimately, in both the South Carolinian and Sicilian cases, the road
to the fulfillment of the regionalist program of autonomy and of extreme
defense of social privileges required the elite's collaboration with the elites
of other regions. In this respect, it is worth noticing that, given the nature of
South Carolina's commitment to slavery and southern states' rights, South
Carolinian planters could only ally with other southern slaveholding elites
against the federal government. On the other hand, given the nature of Sicilian opposition to the Neapolitan—not just Bourbon—governments, Sicilian liberals and democrats could only ally with Italian liberals and democrats
outside the continental *Mezzogiorno*.

In general, in comparison with Sicilian politics, South Carolinian politics
between 1852 and 1860 showed signs of much more superficial political divisions within the elite than the rift between liberals and democrats. South
Carolina's elite divided between a National Democratic faction, whose leader,
James Orr, was committed to forming a proslavery coalition within the
Democratic Party, and a Southern Rights' Democratic faction, which sought
to form an independent Southern Party. Though both factions claimed to
have inherited Calhoun's legacy, the latter was undoubtedly much closer to
his view of politics. Aside from this political difference, extreme regionalists
turned southern nationalists were still stronger in South Carolina than in

the rest of the South, also thanks to the extraordinary 1850s' expansion of the state's commercial agriculture and to the general economic prosperity of the slave system.[105]

The most vocal southern nationalists in South Carolina, not satisfied with the repeated victories of proslavery and expansionist politics in Congress, even went as far as agitating for the reopening of the Atlantic slave trade. Then, during the late 1850s, the emergence of the Republican Party and its progressively stronger influence in Congress rapidly transformed South Carolinian planters' and politicians' deepest fears of a strongly centralizing and committed antislavery federal government into reality. This, together with the increasing radicalism of sectional conflicts over slavery, led to a resurgence of South Carolinians' secessionist propaganda and activities on a large scale, while, as in the rest of the South, politics became increasingly isolated and peripheral. During this period, among the most active and influential advocates of secession in South Carolina was Thomas Middleton Hanckel. In 1859, he published an oration entitled *Government and the Right of Revolution*, in which he supported the creation of a southern nation free from "foreign interference" and argued that South Carolina's task was to "draw the great sword of a sovereign State, and strike for the cause of justice and self-government," leading the South in its great revolution against the Union.[106]

In fact, the idea that the increasingly isolated and peripheral South Carolina was at the forefront of a great revolution was a recurrent theme that reminded people of the American War of Independence against the British Empire—during which South Carolinians had played a major role—and at the same time linked the struggle for freedom from governmental power to the people's right to choose their own institutions. In an 1859 article on the *Charleston Mercury,* J. Foster Marshall—a state senator and fire-eater—conveyed these points with particularly effective eloquence when he wrote that "it is revolution we seek . . . that determined purpose of a people, who . . . find nothing so dreadful as voluntary slavery." Linking the present to the

---

105. See Ford, *Southern Radicalism,* 212–217; Chauncey S. Boucher, "South Carolina and the South on the Eve of Secession, 1852 to 1860," *WUS* 5 (1919): 81–144; Schultz, *Nationalism and Sectionalism,* 26–57; and Smith, *Economic Readjustment,* 53–61.

106. Thomas Middleton Hanckel, *Government, and the Right of Revolution: An Oration Delivered before the '76 Association, and Cincinnati Society, on Monday, July 4th, 1859* (Charleston, S.C., 1859), 12, 17, 30. See also Roberson, "Foundations of Southern Nationalism," 543–546; and Sinha, *Counterrevolution of Slavery,* 125–187.

past, Marshall argued that "it was revolution, in a word, which hating the cowardice of submitting to wrong, nerved our gallant ancestors never to yield until the States became free, sovereign, and independent." Interestingly, Marshall warned to "not confound revolution with change," so as to ensure that the present movement was not against the governmental institutions in South Carolina, because "he who would overthrow the government which rightfully fulfills the purpose for which it was created, is nothing less than an anarchist." Instead, Marshall even borrowed the language of Thomas Jefferson's Declaration of Independence to clarify that, as in 1776, also in 1859, the struggle was about states' rights and not about the rights of different classes within the states, and yet—he argued—it was the right of the people of South Carolina, "nay their duty, to throw off . . . [the abusive federal] government, and provide new guards for their future security."[107]

In his eloquent speech, Marshall summarized the reasons for the appeal of South Carolina's southern nationalist ideology to the majority of the white people of the state: if South Carolina seceded, its people would take part in a new revolutionary war in which, as in 1776, they would take a leading role in the southern struggle for the preservation of liberty against the slavery imposed upon them by governmental abuse and interference with local institutions. The latter were both threats that, together with the increasing loss of importance of the state in national politics, to many South Carolinians had become all the more real with the progressive rise to power of the Republican Party. The powerful rhetorical images evoked by Marshall were familiar to everybody and effectively conveyed the idea that every white male citizen of South Carolina had a reason to fight in order to retain his privileges of freedom and independence. At the same time, Marshall's point that the revolutionary movement should not bring any change in the state's institutions, since its officials "rightfully fulfilled their duty" as representatives of the people, described the essence of the South Carolinian planters' idea of conservative revolution, or "counterrevolution." In the planters' minds, the revolution's aim was to free them from federal encroachment in their exercise of local power over both enslaved African Americans and poor whites, leaving intact their privileges in the access to the highest political offices of the state. Therefore, the rhetoric that linked the 1850s' elitist struggle

---

107. J. Foster Marshall, "South Carolina Should Defend Herself," *CM*, 17 November 1859. See also Roberson, "Foundations of Southern Nationalism," 549–574.

to the 1776 revolutionary war as a great popular movement for freedom served to mask the reality of counterrevolutionary ideas of firm opposition to social change.[108]

On 20 December 1860, the South Carolina legislature gathered in a special convention and unanimously approved the "Ordinance of Secession," which dissolved the state's ties with the Union. The "Declaration of the Immediate Causes of Secession"—an explanatory document that accompanied the Ordinance of Secession—referred to the election of a president (Abraham Lincoln) who belonged to a sectional party (the Republican Party) and "whose opinions and purposes were hostile to slavery." Most of the text of the Declaration focused on the continuous hostility of the northern states toward the slave system and on the right of the individual states to regulate their own internal institutions, arguing that "those [nonslaveholding] States have assumed the right of deciding upon the propriety of our domestic institutions; and have denied the rights of property established in fifteen of the States and recognized by the Constitution." Recalling the argument that was at the heart of the doctrine of states' rights, the Declaration told the familiar story of the colonies which, with the 1776 Declaration of Independence, had proclaimed their freedom and sovereignty as states and had agreed, with a "law of compact," to form the Union. The federal government's interference in the southern states' domestic institution had broken the original agreement between the sovereign states and had prompted South Carolina to secede.[109]

Remarkably, the Declaration of the Immediate Causes of Secession opened with a reference to the Crisis of 1850 and claimed that, even though in 1852 the South Carolina Convention had declared that the federal government's "encroachments upon the reserved rights of the states fully justified this State in then withdrawing from the Federal Union," South Carolina did not secede "in deference to the opinion and wishes of the other slaveholding states." Therefore, the Declaration linked ideally the 1860 conservative revolution with the revolutionary war of 1776, the Crisis of 1850, and also with the ideas at the heart of the nullification struggle. Ever since the foundation

108. See Sinha, *Counterrevolution of Slavery*, 255–258; and George Fredrickson, *The Arrogance of Race: Historical Perspectives on Slavery, Racism, and Social Inequality* (Middletown, Conn., 1989), 15–27.

109. "South Carolina's *Declaration of the Immediate Causes of Secession* (1860)," in Rick Halpern and Enrico Dal Lago, eds., *Slavery and Emancipation* (Malden, Mass., 2002), 348–349. See also McDonald, *States' Rights and the Union*, 190–191; and Ralph A. Wooster, *The Secession Conventions of the South* (Princeton, N.J., 1962), 11–25.

of the American republic, South Carolinian planters' regionalism had been at the forefront of the movement to keep alive the concept of state sovereignty and the right of the individual states to regulate their domestic institutions. Interestingly, Moltke-Hansen has noticed that "the leadership from these two [1776 and 1860] generations came from the same strata and, indeed, often from the same families"; consequently, it was hardly surprising that "in both cases, 1776 and 1860 . . . South Carolina's planter-dominated leadership wanted to control a government which would protect, not threaten, the rights of property of freemen, and so, planter interests."[110]

In 1860, as in 1832 and in 1850, the ultimate aim of the South Carolinian planters' conservative revolution was to create a regional political entity that would protect both the state's sovereignty and the elite's rights to property and to rule over its people, white and black, from a much feared federal government's interference in local affairs. And yet, by 1860, given the transformation of South Carolina and of the South into peripheral political areas—as a result of Republican Party's rise to power and of the consequent increasingly centralizing and antislavery character of the federal government—South Carolina's regionalism could and did find its ultimate fulfillment only as part of the broader movement for the independence of a slaveholding southern nation. Only the creation of a large political entity such as the Confederate States of America—as it actually occurred in February 1861—could guarantee, by force of arms, the protection of southern states' rights from the increasing federal interference and the protection of slaveholding privileges through the provisions set in the Confederate Constitution. And yet, even though South Carolinian planters rejoiced in the formation of the southern confederacy, they did not have to wait long to realize that, due to the pressures of war, both states' rights and slaveholding privileges were to be sacrificed by the Confederate government to the cause of southern independence.[111]

In the United States, during the second half of the 1850s, South Carolina had become increasingly marginal and peripheral in national politics, due to the progressive strengthening of the federal government and to its in-

110. "South Carolina's *Declaration*," 349; Moltke-Hansen, "Protecting Interests," 181–182. See also Steven A. Channing, *Crisis of Fear: Secession in South Carolina* (New York, 1970), 269–285.

111. See McCardell, *Southern Nation*, 332–333; Emory Thomas, *The Confederate Nation, 1861–1865* (New York, 1979), 17–27; and Paul Escott, *Jefferson Davis and the Failure of Confederate Nationalism* (Baton Rouge, La., 1978), 54–93.

creasingly antislavery stance. The state only temporary gained national importance during the secession movement and the initial process of formation of the Confederate nation in 1860–1861. Conversely, Sicily's role in the movement that in the second half of the 1850s prepared the ground for the creation of the Italian nation was crucial in a number of ways. Above all, among the southern exiles who contributed most in catalyzing the attention of the Italian public opinion on southern Italian matters and made possible Garibaldi's conquest of Sicily and of the Bourbon kingdom in 1860, Sicilians played a particularly decisive part.

Unlike South Carolinians, after the failure of the 1848 Revolution, Sicilian liberals and democrats confronted the problem of political repression, and as a consequence many of them joined other southern Italian refugees in exile and attempted to coordinate a program of action against the Bourbon regime. The experience of exile in Turin, the capital of the Kingdom of Sardinia, and the contact with the Piedmontese liberal aristocracy led Sicilian moderate liberals such as Pietro Lanza of Scordìa and Vincenzo Fardella of Torrearsa to the realization that Sicily's only possibility for achieving independence lay in their alliance with the Piedmontese monarchy against the Bourbons. In his 1855 memoirs, Fardella summarized this view by arguing that "our primary concern was the independence and freedom of the island [but] . . . convinced that we needed support, we looked for it in . . . Piedmont." At the same time, toward the end of the 1850s, most members of the Sicilian liberal aristocracy became convinced that the success of a moderate revolution depended on their ability to trust the Piedmontese prime minister, Camillo Cavour, whose plans for the liberation of Sicily from Bourbon rule had a marked counterrevolutionary content.[112]

The premier vehicle for the realization of the moderate liberal program of Italian unification was the Italian National Society. By the late 1850s, Sicilian moderate liberals joined the Italian National Society with the hope of creating an autonomous Sicilian region within an independent Italian state. Summarizing the path followed by Sicilian liberals from 1848 to 1859, Raffaele De Cesare remarked that "if in 1848 the prevalent idea was the independence of the island, in 1859 the horizon was much wider . . . the idea of a [Italian]

---

112. Vincenzo Fardella di Torrearsa, *Memorie* (Florence, 1855), 45. See also Lucy Riall, "Garibaldi and the South," in John A. Davis, ed., *Italy in the Nineteenth Century* (New York, 2000), 139–143; Romeo, *Il Risorgimento in Sicilia,* 354–356; Romano, *Momenti del Risorgimento,* 210–214; and Cingari, "Gli ultimi Borboni," 69–71.

national monarchy." Significantly, De Cesare said that "the first public display of liberal support occurred under the initiative of Corrado Valguarnera," prince of Niscemi, a Sicilian liberal nobleman who expressed his support for the war waged in 1859 by the Piedmontese king, Victor Emmanuel II, and the French emperor, Napoleon III, against the Habsburg Empire.[113]

Yet, to democrats such as Pasquale Calvi and Rosolino Pilo, the moderate liberal program seemed rather narrowminded and conservative. After the failure of the 1848 revolutions throughout Italy, the democrats increasingly looked at the *Mezzogiorno* as the ideal place from which to start the next revolutionary war. Sicily played a central role in these projects because of its explosive combination of anti-Bourbon politics and peasant unrest. Especially after Carlo Pisacane's failed expedition on the southern mainland in 1857, Sicily became the center of the Italian democrats' conspiratorial activity.[114]

In February 1860, Pilo expressed his disappointment at the fact that liberal noblemen such as "Settimo [and] Torrearsa . . . only aspire at the formation of an independent Constitutional Government of the Island . . . and their [idea of] progress does not go further than a Sicilian Kingdom within an Italian federation." Pilo's disappointment derived from the fact that, while Sicilian moderate liberals sought to achieve autonomy firmly within the limits of an Italian federation of monarchies, radical democrats like himself sought to actively collaborate to the creation of a unified Italian republic. And yet, by the late 1850s, moderate Sicilian democrats, such as Francesco Crispi and Giuseppe La Farina, had decided to support the Piedmontese solution in the hope to achieve Italian unification and independence as soon as possible. Significantly, it was under La Farina's leadership that the Italian National Society became a center of both liberal and democratic support for the Sardinian monarchy.[115]

---

113. Raffaele De Cesare, *La fine di un Regno* (Milan, 1969; orig. pub. in 1895), 693. See also Alfonso Scirocco, *L'Italia del Risorgimento* (Bologna, 1990), 377–378; De Francesco, "Ideologie," 408–409; and Raymond Grew, *A Sterner Plan for Italian Unity: The Italian National Society and the Risorgimento* (Princeton, N.J., 1963).

114. See Berti, *I democratici*, 600–648; Franco Della Peruta, *I democratici e la rivoluzione italiana. Dibattiti ideali e contrasti politici all'indomani del 1848* (Milan, 1954); and Alfonso Scirocco, *I democratici italiani da Sapri a Porta Pia* (Naples, 1969).

115. Rosolino Pilo to Francesco Crispi, 15 February 1860, quoted in Romeo, *Il Risorgimento in Sicilia*, 365. See also Lucy Riall, *Sicily and the Unification of Italy: Liberal Policy and Local Power, 1859–1866* (Oxford, 1998), 76–79.

Doubtless, moderate liberals and moderate and radical democrats represented the three different souls of Sicilian revolutionary activism in the 1850s. The three groups' final objectives and their views over Sicily's place in the future Italian nation differed strikingly. Moderate liberals such as Torrearsa and Settimo were autonomists, or former separatists, who agreed that their collaboration with the Italian liberal movement was a means to overthrow the Bourbon monarchy and retrieve control of the regional government. They also thought that their support of the Sardinian monarchy would allow them room for negotiating the extent of Sicily's autonomy within the new Italian nation. On the other hand, radical democrats such as Calvi and Pilo wished for Sicily to be part of a unified Italian republic. Moderate democrats, instead, divided between La Farina's pro-Piedmontese group and Crispi's group, whose associates believed more in Sicily's future as part of an Italian nation than of an enlarged Kingdom of Sardinia.[116]

Though with different objectives in mind, from their exile in Piedmont, both Sicilian liberals and democrats sent their fellow countrymen on the island a clear message on the need to join the movement for Italian national unification. Meanwhile, they began preparing for the organization of a military expedition to Sicily that was to benefit from popular support. Corrado Valguarnera, the young liberal nobleman cited by De Cesare, was just one among a large group of Sicilian revolutionaries who joined Giuseppe Garibaldi and his "Thousand" when they landed in Sicily with the support of the National Society and led the revolt against the Bourbon monarchy in May–July 1860. Members of Sicily's liberal aristocracy, such as Valguarnera, used their position at the forefront of the revolt against the Bourbons to check the degree of change in Sicilian society and transform the popular revolt planned by the democrats into a conservative revolution. Comparable to what planters and politicians did in South Carolina, Sicilian moderate liberals covered their real aims with nationalist rhetoric, arguing that the advent of the new Italian nation would lead to the end of old privileges and to the triumph of liberal principles. Yet, the true nature of the moderate liberals' objectives focused on the elite's recovery of its influence in local affairs, an influence that the Bourbon administration had made a consistent effort to undermine.[117]

116. See Riall, *Sicily and the Unification,* 80–83; and Nino Recupero, "La Sicilia all'opposizione, 1848–1874," in Aymard and Giarrizzo, eds., *La Sicilia.*

117. See Romeo, *Il Risorgimento in Sicilia,* 346–359; Romano, *Momenti del Risorgimento,* 210–214; Giarrizzo, "La Sicilia dal Cinquecento," 763–776; and Cancila, *Palermo,* 56–60, 77–81.

In preparing the background for their conservative revolution, Sicilian moderate liberals had had to guard against the initiatives of the democrats, who sought to liberate the island by exploiting anti-Bourbon feelings and peasant anger against landed proprietors. While the former were the source of much popular discontent—especially after liberal Prince Filangieri's replacement with ruthless and reactionary Prince Castelcicala as Sicily's governor—the latter was the cause of a constant state of unrest in the Sicilian countryside. In early 1860, democrats had increased their conspiratorial activity in order to prompt the peasant masses to start the revolution. The danger of radical upheaval and social change was closer than ever. A failed insurrection had taken place in Palermo already at the beginning April, and conspiratorial activity intensified in other cities and in the countryside, where peasant *squadre* and armed bands overcame government officials in different places. Then, on 11 May, the democratic guerrilla leader Giuseppe Garibaldi landed in Sicily with his "Thousand." With substantial help from a number of *squadre,* he defeated the Bourbon army at Calatafimi on 15 May, declared a dictatorship, and established a new government, at whose head he put Francesco Crispi. Subsequently, Garibaldi succeeded in conquering Palermo and—after a decisive battle at Milazzo—the whole of Sicily, so that by 20 July the island was substantially free from Bourbon rule under his democratic dictatorship.[118]

Despite the democratic threat of social revolution, soon after their arrival, Garibaldi and his followers clarified that they acted in the name of the Piedmontese king, Victor Emmanuel II. Moreover, the new government soon abandoned radical projects of economic and social reform, such as the long-awaited land redistribution. As first Garibaldi and then his successors, pro-dictators Agostino Depretis and Antonio Mordini, ruthlessly repressed peasant unrest, it became clear that the government's intent was far from triggering a democratic revolution. In turn, Garibaldi's clarification of his conservative intent prompted the Sicilian liberal elite to ally with him in the war against the Bourbons so as to stop the growing peasant unrest, restore order, and prevent democrats from provoking radical social change. Subsequently, facing the possibility of social subversion, Sicilian liberals abandoned their separatist positions and rallied in support of the introduction of

---

118. See Giarrizzo, "La Sicilia dal Cinquecento," 778–781; Duggan, *Francesco Crispi,* 213–221; Riall, *Sicily and the Unification,* 62–75; and Giorgio Candeloro, *Storia dell'Italia moderna,* vol. 5, *Dalla rivoluzione nazionale all'Unità, 1849–1860* (Milan, 1964), 427–467.

Piedmontese legislation, so that in less than a month, in August 1860, the entire Sicilian administrative system was remodeled after the Piedmontese one. For the same reason, liberals also supported the move toward immediate annexation of the island to the Kingdom of Sardinia. On 21 October 1860, plebiscites sanctioned the loss of Sicilian autonomy and its annexation to Piedmont. Though Sicilian separatism had played a central role in demolishing Bourbon rule in the *Mezzogiorno,* the island's independence further diminished with its transformation into an Italian province after the proclamation of the Kingdom of Italy in March 1861.[119]

Following a comparable path—a path on which they had initially embarked during the Crisis of 1850 and the Revolution of 1848—South Carolinian planters and Sicilian liberal noblemen and bourgeois merged their projects of regional autonomy with wider projects of formation of supraregional nation-states. In both cases, it became clear to substantial numbers within the two elites that large political institutions were far more effective than small regions in achieving national recognition and in protecting the interests of the upper classes against social revolution. At the same time, the increasing radicalism of American and Italian politics in the 1850s led to comparable accelerations in the concurrent processes of formation of the southern and Italian supraregional nation-states, even though with different characteristics. On one hand, South Carolina's elite, politically isolated and marginalized—together with the rest of the southern slaveholders—by the late 1850s' rise of the Republican Party and by the consequent strengthening of antislavery positions in the federal government, only rose to temporary national prominence at the time of the secession crisis and of the formation of the Confederate nation in 1860–1861. On the other hand, Sicily's elite, whose members in exile in Piedmont became increasingly influential in Italian public opinion during the late 1850s, crowned a period of increasing national importance by playing a major role in the success of Garibaldi's expedition and in the making of the Italian nation, in 1860–1861.

Yet, notwithstanding the different degree of importance in the roles of the two elites in the two national movements, the price that they had to pay to retain their regional power against the prospect of social change

119. See Riall, *Sicily and the Unification,* 83–91; Romano, *Momenti del Risorgimento,* 114–133; Renda, *Storia della Sicilia,* 116–183; and Denis Mack Smith, *Victor Emmanuel, Cavour, and the Risorgimento* (Oxford, 1971), 190–224.

was, in both cases, high. In 1861, the formation of the Confederate States of America strengthened only temporarily the power of the South Carolinian elite both within its region and in relation to the federal government. In the same year, the formation of the Kingdom of Italy contributed a great deal to preserve the power of the Sicilian elite within the island, though only after its unconditional acceptance of Piedmontese rule. Contrary to the two elites' expectations, the two new governments' policies of administrative centralization, which—as a result of both war emergencies and external pressures—manifested fully only in the following years, acted against regional traditions of peripheral autonomy to an even greater extent than the ones previously implemented by the American Union and by the Neapolitan administration.

Making and Unmaking the Confederate States
of America and the Kingdom of Italy

The decisions of the South Carolinian and Sicilian elites to merge their programs of regional separatism with broader nationalist movements triggered sequences of events that eventually led to the American slaveholders' participation in the formation of the Confederate States of America and to the southern Italian landowners' participation in the formation of the Kingdom of Italy. Both nation-states whose creation was sanctioned in 1861, the Confederate States of America and the Kingdom of Italy shared the important characteristic of being the ultimate results of compromises between the two southern elites' needs of protection of their regional privileges and their aspirations to be part of larger, national, political entities. As a consequence, the two new nation-states erected their foundations in the two southern peripheries on very unstable ground.

In fact, in both the American South and the Italian *Mezzogiorno,* the elites supported the process of nation-building with the precise understanding that the new national political entities would interfere with their control of local affairs only to offer protection against either internal or external threats. In both cases, the southern elite considered the new nation a legitimate political formation only insofar as it fulfilled the crucial promises of respect of regional autonomy and protection of regional interests. Yet, in both cases, a combination of factors—among which was the need for centralizing measures due to the emergency of war—led both new nations to the betrayal of the promise to respect regional autonomy not long after the inauguration of the new national government and also to a failure in the attempt to protect regional interests. As a result, almost from the very beginning of their turbulent history, both the Confederacy and the Italian kingdom faced a crisis of legitimacy, a crisis that led to the end of the former and to the near collapse of the latter during the crucial period between 1861 and 1866.

In the American South, the issue of protection of the elite's regional autonomy formed the most important part of the doctrine of states' rights. Being the political ideology at the heart of the creation of the Confederate nation, the doctrine of states' rights succeeded in unifying the regionally diverse elites of the South specifically because of its crucial link to the justification of slavery. As Drew Faust has shown, the Confederate ideology of slavery—as it was represented and celebrated in literature, art, and religious speeches—had its deepest foundations in the idea of a hierarchical nation in which the planter elite exercised a benevolent paternalism over its subjects. At the heyday of Confederate power, the literary sophistication of the proslavery argument, at whose root was the slaveholders' patriarchal-paternalistic worldview, reached its zenith and served to justify the existence of a nation in which slavery effectively functioned as the "cornerstone"—in the famous expression of Confederate vice president Alexander Stephens—of the entire social and political system. At the same time, the justification of the existence of slavery and the acknowledgment of its crucial link with the doctrine of states' rights were the two fundamental features that distinguished the Confederate Constitution from the American Constitution and encapsulated the deep ideological and sociopolitical differences which set the South apart from the North in 1861.[1]

Thus, the existence of the Confederate nation as a legitimate political formation depended on the protection of the southern elite's regional power through the defense of states' rights and on the perpetuation of the patriarchal-paternalistic ideology of justification of slavery. Yet, during its brief existence, the Confederate government—facing increasing pressure from the Union in the Civil War—adopted a policy of centralization that repeatedly violated the rights of the individual states, and toward the end of the war it even approved the draft of African American slaves. The inevitable result was the government's rapid loss of legitimacy in the eyes of the

1. See Drew G. Faust, *The Creation of Confederate Nationalism: Ideology and Identity in the Civil War South* (Baton Rouge, La., 1988), 69–78; Don Fehrenbacher, *Constitutions and Constitutionalism in the Slaveholding South* (Athens, Ga., 1989), 59–81; and Marshall L. DeRosa, *The Confederate Constitution of 1861: An Inquiry into American Constitutionalism* (Columbia, Mo., 1991).

South's regional slaveholding elite. In fact, according to Emory Thomas, the consequences of Confederate president Jefferson Davis's adoption of centralized nationalism in an attempt to cope with the Union's more powerful war machinery were nothing short of revolutionary. Confederate centralization resulted in wartime policies that began the process of revolutionizing southern economy and society, emphasizing manufacturing and urbanization over plantation agriculture, offering new avenues of expression to common southerners against the hegemony of the planter elite and to women against the overarching power of patriarchy. At the same time, Confederate centralization dealt a particularly harsh blow to the belief in the Confederacy as a guardian institution of states' rights with the implementation of wartime measures such as conscription, the suspension of the writ of habeas corpus, and military impressment of both commodities and slaves. As a result, in many states, opposition to Confederate policies led to protracted conflict between the governor—the main agent of Confederate centralization at the regional level—and the state legislature, causing a great deal of political instability in the new nation.[2]

As war progressed and the carnage continued, despite Jefferson Davis's efforts to maintain a tight control over the wartime economy, the Confederate government could not prevent the departure for the front of an increasing number of slaveholders and their sons—which left a number of slaveholding women with the difficult task of running plantations and farms. At the same time, the continuous flow of runaway slaves to the Union lines, besides proving spectacularly wrong the fundamental assumptions at the heart of the patriarchal-paternalistic justification of slavery, brought enormous disruption to the plantation economy and increasing pressure on the heavily agricultural and minimally industrialized Confederate states. By the time Abraham Lincoln released the 1863 Emancipation Proclamation—which nominally freed slaves in all the Confederate territories—the Confederacy's agricultural economy was already under enormous pressure, while most of the resources were diverted to support the army, with disastrous consequences for cities such as Richmond, where riots broke out in the same year. Even before Sherman's Union troops ravaged the Deep South in the 1864

2. See Emory Thomas, *The Confederacy as a Revolutionary Experience* (Columbia, S.C., 1991), 134–135; Paul D. Escott, *After Secession: Jefferson Davis and the Failure of Confederate Nationalism* (Baton Rouge, La., 1978), 212–218; George C. Rable, *The Confederate Republic: A Revolution against Politics* (Chapel Hill, N.C., 1994), 138–165; and Frank L. Owsley, *State Rights in the Confederacy* (Gloucester, Mass., 1961), 150–202.

March to the Sea, in most southern states the slave system was in ruins, while the power of the regional slaveholding elites was increasingly feeble. As the war witnessed its final two years and the disruption of slavery led to the rapid erosion of privileges of the white population, conflicts between yeomen, who bore the brunt of the war, and planters became widespread. In turn, both the increasing atmosphere of class conflict and the betrayal of the states' rights cause became major causes of the Confederacy's deep crisis of legitimacy and contributed decisively to the southern elites' disaffection, if not their outright revolt, against the very nation that they had created.[3]

In March 1865, the Confederate Congress's decision to emancipate and arm the slaves signaled the complete failure of the Confederate government to protect the very basis of power of the slaveholding elite that formed the economic and social backbone of the new nation. Arguably, this was the most extreme measure that the Confederate government implemented in its continuous attempts to cope with the impossible task of fighting a modern industrial war with the support of an agrarian slaveholding economy. Since the start of the war, in order to guarantee the survival of the Confederacy, Jefferson Davis had used an experimental approach to governmental centralization, caring little for major issues such as state sovereignty. Yet, given the fact that the defense of slavery was the most important reason for the existence of the Confederate nation, the Confederate government's contradictory measure to free and arm the slaves would have resulted in its transformation into a very different political institution from the one to which the southern slaveholding elite had sworn allegiance. By then, however, it was too late even for such a radical measure. Incessantly pressed by the Union, the Confederate nation fell as much as a result of the disaffection of the slaveholding elite as of the obvious impossibility of a slave system to cope with a modern type of war.[4]

3. See William W. Freehling, *The South vs. the South: How Anti-Confederate Southerners Shaped the Civil War* (New York, 2001), 141–173; Drew G. Faust, *Mothers of Invention: Women of the Slaveholding South in the American Civil War* (Chapel Hill, N.C., 1996), 9–20; and James L. Roark, *Masters without Slaves: Southern Planters in the Civil War and Reconstruction* (New York, 1977), 21–29.

4. See Bruce Levine, "What Did We Go to War For? Confederate Emancipation and Its Meaning," in Susan-Mary Grant and Brian Holden Reid, eds., *The American Civil War: Explorations and Reconsiderations* (Harlow, 2000), 239–264; Richard Beringer et al., *Why the South Lost the Civil War* (Athens, Ga., 1986), 368–388; and Gary Gallagher, *The Confederate War: How Popular Will, Nationalism, and Military Strategy Could Not Stave off Defeat* (Cambridge, Mass., 1997), 155–174.

* * *

Concurrent with the formation of the Confederate nation in the American South, the Kingdom of Italy proclaimed its birth in early 1861. In the *Mezzogiorno,* the speed and relative ease that had characterized the process of Italian unification were the result of the consensus of the majority of southern Italian landowners over a compromise between liberal demands and administrative centralization. Effectively, the compromise, which focused on the guarantee of restricted parliamentary representation and of governmental protection of local privileges and of law and order, legitimized the hegemonic role of the liberal Piedmontese monarchy in the new nation. Yet, the degree of administrative centralization that would characterize the Italian kingdom and the extent to which the elite of the southern Italian periphery would support or oppose it were both matters open to discussion, even at the beginning of 1861. Since the Piedmontese annexation of Lombardy in 1859, a debate had sparked in Parliament and in public opinion over two opposites views: one focused on the respect for regional institutions and argued in favor of allowing them a certain degree of autonomy, the other simply contemplated the extension of the centralized Piedmontese administrative system—based on the 1859 Rattazzi Law—to the new territories. In March 1861, Minister of Interior Marco Minghetti presented in the Italian Parliament a project of law that guaranteed administrative unity and also preserved a limited degree of local autonomy. However, in August 1862, the plan was rejected in favor of the Rattazzi Law, which was then extended to the *Mezzogiorno* in January 1863.[5]

The move away from respect of regional traditions of local autonomy and toward tighter administrative centralization had a lot to do with the Italian government's inability to maintain law and order in the southern countryside and had the effect of bringing back the problems in core-periphery relations that had previously characterized the Bourbon kingdom. Unable to cope with continuous social unrest and increasing political extremism, the Right governments that guided Italy through the 1860s increasingly turned to authoritarian and repressive measures, alienating the support of a number of representatives of the propertied classes of the *Mezzogiorno*

5. See Claudio Pavone, *Amministrazione centrale e amministrazione periferica da Rattazzi a Ricasoli (1859–1866)* (Milan, 1964), 73–94; Raffaele Romanelli, "Centralismo e autonomie," in Raffaele Romanelli, ed., *Storia dello stato italiano dall'Unità a oggi* (Rome, 1995), 131–140; and Ernesto Ragionieri, *Politica e amministrazione nella storia dell'Italia unita* (Bari, 1967).

who had promoted Italian unification. Though many liberal landowners advocated strong measures to restore normalcy, while democratic politicians and activists continued to divide between advocacy of decentralization and conspiracies to raise the southern masses against Italy's liberal government, both southern Italian liberals and democrats came to resent—to a lesser or greater extent—the exceptional harshness that the Right governments showed in the repression of peasant revolts in the *Mezzogiorno*. Peasants had already revolted in different areas since the time of Garibaldi's 1860 expedition; yet, their activities reached a peak in the period immediately after unification, during the so-called great brigandage of 1861–1865—a civil war that devastated the *Mezzogiorno* and whose causes were extremely complex and multifaceted.[6]

After the surrender of the Bourbon king, Francis II, at Gaeta in February 1861, the demobilization of the Bourbon army, the enforced conscription in the Italian army, and increased taxation forced a number of peasants to flee to the mountains and form outlaw bands to resist the Italian government. Initially, many peasants joined forces with the concurrent legitimist struggle to restore Francis II on the Neapolitan throne. Yet, after the capture and execution of legitimist leader Jose Borjes in December 1861, the peasant revolt acquired a life on its own. In August 1862, when Garibaldi attempted to raise the southern masses to follow him in the conquest of Rome, there was a real possibility that the democrats would take the lead of the brigandage movement and cause a massive social and political conflict throughout the peninsula. Yet, even though the Italian army succeeded in halting Garibaldi, the peasant guerrilla warfare did not show any sign of receding. By then, more than forty mounted bands, each with hundreds of men, terrorized the central provinces of the *Mezzogiorno,* occupying lands, destroying properties, kidnapping landed proprietors, and burning documents that proved the validity of legal and illegal land enclosures. Though many liberal landowners—the peasants' main targets—advocated harsh measures, several of them also acted as what the sources describe as *manutengoli*—individuals who fed and helped the outlaws, or brigands—voicing their discontent against the new Italian kingdom and its Piedmontese ruling class. The Italian government responded to the exceptionality of the situation by declaring a state of

6. See Piero Bevilacqua, *Breve Storia dell'Italia meridionale dall'Ottocento a oggi* (Rome, 1993), 35–36; and John A. Davis, *Conflict and Control: Law and Order in Nineteenth-Century Italy* (London, 1988), 178–184.

siege in the *Mezzogiorno*. Then, in August 1863, the Italian Parliament passed the infamous Pica Law, which charged military tribunals with the power of judging and executing all members of brigand bands and their accomplices who resisted the Italian army.[7]

Despite the democrats' opposition and a parliamentary inquiry—the 1863 Massari Report (*Relazione Massari*)—which demonstrated the importance of poverty as a cause of brigand activity, the government continued to rely on the use of military force. Eventually, by 1865, thanks to the deployment of 116,000 soldiers and a ruthless policy of repression, the Italian army managed to defeat the great brigandage, at the cost of 5,212 official deaths. In the same year, in an attempt to make the administration uniform, the Italian government instituted the "prefect system" in the *Mezzogiorno*. Similar to the Bourbon intendants, prefects were provincial governors nominated by the central government—i.e., the king. Yet, even though there was widespread opposition among southern peripheral elites and the key positions in the municipal governments were elective, prefects held much more power than the intendants; besides being in charge of law and order, health, education, and public works, they could also dissolve elected local councils and put special commissions in their place. Despite this, similar to what had occurred already in the Bourbon kingdom, in the new Italian nation the southern peripheral elite quickly learned to use the new local governmental structures for its own objectives of social advancement through patronage and kin alliances. Yet, the elite also continued to voice its discontent with the excessive administrative centralization enforced upon the southern Italian periphery by the Right governments based in Turin. Then, in September 1866, the western part of Sicily became once again the center of a separatist revolt. After declaring martial law, the Italian army succeeded in crushing the rebels only through a brutal repression, leaving another legacy of ill-will and contributing a great deal to stir the island into a state of endemic opposition to central governmental authorities.[8]

7. See Giorgio Candeloro, *Storia dell'Italia moderna*, vol. 5, *La costruzione dello stato unitario, 1860–1871* (Milan, 1968), 179–211; Alfredo Capone, *Destra e Sinistra da Cavour a Crispi* (Turin, 1981), 43–64; Franco Molfese, *Storia del brigantaggio dopo l'Unità* (Milan, 1964), 215–373; and Roberto Martucci, *Emergenza e tutela dell'ordine pubblico nell'Italia liberale* (Bologna, 1980).

8. See Tommaso Pedio, *Brigantaggio meridionale (1806–1863)* (Cavallino di Lecce, 1997), 97–141; Alfonso Scirocco, *Il Mezzogiorno nell'Italia unita (1861–1865)* (Naples, 1979); Alberto Aquarone, *L'unificazione legislativa e i codici del 1865* (Milan, 1960); and Lucy Riall, *Sicily and the Unification of Italy: Liberal Policy and Local Power, 1859–1866* (Oxford, 1998), 198–221.

* * *

Even though in different ways, after 1861 both the Confederate States of America and the Kingdom of Italy faced crises of legitimacy. The Confederate nation, engaged in the Civil War with the Union, did not survive the crisis. Its central government collapsed, leaving behind it the difficult legacies of the devastating military and moral defeat suffered by the southern people and of the slaveholding elite's hostility toward the victor's imposition of the abolition of slavery, with the consequent transformation of the entire economic and social system that revolved around it. On the other hand, the Italian kingdom survived the crisis through the strengthening of the government's authoritarian character and the indiscriminate use of military force. These measures proved essential in defeating the brigands in the southern Italian civil war, and yet they left the southern elite with a permanent legacy of resentment toward the Italian government's ruthless policy of centralization and toward its inability to maintain law and order. In both cases, the decade after the two civil wars was substantially one of conflict between the southern elite and the central government, and yet one in which no armed rebellion occurred. To a certain extent, it is possible to say that the central government succeeded in both cases in imposing its program of uniformity of governmental institutions despite the aspirations of many members of the southern elites to a higher degree of regional autonomy. Yet, a substantial difference was the fact that, in the American South, governmental centralization was far more radical and with a clearer focus than in the Italian *Mezzogiorno*, where the politics of compromise and patronage characterized the behavior of a largely conservative and corrupt political class.

In general, in the American South the period of Reconstruction (1865–1876) saw a constant struggle between the former slaveholding elites, which attempted to retain their control over both land and workforce, and the emancipated African Americans (or freedpeople), who wished to be economically independent—a struggle in which the federal government sided with the latter with the single-minded objective of helping them in the transition from slavery to nominally free labor. During the years of Congressional Reconstruction—in which Radical Republicans had the upper hand over President Andrew Johnson's compromising policies—the federal government declared martial law in the ex-Confederate states and, with the Reconstruction Acts of 1867, imposed upon ex-slaveholders the formation of state governments with an adequate proportion of African American representatives. Though the freedpeople mostly did not achieve economic independence, since the rumored redistribution of slaveholders' land never took place and the majority of them became sharecroppers on former plantations and farms, the formal cessation of the southern elites' legal privileges occurred with the passing of the Thirteenth, Fourteenth, and Fifteenth Amendments to the Constitution, which sanctioned the abolition of slavery, protected civil rights, and extended voting rights to African Americans.[9]

In comparison with the postbellum American South, no government in the post-unification Italian *Mezzogiorno* ever implemented policies as revolutionary as the ones of Congressional Reconstruction. In the *Mezzogiorno*, the decade after 1866 saw a continuation of milder forms of peasant unrest in the countryside and a recrudescence of conflict between noble and bourgeois landowners. Having been defeated in the southern Italian civil war, peasants continued to be as exploited by the landowners' usurious practices and by the Italian government's fiscal pressure as they had been before. For their part, southern Italian landowners continued to be characterized by deep divisions between aristocracy and bourgeoisie and their different factions over issues of local power and land control, while they still relied heavily on the Italian government for the protection of their regional interests. Yet, in general, even though they profited from the Italian public administration, the elites of the *Mezzogiorno* felt a deep hostility toward it, particularly because the Right governments based in Turin—a far more distant capital than Naples—incessantly sent Piedmontese public officials to the South to substitute local office-holders indiscriminately accused of being Bourbon sympathizers. At the same time, the southern Italian landed elites had relatively few representatives in a parliament that was dominated by northern Italian MPs and northern Italian interests.[10]

In both the American and the Italian cases, the year 1876 signaled the virtual end of the hostilities between the southern elites and the national governments. In both cases, a major compromise over matters of national politics ensured the end of governmental interference in local affairs in the southern regions and the guarantee of respect of southern regional interests. In the United States, in the presidential election of 1876, in return for their support for Republican president Rutheford B. Hayes, the former slaveholding and Confederate elites obtained the complete withdrawal of the Union army from the American South and the end of federal protection

9. See Eric Foner, *Reconstruction: America's Unfinished Revolution* (New York, 1988), 176–346.
10. See Raffaele Romanelli, *L'Italia liberale, 1861–1900* (Bologna, 1990), 163–226.

for African Americans—measures that paved the way to the subsequent, gradual erosion of civil rights in the southern states. On the other hand, in Italy, in the parliamentary election of 1876, in return for their support for the Left's Prime Minister Agostino Depretis, the southern Italian elites obtained the guarantee of greater political representation of their interests and the government's assurance of its policy of nonintervention in local affairs—which led to the subsequent, extraordinary explosion of violence and organized crime in the *Mezzogiorno,* and in Sicily in particular.[11]

In the long run, both American ex-slaveholders and southern Italian landowners renounced their dreams of regional autonomy in the strict political sense in favor of the guarantee of their nearly absolute control over local affairs and in exchange for their support for a national government that promised to either not harm or actively represent their regional interests. This parallel development had important consequences for the subsequent histories of the American and Italian nations. Besides providing a major factor in the construction of a southern question in both countries, it also paved the way to the making of parallel popular myths of the "lost cause"—the Confederate and the Bourbon. In both cases, the myth masked the reality of a compromise that the southern elite had willingly struck with the central government and from which it had gained a great deal in terms of power and influence at both the regional and national levels.

A few years ago, episodes such as the waving of the Confederate flag in South Carolina and the homage to the burial of the Bourbon kings in Naples gave some notoriety to the Neo-Confederate and Neo-Bourbon movements—movements that the media regularly portrayed as if they provided a direct link with the events of the American Civil War and the Italian Risorgimento. However, it is important to remember that the existence of these very active and relatively small groups of individuals has very little to do with the events of the nineteenth century and that, instead, it is far more a result of contemporary forms of protest—white supremacist protest against the 1960s' civil rights gains in the American South and regionally based reaction against the ideological racism of the 1990s' Northern League movement in southern Italy. Yet, if anything, in their own peculiar and distorted ways, both Neo-Confederates and Neo-Bourbons have kept alive a

11. See Steven Hahn, "Class and State in Postemancipation Societies: Southern Planters in Comparative Perspective," *AHR* 95 (1990): 75–98; and Lucy Riall, "Garibaldi and the South," in John A. Davis, ed., *Italy in the Nineteenth Century* (Oxford, 2000), 132–153.

comparable myth of the "lost cause" in the American South and the Italian *Mezzogiorno*; and in both cases, with all its distortions, this myth reminds us that both regions were once, for a shorter or for a longer period of time, independent nation-states ruled by powerful slaveholding and landowning elites.[12]

12. See Tony Horwitz, *Confederates in the Attic: Dispatches from the Unfinished Civil War* (New York, 1998); and Roberto Maria Selvaggi, *Il tempo dei Borbone. La memoria del Sud* (Naples, 1995).

Index

Page references followed by *n* refer to footnotes; those followed by *m* refer to maps.